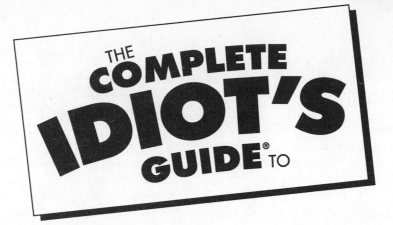

THE COMPLETE IDIOT'S GUIDE® TO

Organizing Your Life

Fourth Edition

by Georgene Lockwood

ALPHA

A member of Penguin Group (USA) Inc.

ALPHA BOOKS

Published by the Penguin Group

Penguin Group (USA) Inc., 375 Hudson Street, New York, New York 10014, U.S.A.

Penguin Group (Canada), 10 Alcorn Avenue, Toronto, Ontario, Canada M4V 3B2 (a division of Pearson Penguin Canada Inc.)

Penguin Books Ltd, 80 Strand, London WC2R 0RL, England

Penguin Ireland, 25 St Stephen's Green, Dublin 2, Ireland (a division of Penguin Books Ltd)

Penguin Group (Australia), 250 Camberwell Road, Camberwell, Victoria 3124, Australia (a division of Pearson Australia Group Pty Ltd)

Penguin Books India Pvt Ltd, 11 Community Centre, Panchsheel Park, New Delhi—110 017, India

Penguin Group (NZ), cnr Airborne and Rosedale Roads, Albany, Auckland 1310, New Zealand (a division of Pearson New Zealand Ltd)

Penguin Books (South Africa) (Pty) Ltd, 24 Sturdee Avenue, Rosebank, Johannesburg 2196, South Africa

Penguin Books Ltd, Registered Offices: 80 Strand, London WC2R 0RL, England

Copyright © 2005 by Georgene Lockwood

International Standard Book Number: 1-59257-413-0
Library of Congress Catalog Card Number: 2005928085

07   06   05   8   7   6   5   4   3   2   1

Interpretation of the printing code: The rightmost number of the first series of numbers is the year of the book's printing; the rightmost number of the second series of numbers is the number of the book's printing. For example, a printing code of 05-1 shows that the first printing occurred in 2005.

Printed in the United States of America

Most Alpha books are available at special quantity discounts for bulk purchases for sales promotions, premiums, fundraising, or educational use. Special books, or book excerpts, can also be created to fit specific needs.

For details, write: Special Markets, Alpha Books, 375 Hudson Street, New York, NY 10014.

Publisher: *Marie Butler-Knight*
Editorial Director: *Mike Sanders*
Senior Managing Editor: *Jennifer Bowles*
Acquisitions Editor: *Randy Ladenheim-Gil*
Development Editor: *Michael Thomas*
Production Editor: *Megan Douglass*

Copy Editor: *Keith Cline*
Illustrator: *Chris Eliopoulos*
Cover/Book Designer: *Trina Wurst*
Indexer: *Angie Bess*
Layout: *Becky Harmon*

Contents at a Glance

Contents

Part 3: Systems for Getting Stuff Done 91

7 Creating a Command Center 93

8 People Who Need People: Interpersonal Systems 107

Foreword

We live in a world in which technology enables us to share information faster than ever before. It has expanded our choices and increased our ability to access anything, anytime, anywhere. This means we have much more to organize, in every aspect of our lives, than ever before. At times, it can make life seem overwhelming and out of control.

Do not despair! You have in your hands a book that can change all that, and help you gain control in your life. It captures the essence of organization. Organization is not about neatness or making things tidy. It is not about being perfect or being rigid. Organization is about being able to find what you need, when you need it.

My personal and professional philosophy is that for organization to work, it must be simple, and it has to be fun. By following the clear, step-by-step advice Georgene Lockwood presents in this book, you will be able to create systems that are tailor-made to your specific needs. Systems that are flexible, that grow and expand as your needs grow and expand. Systems that address the ever-changing needs of this fast-paced world we live in. You will learn how to set realistic goals at work, at home, and at play. But most importantly, you will learn how to keep your systems simple and have fun organizing.

Keep in mind that the adage "knowledge is power" is only half true. The real power of knowledge comes from understanding how to best use that knowledge. To do that, it must be organized. Information and organization in and of themselves have no intrinsic value. Their values are essential life tools. Having both information and organization tools in one place makes this book a truly extraordinary value.

Organization is no longer a luxury; it is a basic necessity in every work and home environment. This is demonstrated in the United States by the growth in membership of the National Association of Professional Organizers (NAPO). Founded in 1985 by five professional organizers, NAPO now has more than 1,100 members (700 of them having joined in the past 4 years). Around the world, professional organizing associations have been formed to help address this global need.

"The most important step on any journey is the first one." You have taken that first step by selecting this book. I assure you, it will dispense wonderful information and be a loyal and trusted friend on your journey to organization. You, too, will thank Georgene Lockwood for sharing her wisdom with us.

—Gloria Ritter, founder and president of PaperMatters and More Inc.

Gloria Ritter, founder and president of PaperMatters and More Inc., has more than 10 years of experience consulting and training companies and individuals in many aspects of organization. She is committed to helping companies and individuals work in an efficient manner to be more productive and therefore minimize stress. Ms. Ritter serves on the board of directors of the National Association of Professional Organizers. She is also president of the National Association of Professional Organizers–Greater Washington/Baltimore Chapter.

Introduction

To have a vision for one's life and to take steps every day toward that vision is where true happiness lies. Ordering our lives to support us in our vision is one of the most profound steps we can take. No matter how many times you've attempted to "get organized once and for all" and have perhaps fallen short of your desires, with some basic determination and this book by your side, you can start where you are and make it happen this time.

To paraphrase George Bernard Shaw, "Hell is to drift. Heaven is to steer." But why do we so often feel out of control? Perhaps it's because we know what we need to do, but we don't know how. Consider the rest of this book as a basic course in life navigation. You're about to become the captain of your own ship and learn how to plot your course through the day-to-day seas of life.

This is not a dictatorial, "do-it-my-way" kind of book. It's more like a Chinese food menu. You know, "Choose one from Column A, one from Column B." I've taken good ideas from wherever I could find them—self-improvement technologies, meditation, visualization, psychology, behavioral studies—whatever I've found that works, either for me personally or for people I know. You pick and choose what makes the most sense for you. Just know that the methods I've shared with you are basic, tried-and-true ones, but feel free to adapt them to suit your own style and personality.

Getting organized isn't something to do "someday"—it's essential to getting ahead and leading a joyful, productive life. The degree to which you need to change what you're doing now to enhance your daily existence and realize your dreams is something you'll have to find out for yourself. Let this book be your guide. I've structured it so you can first set your goals, tackle any immediate roadblocks, decide which areas are really urgent, and then turn to the section that most applies. It's not all work and no play, either. There's lots of fun stuff throughout, and chapters at the end are devoted specifically to life's pleasures and celebrations.

How the Book Is Organized

To make it easy for you to design your own organization plan, there are eight major divisions to help you:

Part 1, "What Do You Mean 'Organized'?" looks at some past experiences or unrealistic ideals that might be getting in your way, and shows you how to figure out what's really important to make an immediate improvement and feel more in control. You also explore some ways to get motivated, to stick to your commitment to organize your life, and to avoid some of the "booby traps" we all have a tendency to set for ourselves. You learn the "basic laws of stuff" and the "basic laws of time," and how stuff and time work together to make your life either smooth or chaotic.

Part 2, "Stuff Simplified," explores some simple ways you can immediately get rid of things you don't really need and get at the things you do, plus some quick-start steps for handling all the paper that comes through the door.

Part 3, "Systems for Getting Stuff Done," moves into the action areas of your life and concentrates on the tasks that will speed you toward accomplishing the goals you set for yourself. You learn how to set up a central area for managing yourself and your family, and you get some step-by-step advice for devising personal systems for your major areas of activity.

Part 4, "Room by Room," examines each room in your house, one by one, and helps you get rid of the clutter and take back your space for yourself and your family.

Part 5, "Money and All That Stuff," guides you through some simple strategies for budgeting and managing your money, examines systems for handling bills and taxes, and asks some basic questions about planning for the future. You'll find concrete ideas for keeping your finances from becoming a tangled mess, causing you aggravation and costing you money.

Part 6, "Getting People Involved," tackles the ways you may let other people sabotage your organizational efforts and helps you get people on your side by encouraging understanding, exploring ways to communicate, and discussing when and how to hire other people to do the work for you.

Part 7, "Now That You're Organized, Let's Keep It That Way!" will help you stay on track with a minimum of effort after you have your plan in place. You'll see how to adapt what you've learned to your particular lifestyle.

Part 8, "You're Ready for Prime Time," focuses on getting the most out of your leisure time and holidays, so if anybody asks "Are we having fun yet?" your answer will always be a resounding "Yes!"

Included at the end of this book are some special resources to take you still further in refining your organizational skills.

Extras

To give you additional food for thought—some shortcuts, tips, and resources to expand your knowledge of certain areas—you'll find boxes scattered throughout the chapters that are indicated by their own special icons:

Wise Words

Humorous and helpful quotes to make your organizing easier.

 Pileups!

Pitfalls to avoid, signs that things are slipping.

 Jump Starts

Ideas for immediate results that just might put your plan in warp drive!

Envisionings

This banner includes visualization exercises to help you clarify your goals and experience the peace of mind organization brings.

 **Resource Files**

This symbol points you to books, audiotapes and videotapes, online resources, organizations, things to send away for—anything I've found to help make you a more powerful organizer.

Acknowledgments

I have a lot of people to be grateful for in my life. Each time I do a book, I'm simply and subtly reminded. First and foremost, I'd like to thank my family and friends for their ideas, feedback, love, and support. As always, you're there and you care. You're the "good stuff"!

Thanks again to the staff at Alpha Books for their intelligence and insight on this fourth edition and helping once again to make a good book better. And thanks to all of my readers who share their stories with me. I'm honored that I can in some small way be a part of making your life more orderly, more fun, and more peaceful.

Special Thanks to the Technical Reviewer

The Complete Idiot's Guide to Organizing Your Life was reviewed in a previous edition by an expert who not only checked the accuracy of what you'll learn in this book, but also provided invaluable insight and suggestions to ensure that you learn everything you need to know to organize yourself for a better life. Our special thanks are extended to Karen Ussery.

The founder and past president of the National Association of Professional Organizers Arizona Chapter, Karen is the owner of Organized for Success. Since 1995, she has written numerous columns on the topic of organizing the office, and is also the author of an idea-a-week book called *Organized for Success: 52 Organizing and Time Management Solutions for Busy Professionals* and co-author of *Maintain Balance in an Unsteady World*. Karen is also a featured professional organizer on HGTV's *Mission: Organization*, and can be reached at www.organizedforsuccess.com.

Trademarks

Part 1

What Do You Mean "Organized"?

Organized people are made, not born. As with other important areas in life, many of us never had anyone to teach us the skills needed to be organized, but with understanding and practice, these skills can be learned.

In these first four chapters, you learn about the beliefs you might have that are undermining your efforts to take control of your time, your relationships, your career, and all the other things that make living worthwhile. You find out how to avoid the biggest trap that seeks to ensnare us all, and the basic rules governing the material things we have and the things we want to do. You also learn how to make your organization efforts compatible with what's really important to you.

The Big Picture: Setting Goals

In This Chapter

◆ Where you got your ideas about being organized

◆ How disorganized are you, really?

◆ The benefits of "getting it all together"

◆ Setting meaningful personal goals

◆ Effective resolutions—New Year's and otherwise

Before you dive in and start writing lists, tearing closets apart, and designing new storage, let's begin at the beginning, which is figuring out how you got into this mess in the first place. Did it just "happen," or are there identifiable reasons your life is so chaotic? Rearranging things on the surface isn't going to create the kind of deeper life changes I suspect you're striving for. You want this to be a permanent step in the right direction, don't you?

Growing Up Is Hard to Do

Imagine a child who was never allowed to make a mess. Let's suppose that child's name is Tony. Tony's parents won't allow him to play with paint because they worry it will stain his clothes or spill. Tony can't play in the dirt because he'll get grimy and disturb the garden. Tony's room is "neat as a pin." There are no stray papers anywhere, no fragments of tape on the walls, and no clothes or toys out of place. To the average outsider, Tony seems like a "model child."

When Tony grows up and leaves home, he figures he's in charge. He decides to rebel against the way it was at home and says to himself, "Now that I'm a grownup, I can make a mess whenever I want to!" In fact, being a slob gives him a distinct pleasure. It feels like delicious freedom. But he is also unable to find the bathroom door through all the debris. Or maybe Tony will continue being super-neat and careful, and rob himself of many of life's pleasures, simply because he can't allow himself to loosen up. Either reaction is just that—a reaction to the way it used to be and not necessarily in Tony's best interest in the present.

How you lived as a child may well help govern how you live now. If someone was always yelling at you to clean up your room, you may still be acting out of your old need to be free from such constraints. You may now be "a messy." Or perhaps you're obsessively neat. (Notice I said "neat," not "organized." We talk about that in more detail later.) Either reaction can get in the way of real freedom.

Envisionings

Close your eyes and imagine yourself in your room as a child. What did your room look like? Did you share a room? How much privacy did you have? Were there things scattered about or was everything "in its place"? Who was responsible for taking care of it? How did being there make you feel? What do you remember your parents saying about it? Add lots of details here. Take your time.

Pay attention to any fatalistic words you hear popping up such as *always* and *never*. These are powerful words and can set the stage for some of your adult attitudes. Also be aware of both verbal criticisms and supportive language. When you set your organization goals, refer back to these memories and see whether some of your goals stem from reactions to past events rather than present needs and desires. You may want to revise them accordingly.

There's also the reverse scenario. Maybe you grew up in a terribly cluttered household and vowed that when you were in control, things would be different. But now you may be going overboard. You may spend time compulsively washing, folding, and tidying all your stuff, rather than enjoying the sunshine or smelling the roses. Your desire to maintain absolute control over your environment can prevent you from having fun, and even keep you from reaching your most important objectives.

Throughout this book, I give you a series of visualizations in the "Envisionings" boxes. When you visualize, pretend you're directing a movie. Add as much detail as you can. Notice any emotions that surface as your "movie" plays on the screen. Write down anything that comes to mind during your screening or dictate your thoughts into a tape recorder. Write an essay or story or draw what you see—whatever most helps you get in touch with your visualization experience. What you see and believe in your mind, you create in the material world. If you want to change what you're creating, one of the first steps is to "see" differently.

You Can't Have (or Do) Everything

Even though we're adults, we may still be trying to gain our parents' approval. This can be especially difficult for women, because housekeeping and making sure the family is well fed, clothed, and successful has traditionally been the woman's job. It's easy to get caught up in trying to be "as good as Mother" (or even better than Mom!), even though Mother might never have worked outside the home or had as many responsibilities or interests.

Recent studies show that although more women are in the work force, and some even make more money than their male partners, most working women still do the lion's share of the housework and child care. Beware of the Superwoman syndrome. It can kill you!

Again, the important thing is simply to notice your feelings and experiences. Ask yourself the following questions:

1. Of the chores that need to be done every day, every week, or every month (don't forget to include tasks such as bill paying, driving kids, making appointments, washing the car, and doing household repairs), how is the work distributed? You may want to make a list on one side of a piece of paper, divide the rest of the paper into two columns, and check off which tasks you do and which ones your partner does. Be honest and fair.

2. How many hours does each adult spend working outside the home? Inside the home?

3. Do you feel that the work is evenly distributed? Are those feelings based on the facts? If you asked the other adults in the household how much of the workload they share, what would they say? How does that fit with your picture of how the work is distributed?

4. If you have children, how much do they contribute?

Note your answers and the emotions they bring up. Acknowledge them, learn from them, and move on. You'll have an opportunity to deal with this more in Chapters 8, 17, and 18.

Superwoman and Superman Are Myths

Not only does your upbringing affect your attitudes about being organized, so do the media and the entertainment industry. TV personalities and the pages of many home and lifestyles magazines present as "normal" certain things that are for most of us impossible ways of living. Don't get me wrong. I subscribe to a few of the magazines. I even watch the TV shows on occasion. But do I really believe the lady on the screen edits her own magazine, does a weekly TV show, keeps several houses, irons her antique linens, shovels manure in her perfectly manicured garden, and single-handedly cooks up impromptu dinners for 50 from scratch? Naaah.

Then there are those guys on the Public Broadcasting Station or the Learning Channel. They know how to fix *everything*. Their Craftsman tools are all in place, and their workshops look like no one ever works there. Of course, that's because after the show is over, someone else comes in, puts everything away, and cleans up for them! And what about those magazines that suggest being a real man means you have to work out, always look great and wear the right jeans, rebuild motors on the weekend, play touch football with the guys, and to top it all off, cook gourmet meals? No sweat, right?

Wise Words

"We are what we think. All that we are arises with our thoughts. With our thoughts, we make our world."

—Buddha

Beware of the images created by movies, TV shows, and advertising. Remember, these people are paid actors. A hairdresser follows them around, their hands never touch a dish or change motor oil, and their homes only exist as movie sets or showrooms.

Advertising especially is about illusions, with sales the ultimate goal. In Advertising 101, students learn how to "create a need" for a new product. If you're "creating" one, that means there isn't one to start with, right? The advertising industry shows you squeaky-clean homes that you feel you must have to be good parents, model homemakers, and acceptable people. In addition to living in a perfect home or apartment, you should have white teeth, perfectly clean hair, sparkling clothes, and dry underarms. Don't let yourself get caught in these marketing traps. See them for what they are: fantasies.

What you're aiming for is a comfortable, orderly, clean, aesthetically pleasing place to live that works well to support your life goals and helps you get the important things, the ones you really care about, done.

How Organized Are You? A Self-Test

Before we continue, let's find out how organized or unorganized you really are. Answer the following questions and you'll have a handle on where you stand:

Yes	No	
❏	❏	Do you find yourself feeling frustrated that you have too little time to do the things you enjoy?
❏	❏	Do you often feel hurried, hassled, or not in control?
❏	❏	When you need to find something, does it often take minutes (or even hours) of frantic searching to finally lay your hands on it?
❏	❏	Do you ever miss appointments or forget deadlines?
❏	❏	Do you have trouble remembering birthdays, anniversaries, important events, and holidays?
❏	❏	Are you usually shopping for special occasions at the last minute (like Christmas shopping on December 23)?
❏	❏	Do you spend your "time off" running errands, playing catch-up, and just trying to keep things from getting out of control?
❏	❏	Are there important things that need to be done to maintain the house or the car that you never seem to get to?
❏	❏	Are repairs made only when something breaks or if it's an absolute emergency?
❏	❏	Do you often pay bills late, not because you don't have the money in your account, but because you just didn't get around to them?
❏	❏	Have you avoided setting up or updating a budget? A will? Insurance? A home inventory? A retirement plan?

continues

continued

Yes	No	
❑	❑	Are there piles of newspapers, unread magazines, junk mail, and various other papers scattered around your house or apartment?
❑	❑	Are you embarrassed to have people see your home or office?
❑	❑	Are mornings hectic, spent rummaging around for clean clothes to wear, gulping down breakfast, and running out the door late?

Pileups!

If you have big piles of paper that are dangerously close to causing an avalanche, you definitely have some organization work to do. Good thing you bought this book!

If you answered yes to two or more of these questions, you can definitely benefit from committing to an "organization overhaul." With this book and a few hours each week, you'll be surprised how quickly you can make a difference.

You know by your answers to these questions whether you're on top of it all or under the gun. I suspect there's a heap of work to be done, and you may be looking for some help. Well, you've certainly come to the right place!

How Would You Change Your Life?

You picked up this book for a reason. You were looking for answers. You were looking for simple, commonsense ways to have your life run more smoothly. Or maybe your existence is out so of control you're desperate for a way out of the chaos. Only you can know where you are in the organization continuum. Getting organized, if it is to be more than a temporary cosmetic solution, is really a change in lifestyle. You're working to change old, deeply ingrained behaviors and adopt new, more productive habits.

Envisionings

Take a minute to visualize what your ideal environment would be like. Close your eyes and walk through your house one room at a time in your mind and imagine each space clean and orderly. Imagine yourself heading out the door to work in the morning with all your clothes ready to wear. See yourself eating a relaxed, nutritious breakfast. Next, visualize yourself commuting to your job and see your office a pleasure to work in. Daydream about what you would like to do with your leisure time. Experience the pride, confidence, serenity, enjoyment, and overall sense of well-being that living in this fantasy place gives you.

So what do you really want to change? Actually, the better question to ask is, "What do you *want?*" I'm not talking about what your parents wanted for you, or what you think you should want, or what the media tells you to want. But what do *you* really want?

Make a list of the top five things that come out of this exercise and post them in a prominent place. Review them at least once a day, starting now. As you begin your plan for getting organized, keep in mind what's truly important to you and make sure the systems you set up support your goals.

Setting Your Personal Organization Goals

Okay, you've been honest with yourself about what your life is like. You've thought about how you'd like things to be different. Now let's decide on some concrete areas to work on—your own personal plan, broken down and in the order of importance that most makes sense to you. When you know what matters most in your life, you can use this book to help you accomplish your goals. You don't need to read it from cover to cover at first. But even if you do, be sure to come back to this first chapter and narrow down those areas you know you need to get a grip on. Concentrating on these right away will have a significant impact on your life.

Doing the exercises I've given you will make the information presented here more effective. Write down your thoughts and make a plan. Consider drafting a written contract. Share your plan or contract with a buddy. Having a "partner in crime" can drive your likelihood of success up another big notch. Make sure you pick someone who'll be "in your face" about what you say you want. Do the same for your partner. Put due dates on your contract or plan and tell your buddy to get on your case when the date is drawing near. Meet in person or by phone with your buddy every week or month to review your progress, and celebrate when you meet a deadline. Have the same commitment to the other person's goals that you have for your own.

Be fair to yourself. You need to look at any special considerations you may have. My husband and I, for example, both work at home in separate businesses. We have a much larger volume of paperwork, supplies, and equipment than the average household does. Managing these areas takes more of our

CAUTION Pileups!

Using your spouse or your significant other as your "buddy" in setting your goals could have some pitfalls. Your partner may be one of the challenges you'll be dealing with later (see Part 6). But if he or she is the supportive, nurturing, team-player type, by all means, enlist your partner's help!

energy than is required by most people. These variables need to be taken into account in our household plan.

Friends of ours own and operate an animal-training business from their home. They need to concentrate on daily cleaning of certain parts of their home and deal with lots of strangers coming in and out. If you have a large family with children of varying ages, your considerations are different from a couple's whose children are all grown and gone. Different still is a household consisting of one individual. While you do your self-assessment, be aware of the realities of your circumstances and know that your plan needs to take these into account. You probably need to tackle the special challenges your particular lifestyle presents first.

As you get serious about setting your goals, think about the rewards. Visualize the final result you're aiming for. Draw a mental picture of how being organized would look in your life.

Wish-full Thinking

Now get out that pad and pencil. We're going to do some broad-based goal setting. Make a separate sheet for these eight major areas of your life:

- ◆ People (you get help with this in Chapter 8)
- ◆ Work (Chapter 9)
- ◆ Food (Chapter 11)
- ◆ Clothing (Chapter 12)
- ◆ Shelter (Chapters 10–14)
- ◆ Money (Chapters 15 and 16)
- ◆ Health (Chapter 21)
- ◆ Fun (Throughout this book!)

On each sheet, make a random list under the main topic of how you'd like that area to be. Don't hold yourself back or censor yourself. No matter how irrelevant or unachievable your wishes and desires may seem, write them down. Include your "if onlys"—the things you'd like to have or do if you had more time, money, or skill. By including everything, you'll get clearer about what you really want.

For example, under Food, your goals might be to eat more healthful foods and perhaps lose some weight. How can being organized help you meet these goals? By having the proper foods on hand, by actually planning your meals to stay within certain nutritional guidelines, and by having the right equipment for preparing those foods handy, your chances soar. If your goal is to become a gourmet cook and start your own catering business, however, your kitchen and your meal planning would look completely different.

Resource Files

Some recommended books to help you further with goal setting and planning are *The Magic Lamp: Goal Setting for People Who Hate Setting Goals*, by Keith Ellis; *The 7 Habits of Highly Effective People: Powerful Lessons in Personal Change*, by Stephen Covey; and two books by Barbara Sher, *Wishcraft: How to Get What You Really Want* and *I Could Do Anything If I Only Knew What It Was: How to Discover What You Really Want and How to Get It*.

On the sheet for Money, your goals might be to get out of debt or secure a better-paying job. Your goals would reflect your desire to change your current situation. Developing a plan and organizing your life around that plan can certainly help you get out of debt or find that new position. If you're debt-free and make enough money in your current job, the way you organize the financial areas of your life might be directed instead toward putting money away for retirement or financing a future project that's important to you.

The point is, if organizing your life is going to be lasting and meaningful, you don't just "get organized"—you *organize with purpose*. It's up to you to discover what that purpose is.

Narrowing Your List

Continue writing your "wish list" for each category until you've completed all eight. Now, on each sheet, circle the one wish that, if it were fulfilled, would have the most significant impact on your life right now. To add a little perspective, think about what would make the most difference in your life if you only had a year to live. I'm not getting morbid here; I'm just trying to inject a little urgency into this exercise. Funny how such a thought cuts through the chaff and gets to the kernel of wheat in a hurry!

As you read this book, use these sheets as a reminder when you begin to list specific tasks taken from each chapter that will help you achieve your goals. You can save the back of each sheet for that, if you like. These are the actions you can take to help you reach the goals you just decided are most important to you. In this way, wishes are transformed into goals, and goals into tasks; ultimately, all this is magically turned into results.

Going back to one of our earlier examples, let's suppose under Food, you listed as your primary goal "to lose 20 pounds and eat more healthful foods." When you turn to Chapter 11, you're going to be looking for the tips and projects that will help you organize your kitchen, and adapt them to cooking healthier meals that will work with your new eating plan. In Chapter 21, you'll learn more about adding a regular fitness plan to your schedule and planning for a healthier lifestyle.

If you put on the worksheet "perform better in my job and set up my office so I can find things," you'll want to pay special attention to Chapter 6, on handling paper, and Chapter 9, on work systems. I know you'll find at least three simple things you can do immediately to get headed in the right direction.

Setting Priorities

Now take your sheets and number them in order of priority, with number one being the most significant for you right now. If you believe the most important immediate area to work on is your relationships, the People sheet will have a number one on it. If your doctor told you to lose 50 pounds or you're likely to have a heart attack, Food and Health might share the number one spot. You get the idea.

How and what you organize first depends largely on your priorities. If you decide that weight loss is a top-of-the-list priority, your kitchen and food systems need special attention, as does your activity level. If your career is in high gear and you want to focus on furthering your education and getting ahead, but you've got the health thing pretty much in hand, other areas jump to the top of the list.

Next on each sheet choose two more wishes (goals) with a very high priority and circle them. That should give you three circled wishes on each sheet. Decide, in order of importance, which should be number two and which takes the number three spot. If you're having problems with goal setting and decide to do some extra work and read one of the books I've recommended, you'll have an even more finely honed set of goals and priorities to work with. *The Magic Lamp* covers all aspects of goal setting, including the things that get in the way, *The 7 Habits of Highly Effective People* focuses heavily on developing a mission statement, and *Wishcraft* and *I Could Do Anything If I Only Knew What It Was* will give you additional exercises to help you pinpoint your goals.

Finally, place the individual lists of three goals for each category on one sheet that you can put in your daily calendar book or on the wall near the desk or table you use to manage your daily affairs.

Pileups!

If you don't have a calendar/planner or a central planning place, you'll make the task of organizing much more difficult than it has to be. We deal with this in more detail in Chapter 7. For now, get an organizer and put it someplace where you'll be able to refer to it often.

Commit or Fail

Let's examine your motivations for a minute. Are you doing this because someone close to you is on your case because your lack of organization has caused that person a problem? Has something happened (such as you blew an important appointment because you forgot or couldn't find the materials you were supposed to bring)? Or did you just spend two hours looking for a wrench you know you have, and finally ended up driving to the hardware store so you could buy a duplicate to complete the job?

Those kinds of aggravating events can sure be the beginnings of getting motivated. But what if you take this trigger incident and broaden it? What if you make a decision to overhaul the larger areas that are out of control, where lack of organization seems to be holding you back and affecting your enjoyment of life? If you look at these incidents in their broader context, the motivation can be even greater and longer lasting.

This is going to take some work on your part, but it need not be overwhelming. You know the old saying: "How do you eat an elephant? One bite at a time." Well, that's what you're going to do—eat an elephant! I'm going to help you, but you're going to have to dig in with both knife and fork. Sure, you can just slap on some quick fixes, and they'll probably make a difference, at least for a while. But think of what a difference it'll make if you work on the big picture and set up organization systems that put your life in high gear. You can have it all if you're willing to make the effort and see it through.

The Master Plan: Keep It Flexible

This is not going to be like the fad diet many of us have experienced—something you go on for a week until you get tired of counting calories or denying yourself what you enjoy. Gradually it goes by the wayside. Why don't these diets work? They're too rigid. Expectations are too high. They make you feel deprived and stifled. They focus on the symptoms, not on making deeper lifestyle changes.

Experts agree that the best way to lose weight is to change your lifestyle to support healthful eating and regular exercise. You need information to make that change. Which foods? How to cook? Which exercise? How to stay motivated? That know-how—some of it general, some of it specific to you (what foods you like and which exercise you most enjoy, for example)—will let you create a plan that will help you achieve a more healthful lifestyle.

It's no different with getting organized. You need to do the following:

◆ Gather general information.

◆ Collect information about your specific likes, dislikes, strengths, and weaknesses.

◆ Identify goals.

◆ Set up a plan.

◆ Break up the plan into simple tasks.

◆ Schedule tasks, and work toward your goals a little each day.

◆ Develop ways to check progress and reward yourself for achievements.

> **Envisionings**
>
> Software programs can help you define your goals. I've heard good things about GoalPro 6.0. This program requires a Windows-based PC running Windows 98SE/Me/2000/XP, and 35MB of hard drive space. You can download a trial version by going to www.goalpro.com/trial.

It's important to do this brain work upfront, before you start tearing apart your closets or canceling all your magazine subscriptions. You've already made a good start in the goal-setting area. And there's an added bonus: The techniques you learn here to get your life in order can be transferred to any other area of your life you'd like to change. Figure out what you really want, make a commitment to get it, get the information you need to achieve your goal, and work at it a little each and every day.

Be willing to adapt your plan as you begin to implement it. Think of your life as continually "under construction," and be open to changing things as you go along. It's been said that life is the greatest do-it-yourself project you'll ever undertake. Acquiring the tools and skills you need will make you a better craftsman.

You Deserve a Break Today

Another fundamental concept for changing behavior is providing rewards when you do what you set out to do. Probably the greatest reward of getting your life organized is having more time to spend doing the things you most enjoy. Why not make a list of these things, and when you achieve one of your goals, reward yourself with some time spent doing one of them? I enjoy certain crafts and playing several musical instruments. When I've done something that was especially difficult or took special discipline, I reward myself with some time in front of the piano or a couple of hours of beading.

Be good to yourself. Changing your old ways will not be easy. We all resist change. It makes us uncomfortable. It can even be downright scary. Reward yourself as often as possible, even if it's just to look yourself in the mirror to say "Well done!" Create small rewards for small things, bigger rewards for bigger things, and don't forget to include some rewards just because you love yourself.

Rewards for getting organized will be inherent. There's the good feeling you get when you can finally walk into your walk-in closet again. The feeling of a burden being lifted when you're out from under all those books and magazines and you can finally face the daily junk mail undaunted can be exhilarating. There's the simple pleasure of spending an afternoon lazing in a hammock with a glass of lemonade in your hand, knowing that the house isn't going to fall down around your ears. You're prepared and up-to-date at work, so when you choose to do something fun, you feel completely guiltless, and everything you need for your downtime will be right there where you put it.

Some rewards are even greater than you may realize. When you're in control of your belongings and your time, it's easier to create a bigger vision and work toward it. You have the luxury of contemplating the grander,

> **Jump Starts**
>
> I want you to have a life you love. I'd like to see you take your dreams seriously and be able to achieve them. You deserve to wake up every morning excited about the day and what it will bring, knowing that you are prepared and clear about the prize you're going after. You deserve to be a *winner*. When you want what I want for you, you'll certainly get a "jump-start"!

more philosophical—even spiritual—things in life. So now is probably a good time to ask yourself, "What's my vision of the future?"

You remember the age-old interview questions: "Where do you want to be tomorrow? Next year? In five years?" Well, ask yourself now. Give serious thought to these familiar questions. Then move on to two even heavier questions: "What do I want on my gravestone? What do I want said in my eulogy?" Whoa! Cosmic, you say? Well, maybe. But answering these questions thoughtfully and honestly should set the stage for you to get the most out of this book and to start thinking with the bigger picture in mind—what getting organized can actually mean for your future.

Putting the "Resolve" in This Year's Resolutions

Each time we replace last year's calendar with a new one, we hear all about resolutions to be made (and probably broken) for the coming year. Usually these involve something we need to give up or deny ourselves, or they highlight bad habits we need to break. More often than not, these are the same resolutions we made the year before.

But from now on, you can look the new year square in the eye filled with excitement and expectancy. You'll view it as a time for congratulating yourself on your achievements and for setting new goals that are meaningful, realistic, and fueled by your innermost desires. You'll expect that the coming year will mean you'll have more of the things you wish for in your life and you'll be doing more of the things you love to do. Now that's a Happy New Year!

The Least You Need to Know

- Your upbringing has shaped your organization skills and habits.
- Setting standards too high actually interferes with lasting change.
- To ensure true success, set goals that are based on what you really want, not what others want for you.
- Being fair to yourself and rewarding yourself often will keep you motivated.

Chapter 2

It's All About "Stuff" and "Time"

In This Chapter

- Taking inventory of what you have and where it came from
- Examining your buying habits
- Making better decisions about the stuff that gets into your life
- Learning about the dynamics of time

You need to consider two essential elements when devising your plan to get organized: *stuff* and *time*. It's simple, right? Well, yes and no. Being honest about how they really operate in your own life can be a challenge. If you're willing to take a little time upfront to examine your personal habits and beliefs, however, you can make some powerful discoveries that lead to far-reaching changes.

Stuff includes all the physical things you own, things you spend time accumulating, maintaining, and disposing of; things you think about, worry about, and protect. Stuff also includes what you want or need to accomplish each day. There's always lots of "stuff to do."

Time is how you measure your life—the minutes, hours, days, weeks, and years. Everyone has the same amount of time in every single day—no more, no less. The difference between people is how they choose to use their time. One of the most compelling reasons to get organized is to have more time to do the things you want to do. No more lost time spent looking for things, fixing or replacing things that broke because they were stored poorly, or going out and buying duplicates because you can't find the originals. By learning the dynamics of time and how to manage it, you can get the "must-do" things out of the way quickly so you can do the fun things. And you can learn to arrange your life so the must-dos really are *musts*.

How Did You Get All This Stuff?

Before we get into the nitty-gritty of organizing your life, we need to start at the beginning—the sources of all the stuff in your life.

Stuff comes into your life in four ways:

1. **You take it.** When you first leave your parents' house to go out on your own, you take some stuff with you. Maybe a small box of books, a few pieces of furniture, stuffed toys, your old test papers and book reports, a scrapbook, and a handful of extra kitchen utensils your mom doesn't need anymore. You know—a little stuff to get you started.

   As you go through your daily life, you bring home more stuff. All those free items (note the magic word—*free*) that agencies, companies, and organizations offer you just for being such a nice person—and a potential customer. Sometimes you pick up stuff in the supermarket from a smiling lady at the door, from a prominently placed brochure rack, or from a shelf, or maybe you send for it in the mail or online (that includes all those downloads and printouts). Still, this is stuff you decide to bring into your life in one way or another. And, hey, it's *free!*

2. **It's given to you.** As time goes by, people give you stuff. There's a chair from Aunt Margaret, Grandma's framed pictures of the Statue of Liberty, Cousin Charlie's used golf clubs. It's hard to say no, and besides, this stuff, too, is *free!*

   Then there are those gifts you receive for all occasions. It starts with gifts for graduation, then your first apartment. Loving relatives and friends send you housewarming gifts. Next there are birthday presents, perhaps wedding gifts, gifts for anniversaries, and, of course, we must not forget Christmas. Maybe the gift is really not your taste, or you have absolutely no use for it, but gee, it's a gift! It's the thought that counts. And, by gosh, it was *free!* So it ends up in the attic, a storage closet, the basement, the breezeway, or any other place you tuck away things you never use.

3. **You inherit it.** Relatives and family friends die. Somehow their stuff finds its way into your stuff. You can't throw away Grandpa's pipe collection, even though you don't smoke. You can't pitch Mother's hand-crocheted doilies, even though you wouldn't be caught dead using doilies. By golly, they're *free!* So you integrate these possessions into your own or store them, keeping them safe to pass on to the next willing (or perhaps unwilling) party.

Wise Words

"Actually, this is just a place for my stuff. That's all I want, that's all you need in life, is a little place for your stuff. You know? I can see it on your table. Everybody's got a little place for their stuff. This is my stuff, that's your stuff. That'll be his stuff over there. That's all you need in life is a little place for your stuff."

—George Carlin

4. **You buy it.** Ah, now here's where it gets serious. When you're given things or inherit them, when someone offers you something for nothing, your desire to please, or at least not hurt another's feelings, and your love for the giver or the departed are strong motivators to keep stuff. But that doesn't explain why you buy so much useless stuff for yourself—on purpose! And if you do it in a wholesale club, you can multiply that inexplicable purchase by a dozen or more!

Why We Buy

How conscious were you when you made your last purchase? How did you decide to buy that item? Had you seen it on TV or in a magazine? Did you notice your neighbor with it and decide you just *had* to have it? Let's look at some of the influences on our buying habits.

As of December 31, 2002, the total number of radio and television broadcast stations in the United States was 26,319, according to the FCC. There are roughly 1,500 daily newspapers and more than 10,000 magazines. All these are avenues that advertisers use to reach potential buyers. Private and public agencies spend approximately $400 billion a year to get you to buy their products or services, change your attitudes, or influence your decisions. That's $1,600 a year just for one person: you.

The average American watches between 30 and 40 hours of television a week. If you fall within this average, in a typical day you watch well over 100 TV commercials.

Besides what you get over the tube, you're exposed to various forms of print media and radio. And let's not forget all those billboards, posters, bumper stickers, bus and cab displays, direct-mail packages, sales calls, spam e-mails, and online ads, not to mention the names and logos of companies plastered on mugs, hats, and memo pads. It's estimated that every day another 100 to 300 sales messages of one kind or another pass by you, either visually or through audio media. Even though Americans represent only 6 percent of the world's population, we consume more than 50 percent of the world's advertising.

> **CAUTION**
>
> **Pileups!**
>
> Don't let today's images of "the good life" in ads, TV programs, and movies pass you by without examining them. Are the images skewed toward a luxurious, "stuff-filled" lifestyle? Just notice what's being presented, and compare it with your own values and beliefs about what "living the good life" really is.

Is it any surprise that you sometimes wonder how that thing got in your shopping cart in the first place? Why your cabinets and closets are crammed with stuff you never use? "Where did that come from?" you ask. "What was I *thinking?*" But instead of admitting you made a shopping mistake, you keep all that stuff, convincing yourself you can't possibly get rid of it, because it's still "perfectly good." Sound familiar?

How to Control the "Gotta Have It" Habit

The first step to controlling the stuff you accumulate is to be aware of how, when, and why you decided to get it in the first place. Take your notebook and keep a running list of the number of times you go shopping next week. Include on it the amount of time spent, what you bought (you can use general categories, but be fairly detailed), and what time of day you went. Notice whether you went alone or with your spouse or a friend, how you felt when you were shopping, whether you went because you had something specific to buy, and whether you stuck to your original purpose or came out with additional items or something else entirely.

Next take a leisurely walk through your house, look at all your stuff, and ask yourself where it came from. If you bought it, try to remember how you came to the decision to buy it. How often do you use it? What purpose does it really serve in your life? What impact would there be if it were lost or stolen? Does it have a definite home in your living space or is it just hanging around?

Notice that I'm not saying you should cover your ears every time you hear a commercial, nor am I asking you to unplug your TV and put it in the attic. I'm not even suggesting that you skip reading your morning paper or tune out your favorite talk-radio host. All I want you to do is to become more conscious of the hidden persuaders around you, and take more conscious control of your buying decisions and your own mind. This is the first important step in organizing your life.

Be more critical of the *way* you view or listen to the mass media, too. The next time you see an advertisement, here are some important questions to ask to help you become a "consumer critic":

◆ What claims does the ad make, both obvious and subtle?

◆ Are the claims substantiated?

◆ What methods are being used to influence your thinking? Pricing gimmicks? Sex appeal? Vivid images? Demonstration? Staged testimonials? Peer pressure? Supposedly scientific studies? Guilt? Fear?

◆ What is the ad's key point? Is it directly related to the product?

◆ How much do you really know about the product from the ad?

◆ Is there some item you already own that performs the same function as well or better?

◆ If this stuff is so great, how come you got along without it until now?

Make it a game when you go shopping with your spouse or kids to keep these questions in mind. This way, you'll help to teach others critical thinking while you hone your own skills.

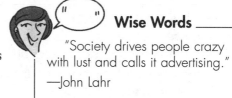

Wise Words

"Society drives people crazy with lust and calls it advertising."
—John Lahr

Buy! Buy! Buy!

The irrational accumulation of things we don't use, don't need, and eventually don't want is what I call the Acquisition Trap, and we all fall victim to it now and again. The Acquisition Trap is a system of assumptions, beliefs, and ideas about the nature of material things and what they can do for us. This system, which often works on us unconsciously, influences many aspects of our lives: where we live, how we work, and who or what we associate with our purchases. The Acquisition Trap seduces us into believing that owning something will make us sexy, or successful, or smart, and that a particular object or possession represents love, happiness, self-esteem, joy, or knowledge.

Resource Files

If you'd like to learn more about living with less and staying or getting out of the Acquisition Trap, check out my book *The Complete Idiot's Guide to Simple Living*. In addition, the Simple Living Network website, www.slnet.com, offers a free e-mail newsletter and lots of resources for a less-acquisitive lifestyle.

Owning a library of beautifully bound books won't make you an educated person. Reading them will. Wearing a certain scent won't make you irresistible to the opposite sex. Your overall appearance and personality is what attracts others. Toting a $500 briefcase won't make you successful in business. Experience, determination, and creativity will.

Be aware of the Acquisition Trap and decide whether you might be caught in it. This isn't about beating yourself up, or feeling guilty—it's just about paying attention to your habits, which can ultimately lead you to living a freer, more organized life.

Less Stuff, More Time

As you begin to apply the ideas in this book, you'll make new decisions about what stuff you have and what stuff you want to devote your time to acquire and maintain. You'll be paring down, examining your work habits, gaining control of your finances, and arranging your life so you can have more fun and spend more time with the people you love. You'll begin to free yourself up to focus on the people and activities that actually give meaning to your life. You'll voluntarily eliminate the excess and concentrate on the good stuff. You'll purge what doesn't work for you and organize the rest. To help you stay on track, I've devised the following 10 Basic Laws of Stuff. Refer to them every time you get the urge to collect more stuff. I hope they'll remind you why you really don't want to!

The 10 Basic Laws of Stuff

Law 1: Stuff breeds. The more you have, the more you need. Well, okay, if you leave two objects in a dark corner, they don't actually reproduce, but sometimes it sure seems that way. Let's suppose you buy a computer system. This basic system consists of a keyboard, the computer itself, and a monitor. Oh, and of course there are all those manuals. After you get the computer out of the box and set it up, the first thing you probably decide you need is a printer. Next you need a printer stand and some paper. Oh, and an extra printer cartridge. Then you need an antiglare screen for your monitor and some stuff to clean it with. But the stuff to clean the antiglare screen is different from the stuff you need to clean the monitor screen itself, so you need to get that other stuff, too. If you have a mouse, you'll probably need a mouse pad and a cleaning kit to keep it working properly. Next you'll start buying software, extra disks, and a CD-ROM drive and burner. And so on, and so on.

Lots of things operate like this. Consider the food processor and all the special attachments, racks, and caddies that go with it, not to mention cookbooks and whatever else you need to get the most out of your appliance. Maybe you're thinking about starting a collection of some kind? All those collector plates need hangers, or holders, or shelves. Those baseball cards need albums or boxes to keep them in. The cute little porcelain figurines need a display case or even a piece of furniture. Even the stuff used to store other stuff, such as Tupperware, just begs for something to hold all those lids when you're not using them!

Law 2: The useless stuff crowds out the good stuff. The more you have that's useless, obsolete, broken, or just plain junk, the harder it is to find (and find places for) the stuff you really value and use often. Finding the good stuff takes twice as much time and raises your blood pressure in the process. The more you have in your life that's extraneous and without purpose, the less time and energy you have for the good stuff.

Law 3: Dust loves stuff. Bugs love stuff. Rodents love stuff. Moisture loves stuff. When you store something unused for long periods of time, odds are that when you finally need it (if you ever do), it'll be useless anyway.

Law 4: Stuff loves to stay where it lands. It takes time and energy to put things away. That's why the coat or sweater that's flung over the chair tends to stay there forever. Inertia is working against you.

Law 5: Stuff expands to fill the space available. The bigger the house and the more storage space it has, the more stuff tends to accumulate.

Law 6: Over time, stuff becomes invisible. Ever notice how after you put something on your bulletin board, in a few days you can no longer see it? Things fade into the background through familiarity. I call this the Disappearing Stuff Phenomenon. After that scrap of paper hangs on the bulletin board for a while, it can be plainly visible, but you still won't see it.

Jump Starts

You can make the corollary to Law 4 work for you. The easier you make it to put stuff away, the more likely it will be. Refer to later chapters for tips on how to coordinate storage space with your daily habits.

Law 7: Stuff costs you money more than once. Don't fool yourself that the only cost of an object is its purchase price. First you pay to buy the item. Now you have to get it home. This may involve driving your car, taking public transportation, or incurring shipping charges. Next you have to store it, which may mean buying a container or a shelf to put it on. If it's valuable, you may need a security system, not to mention paying additional insurance premiums. If you move to another house (which will probably be bigger, because you need more storage), you need to pay to move it.

And if all this isn't enough, finally, your stuff continues to "cost" even beyond the grave, when you saddle your family with the unpleasant task of getting rid of it after you die. Think about the real cost of stuff next time you rush out to grab that "bargain."

Law 8: Stuff has a powerful effect on your state of mind. Clutter can be oppressive and depressing. If our possessions are in need of repair, that can add to our feelings of depression and failure. Stuff can weigh us down. We feel burdened by it and what we have to do to get and keep it.

Law 9: Stuff takes on value only when it is used. Unused stuff is just junk or clutter. How often you use it gives it increased value. Less use, less value. Stuff that may seem not to have any utilitarian value can add beauty to your life and therefore is being "used" by your senses and your soul. These aesthetic additions to your environment should be chosen with great care, to give you enjoyment every time you look at them. If you don't love it, lose it!

Law 10: Stuff doesn't make you happy; you do. I think this law speaks for itself. You know the drill: Money can't buy happiness. Well, it's the same with stuff. Both are just tools to help you achieve your own happiness.

Try spending an entire week without bringing any more stuff into your life. Call a moratorium on shopping, and use what you already have as much as possible. During this time, review the 10 Basic Laws of Stuff and see whether you don't become more aware of how stuff gets into your life.

Envisionings

The following visualization will help you understand how strongly stuff affects your mental state. Picture yourself in a room—for example, your office or garage—where everything is uncluttered, well positioned, and clearly labeled. Take a moment to notice the positive associations evoked by this smoothly functioning and spacious setting. Now imagine the stuff in the room beginning to expand, as paper spills out of the drawers and files onto the floor, labels get switched, and boxes begin to crowd out the elbowroom. What are your emotions now?

The 10 Basic Laws of Time

The other half of the organization equation is *time*. In a way, I discussed time indirectly when I talked about how having less stuff can give you more time to do the things you love most.

But time has its own properties and dynamics. And stuff struggles with time in our lives, requiring us to make constant day-to-day choices that influence how the former affects the latter. Experts tell us how to "manage" our time, but it helps to know a little bit more about its very nature. We couldn't very well have the 10 Basic Laws of Stuff without giving equal time to the 10 Basic Laws of Time, now could we?

Law 1: Time can be neither created nor destroyed. Phrases such as "making time," "buying time," or "saving time" actually reflect the misconception that time is a *thing*. Time is a concept humankind has created to measure and give proportion to the cycle of birth and death. Of course, we need this concept to make sense of our existence, but every now and then, it's worthwhile to remind yourself that your ideas about time are just that: *ideas*. It's up to you to make use of the time you have in a way that's meaningful and leaves you feeling satisfied and rewarded. You are in complete control of your time, even if you think you're not.

Law 2: Nobody gets more time in a day than you do. Ever notice how some people seem to get so much done in a day or week? You'd swear they had 36-hour days instead of the meager 24 the rest of us get. But remember we all have the same period between sunrises. It's just that some people know the secrets for using time to the fullest. Soon you'll know them, too.

Law 3: Time isn't money, it's your life. It's fashionable these days to talk about time as it relates to "the bottom line." I prefer to think of time as a collection of moments, filled with possibilities and beyond price. Certainly we need to know whether our efforts to earn a living are producing an adequate wage for time spent, but along with a growing bank account should be deposits of love and joy in the "bank book" of life.

Law 4: The value of time is created by opportunity and choice. What makes one moment more fulfilling than the next? I'd like to suggest that the opportunities we find or create and the choices we make are what give our time value and pleasure. Even missed opportunities and bad choices can be valuable if we allow ourselves to learn the lessons they can teach us.

Law 5: When time is lost, it can never be reclaimed. When you find yourself "wasting" time watching TV or engaging in idle gossip, remind yourself that these moments are gone forever and can never be retrieved. Imagine how you might want them back if you suddenly find out you have a short time left on the planet. Don't squander your most precious asset.

Law 6: Time invested in planning, preparing, and organizing is vital to making the most of your time. You may rebel at the idea of regularly scheduled planning sessions and careful preparation for both mundane and important events. In the beginning, it may seem that getting organized would take up too much of your time. But by the time you finish this book, you'll understand why time spent planning, preparing, and organizing will more than repay itself in the long run.

Wise Words

"Planning is bringing the future into the present so you can do something about it now."
—Alan Lakein

Law 7: You can always begin where you are. The first step to managing your time and moving toward your goals is to start. You know, "just do it!" Take stock of what tools and skills you have, make a plan, and take action. When you begin the process, you'll figure out what else you need along the way. Recriminations and excuses are a "waste of time."

Law 8: Identifying your personal time-wasters leads to mastery. Who knows where the time goes? You do! If you can't seem to remember, keep an activity log for a week and you'll see clearly where the black holes are that suck up your valuable time. Write down all the things you do and for how long, even the mundane things, and then total the categories up for each day. After you've identified the nonproductive uses of your time, write them up as a list and post it where you can see it each day. Be honest. How much time do you spend watching TV? On the phone? Chatting with your neighbor? Reading through junk mail? Surfing the web? Knowing your time weaknesses will help you avoid them.

Law 9: Time seems to expand when you set limits. The more you make conscious decisions about where, how, and with whom you want to spend your time and energy, the more of these commodities you'll seem to have. Setting limits means saying no to some things and yes to others. Bowing out of activities that don't support your goals and dreams frees up time for what really counts. Taking people up on offers of help or paying someone else to do certain tasks are ways of saying yes to more time for yourself.

Law 10: The secret is to enjoy the passage of time. If you're doing more now and enjoying it less, something's definitely wrong. Just being busy doesn't mean you're productive or happy. Do the work to identify your goals, create systems to achieve them, and allow yourself the time to enjoy the rewards. Time will be your friend, not a high-pressure enemy.

Organization is not an end in itself. You can't do it once and for all. It's an ongoing process, especially if you're an active person with lots of interests, goals, and people in your life. Sure, if all you do is get up in the morning, eat, read the paper, eat, watch TV, eat, stare into space, and go to bed, it's probably pretty easy to be organized.

Wise Words

"This I can report from the front lines: life never calms down long enough for us to wait until tomorrow to start living the lives we deserve. Life is always movement, always change, always unforeseen circumstances. There will always be something trying to grab your attention: the phone call, the child, the fax, the car breaking down, the check that never arrives in the mail. Let's just acknowledge that as far as real life is concerned, we are only one step away from dealing with dysfunction."

—Sarah Ban Breathnach

But if you're running a business, managing a household, pursuing hobbies, doing things with friends, serving in community organizations, taking classes, or whatever else you do, there's a lot more to being organized than throwing out the newspaper each day, washing the dishes, and turning off the tube. In fact, you picked up this book in the first place because you have a busy life. You want to get more out of it and be in control of your time and space. With your sincere willingness, some soul searching, and the information contained in this book, you can transform your life from merely okay to *awesome!*

The Least You Need to Know

♦ Unstuffing begins with understanding how things get into your life in the first place.

♦ The media and advertising have a powerful influence on your buying decisions.

♦ There are basic principles of stuff and time that operate in everybody's life.

♦ Getting control of your stuff and your time is the beginning of gaining control of your life.

3

Excuses! Excuses!

In This Chapter

- ◆ How to break old habits and form new ones
- ◆ Common excuses and how to stop making them
- ◆ Breaking the grip of procrastination
- ◆ Finding the time to get organized
- ◆ The cost of organization

If getting organized is so great, why doesn't everybody do it? Well, nobody said it was going to be a snap. There's effort involved, and sometimes the greatest effort goes into overcoming the obstacles we put in our own way. There are four main reasons people fail to get organized:

1. They have limiting ideas and beliefs about what they can and cannot do.

2. They procrastinate.

3. They believe they don't have the time to get organized.

4. They think the tools for getting organized will cost too much.

Recognize yourself in any of these? Well, in this chapter, we take a closer look at each reason and show that beginning to get organized this very minute is not only possible, but essential to achieving your goals. We also analyze the many reasons we give for why we don't or can't get organized, and expose them for what they are—excuses preventing us from getting what we really want in life.

How Habits Help or Hinder

A habit is what develops when you repeat something often enough that it becomes the customary way you do something. It's "business as usual" in the behavior department. If a habit doesn't seem to benefit us, we talk about "breaking it," much as we talk about taming a wild horse. Habits are hard to break, and the longer you've had them (the more times you've repeated and reinforced them), the more difficult they can be to change. The good news, though, is that you already know how to break an old habit. Really, you do! Because you got these habits through repetition, the way to change them is through the same process—repetition. And if we can break habits, we can also make them. Pick a new behavior, repeat it every day for three to four weeks, and it's yours.

Pileups!

Ideas, assumptions, and habits of thinking that served you in an earlier life situation may no longer be in your best interest now. Holding on to old patterns can block our efforts to make important changes. Be aware and let go!

Bet you don't think of a habit as something you do "on purpose"! Habits can be behaviors that just happen or ones we create consciously. We can create the habits we want to have.

When you're trying to make a major change in the way you do things, another area to look at is your beliefs. We all have automatic reactions to things, and many times we've acquired these reactions, these ways of thinking, *without* thinking. So they may not be suitable for our present lives and goals. It's time to examine some of those beliefs and see whether they might be getting in the way of getting your act together.

Excuses for Stuff

If you're wondering how you ended up with all this useless stuff in your life, read on. These could be some of the things you tell yourself and other people that give you permission to live in a junkyard.

I Might Need It Someday

Maybe yes, maybe no. There are several things to consider here. If you don't throw the item away, will you even be able to find it when you need it, and will it be in any useable condition by then? Chances are, if you haven't used it in the past two years, you won't need it in the next two. On the off chance you do, you can probably get it somewhere else. Besides, you're getting organized for the life you live today. If tomorrow brings different challenges, you can always revise your plan and arrange to have on hand the tools you need.

I'm Just Sentimental

Okay, be sentimental. I consider myself a sucker for things that remind me of the people I love or experiences I treasure. But how about being selective? And how about taking those mementos and turning them into something you'll enjoy every day, like a collage or an album? When it comes to memories, not all experiences and people are created equal. Pick the ones that are truly special and memorialize them. Ask yourself, "Is this really important to me, or am I just keeping it out of habit?"

One way I satisfy my sweet tooth for the past without taking up a lot of space is by keeping a journal. Through my written descriptions of people and things, I can relive my experiences again and again. The composition books I use to record my memoirs take up far less space than boxes of out-of-focus photographs or shelves full of knick-knacks. Some people more artistic than I am add sketches to their journals, and even poems or songs. An occasional photo to accompany the text might be an added way to enhance your personal chronicle. You can reread your journals as part of your annual New Year's ritual. You've created something that has meaning, not just accumulated more stuff. If it's just gathering dust in the attic, what does that say about how much it *really* means to you?

Resource Files

When you are considering buying in bulk, keep in mind the difference between irrational hoarding and wise preparation. Keep on hand whatever you really need in case of natural disaster or other emergencies, but don't turn your home into a warehouse.

More Is Better

The habit of stocking up can come from a variety of sources. It can be a way of feeling more secure—prepared for hard times. People who survive a major economic crisis, whether personal or on a larger scale such as a depression or a war, can overdo it in times of plenty to make up for what they lacked in times past. And wholesale clubs and discount stores make it easier and cheaper to add to the stockpile. We need to apply a little good sense here. How many people are in your family, and how fast will they consume the goods you're amassing? Will you be able to store them in the mean-time, and will they still be fresh when you get around to using them? Do you have room to store them so you can easily see what you have, so that you won't end up buying still more?

So be realistic. It's not a bad idea to store some essentials in case of a natural disaster or difficult times, or to stock up to avoid having to run out to the market constantly. But make sure you rotate older items with fresh ones, and give some serious thought to what you really need.

I'm Saving It for My Kids

This one is closely related to the "sentimental" excuse. If you believe you're filling your attic and basement with things to pass on to your progeny, ask yourself, "Is this something they'd really want?" If you already have adult children or grandchildren, you can ask this question with specific personalities in mind. If you're saving things for children who are yet to be, you might want to honestly ask how likely you are to become a parent or grandparent, and whether the average child of the new millennium will care about this stuff. Remember, tastes change.

> **Jump Starts**
>
> Try to limit your collections to things you can display or store easily; "trade up," getting rid of the lesser examples you have and acquiring better ones as you go along. That's a good rule for decluttering on many fronts. If a new one comes in, an old one goes out!

If you're pretty sure it's something any generation would love, why not pass it on now? Your children or grandchildren might enjoy using these family heirlooms, and you can experience the sense of connection and history that seeing them cared for in the here and now can bring.

One caution. If it's something you're truly ready to give away, do just that: give it away. No strings, no conditions. If the recipients hate it, they should be free to refuse it or pass it on. And promise them you won't be heartbroken if they break it.

It's Really Old

Ah, we've finally hit upon my own personal clutter trap. I love history, and I'm especially attracted to things from the nineteenth century. Victorian antiques could easily be my nemesis. But just because it's 150 years old doesn't mean it's worth having. (I have to keep telling myself this.)

Unless you're actually in the business of buying and selling antiques, even valuable old junk is still junk if all it does is clutter up your house.

It's Still Perfectly Good

It's only perfectly good if it's good to you now. Even if something's in tip-top shape, if you never use it, it's just a perfectly operating piece of junk. Pass it on to someone who really needs it, or sell it at a garage sale, and make room for the things that are truly "perfectly good" because they have usefulness and meaning for *your* life now, or just get rid of it and enjoy the "breathing room."

It Was a Bargain

Need we go back and review the basic principles of advertising we discussed in Chapter 2? Remember, sales are gimmicks to get people into the store. Many times stores run a sale to get rid of something that's going to be discontinued soon, or that a manufacturer has too many of. (Could it be it's not selling well for a reason?)

Unless the item is something you use regularly, or you made a careful decision to acquire something, researched the make and model you wanted, and it happened to be offered at a special price, a sale really isn't a bargain. Consider that when you're clipping all those coupons, too. Same principle. What should get you into a store is the fact that you need something specific and are prepared to buy it. Just think of all the time you'll save when you give up reading and shopping those circulars!

They Call It a Time-Saver

Even if this isn't one of your bugaboos, I bet you know someone who can't resist the latest newfangled thingamajig. Some people are just gadget freaks. They love all sorts of whose-its and whats-its, and can always think of an excuse to get them. Usually it's in the interest of making some task easier, saving money or saving time. Well, always build into the true cost of that gadget the time it takes to earn the money to buy it and to maintain the space you store it in. Add in the time it takes to find it, get it out, and use it, *plus* the time it takes to clean it after the task is done.

The Big Put-Off

Putting off 'til tomorrow what we need to do today is known as *procrastination*. We all do it now and then, but for some it can become a chronic condition. Sometimes knowing why we do something that has a negative effect on our goals and desires can be the beginning of changing how we behave. Now that we've looked at some of your excuses for keeping or acquiring more stuff, let's dive into the reasons you have for just not "getting around to getting organized."

Some underlying causes of procrastination are …

Pileups!

Keep a vigilant eye on the hidden time demands of so-called time-savers. For example, a food processor does a lot of things more quickly than preparing food by hand. But unless you're cooking in quantity, the time it takes to chop onions by hand will be a lot less than the time it takes to take out the processor, use it, clean it, and store it again.

- You're not really committed.
- There's something you don't want to face.
- You don't know how.
- You have some belief that's getting in your way.
- You're setting too high a standard.
- You're afraid you'll fail.
- You're trying to do too much at once.
- You haven't clearly defined your goals.
- Your energy level is low.
- You aren't convinced of the benefits.

The fact that you're reading this book and have gotten this far says to me you're at least somewhat committed to unstuffing your life and getting things on an even keel. If you didn't do the exercises in Chapter 1, go back and do them now, especially if you skipped the goal-setting section. When you have a mission and you know why you're doing something and what the benefits will be when you accomplish it, your excitement will be uncontainable.

If you're still dragging your heels, ask yourself what you're afraid of. Is it a possible conflict with your spouse? Are you afraid you might fail? Is it resistance to change? Let me ask you to put these concerns aside for now. We're going to deal with them in various ways throughout this book, and you'll have lots of small, specific steps you can take to help you confront your fears and accomplish your goals.

Examine your beliefs, as well. Look for things you hear yourself saying often, such as "I can't," or "I always," or "If only," or "Once I have … then I can." Replace this language with "I am," "I want," or "I can and I will." Concentrate on what you have control over, and the skills and resources you already possess. Focus on *acting*, rather than "being acted upon" and "reacting to." Be proactive.

> **Envisionings**
>
> When we don't have the benefits of a course of action clearly in mind, we will it put off. Visualization helps here. Picture yourself at work in a place where you can find everything in your files and never forget an appointment. See yourself dressing in the morning with a wardrobe that's well planned, easy to choose from, and always clean, pressed, and mended. See yourself preparing a meal in a sparkling, efficient kitchen where everything's within easy reach. Use visualizing results and even actions to help you break through stagnation and procrastination!

If your energy level is low, everything becomes a chore. Are you in poor health, not getting enough sleep, partying too much, or experiencing temporary depression? If you answer yes to any of these, give yourself the physical and emotional attention you need first, and then get to work.

Pulverizing Procrastination

Now that you've had a conversation with yourself about some of the underlying causes of your procrastination, here are some tips for breaking through the bottleneck:

- Tackle it head-on. Ask yourself, "What's the real reason I keep putting this off?"

- Take one step. Do *something* right away to get you started. Action produces momentum. Get started.

- Do the hardest thing first. Do the easiest thing first. (See which approach works better for you.)

- Clear the decks. Set aside time, clear a work area, and assemble the tools you need to get started. Make an appointment with yourself and write it in your calendar.

- Break down your plan into small tasks. Write down the larger tasks and divide each into its smaller parts or "bites." (Remember what I said earlier about how to eat an elephant?) See whether the task can be broken down in terms of time or physical space. Do five files, clean one cabinet, set the kitchen timer and spend ten minutes on the task. If you don't have a kitchen timer (the kind that ticks!), get one! We'll be using it a lot on our Organizing Your Life journey.

- Do something toward your goal every day, even if it's a very small thing.

- Set deadlines for yourself. Reward yourself when you meet them.

◆ Set a fixed time to take on a task every day or week, and stick to it. This will help form a habit, and it'll take less energy over time to get it done.

◆ If one way isn't working, try another. Adopt a "whatever it takes" attitude.

◆ Don't let too much attention to detail or perfectionism get in the way. Visualize the end result and be realistic about it.

◆ Enlist some help. Finding someone to share a task with can get you started and keep you going. Enlist your kids, your spouse, or a buddy. Set specific goals, check in with your "partner in crime" regularly, and enjoy a reward together when you follow through.

◆ Do it now! Get in the habit of doing things right away. If you have something to put away, do it. Don't put it on the counter on the way to the garage, or on the stairs to be put away later. Finish it. The sense of completing tasks on a regular basis will reinforce itself.

◆ Increase your rate of motion. Set a timer, challenge yourself, make the time go faster. Create momentum using whatever tricks work for you. Get wise to yourself.

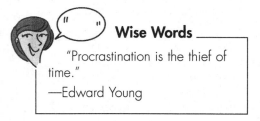

Wise Words

"Procrastination is the thief of time."

—Edward Young

If you keep putting things off in spite of all these efforts, maybe you *really* don't want to get organized. Either shelve the idea until you're ready to commit some significant thought and energy to it or, if you're not ready to give up just yet, hire someone else to do it. Perhaps hiring a professional organizer will be the jump-start you need, and you'll be able to finish the job yourself.

Making Time

Do you think you don't have the time to get organized? Actually, you don't have the time *not* to get organized. Just consider all the extra steps, the time wasted, the duplicated efforts, the frustration, the feelings of losing your grip, the missed appointments and important events, and the lost moments. Getting organized will fill your pockets with time to spare.

But I Don't Have the Money to Get Organized!

Organization is a state of mind, not a thing. It doesn't have to cost a lot of money to get organized. In fact, you can't afford not to. There are lots of low-cost or even recycled storage and organization solutions, and I point them out to you throughout this book. Wherever possible, I give you several alternatives, including budget-conscious ones, for the materials suggested.

However, spending a little extra money on the right tools and equipment will save you gobs of dough in the long run. Quality storage containers and tools quickly pay for themselves. Weigh the cost of something that helps you get and stay organized against the cost of chaos. I think you'll find it's worth it in the long run to spend money on quality items that do the job well and last a long time. Besides, after you read the chapters on organizing your finances later in this book, you'll have the money in your budget to do it right!

> **Resource Files**
>
> Be sure to consult some good books on managing your time, an inextricable part of getting organized. Two good books on time management are *Time Management from the Inside Out: The Foolproof System for Taking Control of Your Schedule and Your Life* by Julie Morgenstern, and *First Things First: To Live, To Love, To Learn, To Leave a Legacy* by Stephen Covey.

So Stop Making Excuses and Go!

Let's face it. People who are always making excuses are a drag. Just think about the people in your life who do it and how you feel about them. Not high on your list of folks to while away the hours with, right?

Don't be one of those people! Start today. Take your first step toward achieving what you truly desire. If you keep making excuses and procrastinating, you give up control. Why drift through life when you could be at the helm, steering? Concentrate on what you can change, and begin.

The Least You Need to Know

- ◆ Habits are made through repetition and can be changed the same way.
- ◆ By looking at your beliefs in light of your goals, you can spot obstacles to your progress.

◆ Procrastination has a variety of causes, and you can immediately take simple steps to combat it.

◆ You can't afford the time or the money it costs to stay disorganized.

Chapter 4

When Stuff Rules Your Life

In This Chapter

- Defining clutter disorder, hoarder's disorder, and compulsive spending disorder
- Understanding the relationship between chronic disorganization and attention deficit disorder (ADD)
- Determining if your relationship with stuff is seriously out of control
- Getting help and support for recovery and growth

Most of us recognize ourselves in the first three chapters of this book. If you weren't struggling with clutter and disorganization, chances are you wouldn't have picked up this book in this first place. Even the most organized people have to do periodic tweaking, can find themselves getting behind, and may sometimes be prone to procrastination. But there's a line beyond which disorganization becomes a debilitating and possibly even dangerous disorder.

In this chapter, we discuss some serious personal issues. It's beyond the scope of this book to fully cover their complexities, so I give you some basic information along with resources to lead you to the real experts—mental health professionals, support groups, and some helpful books. If you're dealing with some of these serious issues, I encourage you to reach out and get the help you need. I hope reading this chapter will be an important first step.

Hoarder's Disorder and a Case of the Messies

For some folks, the terms *messy* or *disorganized* just don't quite express it. The chaos in their lives is extreme and chronic. The debris and mess seriously hamper their ability to function day to day, and may even have a negative impact on their ability to have a happy marriage, parent their children effectively, hold a job, and maintain healthy and satisfying friendships. The problem may be so extreme that their surroundings have actually become unsafe or unhealthy or both. When clutter can mean being evicted from your dwelling or risking losing your children or being fired from your job, it's time to take some drastic measures.

This extreme behavior can come under a variety of names and categories. It's not always easy to diagnose exactly what it is or where it comes from. Sometimes labeled "clutter disorder" or "hoarder's disorder," this is a new area being explored in psychology, and many therapists are not trained or experienced in treating it. Hoarder's disorder is considered an obsessive-compulsive disorder (OCD) by the medical community. This can be caused or at least exacerbated by a chemical imbalance in the brain. Extreme cluttering and disorganization may also be manifestations of other psychological problems or even neurological disorders. But, as with many other debilitating behavioral problems, professionals can be located to provide treatment, and self-help groups—both local and online—have been formed to offer the support and information needed to make great strides in conquering the problem.

According to Sandra Felton, founder of Messies Anonymous and a self-professed "messie," approximately 15 percent of the population is in this category. She describes her life, before she got help, as a real struggle:

> I had big houses, little houses, no children, children, maids, no maids. But under all circumstances I was a messie. This was not only frustrating, but surprising, since I was quite capable in other areas of my life.

Wise Words

"Anything that can get you evicted, get your children taken away from you, keep you from inviting people into your home, or get you charged more by retailers and the tax authorities because you can't find the paperwork needed to pay them on time, is a real problem."

—alt.recovery.clutter FAQ

Pileups!

Ignoring the signs that there's a deeper problem operating in your life can mean serious repercussions later on down the road. People who recognize their needs and seek help are smart and courageous!

Mike Nelson, author of *Stop Clutter from Stealing Your Life: Discover Why You Clutter and How You Can Stop*, puts it this way:

> I had to admit that I was different from other people, that I was powerless over my compulsion, before I could seek help and begin to recover. My life today is hundreds of times better than it was before I faced my cluttering. Cluttering is a personality dysfunction. It has nothing to do with lack of self-control or being a bad person.

Are You a Compulsive Clutterer?

But how do you know whether you're in the "extreme" category? There are warning signs. Ask yourself the following questions, and if you answer yes to several of them, this may be the time to come to grips with what's happening and seek professional help.

Yes	No	
❏	❏	Have you read all the books, hired a professional organizer, and repeatedly tried to get started decluttering your life, yet never seem to be able to do it?
❏	❏	Is the accumulation in your house a severe health or safety hazard?
❏	❏	Do you have a deep fear of people coming to the house and seeing the clutter and dirt? Do you pretend not to be home so you don't have to open the door?
❏	❏	Do you lose sleep over lost papers, money, or other valuable items?
❏	❏	Do you sometimes have to clear a spot on your bed just to be able to sleep?
❏	❏	Do you have to eat somewhere other than the kitchen or dining room table because there no room to put your plate?
❏	❏	Do you chronically miss appointments and important occasions, even though you have the best intentions of making them?
❏	❏	Are you often referred to as unreliable or disorganized by others?
❏	❏	Has the safety of your children ever been compromised because of clutter or disrepair in your home?
❏	❏	Do you regularly pay late payment fees or penalties not because you don't have money to pay the bills, but because you can't find them, can't remember to deposit checks, or are unable to keep track of your checkbook balance?

continues

continued

Yes	No	
❏	❏	Do you avoid leaving the house or cancel appointments for lack of clean or mended clothes?
❏	❏	Do you drive a vehicle with expired insurance or registration, even though you have the money to pay these fees?
❏	❏	Is there so much stuff in your car no one else can ride with you?

These could be indicators that your disorganized habits go deeper than the average person's. If you're not sure, seek the help of a professional, and be open about your behaviors and concerns. There's a lot we don't understand about disorganization and related disorders. Only recently, for example, have they been linked to attention deficit disorder, obsessive-compulsive disorders, and certain speech pathologies, such as stuttering. In the most extreme cases, there may be stacks of newspapers from floor to ceiling; clothes covering all the floors; broken furniture and appliances left blocking doors and windows; and boxes of saved paper, plastic bags, and jars; and cans filling basements and porches. Sufferers may be unable to leave their homes, handle their finances, or have meaningful relationships.

Envisionings

Close your eyes and visualize being enveloped by a huge pink bubble. With this bubble around you, you can be, have, or do anything you want to—you are confident and nothing can harm you. Inside the bubble, you feel bliss and happiness. Imagine that you are unconditionally cared for by others, enjoying their respect and esteem. As you bask in the warmth of your own worth and worthiness, say to yourself, "I am never alone. I have a wise and loving friend within me. If I need help, I can ask for it anytime."

Attention Deficit Disorder and ADHD

A condition that can also manifest itself in extreme cluttering and disorganization is attention deficit disorder (ADD) or ADD with hyperactivity, ADHD. People with ADD often have trouble setting priorities or planning in what order to do a series of tasks or activities. They may start something, but be unable to finish. People suffering from ADD find their mind is so cluttered with competing thoughts and messages that it is hard to function. It's no wonder that mental clutter manifests itself in physical clutter and disorganization.

If you're not sure whether or not you or someone close to you might have ADD or ADHD, there's a quiz available online to give you some clues. You can find it at Mental Help Net at mentalhelp.net. On the left side, scroll down to Resources and click Tests & Questionnaires, and choose the Jasper/Goldberg Adult ADD Questionnaire.

Education professionals are becoming more informed and better able to identify ADD in children. This disorder can severely inhibit a child's ability to learn in a conventional educational setting, and can lead to behavioral problems if not treated. If caught early, however, many positive steps can be taken to circumvent the negative patterns that can develop in ADD children as they grow into adulthood.

Shopping When You Don't Need More Stuff

Compulsive shopping/buying disorder can be another culprit in the fight against clutter and disorganization in a person's life. In this instance, the accumulation of stuff is an offshoot of the problem. The main cause, however, is a compulsive need to buy things, even when they are not needed and they are not serving any purpose in a person's life. Compulsive shopping disorder can cause financial ruin and destroy relationships.

If you're not sure whether you might have a compulsive spending problem, ask yourself these questions:

- Do you continue spending on credit, even though you're unable to pay off your current credit card debt?

- Are you facing bankruptcy or at least serious financial problems, yet are unable to curb your spending?

- Do you often have arguments with your partner, family members, or friends about your spending?

- Do you have a closet stuffed full of clothes you never wear, some with the price tags still on, yet find yourself shopping for more?

- When you're in a store, do you find you cannot leave without buying something?

- Do you spend inordinate amounts of time shopping or thinking about shopping?

- Do you shop to avoid pressure, to escape or fantasize, to increase your self-esteem, or to feel more secure?

Resource Files

Here are two books to help with understanding and overcoming compulsive spending: *Born to Spend: Overcoming Compulsive Spending* by Gloria Arenson; and *A Currency of Hope* by Debtors Anonymous.

Wise Words

"Clutter is anything we don't need, want, or use that takes our time, energy, or space, and destroys our serenity. It can be outgrown clothes or obsolete paper. We may be selective in some areas, but not in others. Objects may be strewn about or wedged into drawers; neatly stacked or stowed in storage."

—The Twelve Steps of Clutterers Anonymous

◆ Do others regularly make comments about your excessive spending?

◆ Do you often spend money you don't have on things you don't need, or perhaps already have several of at home?

If you answered yes to any of these questions, you may be suffering from compulsive shopping disorder. If you're not sure, ask a professional to help with a diagnosis.

Compulsive spending and hoarder's disorder are only two types of obsessive-compulsive disorders (OCDs). Other OCDs manifest themselves in behaviors that are the reverse of disorganization or out-of-control spending, such as compulsive neatness. Both extremes mean that stuff somehow rules your life and interferes with your enjoyment of regular activities and other people. If you can't stand to see something out of place, if you have to constantly straighten and clean, if it's difficult for you to relax without thinking about tidying up or cleaning, you may have OCD. Again, if you're uncertain, seek the help of a professional to get a more accurate diagnosis and devise a treatment strategy.

Other Disorders and Conditions

Other mental health issues and, possibly, infectious diseases may influence an individual's ability to manage his or her life and stay organized. Some of these are depression, bipolar disorder, chronic fatigue syndrome, and fibromyalgia. If you're not sure what may be exerting its influence in your situation, a health-care professional, a professional therapist, counselor, psychologist, or psychiatrist can help you sort it out. If you suspect a particular culprit, by all means share your suspicions with your mental-health professional.

It's important that you identify the source of your problem and get help. You don't have to live with anxiety and chaos! You deserve better. If you or someone you love needs help, lead the way.

Never Fear—Help Is on the Way!

All the disorders and conditions I've mentioned can be treated. There's excellent help out there, and the resources in this chapter should help you at least get started on the road to a better future. There are varying degrees of distress, of course. But for some people the situation is grave, and drastic measures need to be taken.

Don't wait to seek professional help if you feel this is the case. If you believe the situation is less severe, however, you can still take steps to help yourself, armed with good information and the support of other people who suffer from the same problems. In fact, for some, the ongoing support of people like themselves, in addition to working with a mental-health professional, is the best route to real recovery.

> **Jump Starts**
>
> If you join a group, you'll probably find lots of resources available there that you can borrow or share, rather than purchase on your own. This can be the first step toward eliminating clutter in your life. You'll have partners who can catch you when you begin to repeat old, destructive patterns, and cheer you on when you make new, more constructive decisions. You're not alone anymore!

Hoarder's Disorder

One option for recovery is to find a group that is designed to work on your specific problem. Two I've listed here are 12-step groups, similar to alcohol and drug recovery groups and based on the principles of Alcoholics Anonymous. These groups follow a defined structure and set of principles, and have produced some dramatic life-changing results. They're free, and if there isn't one in your area, it's easy to start one on your own. The following are some 12-step groups for clutter disorders:

- Clutterers Anonymous
  P.O. Box 91413
  Los Angeles, CA 90009-1413
  clawso@hotmail.com
  www.clutterersanonymous.net

  For info send a long, first-class SASE with twice the minimum first-class postage.

- Messies Anonymous
  5025 SW 114th Avenue
  Miami, FL 33165
  786-243-2793
  www.messies.com

Founded in 1981 by confessed "messie" Sandra Felton in Miami, these groups use her books to guide in the recovery process. Her latest is *The New Messies Manual: The Procrastinator's Guide to Good Housekeeping*. Felton also offers audiotapes and videotapes and gives seminars nationally.

◆ Clutterless Recovery Groups Inc.
Mike Nelson
13121 South Madrone Trail
Austin, TX 78737-4431
512-351-4058
clutterless.org

Mike Nelson is the author of several books on clutter recovery, and is himself in recovery from hoarder's disorder. This site offers a range of resources and support.

Other Disorders

The following sections list some additional organizations that offer information, referrals, and support.

Obsessive-Compulsive Disorder

Obsessive-Compulsive Foundation
676 State Street
New Haven, CT 06511
203-401-2070
info@ocfoundation.org
www.ocfoundation.org

Resource Files

Bipolar disorder and depression touch people in all walks of life. One of the more well-known personalities who has gone public with her bouts of this mental illness is actress Patty Duke. Her book (with writer Gloria Hochman) is called *A Brilliant Madness: Living with Manic-Depressive Illness*. A second recommended book on the subject is Kay Redfield Jameson's *An Unquiet Mind: A Memoir of Moods and Madness*.

Obsessive-Compulsive Anonymous
P.O. Box 215
New Hyde Park, NY 11040
516-739-0662
hometown.aol.com/west24th/index.html

Compulsive Spending/Shopping Disorder

Debtors Anonymous
General Service Office
P.O. Box 920888
Needham, MA 02492-0009
781-453-2743
www.debtorsanonymous.org

General Emotional Disorders

Emotions Anonymous International
P.O. Box 4245
St. Paul, MN 55104-0245
651-647-9712
info@EmotionsAnonymous.org
www.emotionsanonymous.org

Attention Deficit Disorder

ADDA
P.O. Box 543
Pottstown, PA 19464
484-945-2101
www.add.org

This organization will help you find ADD professionals and support groups in your area, whether you're an adult with ADD or the parent of an ADD child.

Bipolar Disorder and Depression

National Depressive and Manic-Depressive Association
730 N. Franklin Street, Suite 501
Chicago, IL 60610-7224
800-826-3632
www.ndmda.org

Chronic Fatigue Syndrome

The American Association for Chronic Fatigue Syndrome
27 N. Wacker Drive, Suite 416
Chicago, IL 60606
847-748-8288
Admin@aacfs.org
www.AACFS.org

Finding a Local Group

When attempting to locate any self-help group in your area, first check with the headquarters of the proper organization, and ask for a local contact person. If you're close enough, you may be able to join their group. If not, you may want to think about starting your own.

Call the contact person at the national organization or the closest chapter and pick her brain. She'll probably have lots of ideas to share about how she got started, and what to avoid in starting your own group. If you decide you want to do that, put up a notice on bulletin boards at local churches, the library, the post office, Laundromats, health-food stores, and any other public place where you think you might find people who'd like to work with you on starting a group. Leave your name with local mental-health professionals, as well. If you have a community self-help clearinghouse or hotline, let them know of your desire to form a group and ask them to refer people to you.

Put a notice in the public service announcement section of your local newspaper. Consider any newsletters of organizations that might reach people for your group. Contact professional organizers in your area and let them know what you're trying to do. A professional organizer often knows people who might benefit from such a group. To find one, contact the National Association of Professional Organizers, 4700 W. Lake Avenue, Glenview, IL 60025; 847-375-4746; www.napo.net; e-mail: hq@napo.net.

Going Online

Even if you decide not to join a group, you may want to subscribe to an organization's newsletter for support, subscribe to an online mailing list, or check in with an online newsgroup. For online resources, try some of the resources listed in the following sections.

Mailing Lists

Decluttr mailing list

Decluttr@MAELSTROM.STJOHNS.EDU

To subscribe, send this message to listserv@MAELSTROM.STJOHNS.EDU: Subscribe Decluttr (Your) FirstName LastName.

This list and its monthly archives are public. You can subscribe to the list in an index (table of contents) format or a digest (one mailing with all messages for the day) format.

The Flylady mailing list and website

I discovered the Flylady a couple of years ago, and I can't help but sing her praises. Basing her system on the "Slob Sisters" system outlined in the *Sidetracked Home Executives* book series, Marla Cilley has improved on their ideas and created a support system ideal for those who need daily help getting their housework done and clearing their lives of clutter. She recently published her own book called *Sink Reflections*, based on the Flylady system.

To subscribe, go to the Flylady website at www.flylady.net. While you're there, check out the archives and get started on your routines and periodic "27 Fling Boogies." All can benefit from the Flylady's wisdom, but her principles are especially helpful for those suffering from depression, ADD, or ADHD.

Compulsive spenders mailing lists

There are several mailing lists for people with compulsive spending disorder. To sign up, register at group.yahoo.com and type in "compulsive spending" to get a list.

Bipolar disorders information center

Their main website is www.mhsource.com/bipolar/index.html.

Subscribe to the bipolar mailing list at www.mhsource.com/bipolar/mailinglist.html.

Roses and Thorns mailing list

The Roses and Thorns mailing list deals with issues related to diagnosed mood and personality disorders, such as depression, bipolar disorder, and seasonal affective disorder (SAD). To subscribe, go to health.groups.yahoo.com/group/rosesandthorns.

Newsgroups

alt.recovery.clutter

This is a place where people who have cluttering as a problem can discuss methods of dealing with it, share experiences and tips, support each other, recommend books, and find contact information for organizations. It doesn't speak for any particular organization. They have created a FAQ (list of frequently asked questions) available at www.faqs.org/faqs/alt-recovery/clutter.

alt.support.depression.manic
soc.support.depression.manic
soc.support.depression.misc
soc.support.depression.treatment

These four newsgroups are for those suffering from bipolar disorder (also known as manic depression).

Other Online Resources

www.pendulum.org

Bipolar Disorders Portal at Pendulum Resources.

www.cdc.gov/ncidod/diseases/cfs/index.htm

Chronic fatigue syndrome home page from the Centers for Disease Control and Prevention.

If you don't see what you're looking for here, open your favorite search engine and put in any of the terms I've mentioned. You'll find tons of information for each, including help understanding what these disorders are, clues to help you decide what might actually be going on in your own particular case, and resources for finding professional help and support groups in your hometown. If you don't have access to the Internet, check the Yellow Pages of your local phone book, or call the nearest mental-health facility.

Don't underestimate your own ability to do this. After you've identified a problem, you can begin to solve it. Many of these disorders can be overcome or minimized with hard work and persistence. However, if you really try to do it on your own and you're just overwhelmed or can't seem to get out of your own way, reach out and join with others who can help show you the way and support you in your efforts. A support group can give you a sense that you're not in this alone, plus provide some solid ideas and approaches you can try in your own life.

I have nothing but admiration for people who face their illnesses and work on their own recovery. I hope in some small way I've helped you or someone you love find a way. May you gather the courage, energy, and self-love to triumph and be well!

Wise Words

"It is hard to fight an enemy who has outposts in your own head."

—Sally Kempton

The Least You Need to Know

◆ If disorganization and clutter interfere with a person's ability to function on a most basic level, there is likely a more serious disorder that needs to be addressed.

◆ Although each disorder has its own particular symptoms, conditions such as attention deficit disorder (ADD), hoarder's disorder, and bipolar disorder all can lead a person to live a highly disorganized life.

◆ Seeking professional help and joining a support group are effective ways to cope with emotional disorders and diseases that affect the ability to organize and manage one's life.

◆ There are many resources online for information on clutter-related disorders and diseases. Using a search engine will probably provide you with much of what you need, if it's not listed in this chapter or in your local phone book.

Part 2

Stuff Simplified

These next two chapters get you into the unstuffing mode. By reducing the amount of clutter that comes into your space, as well as getting rid of what's already there and in your way, all the rest of your efforts at organizing your life will go more smoothly. First, you learn all the basic steps for managing your stuff. Then we devote some extra time to the bane of our modern existence—paper!

Chapter 5

Utterly Uncluttered Space

In This Chapter

- Simple decluttering principles you can adopt right away for immediate results in any area
- Questions to ask yourself when unstuffing your stuff
- A 10-step program for clearing out the clutter
- The real costs of having too much stuff in your life

You're impatient, I know. So why not get started right this minute? Get out of that chair! Don't even think about going for that remote! Stop whatever you're doing and get the urge to purge!

In this chapter, I'm going to give you 10 quick and easy steps to get you started on the unstuffing track. They're basic principles you can begin using immediately to make the rest of your organization efforts fall right into place. They can be used to unstuff a drawer, a cabinet, a closet, or a whole room. You can use them in 15-minute "quickie" purging sessions or spend a whole day doing a "clean sweep" of an area you just can't put up with anymore. You're in charge. These 10 basic steps are your keys to creating new habits.

Getting Started

Pick one small area to begin. Don't try to do anything too big. It can overwhelm you and then you're back to square one. If you can, pick an area that supports your highest priorities. Key areas would be a corner of your bedroom (to ensure a peaceful night's sleep) or maybe a drawer or cabinet in the kitchen (the hub of the house), but you choose. Just pick a place to start and make it small and manageable.

Decide not to allow yourself to get distracted. Don't answer the phone if it rings. Pick a time when you're not likely to be interrupted. (My best time is early in the morning before the rest of the household wakes up!)

As you note places where buying or building additional storage or buying storage solutions would make a difference, jot them down in a notebook (you might want to have one just for your organization exercises and ideas and for taking notes as you work through this book). Don't worry about any order or deadlines for now. This list will become your Master List (to be discussed further in Chapter 7), but for now you don't need to think about what it's called. Just keep a running list of anything that needs to be done or that you'd like to do someday. Record any ideas that pop into your head while you're plowing through your stuff. If you're purging a drawer and you think having dividers or containers would help, write that down. If you're going through a bunch of papers and think that you need files, make a note of it.

Next set up four boxes. Label them *Put Away/Return*, *Keep*, *Pass On*, and *Fix*, or use your own labels if you like (although we'll be referring to these labels). Have a big trash can nearby. If you have a recycling program in your area, you may want to set up another box labeled *Recycle*, or just bring the plastic recycling bin with you for things such as newspapers and magazines.

Jump Starts

When you do your first timed sort, anything you just can't make a decision about (but try hard to right away) or stuff that needs further sorting can go in the Keep box. Don't spend too much time deliberating, but try to let go of as many things as you can right from the start.

The Put Away/Return box is for stuff that doesn't belong where you found it. It may be other people's junk (or treasures) or simply items that you know belong in another room or somewhere else. If you find books or videos that need to be returned or have borrowed stuff you need to give back to its rightful owner, put those things in this box as well.

The Pass On box is for stuff to hand down, give to charity, or sell at a garage sale—anything you're not keeping that is too good to throw away but that you don't need to keep.

The Keep box is for things you know you need or want. It's also for stuff you just can't figure out what to do with during this speed purge. Maybe you don't have a place for it right now. (You'll need to find one if you decide to keep it around.) Even worse, you may not know what it is (*mystery* stuff)! If at all possible, quickly ask yourself the questions in Step 2 (below) and make a decision now to trash/recycle it, pass it on/return it, or put it away where it belongs. But if you're just not sure where it goes right now and it takes a lot of time to decide, you'll at least have a temporary place for it in the *Keep* box.

The Fix box should only be used for items you really believe are worth fixing. If it's been broken for five years and you've lived without it this long, don't bother. More about this category later.

Now armed with your pad of paper and your boxes, and your trash and recycling bins, you're ready to begin working through the 10 steps.

Step 1: Empty the Space

If it's a drawer, dump everything in a box or container. If it's a closet or cabinet that you've targeted for your first organizing project, find a place you can put the contents temporarily while you work your magic. Now that you've cleared everything out of the space, give it a good cleaning.

Step 2: Use It or Lose It

You're going to repeat this step twice. It's actually the step where you sort through what you have to make decisions about—what to keep and what to let go. The first time we're going to make a game of it. We're going to play "Beat the Clock" and fling as much as we can in 15 minutes.

If you don't have one of those old-fashioned kitchen timers that tick the seconds away, I suggest you get one. The sound of the minutes ticking away is part of the game. Try to touch each item only once during this first quick sort. Pick up the first item and make a decision as quickly as possible. Remember, the clock is ticking!

Challenge yourself to cut the amount of stuff you have in the particular space you've chosen by a third or half. Impossible? Give it a try! As you handle each item (only once) ask yourself the following questions:

- ◆ **When was the last time I *used* this?** The key word here is *use*. If it's been more than a year, give serious thought to putting it in the trash or the Pass On box.

If you're sure you've used it in the last year, go on to the next question. One great way I've heard this question phrased was by professional organizer Peter Walsh on the *Clean Sweep* television show. He asked the homeowner who was holding on to something he rarely used, "Is it a friend, an acquaintance, or a stranger?" Well, which is it?

- **How often do I use it?** If you don't use it very often and it's in a location where regular daily activities occur, put it in the Put Away/Return bin. You need to find a place other than your most precious everyday living space. But, before you do that, ask yourself the next question.

- **If I don't use it very often, could I borrow, rent, or improvise with something else the few times I might need it?** If the answer is yes, put it in the trash or Pass On box.

- **Is it a duplicate?** If it is, you probably bought another one because you were unhappy with the old one or you couldn't find it. If you know you have one that works better, keep the best one and toss or pass on the extra one. Put the one you want to keep in the Keep box or the Put Away/Return box if it belongs in another area.

Pileups!

Don't throw out, give away, or sell anyone else's stuff without asking, as tempting as that may be when you're in the purging mood. How would you like it if someone did that to you?

- **Is it out-of-date?** Examples are canned foods that are past the expiration date or clothing that'll never be back in style. Throw outdated canned items away or add it to the garden compost, and pass on outdated clothes. Expired medicines should be flushed down the toilet for safety's sake.

- **If I didn't have this anymore, what impact would it have on my life?** This is a deeper question, but ultimately one you need to ask. Think worst-case scenario. Imagine that the dog chewed it up or a flood carried it away or a burglar ran off with it. Is this item something you'd have to go right out and replace? This exercise will probably direct still more things into the trash, recycling bin, or Pass On box.

- **Do I value this item?** If the answer is yes, put it in the Keep box. But the word *value* can be a loaded one. Perhaps a different way to put it might be "Do I *care* about this?" Yet another closely related question would be "Would I buy it again today?" If it's just gathering dust or thrown in a heap, how much could you *really* value it? What was once beautiful to you might no longer hold the same luster or excitement. If your tastes have changed or something better has caught your fancy, let it go!

◆ **Is this item in need of repair or damaged?** Put it in the Fix box if it needs a minor repair to make it useable. But be honest about the cost of the repairs versus the cost of replacing the item. Set a time limit of one week to get it done and put that action on your to do list for the week.

◆ **Am I keeping this because I'd feel guilty if I tossed it or gave it away?** Consider that people give you gifts because they want to please you. If you don't use it or like it, pass it on to someone who will. It will make you feel good, which is the whole point of gift giving! Let go of that guilt!

◆ **How easily could I get another one if I needed it?** If it's a hard-to-find item and likely to be used even once in a while, then it may be worth keeping.

One more idea for the Pass On box. How about sharing? Is there someone you know who would use an item more than you do? Give it to that person so that he or she can store it, with the condition that you can borrow it back when you need it. Consider this solution for stuff such as camping gear, bicycles, tools, and sports equipment.

Ding! The timer just went off. How did you do? Hopefully, the trash, the recycling bin, and Pass On box are pretty full already. But now we're going to do a more detailed sort of the Keep box and go through the process once again.

Set aside some more time when you can carefully consider each item and challenge yourself to reduce the stuff you have in the Keep box. Another hour is probably a good objective. Don't try to do too much in any one decluttering session.

Think about the space you have available and what your goals are for that space. Think, too, about the function of that space and whether what you're keeping really serves that function. Indeed, decide whether it serves you in your life and the things you want for yourself. Go through the items now and do a more detailed sort through anything that needed it during your 15-minute blitz purge. Whatever fell into the "mystery" category (what *is* this anyway?) during that first purge needs to be decided on during this second pass. Make a determination; if you can't make a determination, get rid of it. Take your time, but don't labor over this second sort too much. Just do it! Now let's move on to Step 3.

Step 3: Get Rid of It (Now)

Anything you put in the trash, recycling bin, or Pass On box needs to go. Take the trash and recycling out of the house to go in the next pickup. Take those books back to the library and the videos back to the video store. Bag up the items that are earmarked for charity and put them in your vehicle for the next time you run errands. Pack up Grandma's china and give it to your daughter-in-law, *now*. Pack up and ship or haul items that need to be returned as soon as you can. The important thing is to get it out of your space!

Envisionings

Take a moment to visualize the power of 15 short minutes. Mentally walk through your day, picturing all the times when you could easily set aside 15 minutes for your organizing tasks: 15 minutes first thing in the morning, before you fly out the door; the length of a coffee break; a fraction of your lunch hour; half a TV show; the last thing you do before you go to bed. Make a list of the small units of time you could use to declutter that are well suited to your schedule.

Step 4: Group Like Things Together

At this point, all you should have is your Keep box and your Fix box. After you've done your purge of stuff you don't need or want, and you've returned, passed on, or trashed the rest, what you have left is stuff that's worthwhile to have in your space (or it will be after you've fixed it!).

The next step is to sort your stuff so it's easy to find, easy to use, and easy to put back where it belongs. One way to do this is to store like things together. You may need to set up additional boxes or containers here, depending on how much you have for your fine sort. If you're working on a part of your office, for example, you may want to have boxes labeled Supplies, File, Read, Manuals, and Reference or whatever categories make the most sense to you. Look for ways to group similar things in one place.

Keep office supplies in one cabinet, container, or drawer. Having them scattered all over means you have to look several places every time you want a paper clip. Do the same thing with cleaning supplies, canned or packaged goods in the kitchen, tools, craft items, paper, or whatever comes up for the space you're working in. The containers you're using in this sort may not end up being the ones you use for final storage in the end, but they'll help you do your sort. Grouping like things together makes them easier to find, and you'll know what you have so you don't end up buying more when you already have a bunch.

Ways to group might vary. There can be general categories, such as Gift Wrapping Supplies, but they may need to be further broken down into Gift Cards, Bows, and Paper. Be flexible, too, because the best way to group something might be to gather all the things for one task in one container or location. Putting all the things you need to polish your shoes into one container, for example, might be the best way to group "like" things together in this particular instance.

Jump Starts

Don't ignore those mobile clutter catchers such as purses, backpacks, and briefcases. A self-contained space like one of these is just perfect for a 15-minute timed purge. You won't need boxes, just piles, using the same categories previously listed. Keep only the essentials and purge the rest.

While you're working through this step, note whether the categories you're coming up with fit the room and the function of the room. If you're doing the junk drawer in the kitchen, say, and you're finding lots of hardware or office supplies, sort them together, but then put them away where they will be living permanently when you're done.

Step 5: Consolidate and Compress

Consolidating is a natural outgrowth of Step 4. When you start grouping like things together, space seems to appear from nowhere. Putting things that were once scattered in several places into one compact container means they take up less space.

There's a cost associated with being spread out all over the place. The cost is in cluttered, unusable space and wasted time. One way to reclaim it is by consolidating what you have. You might find out you have unnecessary duplicates, including broken items that you've replaced. If you've replaced the broken item already, put it in the Pass On box and give it to Goodwill Industries or a similar charity that repairs broken items and sells them. Your broken item will give work to someone who needs it and money to a worthwhile organization. If you haven't gotten a new one, chances are that because it's been broken all this time, you don't really need it anyway. If you need

Jump Starts

Open your eyes to clutter. Really *see*. Look at your stuff as you begin to sort with a critical eye. Put distance between it and you. Become unattached. This makes it easier to assign true value and to let go of the junk.

the item and it's broken, put it in the Fix box and either fix it or send it out to be repaired this week. But set a time limit and put the task on your to do list (and calendar). Otherwise, if you don't think you'll get to it, throw it out and add purchasing a new one to your list!

If you find lots of duplicates as you consolidate, keep the best ones and pass the others along. If it's something you keep in quantity, such as paper clips or rubber bands, be honest about how many you'll use in six months or a year and share the rest. Unless you're planning to open an office-supply outlet, stocking up beyond a reasonable point is probably a poor use of your space. Here are some other areas where you can consolidate and compress:

◆ Consolidate clothes by getting rid of duplicate, outdated, ill-fitting, and unused items. If it needs mending, start a mending container and either do it yourself or send it out for repairs this week. We tackle your clothes closet in Chapter 12, but this will be a good start.

◆ Use existing containers that are just taking up space, such as jars, drawer units, bins, boxes, sectional boxes and chests, dividers, baskets, caddies, racks, and shelves. If you're not using them, lose them! Look for ways to downsize storage wherever you can. If you have a box with only a few things stored in it, perhaps a smaller container will do.

◆ If you're decluttering something like a closet, remove all the empty hangers and shoeboxes. The idea of consolidating and compressing is to fit the same items into far less space. We look at some storage solutions as we work through each area of your life that work on this principle.

◆ You can also apply the consolidation principle to tasks. Look for shopping areas where you can get a lot done without driving all over creation. Piggyback activities such as shopping and exercise. I park my car downtown and walk to the post office, bookstore, food specialty shops, and the bank. Not only do I get a lot done in a short period of time, I also get some needed exercise.

◆ Look for other areas where you can "fold" or compress time. Cook double batches of a favorite dish at one time and freeze one. You only have to clean the kitchen once, but have prepared two meals.

Step 6: Go for Quality, Not Quantity

Another way to sort and pare down is to keep only the best. This may not seem like a way to reduce the junk in your life, but it very well can be. If you have a tool that works well every time, chances are you won't need another for a long time. You may not think you can afford it, but if you examine the true cost of buying inferior merchandise, you may find it's actually cheaper in the long run to buy the very best.

Let's take the vacuum cleaner, for example. If you buy an inexpensive one or one that's poorly designed and can't handle many jobs, you'll need several other devices to do the work you need to do. One appliance, carefully chosen for its power, utility, and features, should cover almost any job you might encounter. Where do you think all those half-working appliances in your basement or garage came from, anyway? They probably ended up in these way stations because you bought something else that did the job better. Why not do it right the first time?

While you're sorting, if you come across something you just know doesn't work right or you avoid using because it's of inferior quality, toss it and get something that works.

The same applies to the things you surround yourself with for decorations or beauty. Choose the best of what you have. A few truly beautiful things prominently displayed in a place of honor will give you much more pleasure than a lot of so-so knickknacks scattered everywhere.

Step 7: Think Multipurpose

Why have six tools when one can do the job? Marketing experts work long and hard to create new products, but there's a good chance you already have something in the house that'll do the job just as well. Look for appliances and tools that can handle many jobs, not just one. They take up less space, cost less in the long run (although they might be expensive to buy initially), and cut your maintenance time down.

Your Pass On box should be full of items that do a single task that can be done just as well by something else you have on hand for another job.

Step 8: Alphabetize

I never realized the power of this simple step but, believe me, it will help you sail through your day in ways you didn't know were possible. As you work through whatever spaces you've decided to apply the 10 steps to, and after you group things together and consolidate them in containers or on shelves, consider whether putting items in alphabetic order would be an appropriate next step. It's not worthwhile for everything, and I'm not encouraging obsessive-compulsive behavior, but you might be surprised how much easier it is to find things and put them back where they belong when they're in alphabetic order.

Alphabetizing saves me time every single day. I can quickly find a spice when it's on the rack in alphabetic order. Books, videos, you name it—you'll save oodles of time, all the time, if you just use the old A-to-Z method.

Step 9: Label It

This is another powerful tool that produces many of the same results alphabetic organization does. Label everything you can get your hands on. That way you don't have to look through the wrong drawer, because it's labeled. You don't need to wonder what's in that box, because the contents are on the label outside. So now that you've purged and sorted and you're ready to put things away, make sure you can retrieve them again easily (and are more likely to put them back in the same place) by grouping similar things in a labeled container.

Jump Starts

You might consider getting a labeling machine. I'm not a great advocate of gadgets, but this is one that can save a lot of time. Look for one that allows you flexibility in label size, and make sure the type styles are readable from a distance.

Step 10: Put It Away

When you can't find things that are useful or valuable to you, it's like not having them at all. Just like they say in the real estate market—Location, Location, Location!

In this step, you work with your Put Away/Return and Keep boxes. If you have a lot of stuff in your Put Away/Return box, it means that stuff that belongs somewhere else is finding its way into the wrong space. Remember that putting stuff away is a habit. Start today. When you take something out, put it back where you found it. It takes more effort to put something down where it doesn't belong and put it away later than it does to put it in its rightful place. It's a matter of momentum. It's worth the extra steps. When you're about to let something land "just anyplace," ask, "Where does this belong?" and put it there *now*. If it doesn't have a place, that may be part of the problem. When things don't have a home, they end up floating around in your space, adding to the clutter. Applying other principles in this chapter, you'll find a place for it shortly.

Now grab your Put Away/Return box and take the stuff in it where it belongs. Get it out of the space you're trying to organize now. That leaves you with your Keep box. What's left in that should meet three criteria:

- ◆ You use it regularly.

- ◆ You like it.

- ◆ It has a place in the space.

If you don't have a place for it yet—a real home or "address"—you'll need to plan for that. But instead of thinking "Where can I store this?" I want you to think "Where do I use this?" Make sure the place you store the item makes it easy to get to with the least amount of motion. Assess the furniture, built-in storage, and possible storage solutions for the space where you use the item and put any ideas, purchases, or changes on your list in your organizing notebook.

Pileups!

Beware of saving things for garage sales. They either end up accumulating in the garage or find their way back into the house again! If you really have enough for a garage sale, put the ad in the newspaper right away! But honestly, when clutter is a serious problem, I advise getting it out of your space immediately. Bag it up and send it off to charity. Get a receipt and you can recoup a little at tax time. The exhilaration of having it *gone* is contagious. Don't give yourself a second chance to hang on to all that junk!

As you're putting things away, we're going to use a real estate idea again. The storage area closest to where you spend the most time and engage in most of your activities is called *prime real estate*, and it has the most value. Put the things you use most often there. By moving something to where the task is done, you activate it. Be ruthless about this space! Protect it from stuff that doesn't belong there. Make everything that lives there stuff you really need and use or truly love to have around.

Secondary storage is for stuff you use, but not every day. This might be a shelf that's not so easy to get to or the back of a closet. Or maybe it's a shelf in the basement or in the garage.

The *deep freeze* is for rarely used items such as seasonal stuff or tax records. This would be storage that's the most difficult to retrieve stuff from. Be careful of this one, though. It can become a clutter trap all too easily. Remember the key word to keep uppermost in your mind is *use*. If you only think you *might* use it, don't store it at all. Part with it now. Don't get in the habit of putting stuff in the *deep freeze* "just in case." Then it's just clutter.

Now that you've got the three basic categories of space in your mind, the next step is to put your valuable, usable stuff in the right places. When looking for places for things, here are some important principles to remember:

♦ Get stuff in the general area where it will be most useful. Simple, right? But in the course of everyday living, often things end up getting stored in the darnedest places! If you found golf balls in the kitchen junk drawer, put them with the golf clubs. If the hairbrush somehow keeps ending up in the living room, make sure it finds its way back to the bathroom.

♦ Whenever possible, put things in containers with like things. Choose containers that are uniform and covered. Units with drawers are generally better than those that stack, because stacked boxes have to be moved if you're to get to the ones on the bottom. Make sure labels will stick to them or you can devise some other way of denoting what's inside.

Jump Starts

Whenever you've got stuff in your hands, recite, "Don't put it down. Put it away!" Make it your mantra. *Away* means in its place. If it doesn't have a home, you need to make one.

♦ Make sure the location and containers you choose will keep your valuable stuff safe from *The Destroyers*. Who or what are The Destroyers? If you're a clutterer, you know them intimately, I'm sure. They're the natural enemies of stuff such as dust and dirt, moisture, sunlight, and pests. Pests include insects and vermin, and even domestic animals can do damage. Something valuable stored poorly can become junk overnight.

♦ When creating space for the things you're keeping and you find they don't currently have a home, see whether you can add the following:

Shelves

Inserts (step shelves, drawer inserts)

Racks

Poles

Hooks

Pegboards

Containers

Carts on wheels

Add getting these items or doing these projects to your Master List and move on.

And Now What?

Take a break, reward yourself (tea, anyone?), survey your handiwork, and schedule some time with yourself to start again!

Repeating the 10 steps again and again, starting with the spaces that bug you the most or cause you the most pain, is the way to reach your goals. The more times you repeat the process, the better you'll get at it!

Keep going with your purging, sorting, and putting away until you finish a room. Use the room-by-room detailed approach outlined in Part 4 to refine the process. This is not a once-and-for-all thing. You'll probably find yourself unstuffing different areas (sometimes the same ones) several times a year using the 10 steps, but it gets easier as these skills become a part of you and you get in the unstuffing habit. When you experience the uncluttered space you've reclaimed, you'll be more likely to keep stuff from accumulating. Don't let more clutter in the door. Shopping is not a hobby. With each purchase you think of making, ask yourself first, "Do I have a *use* for it?" Then ask, "Do I have a *place* for it?" Put it back on the store shelf unless and until you do.

> **Envisionings**
>
> Close your eyes for a few minutes and imagine the area you've just subjected to the 10 steps. Remember what it looked like when you started? See it the way it is now? Imagine yourself and your family using that area. Imagine opening that newly cleared-out drawer or cabinet and having what you need at your fingertips, exactly where you put it. Congratulate yourself for a job well done. Bask. Luxuriate. Now open your eyes and look at this utterly uncluttered space anew. Well done!

Remember, junk has costs other than money. It robs you of time, energy, peace of mind, and perhaps, ultimately, happiness.

A house filled with clutter is hard to keep clean. It isn't welcoming. We don't want to invite people over because it just takes too much effort to make it vaguely presentable for company. And what's up with that anyway? Why would you want to live in a house that's not good enough for company? Aren't you and your family as important as your company?

Clutter costs you peace of mind. It makes you tired just looking at it. It tears you down and chips away at your self-esteem.

If all this stuff doesn't add to your life and help you accomplish the things you believe to be most important, *lose it!* It didn't get this way overnight, so it's going to take time to clear it out, but you've just learned the process to make that happen. Now plan the next area to give the 10-step treatment. Pick a time and write it down on your calendar. You're off and running, so don't stop now!

The Least You Need to Know

- You can learn basic principles to apply to all areas of organization.
- By applying the 10 steps to any area, large or small, you can get a head start on putting it in order.
- Part of successful unstuffing is identifying the items you simply don't use and getting them out of your space.
- Smart storage habits, consolidation, and grouping like things together can help you streamline your space.

6

Mastering the Paper Monster

In This Chapter

- ◆ Debunking the myth of the "paperless society"
- ◆ How to begin controlling the paper piles in your life right away
- ◆ Filing paper so you can find it
- ◆ Cutting down on junk correspondence and phone calls
- ◆ Using your computer to reduce piles of paper

Way back when, we were told that the computer age would bring about the beginning of a paperless society. With the advent of word processing, databases, electronic spreadsheets, and e-mail, we wouldn't need to put things down on paper anymore.

Well, the "paperless society" is suffering from a paper glut! Some 68 million trees and 28 billion gallons of water are used each year just to produce catalogs and direct-mail sales pitches. Junk mail fills 3 percent of American landfills, and its disposal costs $320 million in American tax dollars annually. Of all junk mail, 44 percent is thrown in the trash, without ever being opened. Add to that all the office paper, personal correspondence, newspapers, magazines, and books and, well, you get the picture.

We all have bills, correspondence, receipts, bank statements and canceled checks, insurance and tax papers, legal papers, reading material, instructions and warranties, business cards, reminders and invitations, keepsakes and photos, recipes, and the list goes on and on. It's whether or not we confront the paper in our lives, deal with it, systematize it, and dispose of it that makes the difference between being on top of the paper pileup or being buried by it. We also need to build in to our paper handling systems a way to protect our identity and privacy.

In this chapter, you take another giant leap toward unstuffing your life and getting a grip on all the paper you get, handle (sometimes again and again), and save (usually for far too long). I give you 10 simple ideas, plus some ways to implement them, that will keep those piles of paper from piling up in the first place.

Idea 1: Stop It!

One way to spend less time and energy handling paper is by reducing the amount that comes into your household. You can lower the amount of junk mail, for example, by stopping it at the source.

One of the fastest and easiest ways to remove your name and address from the many mailing lists that are bought and sold between direct marketing companies (who generate the junk mail in the first place) is to send your name and address on a postcard to the Direct Marketing Association (DMA):

Resource Files

Consider joining the Stop Junk Mail Association. For $20, they delete your name from a variety of sources and lobby to protect your postal privacy. Call or write to Stop Junk Mail Association, 3020 Bridgeway, Suite 150, Sausalito, CA 94965; 1800-827-5549.

Direct Marketing Association
Mail Preference Service
P.O. Box 643
Carmel, NY 10512-0643

You can do it online as well, for a $5 fee at www. dmaconsumers.org/cgi/offmailinglist. Even if you decide to use the old-fashioned method, there's lots of good information and answers to commonly asked questions on their website.

Make sure you give them all the different incarnations of your personal mailing information. If your name appears sometimes as John Doe and others as J. P. Doe and yet again as John Doe, Sr., you need to let them know. Your name and address in various forms will be added to the Direct Marketing Association's delete file, and its 3,600 members will be notified. It may take several months for you to see results, so be patient. You need to repeat this procedure every five years, because that's how long your information remains in the delete file.

If you notice a reduction in some mail, but continue to receive other unsolicited mailings, that may mean a particular company doesn't participate in DMA's program. In this case, you have to contact the company directly. You can easily compose a form letter and simply make copies, filling in the name of the company as needed.

Dealing with credit card companies requires a slightly different approach. The law requires that these companies refrain from disclosing a customer's personal information for marketing purposes if the customer requests. Call your credit card company's 1-800 number for customer service or write to them directly and ask them to keep your name and information private. You can also attack the problem from another angle, by contacting credit bureaus. Depending on which state you live in, these bureaus may be required by law to delete your name from their marketing mailing lists if you request it. There are three major credit bureaus you should contact—Equifax, Experian, and TransUnion—and all three can be reached with the same toll-free number: 1-888-567-8688. You'll be calling the "Opt Out Request Line," and by giving them your information when asked, you kill three birds with one stone.

Another place you might want to contact to have your name deleted is National Demographics and Lifestyles. This company collects buyer profiles and sells the information. Write to:

National Demographics and Lifestyles
List Order Department
1621 18th Street, Suite 300
Denver, CO 80202

Staying away from buyer's clubs or special buying programs is another way to reduce the number of promotions and coupons sent to your home. Another source companies use for mailings is the telephone book. Having an unlisted number, or having only your name and number (no address) in the book, is another way to cut down on the number of solicitations you receive.

According to the website www.obviously.com, which outlines a detailed step-by-step procedure for reducing all kinds of junk communications—mail, phone calls, and electronic solicitations—these steps also help:

◆ Whenever you donate money, order a product or service, or fill out a warranty card, write in large letters **"Please do not sell my name or address."** Most organizations will properly mark your name in their computer.

◆ Product warranty cards are often used to collect information on your habits and income for the sole purpose of targeting direct mail. These cards are not required in most situations—avoid sending them.

◆ When ordering on the telephone, say **"Please mark my account so that my name is not traded or sold to other companies."**

◆ "Contests" where you fill in a little entry blank to win are almost always fishing expeditions for names. If you fill one out at a football game, for example, expect to get a catalog of football merchandise within a few months. Avoid these if you don't want the mail.

Resource Files

If you order or request a catalog from a mail-order company, ask that the company not pass your information on to anyone else. Otherwise, your mailbox will begin to fill up with unwanted junk mail all over again. Make it a habit to "just say no" right from the start.

Whenever you get the chance, make a formal request that your name be kept private and that no mailings other than those you specifically request be sent. Here are some other big list sellers that you might want to write or call:

ADVO, Inc., Delivery Services
6955 Mowry Avenue
Newark, CA 94560

You can obtain a form to print out on their website (in PDF format) at www.advo.com/document/remove.pdf.

Donnelley Marketing
Database Operations
416 South Bell
Ames, IA 50010
1-888-633-4402

Metromail/Experian
List Maintenance
901 West Bond
Lincoln, NE 68521
1-800-228-4571

Even the post office sells your name and address! Didn't know that, did you? When you move and fill out those little change of address cards, they sell the information to bulk mailers. Better to skip those cards entirely and contact your correspondents individually.

This may all seem like a lot of effort, but it really doesn't take more than writing a simple form letter, addressing a few envelopes, and sticking them in the mail. The reduction in unsolicited mail can be dramatic. Remember to keep a list of the companies I've given you (or refer back to this book), because you may need to repeat the process in five years or so.

Another important paper-reduction technique is to cancel subscriptions to publications you don't really read. Consider combining subscriptions with someone else who shares your interests, or using the library. I'd bet if you had to make a trip to the library to read publications, you'd see in a hurry which ones really mattered to you!

And finally, when you're out and about, get into the "no paper" habit! Free paper is everywhere, just for the taking. You can grab flyers, brochures, coupons, and publications by the dozens on any given day. Don't! Unless it's something you're sure is really valuable to you, don't touch it, don't take it, and don't bring it home.

Idea 2: Decide Now

When paper in its many forms first comes through the door, you need to make a decision about it right away. Don't allow it to pile up. This is the first step in conquering the paper-piling habit. After you change that to the "immediate decision" habit, I can show you how to set up a system to keep it moving, and you'll know immediately where in the system it goes. Probably the single worst thing you can do when it comes to paper is to put off deciding what to do with it. That's how the piles got there!

Why do we put off deciding about paper? Often it's a result of our anxiety about losing information we might need later or a false sense of security in believing we'll be able to back up everything we do. Well, if you're choking in paper, you won't be able to do either of these things.

Jump Starts

Because warranty or product registration cards might generate more junk mail for you, consider not sending the card next time you buy something new. You're covered by the manufacturer's warranty whether or not you send it in. If you feel you must send in the card, fill in the bare minimum and indicate you do not want your information passed on. Keep your receipt along with the product model and serial numbers for warranty and recall purposes.

The antidote for these feelings of insecurity is knowledge. When we know what we really need to keep and have a system for retrieving it quickly and easily, the more we can liberate ourselves from the paper-pile monster.

Sorting Into Three Categories

Paper falls into three basic categories: *Action* (respond or file), *Throw Away* (challenge yourself to send as much as possible directly into the trash barrel), and *Pass On* (stuff that needs to be handed or sent to someone else).

An Action might be to read it, do something with it (such as pay a bill), or respond in some way. It might go in a tickler file, you might need to transfer the date to your calendar and then throw the piece of paper out, or it may need to be filed for reference. Maybe you need to write a letter in response. Whatever the Action is, those papers are the ones you keep. The rest get trashed or given to someone else. When the piece of paper first enters your life, ask yourself the following:

- ◆ Would I miss this? What would I do if it were gone?

- ◆ Can I get this somewhere else?

- ◆ Does having this piece of paper support the goals I've set for myself?

- ◆ Can I reduce or consolidate this?

- ◆ If I decide to keep this, how long will I need it?

- ◆ Where can I keep it so I can find it when I need it? (This last question leads into how you sort and file paper, which I discuss shortly.)

Don't Open It!

Get in the habit of sorting your mail over the trash barrel and recycling bin. Whatever can go directly into one or the other should go there unopened. This is especially effective with expiration notices for magazines you've decided not to renew, contests, catalogs, and offers. Rip up or shred credit card offers without reading them. Some of your junk mail should definitely be shredded, and I highly recommend getting a good paper shredder. This is essential in today's world where identity theft is a real concern. Chapters 15 and 16 cover this topic in more detail.

You've probably heard organization experts say you should handle paper only once. This is a guideline, not a rule. It's often impossible to handle a piece of paper only once, but you want to make a decision as quickly as possible about where it goes. Don't allow it to pile up, handling it many times, moving it from here to there, from pile to pile.

Pileups!

Don't throw away unopened mail unless you're *absolutely sure* it's not something important. You may be throwing away a check or a bill!

Move It Along

If paper belongs with someone else, get it going! Have envelopes and postage handy (plus a chart of rates for various sizes and weights, and a postage scale) so you can hand off things as quickly as possible. I keep folders in my filing system for people I regularly send things to. When I see an article, get a flyer, or print out a useful message from the Internet that I know they'd find useful or enjoy, I immediately put it in their folder and once a week or so I send off these items to them. It's an important way to let them know I'm thinking of them, but I don't want it to turn into a "paper problem" for me or them, so I'm very selective about what I choose and I empty their folders on a regular basis.

A good idea is to pre-address some envelopes for the people you regularly send items to. You're more likely to keep up with it if you've got everything prepared in advance.

Another way to "pass it on" is to recycle. That may mean actually sending your useless paper to a recycling center or simply giving items you've finished with to someone else who might have use for them. Give old magazines to doctors' offices or nursing homes. Our local library accepts donations of some magazines and books and sells them to raise money.

Resource Files

Sharing is a great way to reduce the paper in your life and even save money. I share my copies of *Publisher's Weekly* with writer friends in my area, and they pass them on to the local writer's club when they're done. Consult professional associates or people with the same interests who might be willing to do the same. Knowing that someone else is waiting for your magazines is also an incentive to get them read and out the door.

If you make the effort and implement Idea 2, you'll find you're physically dealing with paper far less. If you constantly police yourself, reduce the amount of mail you get by following the suggestions in Idea 1, and apply the principles in this chapter daily, you'll spend less time shuffling paper and more time doing the things you want to do.

Idea 3: Purge, Sort, and Systematize

Ideas 1 and 2 are aimed at the new paper coming into your life every day. Idea 3 is the first step in handling what you already have in piles and files all around the house and what's left each day when you've applied my first two ideas.

Just as we did in Chapter 5, we're going to unstuff your paper piles. First we're going to use the quick sort technique you've already learned. Set the kitchen timer for 15 minutes, or more if you have the time. Using the categories in Idea 2, take a pile and work through it in rapid fire, putting each piece of paper in the Trash (or the recycling bin), in a pile to Pass On to someone else, or in a third pile that requires you to take additional Action. Use boxes or baskets if you have a big pile.

The Action pile roughly corresponds with the Keep pile from Chapter 5. You want to make it as small as you possibly can in your initial sort, but you have a chance to reduce it even further when you do your final, more detailed sort, which happens next.

Dealing with What Remains

After you make the first set of decisions about what to act on, what to trash, and what to pass on, you need to decide what to do with what you have left.

This is the second sort. Here you need to map out a bit more time. Depending on the size of the pile you started with and what you ended up with that wasn't trash, you may want to set aside half an hour or more. But, as before, don't spend more than an hour or so. You didn't get here overnight, and you're not going to dig out in a day either. Be realistic, be kind to yourself, and take small steps that add up to big results.

First take care of the Pass On pile. If the item needs to be mailed, get it ready to go. If you just need to give it to someone when you see her next, put it in a prominent place so you won't forget.

Next you need to refine the Action pile and set up systems to handle the paper that falls in that category from now on. These systems need to be flexible and maintainable. They need to be easy to use so you *will* maintain them, and they need to fit your personality and lifestyle. After a piece of paper enters your system, you need to be able to find it again quickly and easily.

The backbone of your paper-handling system is your filing system. Depending on your needs, your filing system will be bare-bones or it might be quite extensive. In our house, we run three businesses out of our home, so we have more files than the average household. But just like everyone else, our household filing system is the hub and center of it all.

In Chapter 7, we talk about setting up a central area where you manage your household affairs, the Life Management Center. If at all possible, this is where you want to locate your household files. If it's not, get yourself a rolling file cabinet and set them up there, so you can bring them wherever you make your phone calls and pay your bills as needed.

The contents of your household filing system may vary somewhat from your neighbor's, but generally it will follow the basic categories you use to file your taxes at the end of the year along with some additional files for receipts and household records that may not be tax related.

We talk at length about household financial files in Chapter 16, but as you sort through the piles you're going to see some patterns developing. At least begin setting up some preliminary files based on what you find. You want only the current files in this preliminary system. Anything that you think you need to keep, but goes back beyond the current year or previous tax year (if it's prior to April 15), should go in its own pile. Remember what I told you about *prime real estate* in Chapter 5? Only your current files should be there.

Personal Action Items

The next decision level concerns your own personal action items. Decide now how you're going to sort all your own personal paper—past, present, and future. The usual categories most people use are *To Do*, *To Pay*, *To Read*, and *To File*. Some people add a *Pending* category, as well. That can become a catchall and a "black hole" for paper, however, so be careful. If you do decide to have a Pending or Holding file, make sure you're going to check it often; if not, skip it.

CAUTION

Pileups!

Be careful about bulletin boards: they can become catchalls instead of organization tools. The items on them can all too easily become strangely invisible. If you must, use a bulletin board only to post material you refer to regularly, and make a vow not to clutter it with anything else.

Get yourself a stacking basket system for your Action items. I like wire baskets because you can see what's in them. Make sure you can label each one. You'll probably want three baskets—one labeled To Do, one for bills labeled To Pay, and one that's labeled To File. Because I handle bills for another person, I have an extra category and separate those bills. You may have a similar circumstance or may want to separate business bills from household ones. Adapt your system to your life. What's nice about these stacking baskets is you can add or subtract based on what works best for you as you test these ideas for yourself.

Reading material can go in another basket, or you may want to have something portable for magazines and newsletters, such as a wicker tote or basket that sits on the floor near your desk. This will allow you to take your reading material to another location. Decide now that you will only allow one basket of reading material to accumulate and no more. If you don't get to it before the next issue arrives, let it go. If this keeps happening, you need to take a serious look at the number of subscriptions you have and be realistic about how much time you can devote to keeping up.

You deal with the filing basket in even more detail when you get to the chapters on work and finances. What you're working on here are some general systems to get you started. As you sort your Action items, ask these questions to help you get rid of still more paper, *before* it finds its way into your action system:

◆ Is there enough time to do this, or is it already too late?

◆ Do I really want to do this? Do I *have* to do this? Does this support the goals I've set for myself?

◆ Will doing this really make a difference for others or myself?

◆ What would happen if I never did this (worst-case scenario)? What would happen if I never read this? What would happen if I never filed or replied to this?

Envisionings

Playing the Worst-Case Scenario game is an extremely useful tool when you're trying to break old habits that have held you back from getting clutter out of your life and getting organized.

When you're stuck and can't make a decision about a piece of paper, stop and use your visualization skills. Close your eyes and imagine the very worst thing that could happen if the item were lost forever. Really see it happening. Could you call the bank and get a copy? Could you find it in the library or online? Would your lawyer, accountant, or financial planner have a copy? If you can see yourself solving the problem, then maybe you don't need it after all.

Decide now to schedule a regular bill-paying day each week or at least twice a month. In our house, Friday is bill-paying and filing day. What's your day?

Next put all the items you need to call about in a file folder marked *Call.* For now, put that by the phone and schedule a time to catch up on these. In the future, you'll be doing this each day at a designated time. Think about when might be a good time for you. Experts say the best time to return calls is the half hour before *their* lunch hour and the half hour before *their* quitting time. Keep this in mind when you set your calling times.

Now on to the To File pile. If you have paid bills in the pile, file them. If you don't have a filing system for paid bills, put aside some time to set one up. It took me all of one afternoon to set up my own files. I included both household and business, and organized them according to the categories I use in my Quicken personal finance software. These are set up for tax purposes, so they make what used to be an end-of-the-year scramble a breeze.

Jump Starts _____

If the thought of setting up a household filing system just overwhelms you, there's help out there! You can purchase a prefabricated system, complete with preprinted labels, tabs, file folders, and even a portable file box or rolling cart, all for less than $100! You'll probably have to tweak it a bit, but at least it's a start. The EasyFile system is available at www.simplfiedsolutions.org or call 386-673-5574.

You may want to look at how your taxes were prepared for some of the categories, and then include anything else you'd like to track or need to be able to put your hands on quickly. (We talk more about taxes in Chapter 16.) Adapt and adjust your system to your personal needs, and always remember you can change and improve it at any time.

Reading Material

So you threw out all those back issues like I told you to, right? If you didn't, be honest with yourself and get all that paper off the floor and off your back. Just let it go. Unread stuff is a burden. It's just that—stuff!

Now honestly evaluate the periodicals you subscribe to. Which ones do you look forward to reading when they come in? Which ones always seem to have at least one article you truly enjoy or that pertains to your work or lifestyle? And which ones do you just never seem to get to?

Cancel the last category. Do it now. You can always pick up a copy on the newsstand now and then or check out the table of contents the next time you're at the library. If you're not reading it, you don't need it in your space.

Now that you've pared down what arrives regularly in your mailbox, you need a system to keep up with the reading material you've decided you truly need or enjoy. If you can't stay on top of it, you have too much. You'll never get to it anyway, and when it's in huge piles, you won't want to.

A good rule is to have no more than two or three issues of any one publication at any one time. If it's a publication you need for reference, you need to provide a way to store it, and usually a year's worth is all you'll ever need. Photocopy the table of contents for each issue and keep those copies in a place where you can find them quickly and easily. That way you'll know what's in which issue without having to pull each publication out.

Beyond a year, the information contained in these publications usually becomes outdated, and you can obtain back issues another way if you really need them. Some online magazine databases enable you to retrieve and print out articles for a small fee. If you're saving magazines with projects for hobbies, remove and store only the projects you really think you'll make and trash or recycle the rest of the magazine.

Use the table of contents. Why thumb through the whole magazine if only one article really pertains to your topic of interest? Besides, you'll miss all the ads (remember the Acquisition Trap?). If you don't have time to read it right away, tear it out and put it in your To Read basket, and then trash or recycle the publication right away.

Jump Starts

Why read it when skimming will do? Much of what we put aside to read only needs a quick perusal for pertinent information. Skim with a highlighter in your hand. If it's information you need to file, maybe you only need a small portion of the article. Keep a pair of scissors nearby.

I make a habit of reading through the day's material most evenings after I've put away my work and while I listen to the TV news in the background. Those are two activities I can easily do simultaneously. If certain reading material requires more serious concentration, I might put it on my bedside table and read it before I go to bed or over my morning cup of coffee the next day. What system for your reading material would work best for you? If you commute daily to work, how about using that time to catch up on your reading? If you spend a lot of time waiting for appointments, maybe those can be some "found" moments for catching up on your reading.

The important thing is to set up a process that helps you make immediate decisions regarding the paper in your life. Get your system up and running right away, and reevaluate it in a couple of weeks. I say "right away" because paper is the single greatest contributor to clutter and disorganization in our lives. If you find you still have piles of paper around, critically examine what the paper is and where the system has broken down. Then fix it!

Idea 4: Distinguish Between Short and Long Term

We all have paper we need to save for various reasons, but most of us end up hanging on to it much longer than we have to.

Find out from your tax preparer, financial advisor, and lawyer what documents you need to keep and for how long. We discuss this at length in Chapters 15 and 16, but you might want to start asking some of these questions now, because this is the "quick start" part of your organization plan. Weigh the cost in storage space and time required for you to hold on to these documents against the costs involved in re-creating them in the event you might need them in the future. What is the likelihood you'll ever need them? How difficult would it be to obtain them again?

A Three-Category System

Remember that paper is the same as other stuff as far as storage is concerned. What you need at your fingertips should occupy *prime real estate*. Other paper that needs to be accessible, but isn't used as often, falls in the category of active files and occupies *secondary storage*. And, last, you will have some paper that belongs in the *deep freeze*, of which there should be *very, very little*. All I keep in the *deep freeze* is support material for books I've already completed and previous years' tax information. The rest is either *active* or *essential*, and those are in systems that are easy to access and regularly purged.

A basic filing system falls into three categories: *working*, *reference*, and *archival*.

Working files get prime real estate, the space that's closest to you. Depending on whether you have a home office or not, these might be in your office or at your central planning area or Life Management Center. We talk lots more about the Life Management Center in the next chapter, but just be aware that you need a central place to store the supplies and information you rely on to keep everything operating smoothly in your life. Working files include current projects and current financial information.

Next are your reference files. These are the things you need to refer to fairly often, but they're not part of your daily life. These files might include information on hobbies, career, housekeeping, your family history—whatever is currently in your life, but not essential to the daily workings of your household. If you have room to keep both the working files and the reference files in the same place, that's great. If not, reference files should still be accessible.

The final part of your filing system is the archival files, and there should be practically nothing there. In our household, because I'm a writer, we probably have more in this category than most people. I need to keep support files for the books and articles I write. I weed them out, and then they go into cardboard banker boxes and get stored in the garage. As I mentioned earlier, the only other deep freeze files we have are past years' tax records and support material.

Envisionings

Imagine what would happen if everything you own were destroyed in a fire, flood, or other disaster. What would you need to pick up the pieces? How would you identify yourself? If you died, how easily could your survivors handle your estate and other affairs? Visualize what would happen. Then take a look at your files and records and come up with a plan that would deal with these two circumstances. Consider off-site backup and who should know where things are (and what that person might need). We deal with this in more detail later on, but having this visualization will help get you started in the right direction now.

Make sure to purge your files regularly (every three to six months), using the guidelines your professional advisers give you. Mark the date on your calendar as an appointment with yourself. I like to key my purging with key seasonal events. I do one purge right after New Year's in preparation for preparing our tax returns. The second purge coincides with mid-year cleaning. Figure out what works best for you. It's easy to forget and just allow these mounds of paper to accumulate and your files can become clogged with useless paper, too. Experts say that 80 percent of what's in the average filing system is never looked at again! If you keep going through them regularly, you'll still only need the same amount of storage. You'll learn how to rotate your long-term storage out the door as older tax files become obsolete and more recent files go into long-term storage for a defined length of time. That means that after you set up storage systems for these long-term records, you'll probably never have to add to them to any appreciable extent.

Idea 5: File So You Can Find It

There are many filing systems—some so complicated only the person who set them up can use them. But you want your filing system to be easy and simple, right? So let's spend some time discussing how to set up your own household filing system—one that works.

My basic advice is to keep your system as streamlined as possible, make it alphabetic wherever possible, label everything clearly and boldly, and be sure it is easy for other people to use. It should be self-explanatory, meaning someone besides yourself can open a file drawer and "get it" right away. What if you're stranded in Bora Bora and need to tell someone how to get a copy of your birth certificate to you? It should be simple for anyone (even the house-sitter) to oblige if your files are set up right.

 Jump Starts

As you sort through your paper piles, you can help speed up the filing process later on by either highlighting a word or two in the document that refers to the filing category it best fits into or by writing that category on the top. This will get easier as your filing system is developed and you get used to using it regularly.

Next let's talk about categories for your household files. Here's a list of those I think almost every household should have. We discuss several of them in more detail when we get into organizing your financial life later on in this book, but for now, consider setting up hanging folders for each of these categories right away. You want hanging folders, which you never remove from your file drawer, *and* regular file folders. Some people may disagree with this, and if space is really at a premium, you may not be able to do it this way. The reason I like this redundant system is that it practically maintains itself. When you take out the file folder, the hanging folder remains in its alphabetic spot. When you go to put the file folder back it's easy to see immediately where it goes. If a file folder is missing, that's easy to see, too!

Now for the categories:

- Auto (gasoline, loan information, repair records)
- Bank Statements
- Birth and other important records (copies of birth, marriage, divorce, adoption, citizenship, death, and military records would go here; keep originals in a safety deposit box)
- Budget

- Contributions/Charities
- Credit Cards
- Heating (fuel and service)
- Home Repairs, Improvements, and Equipment
- Income Tax (current year and prior year's form as filed)
- Insurance (auto, homeowner or renter, health, business, life)
- Inventory (a copy of this should be kept in a safety deposit box, along with supporting photos and/or video)
- Investments (stocks, bonds, pension, mutual funds, savings; you might want to break this out into separate sections if you have a lot of investments)
- Medical (divided by person; receipts; you might want to include dental or break that out into a separate folder)
- Safety Deposit Box (information on the box itself, as well as copies of important documents kept there and an inventory of everything in the box)

Wise Words

"Order marches with weighty and measured strides; disorder is always in a hurry."

—Napoleon I

Some other files you might have include the following:

- Legal (case information, including expenses)
- Pets (this could also be a subcategory of Medical)
- School (transcripts, registration information)
- Social Security

This is just the beginning. Have filing supplies handy and add to your system as needed. In the beginning, you'll probably have to set aside some time regularly as you apply Ideas 1, 2, and 3 to those paper piles all over the house!

Another important point: Whatever categories you choose, make sure they'll make sense to you six months from now. Start with general categories and refine them later. Keep in mind that you may not be the only person who needs to be able to find something in your filing system. Choosing logical categories for your files that will help you find pieces of paper you need in the future is a key step in setting up an effective filing system.

Don't Forget Computer Records and Documents

Even if your computer records and documents aren't in hardcopy form, they may still be important pieces of information that need to be organized and probably backed up. Make printouts of documents that really belong in your files and would be hard for a person who's not computer-oriented to find. A man we know died quite suddenly, and all his financial information was on his computer, which no one else in the family knew how to operate. It took months for his widow to learn that she had been well taken care of, so she could stop worrying. If you do keep important records on computer, make sure someone else knows how to access them, or back up the critical ones with actual paper printouts that are clearly labeled and filed so anyone can find them.

Here again, file stuff on your computer or disks using filenames that make the information easy to retrieve in the future.

Paper with Deadlines

You already know where to put things such as permission slips, invitations with RSVPs, and anything else that has a deadline on it. It's an Action item. But sometimes these pieces of paper need special handling. The systems you set up will depend largely on the needs of your household and what kinds of things are most common for you. If you have kids in school and there are lots of papers and permission slips to sign, you might consider setting up a special box or basket just for those. Train the kids to deposit these items daily in the designated place so you can handle them by the following day. If you do a lot of traveling on business, you may want a separate folder for travel documents. I have a "Trips, Upcoming" folder in the file drawer closest to where I work, and everything relating to my travel plans goes in there. If you go to a lot of concerts or theater performances, set up a system for keeping track of these time-sensitive events. This may be a good use of that bulletin board for you. This wouldn't work for me. I once spent hours looking for airplane tickets that had been pinned to the bulletin board and somehow became "invisible." But that's me!

To ensure these crucial pieces of paper don't disappear into your new filing system, make a note of the dates connected with them on your calendar. (We talk more about this later.) Also note where the documents connected with the event are stored. (You could use a Post-It note for this.) Eventually you may not need to take this extra step, when your system is refined and you have it committed to memory and habit; but while you're making these initial baby steps to get organized, a redundant system such as this will help.

Idea 6: Keep It Where You Need It

If you often use certain information that's on paper, put it where you need it. I keep a file near the kitchen for all my instructions for electric tools and appliances. The file is close to most of the appliances we use, which are in the kitchen, the laundry room, and the garage just off the kitchen. I have a separate one in my work area for all the office equipment and computer stuff I use there. It's clearly labeled, so if someone needs to run the equipment when I am not around, he can quickly and easily find the information he needs to do it.

Remember, current action files belong in prime real estate. All other files should be in secondary storage or the deep freeze. If it's in the deep freeze and your tax consultant or lawyer hasn't told you that you need to hang on to it, maybe you ought to consider getting rid of it.

Keep phone message pads by the phone. Ditto with the family address and phone file and the phone book. You'll be making a User's Manual for your household in Chapter 7, which you will want to keep close at hand. Keep the TV, cable, or satellite guide by the TV. If you have places designated for these things, they're less likely to walk away. Just keep in mind the idea of prime real estate and the importance of location, and you'll find you can lay your hands on the important papers you need when you need them.

Idea 7: Tailor Systems to Special Needs

Some activities involving paper require special handling. Perhaps you work at home, or maybe you work outside the home but handle the paperwork for your job at home. Some paper just doesn't quite fall into the usual categories; examples include greeting cards, recipes, photos, or your kids' school projects.

Jump Starts

If you're most likely to read magazine articles while relaxing at night, soaking in the bathtub, or waiting for appointments, tear them out and keep them where you're most likely to read them, and then get rid of the rest of the publication. This is one way to help keep magazines from piling up.

As you examine, purge, and sort the many kinds of paper in your home or workplace, these are the items you might not know what to do with. These types of paper may need special systems to handle them in a way that preserves them and makes them easy to get to.

I specifically tackle home office solutions, recipes, photos, and keepsakes in later chapters. You may want to skip ahead if you're really motivated, or for now you can simply start grouping items together in temporary containers until you reach those sections. Boxes from computer paper, stationery, or file folders work great for this. Shoeboxes work well for receipts and smaller pieces of paper. But please *do* sort them and contain them. *Don't* just throw them in a jumbled paper pile again!

Idea 8: Use Computers to Cut Paper, Not Make More

You already know that computers haven't eliminated wasteful paper. Far from it! If you're a computer user, you know from experience how much paper it can generate. Luckily, computers can also reduce paper if we think before we print and remember the principles we've already learned in this chapter.

Think seriously before printing something out. It can become a bad habit. Before you click the Print button, ask yourself the following:

◆ Can I work with this onscreen?

◆ Do I really need to save this? What are the chances I'll need to refer to it again? What's the worst-case scenario?

◆ Can I archive this on a disk rather than make a hard copy?

A lot of information we used to get in print form is available and, actually, more useable in online form. For example, just this year I stopped several subscriptions and now use online newspapers and magazines to get most of my news. If there's something I want to save or have someone else read, I can print out only that item or e-mail it on to a colleague or friend, but I can be very selective. Sure, I'm generating some paper, but far less than I had with the paper subscription. Are there any areas where this might work for you?

Envisionings

Put your imagination cap on, pick a room, and scan it for any paper items that fall into the "special" category. Can they be grouped together in categories? Can they be integrated into the filing system you set up earlier? If not, what storage or display format would make them most useful to you? Consider things such as photo boxes, albums, display cases, frames, magnetic strips or boards, and anything else that might be used for that purpose.

Incidentally, things get lost on disks because of poor filing, just as they do in paper files. The same rules apply to both: purge often, label clearly, and only save what you really need.

Use e-mail to reduce the amount of paper coming into your mailbox. Don't feel compelled to print out and save every message. Of course, one of the advantages of e-mail over, say, a telephone conversation is that you can make a hard copy of what was communicated for future reference. This proves especially handy for job-related information, directions, travel information, and the like. Again, ask yourself the important questions and don't hang on to these printouts longer than you need to. Question whether you need to make them at all.

With online banking and investing becoming commonplace, much of what we used to do on paper can reliably be done online. Arrange for fixed monthly bills to be paid automatically, directly from your bank account. Still other bills can be put on a credit card monthly so you pay only one bill rather than several. Many banking and other financial records can be archived electronically and printed out only in the event you really need them.

Idea 9: Put Paper in Its Place

Many of the same principles I gave you in Chapter 5 for dealing with stuff apply just as well to taking care of paper. Consolidate and compress. Put it on one sheet. Reduce it with a copier. This technique is especially effective with keepsakes—keep a part of something sentimental. Keep the best pieces of artwork your child produced in kindergarten, not all of it. Ask him to choose his favorites. Choose just a few pictures that are representative of an event, not every out-of-focus shot. Consolidate keepsakes—put them in a scrapbook or album or make a memory wreath or collage. You decide what paper to keep and set up the rules. That way paper doesn't rule your life. Put it in its place and keep it there!

Jump Starts

Be creative when thinking up ways to save space. Take a tip from a clever quilter who selectively reproduced various images of her parents and transferred them using computer technology to a quilt for their fiftieth wedding anniversary. Included in the quilt's fabric were swatches from old dresses, tablecloths, and baby clothes. She chose the best, turned it into something special, and let go of the rest.

When we finish with Chapter 7, about setting up a Life Management Center, you'll reduce your paper even further, because you'll have a simple system for keeping important information in one place all the time. You'll stop putting notes on a zillion different snippets of paper, and you'll learn to have a single place to plan and keep track of details.

Idea 10: Create Mobile Paper Systems Where You Need Them

As if the paper piles at home weren't enough, most of us have traveling paper problems, too! Let's see—how are your systems for handing paper between home and office working for you? What does the glove compartment in your car look like? If you travel for your career, how are your systems for handling travel documents and receipts working?

If these mini-systems are a mess, they can become real bottlenecks in your efforts to maintain order at home and in the office. After you've got a basic household filing system in place, you'll want to tackle some of these "floating" paper piles before they begin to cause problems for you.

Get yourself a portable file box for files that need to come home from work and go back again. Don't keep these in your briefcase, which should contain what you need for the most current activities.

A small accordion folder that has tabbed sections and fits in your glove compartment is a handy thing to have for documents such as your vehicle registration, insurance information, emergency road information, and directions or a local map.

Keep an envelope for receipts when traveling on business and label it with the trip/client/date and whatever else will help you later when you need to fill out an expense report or file them for the IRS. A little thought and organization upfront will save you time and effort later on.

Right now reward yourself for making important strides toward getting on top of your own personal paper mountain. If paper starts to build up again, stop it in its tracks! Now you know the way. Set aside some time every day at home and at work to do your paperwork. Use small bits of time (remember the power of just 15 minutes and your timer?) to handle it throughout the day. The amount of time you gain by getting control of paper is enormous. The joy of being able to put your hands on the information you need, when you need it, is real and will make your life better. It will serve you well every single day.

The Least You Need to Know

♦ Paper can support or hinder you in achieving your goals.

♦ You can't get organized until you get control of paper.

♦ You can reduce the amount of paper you handle every day by stopping it at its source.

♦ Systems can be set up to sort and file paper, keeping it under control and easy to retrieve when you need it. Tailoring these systems to your needs will help you maintain them.

♦ Some kinds of paper need special systems to be handled effectively.

♦ Applying the 10 ideas regularly will help ensure that you never again end up with a paper pileup.

Part 3

Systems for Getting Stuff Done

In Part 3, you develop systems for accomplishing goals in three crucial areas of daily life.

First, you carve out a place at the helm of your ship, a hub or center from which to manage your life. You also create a portable system you can take with you wherever you go. Next, you zero in on your relationships—the people who matter most in your life. And last, you focus on your work life, both where you are and where you want to be. When you finish this part, you'll see even more dramatic changes in your day-to-day life. So roll up your sleeves and let's get to work!

Creating a Command Center

In This Chapter

◆ Carving out an efficient place to run your life

◆ Schedules, lists, and time-management systems

◆ Commanding, delegating, and co-managing

◆ Taking it all with you

Many people have likened life to a ship on an ocean. And if life is a ship, then you're the captain, and somewhere on board there needs to be a "bridge." The bridge of a ship is where the captain (supported by a highly trained and obedient crew) navigates and handles crises. This is Information Central, where all the various departments of the vessel report and get their orders.

To manage your life effectively, you need to create your very own "bridge." You can call it whatever you like: the hub, the nucleus, the Office of the President—you may even want to make a sign so there's no mistaking it. Around our house, we call it the Command Center. For the purposes of this chapter, we call it your Life Management Center.

A Room All Your Own

Where you locate your Life Management Center is up to you. Just make sure it's in the center of your life's activity. If you share your space with other people, it needs to be a place accessible to everyone. This is where you funnel all the information about everyone's schedules, chores that need to be done, mail that needs to be sent, bills that have to be paid, and everything else that goes on in your household.

Ideally your Life Management Center will be located near a phone, and it will have a good-size uncluttered working surface to write on with some wall space to hang a calendar and any other information that needs to be posted, such as lists of chores. If at all possible, your current files will be located there as well. If that's not feasible, consider having a rolling cart that you can store elsewhere and bring to your center when you have filing to do or need to refer to something. If you have room for a shelf or bookcase nearby, that would be real plus.

Good locations for your Life Management Center are a spot in the kitchen, a corner of your home office, or perhaps a spot tucked somewhere near the main door of your home. What you want is to create a hub where you can launch your life and keep track of it on a daily basis.

Stocking Up: Basic Life Management Supplies

Certainly an effective manager or captain needs to have the "right stuff" to get the job done. Basic tools and supplies kept all in one place make it more pleasurable to do the job, and more likely you'll want to start it in the first place.

Here's a list of some basic supplies you'll probably want on hand:

Paper/letterhead

Business envelopes

Mailing supplies, including overnight mail forms and supplies if you use those services

Letter opener

Stamps in denominations most often used

Supply of greeting cards, note cards, and postcards

Ruler

Pileups!

Don't let yourself get distracted by others who inadvertently take your supplies without returning them. Tell the others in your household that things taken from your Life Management Center need to be returned and replenished. You might even want to consider putting a long string on your scissors, stapler, and tape dispenser so they're less likely to "walk away." Make it known that anyone caught with the captain's stuff will have to walk the plank!

Stapler

Glue stick

Pens and pencils

Highlighter

Tape

Post-It notes

Paper clips

Scissors

Calendar

Bulletin board for posting schedules and other important information (and nothing else!)

If you use a computer for your planning and/or finances, you may want to locate it in your Life Management Center. If you have a laptop computer, you can bring it into your Life Management Center when you need to. There's always room to adapt your command center to your particular situation.

You've Got Mail (or Other Messages)

If handled poorly, phone messages and written notes from members of the family can be a major source of frustration and even disaster. If members of the household need to communicate and are on different schedules, ensuring that these messages are passed on is imperative. One thing you can do is set up a message board in a prominent place, either one that can be written on and erased, or a bulletin board sectioned off with a space for each person. Or you could use a horizontal compartmentalized organizer

Resource Files

If you have multiple phones in your house, lost phone messages can become a problem. Consider getting carbon phone message pads. As you write down the message, tear it off, and pass it on to the right person or to your Action file (see Chapter 6). If a message gets lost in the shuffle or misplaced, there's always the carbon record to refer to. Put one by every phone in the house.

and assign a slot for each individual. You can also make a board with several large clips, putting each person's name above his or her clip. There they can check for mail, notes, or phone messages whenever they get home. Find the solution that works for your household (experiment) and stick to it.

Whatever method you choose to take and receive messages, make sure everyone is aware of the setup, and give it time to be adopted and become a habit. The more permanent and prominent the message center you create, the more likely it will be a success. Magnets holding up messages on the refrigerator may work for some, but setting up a communication center for a busy household is usually a better solution.

This Is the Captain Speaking!

One more aspect of setting up a Life Management Center is adapting it to your life situation. One essential question in any enterprise is "Who's in charge?" There can be many answers to that, depending on your living arrangements. But one thing is for sure—when it comes to your own personal responsibilities and interests, the answer is *you*. You are always the one in charge, and the more you accept and believe that, the more empowered you'll be in your life.

But what about the spheres outside of your immediate influence? Let's take where you live, for instance. If you live alone, the answer's pretty obvious. You decide how everything is organized, what you eat, what color the sheets are, when the bills get paid, and what TV shows to watch. But many of us share our space with someone else. It could be a significant other, a roommate, or an entire family. Now the question of who's in charge becomes a little more complicated.

When you set up your Life Management Center, it's important to consider other people and examine the real dynamics in your particular household. In our house, for example, I'm pretty much the home manager. When my husband and I were first married, I tried different approaches, but it became obvious that he preferred letting me handle the organizing, scheduling, bill paying, and most other activities involving the running of the home. He liked to be consulted, and he was always willing to help, but he preferred to let me handle the details. At first I resisted the responsibility, but then I realized it gave me a lot of freedom to manage things the way I wanted. I also knew I was probably more skilled in these areas.

If you're "in command," so to speak, you'll be doing a lot of delegating as well. You may delegate to your partner and children, and you may also delegate to various outside contractors to handle certain jobs that no one in the household wants or has time to do.

In another living arrangement, two or more adults may be more equally involved in the home management process. It's very important here that you consult the other people in your life when you design these basic systems. First of all, they'll be more likely to use them if they've been part of the planning process. Also they may have some good suggestions for making the system work better. You may need to divide areas of responsibility for it to work effectively.

Add children to the household and you have yet another wrinkle (or two or three). Depending on the age of the child, you may do more delegating (and following up) or work more in partnership. You need to devise systems they can use as well. It may be as simple as positioning the message board at a lower level, or printing lists and labels rather than writing in script. A system of incentives and rewards will likely become part of the mix as well. Be sure to include children, even young children, in the organizing process.

Schedules, Lists, and Time-Management Systems

As soon as you hear the word *schedule*, does the hair on the back of your neck stand up? Are you unpleasantly reminded of school, or punching a clock, and does every fiber of your being revolt? Try to keep an open mind. I promise we won't divide up every minute of your day. But having schedules and lists, and some kind of a system for keeping track of them, is essential for getting your life under control.

One tool you certainly need is a planner/organizer. Think of your planner/organizer as your mobile command center, an extension of the well-organized Life Management Center hub you've established at home. If you set it up right, it'll give you ultimate control, whether you're at work, traveling, or pushing a cart at the grocery store.

> **Envisionings**
>
> The major personal planner companies are on the World Wide Web, complete with product information and lots of helpful articles and tips. Check out Day-Timer at www.daytimer.com, DayRunner at www.dayrunner.com, and FranklinCovey at www.franklincovey.com.

A planner/organizer eliminates all the little scraps of paper scattered all over your desk, in your pocket, on the kitchen table, and stuck to the visor in your car. You'll save hours of time you would have spent looking for things, or trying to re-create what happened last week. Everything will be at your fingertips in one central place.

You can buy many prefabricated systems through the mail or at an office-supply store. Or you can set up a notebook of your own if you think that would work better for you. Just make sure it's a size that's portable and flexible, yet large enough to handle all the aspects of life management we're going to discuss.

I've used several different planners over the years, and for a long time I've found one of the smaller versions of the Day-Timer to work best for me. It was large enough to give me room to write, yet small enough to fit in a purse or briefcase. Other excellent planning systems include DayRunner and FranklinCovey.

Most paper-based planners are supported by various computer software programs that not only complement the paper planner, but also can be used to print out the forms for them. You'll find addresses and phone numbers of the major companies that offer organizers in Appendix A, so you can send for information or order products through the mail or online. You can also look for them at your favorite business products supply store.

The cheapest alternative to buying a premade planning system is to use a small ringed binder with dividers. However, you may still like the convenience of having preprinted forms that you can use however you wish. Just make them up yourself and photocopy more when you need them.

Planner/Organizer Essentials

Whichever system you choose, make sure it has the following features. Your ideal system …

- Is portable enough to take anywhere.
- Is refillable. (A spiral notebook won't do.)
- Is durable and can be kept secure.
- Has a calendar section with options for daily, weekly, monthly, and annual calendars.
- Has calendar pages with ample room for appointments, phone calls that need to be made, and a daily To-Do list.
- Has a section that's divided alphabetically with tabbed sections. (You'll see why in a minute.)

◆ Has address/phone pages. (Usually this is the alphabetically divided section.)

◆ Has a variety of other preprinted forms you can use if you need them, such as expenses, mileage, sources, and notes.

The two obvious uses for your planner are to keep track of appointments and schedules on your calendar, and to record addresses and phone numbers. But this isn't using your system as a true life-management tool. Your planner is a way to constantly remind yourself of your mission, your goals, and your priorities. It's also a convenient way to chart your progress.

The alphabetically divided address/phone section is a sophisticated database. Say what? That's right! It may not need a computer chip or power supply, but it can function as your own personal databank. Think of it as an alphabetic filing cabinet for all the information you want to have at your fingertips, no matter where you are. This A-to-Z filing system can empower you to make decisions on the spot, save you time over and over again, keep you on track, and make managing projects a breeze.

Here's how to make it work for you: Make a list of all the information you might need if you were suddenly stranded in a faraway city and forced to manage your life from a hotel room or simply "on the road" for the day. Your list might include these categories:

◆ Banking (account numbers, phone numbers; don't write your PIN number, though!)

◆ Computer information/settings/support phone numbers

◆ Family (clothing sizes, birth dates, blood types)

◆ Food (master shopping list, weekly menus, allergies)

◆ Home repairs (vendor and service tech phone numbers, account numbers, list of what was done and when)

◆ Investments (list of stocks with symbols, phone number of broker, account information, rollover dates, and so on)

◆ Legal (attorney's phone number and address)

◆ Medical (list of doctors and dentists, medical history, health insurance information)

> **CAUTION**
>
> **Pileups!** _____
>
> Try to avoid all the extra sleeves, pockets, checkbook organizers, and credit card holders that just add bulk to your planner. They not only can be a nuisance, they are also costly—if you lose your planner, you lose all your important cards and checks, too.

You get the idea. This list is just to get you started. Add your own data as you see the need. When you begin thinking of your planner this way, you'll come up with more and more categories. I have a personal wish list (filed in the *W* section) for things I'd like to have or accomplish, and I even have a rewards list to remind me of nice things I can do for myself when I've done a job well. This is filed under *R* for rewards, of course.

If you're working on a particular project, or serve in a leadership position in an organization, it's helpful to have the pertinent information all on one sheet. Then, wherever you are, you can turn to your planner and handle whatever comes up. For instance, you can go down the list and call each member to schedule a meeting. Use the blank sheets provided with your planner creatively or adapt one of the preprinted forms. DayRunner has a form called Sources and another called Project, either of which could be adapted for this purpose. Have important lists, forms, corporate objectives, or records reduced at the copy shop, punch holes (there are miniature hole punchers just for this purpose), and file them in your "databank."

Pretty soon you'll be relying on your planner/organizer as you would a partner. It adds confidence to know that wherever you are, you can quickly put your hands on all the important information you rely on in your everyday life. It helps you handle emergencies, and it enables you to take advantage of waiting time. Just grab your planner/organizer whenever you leave the house, and you're all set.

The power of any planning/organizing system is imparted only when you use it! If you think of it as your partner, you'll want to consult it on a regular basis. Use it for as many aspects of your life as possible. Make it user-friendly by setting it up in a way that works for you and pleases you as well. Use forms and paper fillers that encourage you to use them. A little color may add to your enjoyment.

For starters, you'll probably want to consult your planner/organizer first thing every morning and at the end of the day. As time goes on and you customize it more, making it more and more useful, you'll find yourself turning to it throughout the day.

As with any filing system, your planner/organizer needs regular maintenance. Go through it periodically (a great use for one of those 15-minute snippets of time I keep reminding you about!) and update or purge information. Put some planning time into your schedule—whatever works best for you. How about Sunday evenings before the workweek begins?

> **Jump Starts**
>
> Whatever time you choose for updating your planner/organizer, make sure you add it to your routine. Use it to review your goals, track your progress, and reward yourself.

Or Friday afternoons, when the week is drawing to a close? Maybe short periods every morning or evening will work best for you.

Electronic Planner/Organizers

Electronic devices for keeping track of calendars, contacts, appointments, and just about everything else have come a long way. These little mini-computers actually have more processing power than the ones that took the Apollo astronauts to the moon. The Palm handheld and the Blackberry are two popular brands. Not only can these devices help organize your life, some have built-in music players, digital cameras, phones, and voice recorders. You can use them to make phone calls one minute and play poker the next.

Depending on your lifestyle, how computer-oriented you are, and how much you actually have to keep track of, you may find a personal digital assistant (PDA) the perfect solution. They are pricey, however, and can be complicated to use. For many of us, a paper-based system is all that's needed. In fact, it actually simplifies our lives more than an electronic device would. For others, the reverse is true. The power and convenience of an electronic planner or PDA is worth the money and the time to learn how to use it wisely.

If you're thinking of purchasing a PDA as a life-management tool, do your research. Compare the different models close up and personal. Make sure you both have the different choices demonstrated for you and then try them out yourself. Consider functionality, operating system, display, memory, battery options, input options, size, connection options, expandability, and cost. There are some excellent books on the subject to help you evaluate whether you actually need one and, if you decide you do, how to get the most out of yours.

Resource Files

If you're thinking of going digital and purchasing a PDA, research your options. To learn about these popular products, borrow a copy of *How to Do Everything with Your Palm Handheld* by Dave Johnson and Rick Broida, or *How to Do Everything with Your BlackBerry* by Curt Simmons.

The Master of All Lists

One of the most important lists you'll keep in your planner/organizer is what I call the Master List. You actually started it in Chapter 5. This is a type of To-Do list, but it knows no priorities and no boundaries. This is where you dump anything that comes up requiring action during the day—tasks you either want to do or feel you need to do that suddenly pop into your head in no particular order. Don't worry about when you'll get to it, or whether it's urgent or not—just get it down on paper. You consult this list when you're actually doing your planning and scheduling. At that time, you set priorities and decide which activities most support you in meeting the goals you set for yourself in Part 1 of this book. This list is simply a repository for all your ideas.

Your Master List will contain everything from making important business calls to cleaning the gutters, from fixing your daughter's bike to making a doctor's appointment. The purpose of the Master List is to catch the fleeting thoughts you have that reveal your motivations and desires. Your brain is working on many different levels, even when you're occupied with something else. It's a powerful computer and is often triggered by associations or visual input in an unpredictable way. The beauty of the Master List is that you capture the thought *and* get it off your mind by putting it in writing.

Some things stay on my Master List a long time. Some things never get done because I later decide they're not important. That's the key word—*decide*. The Master List lets me decide what to do about each item, and that puts me in control.

The Calendar

The rest of your planner/organizer should contain a calendar section. I prefer a weekly form that lays out an entire week on two opposing pages. If you have a lot of appointments, you may prefer having one day per page. Whatever your style, you need to have enough room to put down your appointments and things to do. I divide each page into three sections: Appointments, To Do, and Phone Calls. Because I make all my phone calls at one particular time of the day, I like having a list of people to call in one place. I recommend you write down all appointments in your planner, rather than trying to rely on your memory.

Pileups!

Try not to make notes on your calendar pages. For this purpose, use a separate pad or notes sheets. This will make your calendar more useful for later reference.

Whichever method you choose, keep your calendar section clean and functional. You never know when you may need it to re-create the past. The one and only time I was audited by the IRS, I brought in my bank records and my planner/organizer. After just a few minutes, the auditor could see I had a record of every trip, every business lunch, and every appointment. He told me to go home, and that I kept very good records. Most of it I could hold in one hand!

Although this isn't a book strictly about time management, many of the tools and concepts are the same. If you feel time management is an area where you need more work, several good books are available to help you. I've listed some of my favorites in Appendix A. But here I give you some of the basics, which should get you well underway.

Backing Up Is Smart to Do!

Make sure you have a backup for all the essential information you keep in your planner/organizer. Just as you would need to recover from a disaster that destroyed your records at home or at work or in a computer crash, you'd likewise need to re-create the important information in your planner/organizer if it were lost or stolen.

One simple way to back up is to keep a file folder with photocopies of the important information in your planner. For me, these include the telephone/address section (updated periodically to include new additions), specialized phone lists, family information, and a few information lists that I could re-create, but only with some serious time and effort.

If you're working from a computer program and printing out your pages from there or using a PDA with computer interface, you can easily create an automatic backup, which is one of the advantages of this arrangement. My only caution here is that you could end up using two systems, but fail to have all the information on both. If you're not diligent about transferring information back and forth, it could cause confusion and missed appointments. You need to be sure information is shared between both systems or devices on a daily basis.

A User Manual for Your Life

Just about everything you own has a user manual or instruction book to go with it. How about your life? Well, if not, that's the next project I'm going to ask you to tackle.

Call it your user manual, household management book, control journal, or captain's log—whatever you call it, the binder you're going to create will be an invaluable tool not only for you, but for everyone in your family and anyone who helps you take care of your home.

Get yourself a three-ring binder, some tab dividers, and some plastic sheet protectors. Choose the size binder that suits the size of your family and the amount of information you think you'll have to keep in it. This book will provide you with all the information you, your family, and anyone stepping in to take care of your household might need to refer to. That goes for day-to-day information, as well as instructions on what to do in an emergency. This book will become a repository for critical information about your family and home.

Your planner/organizer is for you. Your family user manual is for everyone else. Don't worry about putting this together all at one time. Just get started and as things come up you'll begin adding them to your binder. Having the information in your computer makes it easy to revise the various information sheets and print out a fresh copy as needed. Here are some of the categories you'll want to create:

◆ Emergency phone numbers—include cell phone numbers, doctor, veterinarian, hospital, poison control center (add a reminder to call 911 first)

◆ General household numbers—utilities (gas, water, electricity), schools, relatives, plumber, electrician, carpenter, etc.

◆ Security alarm system instructions and information

◆ Pet instructions—who's who, food, walks, litter box, idiosyncrasies, house rules (on the couch or off? outside cat or not?)

◆ House rules for kids—bedtimes, mealtimes, school/homework, TV

◆ Important things to know—turn-offs for water, gas, hot water, electricity; that the furnace makes a weird noise when it turns on and off!

◆ List of important documents (birth and marriage certificates, passports, etc.) and where they can be found, which should be a secure place, such as a safe or safe deposit box.

◆ Instructions on what to do if you become incapacitated or die—who to call first, where the will is located, the names and phone numbers of your estate attorney and financial advisor

Jump Starts

Want to get a "leg up" on putting your family user manual together? There's at least one company that's thought of everything for you. The Family Facts Family Life Organizer has all kinds of predesigned forms you can use to create one tailored to your needs. Their website is www.family-facts.com.

You know your life better than anyone. Ask yourself "What would someone need to know if they had to walk in and take over for me?" Label this boldly and keep it in your Life Management Center. Every family member should know where it is and what's in it. You may want to have an abbreviated version for when the baby sitter, house sitter, or pet sitter comes; put it out for them and explain what's in there. The kids will probably have ideas to add.

Personal Management for Road Warriors

If you're one of those people who spend a lot of time on the road, your Life Management Center will most likely need to be a mobile one. The principles are still the same, however, and you simply need to have a scaled-down system for handling the same tasks. If you use a cell phone or receive a lot of phone calls at your hotel room, you need a way of taking down messages so you don't lose them. If I'm traveling, I prefer to keep everything in one place, including phone messages, so I keep them in my personal planner. That way, there are no little pieces of paper to lose.

You need some sort of portable filing system to keep track of important receipts and papers generated during the day. These could include personal and household items, as well as those related to work. Labeled folders in one of those portable plastic file boxes is a workable solution. Instead of having receipts in your pockets or flying all over the car, you'll deposit them in their folders—one for business, one for personal. Of course, you can organize this in whatever way most suits your particular situation, but you get the idea.

If you use a PDA and/or a laptop, these can contain a digital version of your life-management system. If you're a laptop user, much of your information can be kept electronically, including personal files, so you can manage both your work and personal life on the go right from your computer. If you're using personal organizing software, this may be the place to keep it, rather than on your desktop at home. Just make sure that whatever option you choose (laptop, PDA, desktop, or paper), you use it consistently and don't have partial information in a variety of different locations. Instead of making life less complicated, this fragmented or duplicated approach can really foul you up. If one system doesn't seem to be working, try another, but commit to one at a time and use it fully and consistently. Simpler is usually better.

Make It So!

Now that you've got control of your ship, you can explore any territory with confidence. You now have one place to handle your finances, plan the week's menus, check on the kid's soccer game, or plot the overthrow of your company's competitors. With your Life Management Center and its satellite, your planner/organizer, you're ready for any mission. And with your family user manual safe at home, anyone can keep the home fires burning and handle just about any emergency in your absence.

The Least You Need to Know

◆ Setting up a central place for managing your affairs gives you control and saves you time.

◆ Having basic supplies on hand helps your Life Management Center operate smoothly.

◆ When setting up your Life Management Center, be sure to take into account your personal living situation.

◆ Having a personal planner/organizer will make you more effective at home, at work, and on the road.

◆ Your family user manual will make it easy for you, your family, and anyone taking care of your house, children, or pets to help keep your life running smoothly, even in an emergency.

People Who Need People: Interpersonal Systems

In This Chapter

- ◆ Priority one: taking care of yourself
- ◆ Nurturing relationships as part of your organization plan
- ◆ Setting people priorities
- ◆ Keeping track of important dates and events
- ◆ Using organizational tools to have more fun with the people you love

We've spent a lot of time so far talking about organizing "things." But besides getting control of your possessions, an important aspect of organization that most experts overlook is getting control of your relationships. What do I mean by *control?* I'm talking about establishing successful, rewarding relationships with the people you value most in your life through planning, scheduling, goal setting, and plain old-fashioned organizing. You didn't think organizing your life could help you with your relationships? Think again!

Who's Looking Out for You?

The first person you need to provide for in your overall organizing program is *you*. The very fact that you're reading this book and taking steps to carve some order out of chaos shows you care about yourself and are trying to make your life better. Let's begin, then, with the premise that you're no good to yourself or anyone else—family, friends, co-workers, *anyone*—unless you're "taking care of business" with the most important person in your life—you.

Maybe you have trouble thinking of yourself as number one, but you are. You are, and you have to be. Your goals regarding health, mental attitudes, physical appearance, and spiritual well-being all need to be essential parts of any organization plan.

> **Wise Words**
>
> "Friendship with oneself is all-important, because without it one cannot be friends with anyone else in the world."
>
> —Eleanor Roosevelt

In Chapter 21, I share more information on organizing for health and fitness; but in a discussion about planning for the people in your life, it is extremely important to get you thinking about yourself and your own well-being as you engage in the organization process.

"Unstuff" Your Relationships

Just as your home or office can be full of stuff that falls into the category of "junk" (useless things that only get in your way) so, too, your social life may be filled with "junk relationships." This can be a hard thing to face honestly. None of us like to discard people, and we don't want to be discarded. But if we haven't been steering our own ship well in other areas of life, it's likely that our relationships, too, may be foundering on rough seas.

There's no polite way to say it—you need to get the people who don't support your goals and share a positive outlook out of your life. You need to learn how to say no to these people and concentrate your time and energy on those who add substance and sustenance to your life.

Relationships, like "stuff," tend to fall into three categories:

1. There are the people who deserve to occupy *prime emotional real estate*. They're the closest to you and often the ones you're most likely to take for granted or ignore. Sometimes they're not as demanding as people who are actually less important to you.

Although we constantly hear that the world is becoming smaller and technology is making it easier to stay "in touch" and "connected," technology also brings with it increasing demands on our time. There are lots of stimuli vying for our attention. We may spend more time with TV people than with the people we say are most important in our lives. You can use your organization program to see that this doesn't happen.

2. Then there are *secondary* people. You like them and care about them, but they're not fundamental to your existence. They're not at the core of your life. This probably includes people you encounter at work, in your community, at your place of worship, or while pursuing your various interests. You enjoy their company, they play an important part in these particular spheres of your life, but if you were to lose contact with them through a move or other change, you might not see them regularly, or might lose track of them altogether.

3. Last are the people who are better put in the *deep freeze*. I know that sounds harsh, but I think you know what I'm talking about. It's essential that you have an honest talk with yourself about the people you devote time and energy to who might fall into this category. Do some people you spend time with add nothing to your life?

Envisionings

Close your eyes and clear your mind. Visualize the people you spent time with this past week. If necessary, write down a list before you begin this visualization. Put the face of each person in front of you, one at a time. Note how you feel when you visualize that person. Recall what time spent together was like. Was it rewarding? Do you eagerly await seeing that person again? Is this a person you've identified as one of the key people in your life (see "Creating a Quality Circle," further on in this chapter)? How much time did you spend with the ones you love and enjoy most?

I look at it this way: the people who are most important to me are held in the highest esteem in my life. I give them priority over all others. What's left goes to the next level of relationships, and I simply don't have a place in my life for the third kind.

Take a "People" Inventory

At the beginning of this book, we spent some time talking about your personal challenges and your mission in life. This was a "broad-stroke" process to help you identify what's important and what you really want. Now I'm asking you to take a similar inventory of your relationships and implement some incremental changes to make them better and stronger than ever before. The goal of this book is not just to help you be an organized person. There are plenty of sharply dressed people with tidy offices and showplace houses whose lives are falling apart. I want you to have it *all*, and the only way for you to do that is to include it *all* in your Life Plan.

Jump Starts

When you "de-junk" your relationships, you have more time to nurture those with potential to be more rewarding. With more frequent visits, phone calls, or letters, could you grow closer with certain relatives or friends who have gotten pushed into the background? You might be surprised what happens when you make the effort!

Take a look back at the past week. Who did you spend time with? How much time? Write down the names and, next to them, the approximate times. Use the visualization exercise I've given you to help you accomplish this. Now look at your schedule for this week. Who are you planning to see? Add these people to your list if they're not already there. Next make a list of the people who are most important to you. Your spouse, partner, or person you're dating? Your children? Your parents? Siblings? Extended family? Friends? Co-workers? List them on a separate sheet in the order of their importance. How does what you're actually doing stack up against what you say is most important to you?

Now that you've taken your people inventory, the next step is to decide what results you want with the people who mean the most to you. To get you started, try asking these questions about the key people you've identified. Again I suggest you write the answers down so you can get a clear overall picture. For each person, ask the following:

- What's the current state of our relationship?

- Do we communicate often enough?

- What are some of the areas between us that could be improved?

- What would I have to do to make those improvements?

- How would improving that relationship make me feel?

- What are five small things I could do today to contribute to making that happen?

- How can I use my current organization plan to improve my relationships with this person?

- Is there a phone call or visit I need to make? A letter or card I really need to send?

Maybe you need to schedule a night out with your spouse. Many people have a regular weekly "date night." Maybe you could improve the interaction between you and a partner or your kids by streamlining some of the daily chores and working together on the process. I'll bet if you start today to focus regularly on your "people priorities" and include them in your daily and weekly planning sessions, you'll see some immediate results.

Creating a Quality Circle

In the 1970s, an idea was introduced to American management from Japan that many people believe helps improve productivity and quality, especially in manufacturing. The concept was called "quality circles," and it has helped build strong project teams and strengthen communications. I'd like to suggest applying a modified version of this principle to your relationships.

Somewhere I read that we can't have quality relationships with more than 10 people at one time. I'm not sure I can even manage 10! That's not to say we can't know and interact with more, but we can only give of ourselves to 10 people or fewer in a deep, intimate way.

Let's look again at your list of the most important people in your life. How many people are on it? Are you certain these are the people who are vital to your happiness, who truly mean the most to you? Are they at the core of your life? Do you hold a similar place in their lives? If not, pare your list down to those relationships that are key to your happiness. I'll bet when you're finished, you'll have 10 people or fewer by default.

Think of this as your own personal quality circle and nurture it every day. Hold these people in the highest esteem and give them the best you have to offer. Organize your life around them. They form your support system in difficult times and are the ones you celebrate with in joyful times. Being committed to their happiness and well-being will help ensure yours.

You Remembered!

Just by focusing more on the people you care about and eliminating unrewarding relationships, you'll find it easier to remember and keep track of important events such as birthdays, anniversaries, school plays, or whatever. But if you tend to be forgetful or remember too late to make the occasion as special as you'd like, I have a foolproof method for always being on top of remembering these milestones.

What makes it foolproof is that it actually involves several systems, not just one. It's what they call in computer jargon "redundancy." Most of the time, organizing involves eliminating duplication, but in this instance duplication works in your favor.

Here's how I do it. In my personal planner, I keep an events calendar. It's really just a list of regular events that occur each year pretty much at the same time. Toward the end of any given year, I use my events calendar to fill in important dates for the coming year on my daily calendar pages. I put the actual date on the calendar *and* an early reminder 10 days before. I *also* put these dates on the communal family wall calendar for the year, so I can help my husband keep track.

I also have a calendar program on my laptop. Any annually recurring events such as birthdays and anniversaries need only be entered once. The program keeps them perpetually year after year. I set the program to sound an alarm to remind me, too. Most PDAs have similar features with the added redundancy of a backup to your computer. The 10-day lead time allows enough time to order a gift or send a card, and the second reminder the day of the event will give you nudges to call and wish your favorite aunt a happy birthday, too.

If you're strictly using a paper system, one way to create "redundancy" is to put all these events on both your family wall calendar and your personal planner. Remember to build in the 10-day cushion so you have time to get a gift or send a card by noting that on the calendar as well.

Resource Files

If you don't use a computer that often, you might consider a telephone or mail reminder service. Look in your Yellow Pages under "reminder services" or "personal assistant" or check into one from a nearby city if you live in a small town. Some personal assistants will even buy gifts, send cards, and run errands for you (for a fee, of course). There are even free e-mail reminder services. www.memotome.com is a popular one.

Another good idea is to keep a list in your planner/organizer (under "G" for "Gifts") of outings, books, or gifts you hear people say they'd like—their personal "wish list" kept by you. If you come across something in a magazine or on TV that you think they might like, jot down the information and transfer it to this list. You could also have this in a file folder if that's more convenient for you, but I find that having it with me in my planner/organizer allows me to act on it whenever the opportunity arises. If I'm in a store, for example, and I have some time to browse, I refer to my list so I have my giftees in mind. At the beginning of the year, I review that list and put out feelers to see whether these things are still appealing to my giftee. If not, I cross it out; if so, I decide whether I need to do some advance planning and build that in to my calendar.

When a new year begins, set aside some time to review special events coming up unique to that year. Note, especially, landmark events, such as twenty-fifth or fiftieth wedding anniversaries, decade birthdays, baby's first Christmas, confirmations, bar mitzvahs, and similar once-in-a-lifetime events. This gives you even more time than the usual 10 days to plan something really special. Draw up a plan and schedule various tasks into your calendar.

One year for a special Father's Day, for instance, I decided I wanted to do something really different for my husband. I investigated a Jeep tour I'd read about. He's a Western history buff, and the tour involved traveling over some rough road to an old mining town and following a historic Arizona stagecoach route. I found out I needed to book at least a month in advance and had to have at least four people to go on the tour. I had time to invite one of our favorite couples and make it a total surprise. This took some advance planning and organization, but because of my system, I was able to pull it all off without a hitch and in plenty of time. No telling what might happen next year!

Something else that will save you time and keep the pressure off is to buy greeting cards in advance. You can keep them in a box with dividers especially for that purpose. Because you have your personal planner with you, you'll know which events are coming up and who you need to have cards for. If you do buy cards in advance, make sure you have a place to keep them where they won't get soiled or wrinkled and where they're easy to find any time. You might organize them by month and put a sticky note on ones you have specifically earmarked with certain individuals in mind. Then when you reach your 10-day reminder, you'll just go into your box and grab the card you planned for in advance. Don't just buy for specific occasions—have a few extra for those unplanned-for times when a get well, birthday, or "thinking of you" card would come in handy.

Letters! We Get Letters!

Do people really write letters anymore? Well, *I* do! Granted, I write far fewer letters than I used to, with e-mail being so handy, but there's just something special about a handwritten note, and it's important to create some time for it in my life. When you simplify and organize your life, you have time and energy for some of the social graces that make daily living kinder and gentler. With more reliance on the telephone and e-mail, I certainly send letters through the mail ("snail mail" as it's often referred to in cyberspace) less often than I used to, but it's still a part of my daily life.

Sometimes I write because I have to clear up a question on a bill or change an address on an account or for similar reasons. This generally falls into the category of business correspondence, and I discuss that later in Chapter 9. But on some occasions, a personal note, postcard, or letter is appropriate.

Be creative in thinking of ways to keep up with your correspondence. Sometimes I sit out in the hammock and jot off a short postcard message to a friend with a quote or a thought to let her know I'm thinking of her. You might write letters for an hour or so in bed, just before drifting off to sleep. Or you can bring your basket of stationery supplies and write while others might be watching a TV program you're not all that interested in. Remember those small 15-minute gems of time I mentioned earlier in this book? When you have your letter-writing supplies handy, it's easy to make use of those 15 minutes to stay in touch with loved ones.

There are lots of systems for keeping addresses and phone numbers, from the most old-fashioned (a handwritten address book) to the most newfangled (contact software or on your PDA). I'm of both the old and the new school here. I keep an address/ phone book in my Family User Manual (you now have one, too!), which stays in the kitchen and which everyone has access to. It's actually just a printout from my computer contact program. I also keep a Christmas card list (redundancy again) in a label program in my computer, which I update every year. This allows me to generate labels anytime for most everyone we stay in contact with.

> **Jump Starts**
>
> One way to encourage personal letter writing and make it quick and easy is to have all your supplies—stationery, stamps, return address labels or rubber stamp, stickers, and pens—in a box or basket you can take with you anywhere.

Some people favor a 3×5 card filing system for addresses so they can make notations on the cards. Others keep everything in a computer program or PDA and make notes there. You decide what's best for you, but be sure your system is portable and easy to update.

Escalating E-Mail: How to Keep Up

With the rapid increase in the number of people who have computers at home and in the office, the use of e-mail has skyrocketed. Depending on how you use and manage it, e-mail can make a big difference in how well you stay in contact with the people in your life who really matter, but who may not be close at hand. If mishandled, however, e-mail can become just one more cluttered mess choking your computer and stealing your time.

The Benefits of E-Mail

I find e-mail indispensable for both personal and business correspondence. Benefits of e-mail include the following:

- ◆ It's easy.

- ◆ It's cheap.

- ◆ It's fast. In fact, in most cases it's immediate.

- ◆ E-mail gives the people you write to a hard copy at the touch of the button, but generates paper only when they choose.

- ◆ You can send items of interest, photos, and sound and video files as attachments to e-mail.

- ◆ You can use e-mail to transmit short messages that would otherwise end up in chatty phone calls taking far more time out of your schedule.

E-mail is great for firming up visiting arrangements, and for transmitting directions and flight information. I urge caution here, however. Print out the information, and always confirm by telephone closer to the date. That's good e-mail etiquette in any case, and will prevent misunderstandings. E-mail just doesn't have the urgency or impact that phone or face-to-face communication does. In some instances, it's a great supplement to voice communication, but not a complete substitute.

Resource Files

For a nifty selection of electronic greeting cards, check out the Blue Mountain Arts site at www.bluemountain.com. There's something to send for just about any holiday, including those that might be obscure to many of us, and there are some greetings available in French, Spanish, and other languages.

Things to Watch Out For: "Netiquette"

Just as there are polite rules of behavior in other areas of social interaction, there are also rules (commonly known as "netiquette") governing communications in cyberspace. Here's a short list of do's and don'ts for e-mail correspondence:

- ◆ Do read over an e-mail message you've composed before you send it. Remember, there are no emotional clues, no voice inflections, no pauses or facial expressions to tell the reader that something's intended with humor or being said with a smile or a sarcastic grin. Make sure there can be no misunderstanding.

Jump Starts _____

It's bad enough that your virtual mailbox is stuffed with unsolicited offers and advertising. The other big culprits in creating unwanted e-mail are your friends and family! If you don't want your e-mail stuffed with junk, ask others to take you off their joke-of-the-day, recipe, or other mail list. It's just a waste of your time if you don't enjoy it. Likewise, don't subject other people to your own mail list without their permission.

CAUTION

Pileups! _____

Be sure the person you're e-mailing is a regular user of his online connection, especially if you're contacting that person with time-sensitive information. Otherwise, your message can sit there forever, and you'll wonder why you haven't gotten a response. The reverse is also true. Don't send an e-mail message or give out your e-mail address and then not log on for two weeks.

◆ Do learn to use emotion symbols (known as "emoticons") whenever truly useful. Many use <g> to mean "grin" or :) to mean "smile" (look at it sideways and you'll see a vsmiley face). For a comprehensive list of emoticons and other e-mail shorthand, go to www.computer-user.com/resources/_dictionary/emoticons.html. You can also use descriptive words in parentheses to make the meaning clear if you're not sure it will be clear to the recipient.

◆ Don't forward long posts or files unless you really think the recipient will benefit from or enjoy them.

◆ Don't send chain letters or information about multilevel marketing schemes. It's rude and, again, takes up a person's time even if it's just to open your message, read part of it, and delete it.

◆ Don't rely solely on e-mail when making important arrangements. Always confirm or reiterate via phone or in person.

◆ Do quote part of someone's previous message when replying to his e-mail; this reminds him of the "thread" of the conversation. Many e-mail programs automatically duplicate the message being replied to in the body of the reply. But don't overdo it. Having to read through the entire message again is a waste of time. Just quote the pertinent parts.

◆ Do exercise care with grammar and spelling. Not only do poor communication skills reflect on you, they also indicate how much you value getting a clear message across to the recipient. The less clear the communication, the more room there is for misunderstanding.

◆ Don't use all capital letters. It makes your message LOOK LIKE IT'S BEING SHOUTED! And we all know it's rude to shout.

Unsolicited commercial e-mail or spam is a growing problem and it wastes our time every day. Use a spam filter and learn some tips on how to cut down on spam from spam.getnetwise.org. Use some of the same techniques with electronic junk mail that you learned for handling paper junk mail. Stop it at the source (ask the people you know, politely, who regularly send irrelevant e-mails to please stop), don't open it, and for goodness sake, don't waste your time reading it!

Putting People in Their Place

What do you do when you really need to tell someone to give you some space or let others know they're intruding on your privacy or time? If you're truly committed to simplifying and organizing your life, this may well be necessary at some point.

Generally I find honesty is the best policy. If it's not a good time for people to call, say so. If they just drop in without asking, tell them you can't see them right now and ask them to call next time. If you need uninterrupted time to get something done, don't answer the phone. Let your voicemail or answering machine take it. You decide who has access to you and when. Use the various means available to you to control your time and your life.

I have caller ID, for example, as well as an unwanted call screen, and I use them to eliminate calls from telemarketers and control calls from people I know who are habitually inconsiderate of my time and my needs. My home is my castle, my quality circle is my first concern, and my time is precious. I use every trick I can find to protect them and me. You can, too.

Scrapbooks and Other Memory Devices

Because we're on the subject of people, let's talk about the things we tend to accumulate as keepsakes to remind us of special people and important moments we spend with them. This is especially true of those who have passed away. These can include letters, cards for special occasions, photographs, memorabilia, and just about anything else that reminds us of a special event or person. But these things can accumulate, and unless they're selectively organized in a meaningful way, they just become part of the clutter.

The first thing to acknowledge is that a collection of "things" is not the person or the memory itself. By paring down what you keep to remind you of the past, you are not dishonoring it. In fact, by clearing out the clutter, picking only the very best and featuring it in a special way, you are honoring that person or event.

A "new" trend (actually, it's quite old-fashioned) is the making of scrapbooks or "memory books." This is a great way to unstuff your life of sentimental clutter and keep only the best or most memorable things. You discard a lot. What you *do* save goes into an archival quality album made with acid-free paper, so you're protecting your precious memories from the ravages of time. You can add sentimental value by adding your own personal comments and artistic sense, and putting photos and keepsakes into a form that can be passed on and appreciated by the whole family and future generations.

> **Jump Starts**
>
> There's really no need to keep negatives anymore. If you want to make a duplicate of a photograph, all you need to do is scan the photo (or have it scanned) and print it out. And ditch those "outtakes"—fuzzy, poorly composed pictures that just become clutter. If you can crop out the bad stuff and use the photo on your scrapbook page, fine. Otherwise, ditch it!

Keep scrapbooking materials to a minimum, even though that may be hard to do. There are lots of products on the market to enhance your scrapbook—stickers, rubber stamps, special papers, glitter, and much, much more. Just keep it simple and basic, buying only what you need. Put your best photos and mementos in your album and get rid of the rest.

If you use a digital camera, remember to purge the less-than-wonderful shots from there as well. Make a decision when you take the shot if at all possible. Organize your digital photos and create something worthwhile with them—a digital slideshow or a scrapbook page.

If your photos are in a jumble in boxes and bags, they're just going to get damaged and aren't serving any real purpose.

Photos generally fall into three categories: archival (historical family photos), snapshots (everyday photos to record and remember important events), and special photos (wedding and baby pictures).

Archival photos should be sorted and stored in archival boxes (these products will say somewhere on the label "acid free," "PBS free," or "archival safe") with acid-free tissue in between (keeps photos from flaking). Categorize them in separate boxes and label. Seriously consider taking them to a photo studio and have them transferred to a CD-ROM or do this yourself.

Snapshots or everyday photos need to be sorted regularly. What are your criteria? Are there duplicates? Is it a bad picture? Does it evoke a memory? Does it really capture the moment? Does this photo record your memory (or someone else's)? Do you have enough of that memory? Ten photos are usually enough to capture any event or memory, so be selective and keep the photo clutter to a minimum.

Special photos belong in a special place and should be stored carefully. Again, you'll want archival quality albums for things such as wedding photos and baby pictures. If you've started an album, but never finished, schedule this as a fun project and maybe enlist some help from the family.

Another way to pare down keepsakes is to incorporate them into a collage or other display that, again, only uses the best or most memorable objects. Still another idea for kids and adults alike is to keep a "memory box." Use the size of the box to limit what is retained, and weed it out periodically so it contains only the most special trinkets and photographs. I also find that my personal journal and the descriptions of events I write there often make it less necessary to save these things. An illustrated journal (a few choice photographs can be added to enhance the text) makes an even more personal way to remember the past without cluttering the present and future. A scrapbook can also be made richer by the addition of journal-like commentary on its pages.

Resource Files

Lots of books and magazines on scrapbooking are available. One that's aimed at beginners is *Quick & Easy Scrapbook Pages: 100 Scrapbook Pages You Can Make in One Hour or Less* by Memory Makers. Your scrapbooks don't have be elaborate, but they're a meaningful way to make just a few photos evoke the memories as you intended when you took them.

Scheduled Spontaneity?

Making an inventory of people in your life and planning time around them may seem too structured, too scheduled, not spontaneous. That doesn't have to be true if you make sure there's unstructured time in your plan. This may seem like a contradiction—organizing yourself to be spontaneous? It isn't. By getting physically organized and mentally focused (they reinforce each other), you get the "must do's" done more efficiently. You release yourself from the nagging feeling that things are out of control and getting further away from you. You feel confident knowing that you're making time for the people and activities you really care about. This actually allows you to be more spontaneous and provides the emotional freedom to let go.

One important point about intimacy and romance—I believe it's essential to have planned times for intimacy, as well as spaces in your life where the unexpected can happen. Think how much more passionate you can be when you can relax and know that your life is humming along on an organized plan. You'll feel strong and ener-gized knowing you're well on your way to achieving the goals you've set for yourself. Bet you didn't know that being organized can be sexy!

Resource Files

Want some terrific ideas for gifts (many of them "nonstuff" ones) you can give the one you love? Get yourself a copy of Gregory Godek's *1001 Ways to Be Romantic* and his sequel, *1001 More Ways to Be Romantic.*

My friend Karen and her husband actually schedule at least half an hour every day to snuggle. They usu-ally set time aside around 5:30 P.M., when they're both done working for the day (they both work at home), as a way to connect with each other. It's absolutely precious and jealously guarded time for them. No phone calls, please!

People Time, Alone Time

There's a time to be with people and a time to be alone. And time alone spent in silence is especially healing and renewing. Remember, included in your quality circle is *you!* Make sure you schedule time each day (yes, I said *day,* not *week!*) to listen to your own inner voice. That's how you know if you're on the right path and you've got your goals and priorities in the right place. That's how you know whether your people time is being spent wisely and whether you're happy.

So tend to the people you care about most, but always leave time for solitude and having important (or even frivolous) conversations with yourself.

If You Can't Have Fun, Why Get Organized?

Getting your life in order may seem like hard work. And in fact, it *is* hard to honestly assess what you're doing that isn't working for you and change old, deeply ingrained habits. But as I'm sure you're beginning to see, the rewards are enormous. Granted, cleaning out your dead files, throwing out old newspapers, and getting a PDA won't automatically make you spouse of the year, superdad, and megafriend. But let me ask you a question: if you have more time to spend with your loved ones, if you're more relaxed when you're with them because your life is under control, and if you're mak-ing sure you include them in your overall Life Plan, could this possibly *hurt?* I think you know the answer!

The Least You Need to Know

◆ Your own health and well-being are the center around which your entire organization plan revolves.

◆ There are three types of relationships. The first type is most important and occupies prime emotional real estate; the second type is maintained with what remains; and the third type should be eliminated entirely.

◆ A redundant reminder system will ensure you never again forget an important recurring event.

◆ Correspondence is easily managed by assembling all the supplies in a central place and using small blocks of time.

◆ E-mail can be an effective way of keeping in touch if you observe a few basic rules.

◆ Spontaneity (and even romance!) is made possible by organization and planning.

Chapter 9

Work Systems: Getting Ahead Without Getting a Headache

In This Chapter

- ◆ Applying basic organization principles to your work life and career goals
- ◆ Unstuffing your office
- ◆ Getting control of the paper piles in your office
- ◆ Organizing your home-based business

When people are disorganized at work, they live every day feeling overwhelmed, ineffective, and pressured. Not sure whether you're disorganized in your job? Check whether any of these has happened to you recently:

- ❏ You missed an important appointment or meeting because you forgot or lost track of time.
- ❏ You forgot to return a phone call and the caller had to phone you a second time.

Pileups!

Besides taking a toll on your own mental and physical well-being, both the reality and the perception of you as a disorganized person may be keeping you from a promotion or from moving into the career you really want. How likely would *you* be to trust additional responsibility to someone you thought of as "disorganized" and "scattered"?

❑ You had to do something over because you couldn't find the original work.

❑ You missed an important deadline.

❑ You spent hours looking for a piece of paper you needed in a hurry, only to find it sometime later in a pile on your desk or stuffed in an obscure file folder.

❑ You passed up an opportunity for a better job or promotion because it was too much trouble to put your resumé in order.

❑ You spent evenings or weekends working at home because you couldn't get the job done during regular business hours.

If you checked one or more of the above, you probably have a less-than-perfect work life. If you checked three or more, it's probably darn near out of control, and you're way more stressed out than you want or need to be.

Never fear. Together, you and I will conquer the work front the same way we began whipping things into shape at home. So stop making excuses, stop procrastinating, roll up your sleeves, and let's get to work on work.

Goal Setting Fine-Tuned

More goal setting? Absolutely! Only this time you're moving into advanced goal setting, fine-tuned specifically for work and career. Let's start with a few questions first (and feel free to write your answers on the lines provided or on a separate piece of paper):

◆ How satisfied are you in your current job? Do you plan to be there a year from now?

_____

_____

◆ If you're dissatisfied with where you are now, what are you specifically dissatisfied with? Could any of these be related to your own performance or lack of organization? How could getting organized improve your present job satisfaction?

_____

_____

◆ If you plan to seek a new job in the next year, how would getting organized right now support both your job-hunting efforts and your goals in your new position?

_____

_____

◆ What are your broader career goals? Where do you want to be 5 years from now? 10 years? 20? What additional skills, education, or experience do you need to realize these goals? How would getting organized support you? Do you have a career strategy or plan for getting where you want to be? What would one look like if you did?

_____

_____

◆ Look at your current working environment. What feelings does it create for you? Which elements do you have the freedom to change? (Look at "Designing Your Work Environment" later in this chapter for some specific areas to consider.)

_____

_____

◆ Can you take the basic principles of organization you learned in Chapter 5, Chapter 6, and Chapter 7 and apply them to work? (Don't worry if the answer is no on this one. You'll be getting some additional help!)

_____

_____

Envisionings

Would thinking of yourself as an entrepreneur, even though you work for someone else, have an effect on your attitude and ultimately your results at work? Close your eyes and visualize your present job position as your own small company, with you as president and CEO of your job. Imagine you are solely responsible for making the company grow and that all of the people you work with are part of your corporate team. Imagine you are responsible for motivating these people to help you grow your business. How does this feel? How does this shift in viewpoint change the way you see your job? Act on this shift in perception and see whether it doesn't improve your attitude and performance.

Unstuffing: Work Version

Before you try to get organized at work, you need to get rid of the clutter that's getting in your way. Sound familiar? This unstuffing stuff seems to apply to *everything!* Commit to getting rid of the clutter and junk around you and streamlining your work space, just as you've already begun to do in other areas.

Start by mapping out some time. Come in an hour early. Stay an hour late. Use your lunch hour or a series of breaks to get started. Whenever you choose to make time, focus exclusively on implementing your organization plan and don't allow any interruptions.

Remember the boxes for sorting you used in Chapter 5? We're going to use the same basic system for unstuffing your workspace. Your boxes will be labeled *Trash* (or you can just use a large wastebasket), *Put Away* (this is stuff that doesn't belong in your office. Most likely you'll be taking it home), *Pass On*, and *Keep*.

Do the same thing here that you did earlier with your living space. Tackle one small area at a time (a drawer, cabinet, or shelf). Remember the power of "just 15 minutes"? Use the same double sort technique, too. Bring your kitchen timer to work and use it to do an initial "quick sort." That should leave you with a full trash can, a box of stuff to get to other people, a box (small, I hope) to take home, and a box of stuff to keep. Ding! Time's up.

As you do your initial sorting, ask the same basic questions you asked when you unstuffed your home space:

♦ When was the last time I used this?

♦ How often do I use it?

♦ If I don't use it very often, could I borrow it the few times I might need it?

♦ Is it a duplicate? If so, which one works best? How many copies do I really need?

♦ Is it out-of-date?

♦ If I didn't have this anymore, what impact if any would it have on my work? What's the *worst* thing that could happen if I tossed this and then found out I needed it?

As you answer these questions, more should be finding its way into the Trash or Pass On bins or boxes. Be ruthless. Remember, just because someone sent it or gave it to you doesn't mean you have to keep it.

Next follow the "directions" on your Trash and Pass On bins. That's easy—just do it. Now let's take a look at the Keep box. Chances are you're dealing mostly with paper here, but there will also be supplies and personal items. Are you hoarding things such as artwork, knickknacks, photographs, funny calendars, souvenirs, sneakers, umbrellas, food containers, or coffee mugs? For now, just group these personal items together in piles of similar items and put them aside.

Take a look at your pile of supplies. You may find you actually have three rulers and two staplers. Look for duplicates, keep the best, and either pass the others on or trash them if they don't work well. Decide on a place to keep supplies. You'll probably end up with two places: one for what you need right at your fingertips, such as tape, a stapler, staple remover, and pens; and one for supplies you don't need very often, such as tape refills and extra staples. Keep *prime real estate*—the drawers, shelves, cabinets, and surfaces closest to you—for the most frequently used things.

Even if your company won't supply a rolling cart, you may want to consider buying one for supplies. I use this in my home office and couldn't be without it. It cost about $30, has five drawers, and sits on casters, so I can move it out of the way when I don't need it. Remember to label the drawers so you don't have to rummage through each one looking for a pair of scissors or a letter opener.

If the rolling cart idea doesn't work for you, consider drawer dividers and step shelves for cabinets to maximize your storage space. Again, if your company won't pay for them, it's worth getting them yourself. You can always take them with you, and when others in the company see how well they work, you may even be reimbursed.

Keep personal items to a minimum. Make them simple and meaningful.

Resource Files

Check the resource guide in Appendix A at the back of this book for lots of mail-order and online companies that sell office and organizing supplies. You'll find filing supplies, rolling drawer carts, rolling file carts, baskets, racks, office furniture, phone equipment, and just about anything else you can think of to help organize your office space just a click or a phone call away.

What's left in your Keep box is probably paper. In this second sort, you divide into the same categories you did before—*To Do, To File, Pass On,* and *To Pay.* If you own your own business, you may actually have bills to pay at your office. Otherwise, these should be sent to the proper department or individual. If you found more paper that needs to go to someone else, pass it on. That leaves you with To Do and To File.

Your Files Aren't Another Trash Can!

How much of what's in your files is outdated or no longer useful to you? Probably about 80 percent! As you clean up the stuff strewn around your office, file only what you really need. Then set up a time to go through your existing files and do some serious weeding out. When that's done, commit to purging them at least twice a year, and more often if you can. Perhaps you can key those purging sessions to events such as the new year and "spring cleaning." You don't have to do your file purge all at once. Take 15 minutes and do a little every day. Before you know it, you'll have more file drawer space than you ever imagined possible.

Another important issue is whether it's easy to find something after you file it. My advice is to keep your filing system simple. Not only does it save you time, it also makes it easier for someone else to handle things in your absence. In fact, when you get that promotion, it'll make it easier for the next person in your position to take over!

Here are some tips for improving your filing system:

♦ Alphabetize. Don't separate individual files into various conceptual divisions and then alphabetize within them. If it makes sense, use separate drawers for broad divisions such as Projects, Personnel, and so on, and alphabetize the whole drawer. Of course, sometimes you may need to use another type of system, but for most filing, alphabetic is the way to go. If you use subcategories, alphabetize those, too.

♦ Label clearly and boldly. Make sure you can read the subject headers quickly and easily, even from a distance. Black and bold is best. There are label programs for your computer and handy labeling machines that allow you to select an easy-to-read font in any size and print out labels whenever you need them.

♦ For each item you're filing, ask what word comes to your mind first and use that as your category. Use a noun for file categories. For example, "Files, Organizing," not "Organizing Files." Remember that the word you choose to be first will determine where the file goes alphabetically. File so you can find it!

♦ Be careful you don't duplicate categories—Records, Medical and Records, Health, for example. Pick one and be consistent. Use the same filename for both paper and computer files.

♦ At least in the beginning, consider keeping a list of all your file categories. That'll prevent you from creating duplicates and make the system easier to revise.

Jump Starts

If your secondary storage space is limited, you may want to keep only a bare minimum of extra supplies in your office and go to the supply room when you start to get low.

◆ File the most recent document in the front. When you open the folder, your documents will always be in chronological order.

◆ Use a hanging folder and a regular folder for each subject. This may seem like extra work, but in the long run it isn't. If you never take the hanging folder out of the drawer, you'll file the manila folder in the same place every time and filing will be quicker and easier. Guaranteed!

◆ Consolidate and compress wherever possible. Can you make a list on one piece of paper and eliminate several sheets? Can a document be reduced or copied double-sided? Can several pieces relating to the same project be pasted together and copied on one sheet?

> **CAUTION**
>
> **Pileups!**
> Avoid having files called Miscellaneous or Other. These are traps, and you usually can't find things in them anyway.

Don't forget to unstuff your computer files, too. Many of the same principles apply—file things under names you'll find easily, avoid catchall filenames such as Miscellaneous or Stuff, consolidate files, and avoid duplicates. Use the Search or Find File function to find files when you can't. Use a compression program to save on disk space. A software program such as Norton Utilities can help to regularly "defragment" your hard drive to optimize space as well. Keep your computer desktop clean and uncluttered. Purge computer files when you purge paper ones.

And Speaking of Paper

In Chapter 6, we talked at length about controlling paper at home. Now, how can you apply what you learned to handling paper in the workplace? Let's review.

Stop It!

Get rid of as much junk mail at work as you can, using the technique I've already shown you for the home front. Ask to be taken off mailing lists. Stay away from surveys and questionnaires. And when you subscribe to a publication, send a form letter requesting to be kept off mailing lists and not to sell your information to anyone else.

In addition to junk mail delivered by the post office, you may also need to combat junk e-mail, also known as spam. This fast and cheap way to target upscale consumers has lots of e-mail subscribers up in arms. It takes valuable time to download, open, read, and then trash those useless messages, and it overloads online resources already pushed to the limit carrying important stuff that we really want! We talked briefly about spam in your personal e-mail in Chapter 8.

Here are some additional steps to stop spam at work:

1. If the sender gives you a way to "opt out" in the message, you can do so. I feel that it should be the other way around—we should decide whether we want to receive the stuff in the first place—but at least you may be able to stop more from coming. Some determined spammers only use your reply to confirm your e-mail address and sell your name to still more spammers!

2. Go to the Junkbusters site (www.junkbusters.com) and download their free Internet Junkbuster software. There are lots of good tips here, too, about getting rid of all kinds of junk mail, including tons of sample letters you can use to send to marketers. Just add your own name and address and it's all done for you.

3. If there's a toll-free number in the spam you get, call and complain.

4. Complain to your own Internet service provider (find out who the right person is). Some ISPs have standard addresses for this purpose, such as postmaster@*yourisp*.com or abuse@*yourisp*.com. You can ask that your provider install a junk e-mail filter, which will filter out spam from known offenders. Most ISPs are already doing this and putting suspected spam in quarantine so you can trash these unwanted e-mails without reading them.

5. Be careful about registration forms and surveys on the Internet. If you fill one out to access a site, give as little information as possible, and tell them you don't want your information to go anyplace else.

Internet activists are attempting to get Congress to regulate online marketing and the proliferation of spam. Until they do, you can at least take some steps to reduce the amount you get clogging your e-mail box.

Review your subscriptions at work and see whether you can't cut them in half. Be realistic about the time you actually have for reading. If you've got reading material backed up for more than a week, trash it and start fresh.

Can you use an electronic or paper clipping service or specialized, closed Internet mailing list to stay on top of subjects you need to track? Is there a printed or electronic newsletter that does a good job of summarizing the latest developments in your field? Even though some of these options may seem somewhat expensive initially, in the long run they'll save you precious time and money. (Add up the cost of all those subscriptions, for instance.) In addition, information is often easier to absorb on one particular subject when it's gathered in one place.

If you have a secretary, see whether your mail can be opened and sorted before you get it. Deal only with priority mail during the business day, and quickly sort through the rest at the end of the day, during your homebound commute (if you don't drive to work), or during your afternoon break.

Jump Starts

If you're on a publication pass-on list within the company, try requesting to be taken off the list if the information in the publication isn't crucial.

Don't be a paper generator. Limit memos and letters whenever possible. Try to avoid getting into the "CYA" habit. Most of the time this causes unnecessary accumulation of paper to prove something actually occurred, in case you're asked to defend yourself. If this is really a constant necessity in your present company, you might want to think about changing jobs. Don't print out e-mail messages or online information unless it's absolutely necessary! Whenever possible, file it digitally.

Decide Now

When you sort through mail or other papers, put them into categories as quickly as possible. Be ruthless. The paper in your hand either gets trashed, is passed on, or goes in one of three compartments: *To Do, To File,* or *To Read.*

If you decide something needs to be filed, make sure it's something you really need to keep. Keep it only if it meets one or more of these criteria:

◆ Can't be found elsewhere

◆ Supports you in the goals you've set for yourself

◆ Has been reduced or consolidated as much as possible

◆ Is up-to-date

Make sure you file it where you can retrieve it when you need it. Have a clear idea of how long you really need a particular piece of paper. If you purge your files every six months (or more often, if you can manage it), after a particular item's usefulness has passed, you'll be pitching it in the circular file, and freeing up space on a regular basis.

File So You Can Find It

Treat your files at work the same way you do at home. There are your current *working* files, *secondary* or *reference* files, and *archival* files (the *deep freeze!*). Keep your working files close at hand in your prime real estate. You may even want to consider one of those rolling files we talked about earlier, or a divided holder next to your desk.

Secondary files that you only refer to periodically can be less accessible. Archival files should be put in storage, preferably out of your office, and should be kept to an absolute minimum.

Whatever you use for current project files, make sure it's not a catchall. Some people like having some sort of rack or holder to keep them in view. Rather than having a holder out on the desk for current files, other people prefer an in-the-drawer system or rolling file. This is an especially good option if you're easily distracted. In the morning, the desk is clear and you can focus on whatever tasks you decide should get your attention first. Then in the evening, everything can be put away off your desk for a fresh start in the morning. I've tried both systems, and both have advantages and disadvantages. You decide.

Everything's filed in alphabetic order using a hanging folder first with an identically labeled manila folder within it. If there is more than one subdivision within a hanging folder, then the manila folders are also filed alphabetically. That's the simplest and quickest system I know, and it works best for most people. In some cases, you may need to use a chronological or numeric filing system instead.

Be sure your documents are dated and the source is identified before you file. This is especially important when clipping newspaper or magazine articles. Should you later need to quote the piece or place it in a chronology, you'll be glad you took the time.

Pileups!

Before you make any radical changes in the way you handle and store files and records, be sure to review your company's policy (and your department's) to make sure you comply with their financial and legal requirements.

Observe good filing practices with your computer, as well. Use color coding only if it really helps. Keep files and folders off your desktop and tucked away under pertinent category folders on your hard drive. Purge often. Put as much in the trash as possible, use portable media (floppy disks, larger disk media, tape cartridges) to "file off" and store a big chunk, and then organize the rest on your hard drive. Don't duplicate digital with paper files unless absolutely necessary. Choose the file form that makes the most sense.

Back Up or Else!

Another important consideration for electronic files is backing up. We all know we should do it, but most of us back up sporadically at best. I suggest you keep two sets of backup disks for your files. One set you will leave at work, and the second set you will take home with you and rotate once a week. That way, you're always assured a fairly recent copy of your work regardless of any disaster that might occur. Because I work at home, I exchange a set of backup disks with another home worker. We meet for breakfast once a week and exchange our latest versions. If you don't have someone to switch with, consider keeping a set in your safety deposit box. Especially if you own your own business, having backup can mean the difference between surviving and going under in the event of a fire or other disaster. You may even want to consider a commercial off-site backup service.

If you tend to forget to make a backup, make it a ritual. How about every Friday afternoon? Or every Monday morning? I generally use Fridays for "housekeeping" in my office—filing, tidying up, bill paying, and nonurgent correspondence. This is my time to do a weekly backup. On important documents, I back them up to a zip disk every day. There is also software you can buy that automatically reminds you to back up. Whatever you do and however you do it, remember to back it up!

A final note: Be careful about taking digital or paper files out of the office without adequate backup. Think of the hardship it would cause you and your company if these files were lost or damaged. Make sure you have duplicates of absolutely critical files.

Life Management Center: Work Version

In the office, you'll have a different version of the Life Management Center you set up at home. This one is specifically geared toward supporting you in your career goals. Depending on what kind of work you do, it may involve a planning board, a project calendar on the wall, or other specialized tools.

You also need a way to integrate the schedules of other people in your department and overall deadlines. Some companies do this through software on a networked computer system. If yours has one, learn how to use it effectively and train others, too.

Jump Starts

If you use a paper planner/organizer, use a pencil for writing down appointments and to-dos that may change. Try a colored pen or highlighter to emphasize important appointments or reminders.

An indispensable tool, however, will still be the planner/organizer that you set up in Chapter 7. This is what integrates all the things that are important to you in your life, and helps you keep a balance between work and home. Enter everything that comes to mind that you need to do on your Master List as you think of it. You can keep a separate one for work and home if you like, but I prefer to keep everything on one list, so I'm sure to include both when I'm planning.

Your Master List is simply a databank of things you want or need to do. You're the sorter. Review your Master List whenever you do your planning (I recommend mini-planning sessions first thing in the morning and last thing in the evening, every day) and see what should be transferred to your daily to-do list and when. Make sure you include deadlines and phone calls you need to make (or times you've asked others to call you), as well.

Pileups!

What seems to be most urgent is not necessarily what's most important. Keep repeating this over and over to yourself. Don't let only the "squeaky wheel" grab your attention. You decide what's important.

Prioritize the tasks on your daily to-do list. Some people like the A-B-C method:

A—Top-priority items.

B—These things are important but don't absolutely have to get done today.

C—It would be nice if these things got done, but they could probably be put off indefinitely.

Personally, I don't think any C items should be on your list at all. Keep them on your Master List and only add them to your daily one when you decide they're important enough. So all that's left are As and Bs. I prefer to number them in order of priority, from number one to whatever. Anything I don't get to at the end of the day gets put on the next day's list and most likely gets a high-priority number.

Assigning a task number one priority doesn't necessarily mean it's the one you do first. It simply means that of all the tasks on your schedule for that day, it's the one that you most want or need to get done. Take advantage of your peak performance times for tasks that require the most concentration or creativity.

Remember, what determines priority is the place a particular activity has in supporting you in your goals, not whatever comes up first or shouts the loudest.

Use the organizing principles you learned in Chapter 5. Group like things together when you plan your time. It's often more efficient to do all the things that require certain tools or skills at one time, such as writing letters or making phone calls, than it is to scatter them throughout the day.

Don't forget to write down planning time on your schedule, block out time to be with family and friends, and make appointments with yourself to take care of your needs for relaxation, learning, and spiritual development. Always keep in mind the whole picture of who you are and are aspiring to be, and integrate that into your daily work planning and organizing.

If you're not accomplishing all the tasks you set for yourself in a day on a regular basis, that usually means you're wasting time, asking yourself to do too much, allowing too many interruptions, or suffering from the big P: procrastination. If it's the latter, go back to Chapter 3 and review the section on procrastination. You can't afford not to conquer it.

In conjunction with a planner/organizer, some people have a "tickler" file. A tickler file is simply a set of 31 numbered files representing each day of the month and a set of 12 files behind them for each month of the year. As invitations, tickets, conference brochures, or anything with date-specific importance comes through your hands, you can file it in your tickler file. When the event draws near, you have all the information you need. Make sure to file the information in the file for the date you need to act on it, *not* when it's due. If you get a memo about a project that's due two weeks from now and you don't intend to work on it for another week, for example, put it in the numbered file for seven days from now, to remind you to start on it. Keep information for later months in the 12-month folders. Be sure to check your tickler file every day. It's not a bad idea to check ahead for the following week on Monday morning and Friday afternoon, as well.

Jump Starts

A tickler file system should occupy prime real estate (as in, under your nose), and checking it must be a habit. The system only works if you use it regularly. If you forget to check it, things can get lost, and you can forget to take important actions when needed.

Tickler files don't work for everyone, but if your work is very date-oriented, it might be the right system for you.

Designing Your Work Environment

The environment you create in your workspace has a direct effect on how well you work. That applies to offices away from home as well as home offices. Often, if you work for someone else, you simply accept the environment you're given and fail to realize how much you can actually do to adapt it to your own needs and working style.

Look around your office or cubby and ask these questions:

♦ What's the furniture in this room really like? Is it functional? Is it in the best spot? Is it attractive? Is your desk the right height? Your computer keyboard? Do you have space to spread out? Is there ample room for you to stretch out your legs or lean back? How comfortable is your chair? What are your options in this company as far as furniture is concerned? Can you make changes? If not, what can you do to adapt what you already have using add-on drawers, step shelves, desk pads, chair pads, or other removable accessories?

♦ What are the predominant colors in this room? How do you respond to them? Is there a way to add color through wall decorations, furniture choices, or office accessories?

♦ How does this room filter out sound? Is there a way to improve it? How does sound affect you when you work? If there's music piped in, does it help or hinder you? Can you eliminate it if you want to? When might you need to do that? Is there a quieter place you can retreat to when noise becomes a serious distraction?

♦ Where are your light sources? Is there any natural light? What kind of blinds or curtains do you have to control natural light? What kind of light fixtures do you have? Are they adequate? Are they located in the best places? Are they fluorescent or incandescent? (Incandescent is easier on your eyes.) If you have a fluorescent fixture, does it buzz? (If so, the ballast may need to be replaced.) What is the strength of the light bulbs in your fixtures? What are your options for changing and improving your office lighting? Are there any ways you could improve the lighting in your workspace?

♦ What's the temperature in your office? Is it too cold? Too warm? Does it fluctuate? Can you control it in any way? Can you control the sunlight into your office, thereby having a certain amount of control over the temperature? Would the addition of a small fan or space heater help? Would wearing layered clothing that you can add or shed make a difference? Do you include getting some fresh air as part of your daily routine? Is there a way to get fresh air into your workspace?

♦ How about humidity? Is it too damp or too dry? Would the introduction of a room humidifier or dehumidifier be an option?

♦ What's the location of your phone jack? Is it conducive to where you want your desk and computer to be? Can you have your phone jack moved or an additional one put in? Can you go wireless? How about electrical outlets? What are your options here? Can you get extension cords or power strips? (Be careful about overloading electrical circuits, protecting critical equipment, and the safe locating of cords and wires.) Would the addition of a headset, cordless headset, or speaker phone enhance your comfort and efficiency?

◆ Do you store food in your office? How does that affect your working environment, and does that support you in your health and fitness goals? Does having food nearby distract you or encourage you to procrastinate? Do you tend to eat lunch and take breaks in your office, rather than resting your eyes and your wrists or stretching your legs?

◆ What comforts or accessories can you add to make this a better workspace? A better chair, a cushion, or backrest? A wrist pad or more ergonomic mouse for your computer? An antiglare screen? A mat or footrest? How about a rolling cart for supplies or a rolling file cart?

◆ Do you have your space set up to maximize your movements, and have you allotted prime real estate to the things you need for the tasks you perform most often? Are all the supplies you need to perform a task located in the right place? Can you obtain more or better storage to accommodate your needs? Can you make better use of vertical space (think *up!*)?

◆ Have you managed your total work environment to bolster your energy level and help you stick to your health goals? Are you taking regular breaks from your computer screen or other work? Are you getting up from your desk regularly and moving? Have you considered buying equipment such as an air filter, ionizer, or aromatherapy diffuser to enhance your work environment? Make sure these things would be allowed before bringing or purchasing them.

◆ Have you given consideration to the care and feeding of your mind, heart, and soul when you survey your work environment? What's your overall sense of well-being in your current workspace?

◆ Are your goals, dreams, and visions somehow projected and presented for you on a daily basis?'

Resource Files

For suppliers of office phone equipment, check out your local business-supply store or chain, such as Staples (www.staples.com) or Office Max (www.officemax.com), Radio Shack's Duofone products (www.radioshack.com), and the Quill business-supply catalog (www.quillcorp.com). There are also some excellent sources that specialize in headset phone equipment, such as www.headsets.com.

By the time you're done asking yourself these questions, you'll probably have a list of things to do and requests for your purchasing department or office-supply center (or you may need to buy things personally). Don't delay, because these "environmental" improvements can have an immediate impact on how well you perform your job and how you feel about it. These things are so easy to take for granted or ignore. Take a few minutes today to focus on them and make the necessary improvements.

People Power

Do you manage people? Work in teams? How's your relationship with your boss? Your secretary? The mailroom personnel? How can you organize yourself to make these relationships better? Being organized reduces stress, not only for you, but also for the people around you. Order increases efficiency and promotes creativity; it has a definite effect on your ability to perform and your level of satisfaction. Here are six strategies for increasing your people power:

1. **Delegate.** Delegating means giving other people the authority and freedom to do a task that you might otherwise do yourself. Make sure you thoroughly explain the task, communicate what's expected, and empower the person you've asked to do the task to perform it thoroughly and well. Agree on when and how progress will be reported and reviewed. If you learn to delegate effectively, you'll have more time to attend to higher-priority tasks, and the person you've delegated to will have a valuable opportunity to learn and grow.

> **Resource Files**
>
> Use professional organizations as a means of networking. Locate the most prominent in your field and find out what resources they offer. The International Association of Business Communicators (IABC), for example, gives briefs on various types of communications programs and holds regular networking meetings, as well as national conferences. Check them out at www.iabc.com.

2. **Network.** Use your friends' and colleagues' knowledge and experience. If you're asked to do a project or implement a program that others you know have done, pick their brains. And make yourself available to them for the same purpose. I regularly let writer friends of mine know what projects I'm working on. Because they see a lot of information daily on a variety of topics, just as I do, they often pass on news or magazine clippings or make me aware of experts, books, or online sites I should know about. I reciprocate in kind.

3. **Collaborate.** A "buddy system" often makes tasks easier or helps you stick to a particular project. Is there a colleague you can get to work with you? How can you make it to his or her advantage to do so? This technique is effective at work, but can also be applied to many other areas of your life.

4. **Prepare.** Organize and plan carefully for meetings ahead of time. They'll be more productive and take half the time. If your department has regularly scheduled meetings, try eliminating one and see whether it really makes a difference. You may just be meeting out of habit, rather than need.

5. **Listen.** Apply Stephen Covey's rule in *The 7 Habits of Highly Effective People:* "Seek first to understand, then to be understood." By listening carefully and fully comprehending the problem before you try to give advice or attempt a solution, you'll save time in the long run and be much more effective in your dealings with people in all areas of your life.

6. **Learn to say no.** Just because someone calls, walks in your office, or asks you to do something doesn't mean you have to give him your time right then. Make decisions about how to organize your time, and be firm about not allowing other people to sabotage your efforts. Be polite, but don't be afraid to say, "No, I can't do that," or, "I'll talk to you about it later." If it's something you want or need to do, but you're busy with something else, schedule a time then and there when you'll meet with or call the person to discuss it. Thank the person for respecting your time.

   If you already have too many commitments, resign or beg off of some. What committees or boards are you on that don't really serve you or make the best use of your time and resources?

Envisionings

Saying no is very difficult for some people. Close your eyes and imagine yourself in various situations (be as specific as possible) where you might be asked to do something where saying no would be a good idea. See yourself saying no firmly and politely. Say it out loud when you're by yourself, and hear yourself taking control of your time and what you need to do. Repeat the process over again until you really feel comfortable doing it, and then try it out. Notice how powerful the word *no* is.

Shortcuts

What can you streamline? Standardize? Customize? Computerize?

Look for ways to standardize forms, formats, routines, and checklists. Create procedural manuals whenever possible. This saves time with new employees. (Make sure it's kept up-to-date.) Create form letters for regular types of correspondence. You can change them slightly if need be, but you won't have to put in the mental energy creating a new letter each time.

Set up style sheets for regular correspondence or flyers in your desktop publishing or word processing software, so you don't have to reformat each time. Keep a file with directions to your office or meeting place and send it with confirmation e-mails, or print out and send a copy with written correspondence. This eliminates those "how do I get there again?" phone calls and e-mail messages.

Use checklists. When you travel, use a packing checklist. When you make a sales call, use a checklist or a phone interview sheet to make sure you've covered everything.

Make up a fax cover sheet that you store in your computer. Copy enough to have on hand when you need them.

Jump Starts

Write thank you and follow-up letters while you're on the road (a great way to use flight time); at least do a draft, which you can tweak after the event. You can address envelopes ahead of time, too.

Use binders when they make sense. You can use all kinds of inserts and plastic sheets to customize a binder to suit any number of purposes. A binder can be used to organize business cards, slides, computer disks, specific business trips, news-letters, professional organization information, and any sheets of paper you want to last a long time. (Use plastic sheet protectors.)

Learn how to use all your fax machine or fax software features. That goes for all the office equipment you use regularly. Some time spent upfront will save you time every day.

Make an effort to really learn your computer's capabilities. Take the time to read software manuals to help you understand program features. You'll be amazed how little of your computer's power you're actually using! Get help with a tutorial, a book, or a class that addresses your particular software. It's not cost-effective to spend $500 for a program and only know how to use a fraction of its features. When you know what it's capable of, you can make an intelligent decision about which features are most useful for you.

Ring Around the Workplace: Phone Control

The telephone is a tool. In fact, it is your servant! So how come it feels like it rules your life? Take charge and use these techniques for a happy, productive "phone relationship." Get control of your phone and you get control of one of the greatest sources of interruptions and wasted time:

◆ Have a specific time for making and returning phone calls and a specific time when you can encourage other people to reach you in your office. If possible, have your answering machine, voicemail, or secretary take messages at other times.

◆ Change your voicemail message as needed to let people know your schedule and when they should call; then make sure you're available when you say you'll be. Don't answer except at the allotted time. Do the same for returning calls, and keep your word.

> **CAUTION**
> **Pileups!** _____
> Don't let disorganized phone time eat up your day. Set up telephone appointments, just like in-person appointments. Say, "I'll call you at 2 P.M." and do it.

◆ When recording a phone message on someone's answering machine or voice-mail, leave a specific time when she can call you back. Always repeat your phone number, even if you think she's already got it, and give your full name.

◆ Do phone messages have a way of disappearing? Use a two-part carbonless phone message book available from business-supply stores. This ensures that if someone misplaces the original message, there's always a backup.

◆ If you make a lot of telephone calls or make extensive notes from your calls, consider buying a telephone headset. It frees your hands to do computer file maintenance, open mail, write short letters, or sort papers while you're on hold, and it beats scrunching the phone between your shoulder and ear. Besides, you look mighty funny that way and your neck will thank you!

◆ Learn to make phone calls quickly and get to the point. Answer phone calls the same way. Decide on the focus of the call, prepare (make a list of points to cover before you dial), and stay on track. If you know you're going to be calling some-one who tends to chat a lot, make the call just before lunch or a few minutes before quitting time. Hunger or the desire to go home can be great motivations for keeping it short. This is also a good time to call someone who's difficult to reach.

◆ Treat e-mails and faxes the same way you would other mail or phone calls. Pick specific times to go online and collect your e-mail (twice a day is the minimum). Respond immediately to anything you can, and add to your schedule those that are really a to-do. If an e-mail message contains information you need to retain, print it out and put it in the To File slot right away. (Do this sparingly!) If you need to pass it on to someone else, either forward it electronically or print it out and forward it. The same basically applies to faxes. They either go in the To Do slot, where they are scheduled in your planner/organizer, or they get filed, passed on, or discarded.

Business Correspondence Made Easy

Now let's move on to organizing your business correspondence. We've talked a little bit about e-mails and faxes, which, along with letters and memos, make up the bulk of your correspondence. You can apply your basic sorting system to all of them. Some goes directly in the trash. Some might need a short notation and can then be returned to the sender or passed on to the appropriate person. Some may simply need to be filed. And some requires action, which might include a more extensive reply. Throughout the day, think of these categories—Trash, Pass On, File, To Do—and continually get things off your desk or desktop and into the appropriate place.

Jump Starts

Make your daily commute count in your quest for organization and peace. Use it to set yourself up for a great day and to start unwinding the moment you leave your office. If you drive, give some creative thought to providing an orderly, pleasant environment each morning and evening. If you use public transportation, organize yourself so you can use that time to prepare for the day, relax, or pursue a favorite hobby. And don't use your morning commute for breakfast. Get up as early as you must to prepare a nutritious breakfast at home. You'll save money, eat better, and help your digestion!

Now for some tips to lighten your load when it comes to business correspondence and to streamline the process:

◆ When only a brief reply is needed and the original doesn't need to be kept on file, return the original letter with your notation at the bottom. That gets it off your desk, saves paper, and reminds the sender what was said originally.

◆ Use e-mail to reply whenever possible, rather than a written letter. It's quicker to write, doesn't generate paper, and is cheaper and instant. Make sure the recipient is someone who checks his e-mail frequently, however, if the message is urgent.

◆ Schedule time to fully learn your e-mail program. These programs are being updated all the time, and newer versions may have powerful features you may not even know about.

◆ When you have a choice between a written letter or fax and a phone call, choose the telephone. When you have a choice between an e-mail and a phone call and the e-mail will work just as well, choose e-mail.

◆ Write in clear, concise English using action verbs and nouns. Write short sentences and paragraphs. Poor communication wastes time—yours and everyone else's!

◆ Don't create more information in your written communications than anybody needs! Don't write a 10-page proposal when 1 page will do. Aim for tighter writing. It promotes clearer thought (you have to focus and be clear yourself to write concisely) and results in greater understanding.

◆ Don't print e-mail messages unless you really have to. Enter the information in your planner if it's about an appointment or a meeting. File electronically whenever you can. If you must file a hard copy, print it out and put it in the To File bin immediately.

Resource Files

Need some quick help with your writing style? One of the best books I know on effective business writing is Robert Gunning's *How to Take the Fog Out of Business Writing.* You know if your writing can use help. If it can, get it!

Envisionings

Imagine yourself in total control of your work environment. See yourself using your time effectively, meeting your deadlines and handling crises. Make it real. What are you wearing? How do you feel? Visualize yourself walking through your workday with all the right tools at your fingertips. What does this picture do for your self-confidence? Where can you imagine it leading? List all the ways not being organized and confident will cost you, financially and emotionally. List all the benefits you'd gain.

Taking It On the Road

Many of us are going mobile. Travel for both business and pleasure creates its own organizational challenges. Going on a business trip to a trade show or an industry convention doesn't have to mean coming back with a backlog of paperwork, tons of phone calls and correspondence, and a general feeling of disorganization and inefficiency. Don't put off dealing with the accumulation of business cards, literature, receipts, or papers to be sorted through. When you delay making decisions, clutter builds up.

Use travel time and evenings in your hotel room to keep on top of it all. Have folders that duplicate your office sorting system in your briefcase: To File, To Do, To Read, Pass On. As you sort through paper for filing, especially if you can't do it right away, highlight or jot down the filing category on top. This speeds up filing when you get back to the office. On your first day back in the office, schedule time to deal with the accumulation of mail and paperwork. Don't put it off or it will soon grow into a mountain instead of a small hill.

Keep an envelope for your receipts, and write notes on them while the purpose or other details are fresh in your mind. Write notes on the back of any business cards you get—anything you've agreed to do, where you met the individual, or any other pertinent information. Then transfer the card information to your computer contact software, or put the card in your office card file, after you've taken any necessary action.

Make sure to add to your planner/organizer any deadlines or promises you made. Any other ideas that come up can be added either to your idea list or your Master List of things to do.

Jump Starts

Mail literature you've accumulated from trade shows. Don't carry it home! Trade show companies sometimes provide boxes and mailing points specifically for this purpose. If you only need to glance over some of the literature and have room for it, read it over on the flight home and dispose of it at the airport when you arrive.

Use e-mail to your advantage while you're traveling. You can stay in touch with the office when it's most convenient for you. These days, most hotels have high-speed Internet connections. If so, make sure you're set up to take advantage of this service. Write snail mail letters and e-mail them to your secretary to mail out while you're gone. By the time you return, you'll either already have a reply or will have one shortly. Use e-mail to keep in touch with family when schedules conflict. It's not a substitute for a phone call, but can be a great way to help keep the home fires burning when you're far away. E-mail is just one more way of keeping our people priorities straight. It's also a good way to reinforce your commitments to employees when you can't be in the office.

Don't forget to send thank you notes and e-mails.

When Home Is Your Office

If you're new to working at home or just considering it as a possible alternative, you need to realize it takes time to adjust to this new lifestyle. You have to set all sorts of limits on other people—like the neighbor who figures that because you don't have a "real" job you can let in the plumber and walk her dog. This includes your own family, as well.

In the beginning, allow yourself room to experiment. If at all possible, plan for becoming a home-based worker in advance, set up your workspace, and ease into at least a partial routine before you give up your off-site job.

Get your equipment and supplies, design your office space, write your business plan, and have your stationery printed before you quit your job. Consider using your days off to try things out and get a handle on the challenges you'll face. Take notice of your energy patterns, what distracts you, and where your time goes; you might even keep a log at first.

Go through the questions list in the "Designing Your Work Environment" section earlier in this chapter and broaden it to take advantage of the freedom being a home-based worker affords you. You can repaint, remodel, accessorize, and furnish to your heart's (and budget's) content. It's up to you to make the choices and keep your focus at the same time.

Resource Files

I highly recommend the book *Working from Home: Everything You Need to Know About Living and Working Under the Same Roof* by Paul and Sarah Edwards. It's the "bible" of the home-based business movement. Another very good book on the subject is *The 30-Second Commute: The Ultimate Guide to Starting and Operating a Home-Based Business* by Beverley Williams and Don Cooper.

Because someone else doesn't structure your workday, *you* have to define it. Use your Life Management Center and your planner/organizer to give your work life structure. Set regular hours with room for planned deviations. Create routines and rituals that help you stay focused. Some experts even suggest dressing a certain way for work, even if it's just wearing a particular sweater or pair of tennis shoes. If you wore a suit to work before and it puts you in the "work mode," wear a suit at home, at least in the beginning, until you establish some kind of routine. One man even got dressed, walked out the door, got in his car, drove around the block, and then came back to work in his home office to get himself in gear. Hey, whatever works!

Pileups!

If you work at home, you don't have to go overboard devoting permanent space to meeting with clients or colleagues. If there isn't adequate space at home, meet at their location, at a rented suite (in some areas, office suites can be rented by the hour or the day), or in a restaurant or club.

Set regular deadlines for yourself. If all you have is the deadline for the completed project, break it down into smaller, manageable chunks and assign deadlines to those. Add them to your planner/organizer.

Define your work area as well. If at all possible, physically separate your office from the rest of the house. You can possibly turn a spare bedroom, a rarely used dining room, a large closet, garage, attic, basement, or finished porch into the perfect office space. It helps if it has a door you can close or even lock or some other way to mark off a separate space and indicate that you're working and don't want to be disturbed.

Working at home is about taking full responsibility for your work life, especially if you're self-employed as well. So take responsibility for …

- Preventing interruptions.

- Creating a supportive working environment.

- Getting the right tools.

- Creating the image you want for your business.

- Learning about new technology and using it.

- Keeping up with your field or industry.

- Finding local services and vendors and establishing a good business relationship.

- Making a business plan and reviewing it regularly.

- Finding a good business lawyer, tax preparer/accountant, and financial planner.

- Filing the appropriate papers and obtaining necessary licenses, such as a local business license, resale certificate, seller's permit, employer ID number, business name registration, partnership agreement, or articles of incorporation—find out from your lawyer what you need and then get it!

◆ Investigating and using telephone company services such as call forwarding, call waiting, voicemail, and built-in (often free) accounting features if these will help you run your business better, stay focused, save time, and help organize you.

◆ Backing up important print and computer files.

◆ Preparing your business for fire, flood, theft, or other disasters.

◆ Giving yourself time to dream, plan, think, and create.

◆ Rewarding yourself and sharing your success with others.

Take responsibility for your own success. You wanted to be in charge. So take charge!

On the Lookout for Your Next Job

How prepared would you be if you got fired or laid off today? If you're currently working at home, what if you decided to get an off-site job? How quickly could you begin to make the transition? What if a head hunter called with the job of your dreams, but you needed to get a resumé in today's express mail? Or what if a job opening was announced today within your company that you really wanted? Would you be able to act on it in a hurry?

An important benefit of being organized is that it allows you to be proactive, rather than reactive. *Proactive* is really just another word for prepared. If an opportunity arises, you don't need to "throw something together"—you've already *got* it together. Have a file both at home and at work that contains your employment records, references, letters of praise, and an up-to-date resumé. If you don't have a resumé, write and design one. Get professional help if you need to.

Review your job readiness every few months. Set up a plan to have enough money in the bank to cover four to six months of unemployment. If you're not in a financial position to do that right now, start working toward it. Chapters 15 and 16 in this book can help you. Even if you switch jobs, you still may need extra money to make the transition between your last paycheck at your old job and the first at your new one soon.

Resource Files

Buy or borrow the book *What Color Is Your Parachute?* by Richard Nelson Bolles. This is *the* classic guide to career planning and job hunting. You'll probably want to reread it periodically, because it's so informative, entertaining, and uplifting. It turns "looking for work" into "discovering your life's work."

Keep a diary of your job accomplishments with specifics: How much did you actually save the company? How many people did you oversee on that project? What were the results? Who? When? What? Where? How? Why? You'll have everything you need at your fingertips if you need to back up a request for a raise or for your next job interview.

Don't just organize for the job you have. Organize for the job you want. Think of the peace of mind you'd have today just knowing you could handle any change in your job situation and respond to any opportunity.

Your work life is your life. Identify how it fits in to your mission statement. Make it part of your overall organization plan, and you'll not only be more productive, you'll also be a happier person.

The Least You Need to Know

- The same principles and techniques you use to organize yourself at home can easily be applied to work.

- Using a planner/organizer effectively helps integrate your work and home lives, and keeps larger goals in front of you.

- Even if you work for someone else, you can customize your office space to make it more comfortable, efficient, and enjoyable.

- Working at home offers more freedom and creates unique challenges. Taking responsibility is a key element in being a successful home-based worker.

- Keeping up with basic organizing tasks on the road will make your first day back in the office a snap.

- Being prepared for unemployment or new job opportunities alleviates worry and creates possibilities.

Part 4

Room by Room

Each room in your home plays a different role in your overall organization picture. In the next five chapters, we take them, one by one, and examine their form and function in your organized life.

Imagine how different your life would be if your kitchen supported you in your health and fitness goals. What if your bedroom were a serene retreat and your bedroom closet were filled with attractive, wearable clothes that you love? Well, together we can make over every space to give you breathing room and good vibes every time you enter it.

10

Bathroom Organization: Methods for Your Morning Madness

In This Chapter

◆ Starting the day the organized way

◆ Saving time on grooming and makeup routines

◆ Keeping a lid on clutter

◆ Using a modular system to end the "handbag from hell"

What is "beautiful" or "handsome"? You won't catch me opening *that* can of worms! But I think we can agree that "looking good" not only makes us feel good, it can also help create the confidence we need to be more successful.

This chapter will help you make "looking good" easy and fun, by showing you how to pare down and devise simple routines, as well as giving you tips on how to organize the stuff you use to get the look you want.

Unstuff the Bathroom!

First things first. Before we talk about ways to organize what you have, let's get rid of what you don't need. Most bathrooms are booby-trapped, with bottles and tubes of goo tucked everywhere—some of it from another decade. It may be hard to find the sink; you have to duck when you open the medicine chest. The vanity cabinet under the sink is a jungle of pomades and potions and tangled electrical cords.

Out It Goes!

Step one is to go through your cabinets, bathroom drawers, linen closet, medicine chest, dressing table, bureau—wherever you keep various personal care concoctions, bath brews, face paints, nail polishes, hotel samples, and hair tools. Clear them all out (bet they'll fill a clothes basket), clean the drawers and shelves, and then start to weed out the pile using the sorting method you already learned in Chapter 5. Sort into *Trash*, *Keep*, *Pass On*, and *Put Away*. Do the initial sort quickly with the kitchen timer ticking away. Then refine the Keep pile by putting like things together.

Get rid of old cosmetics and personal products. Here are some guidelines for how long you can keep common items and the best way to store them:

◆ Creams and lotions can be kept up to two years. Pump-type dispensers are best because fingers never touch what's left in the bottle, so you don't add bacteria. Otherwise, dab what you need on a cotton ball.

◆ Sunscreens usually have an expiration date. If there isn't one on the containers, ditch them if they're older than one year. Remember, when you head for the beach, sunscreen should be kept in a cool, dry place—not in a hot glove compartment or basking in the sun.

◆ Toothbrushes should be replaced every three months. Store them so they dry quickly. Dampness breeds bacteria.

◆ Nail polish may thicken or separate with age. Shake it to blend. If that doesn't do it, you'll know it's time to toss it.

◆ Mascara is a real villain for transmitting bacteria that can cause infections. Don't keep it more than three months. Use a permanent marker to note on the tube the date you bought it. You can do the same for toothbrushes. If you're not sure how old it is, toss it out.

♦ Foundation, cover-up, lipstick, eye shadow, blush, and powders are generally safe for one year. Why not make an annual purge on New Year's Day or just before the holiday season?

♦ Hair color has an expiration date on the package. It should be kept out of light and heat.

Keep in mind three more general points:

♦ If you can't remember when you bought it, throw it out!

♦ Get rid of duplicates, items that are broken, and those that just don't do the job.

♦ While you're tossing outdated, redundant, and useless personal-care products, add expired prescription medicines to the pile. Don't play doctor and medicate yourself with old medicines. Get proper medical advice and the right medication. And never, *never* transfer prescription medicines to different containers. The results could be dangerous or even fatal. Flush outdated medicines down the toilet.

> **CAUTION Pileups!**
>
> Don't limit yourself to single-use products. By choosing products with multiple uses, you can cut down on bathroom clutter. For example, as most outdoor enthusiasts know, Avon's Skin-So-Soft bath oil does double duty as an effective bug repellent. Petroleum jelly has a host of applications. And many moisturizers and makeup bases have sun protection built in.

By following these guidelines and getting rid of old products, you've already done yourself a favor. You can further reduce health risks by becoming a label reader. If a product causes burning, a rash, or breakout, note the main ingredients and move on to something else that doesn't list those ingredients.

An allergic reaction may also be due to preservatives or even an old product whose chemical composition has begun to break down—all the more reason to dump cosmetics and personal-care products that are past their prime.

Another word about labels: don't be fooled. The government doesn't regulate use of the term *hypoallergenic*, so don't assume you won't have a reaction when you see this word on the label. "All natural" doesn't necessarily mean allergy-free, either. Some natural substances are just as irritating as commonly used chemicals, if not more so.

Never share your cosmetics or personal products. This is really asking for trouble. Remember to be conscious of this rule when trying on cosmetics at the store counter. Use personal samples only.

Stow It! Bathroom Storage Solutions

Now that you've unstuffed your beauty and grooming products, and have them sorted by type, you need to find a better way to store them. We all know that bathroom cabinets and drawers were devilishly devised to make it impossible to retrieve what you want, when you want it. Here are some storage suggestions that may work better for you:

◆ Store regularly used products such as shampoo, conditioner, and cleanser in the shower. In a smaller shower, consider one of the many over-the-showerhead organizers. In a larger stall, a spring-loaded floor-to-ceiling unit with multitiered shelves works well.

Jump Starts

Can't seem to find any more space in the bathroom? Try hanging a shoe bag on the back of the bathroom door. This is a great caddy for small things you need at your fingertips. Make sure the compartments are clear, so you can see without rummaging around, and group like things together in one compartment.

◆ Divider trays in drawers keep smaller items under control. To clean the drawers, you just take the trays out and wash them.

◆ One way to organize drawer contents is by assigning each drawer or drawer section to a particular part of the body. How about one drawer for hairbrushes, combs, and accessories, one just for the man of the house's shaving paraphernalia, and another just for special pampering accoutrements—complete with bath oils, scrubs, and moisturizers.

◆ In some instances, a tackle box, art-supply caddy, or box made especially for holding cosmetics or grooming products might make the most sense. This is especially true if you're sharing a bathroom with several other people and need to look for an alternate place to get ready when the bathroom's occupied. You can take your "paint box" anywhere, even when you travel.

◆ Consider a Lazy Susan to move things easily from the back of the cabinet to the front.

◆ Group like things together in bins or baskets.

◆ Hang hair dryers, curling irons, razors, and electric toothbrushes in special caddies or racks specifically made for affixing them to the wall.

◆ An old-fashioned vanity or dressing table gets you out of a shared bathroom for certain parts of your morning routine. Make sure it's well lit, has a good mirror, and has places for all your makeup, perfume, and hair-grooming supplies.

Get a Routine

The time you spend in the morning showering, shaving (for you guys), fixing your hair, dressing, and putting on your makeup can get you ready to meet the world with your best face forward. But if it's hurried and chaotic, you'll start out with a frown. Here are some tips for avoiding "morning madness":

♦ The best way to make your morning production smooth is to standardize what you do. By creating a routine, you'll save time, you'll narrow down the products you need, and you won't be faced with making new decisions each morning. Do the same steps each day and your morning ritual will eventually become second nature. Write down the steps to start with, if you need to.

> **Pileups!**
>
> Make sure to leave enough time for your makeup routine. Applying mascara while driving is an absolute no-no. At the very least, you could soil your clean clothes. At worst, you could have an accident or blind yourself (no kidding).

♦ Being well groomed today means more for men than just having trimmed hair and clean fingernails. Many men today have all the gels, mousses, lotions, shampoos, sprays, spritzes, soaps, salves, scrubs, mists, and masks that women do. There are even makeup and hair-coloring products especially for men. Decide what your "bottom line" is and build it in to your daily routine.

♦ Maybe the shampoo bottle says "wash, rinse, and repeat," but unless your hair is especially oily or dirty, once is probably enough. It's also a good idea to change hair products periodically. It seems to prevent a buildup. There are also special products on the market that eliminate buildup caused by shampoos, conditioners, and styling products. Or try a diluted vinegar rinse.

♦ Use only a small amount of conditioner, and concentrate on hair ends, not on the scalp.

♦ Some men find sporting a beard saves time and is easier on their skin. And they like the look.

♦ Pay attention to the weather and climate conditions. Choose your hairstyle for the day accordingly. Take steps to protect yourself from sun, heat, wind, and cold. Choose daily skin-care products that contain sunscreens and moisturizers.

♦ Switch to a simpler hairstyle. For women, long or short is easiest, but a classic bob is relatively easy to care for as well. Long hair can be swept back, put up in a French twist, or made into a braid that's tucked under at the nape of the neck. These sleek hairstyles look best on women with high cheekbones and fairly delicate features. Find something that's flattering (get professional help if you need it), and practice fixing it until you have it down to a few simple steps.

Men have similar choices. If you choose to wear your hair long, it can be slicked back and pulled into a ponytail. Shorter hair is probably the easiest of all.

> **Jump Starts**
>
> One time-saver is to brush your teeth in the shower. It's easy to rinse thoroughly—just put your head under the water! Be careful, though, that your toothbrush doesn't stay damp and become a breeding ground for nasty germs. Let it dry completely between brushings.

Morning Makeup

In my opinion, less is definitely more when it comes to women and makeup. I'm not a purist, mind you, just a minimalist.

Cosmetics definitely have their place. Makeup can conceal defects such as hereditary dark circles under eyes and even birthmarks or disfiguring scars. Makeup can be used to enhance good features and minimize less-attractive ones. For some women, wearing makeup makes them feel more confident and prettier. And some products can have health benefits, such as protecting against sun and wind damage. If it has that effect for you, then I'm all for it. To my mind, however, there's no substitute for regular exercise, adequate sleep, and healthful food. Good health is the prettiest makeup of all.

When creating your makeup strategy, find a selection of products that work for you, and get rid of those that don't. Practice applying them (there are plenty of books and magazines to show you how) until you have it down to a quick set of steps. You might even consider making an appointment with a cosmetician or color consultant (something to add to your Rewards List) with the idea of finding a simple routine that makes the most of your makeup time.

What should your routine consist of? One school of thought is to pick neutral colors (your consultant can help you choose which ones are best for you) and use them for everyday. Choose from browns, taupes, grays, champagnes, beiges, gold tones, coppers, and silvers, all of which go with everything.

Then use color for dress-up, adding reds, plums, berry colors, pinks and oranges, or blues and greens to your special-occasion makeup wardrobe.

Ladies, take a tip from the stars. Their makeup artists often pick one strong feature and play it up, then minimize the rest. Do you have especially interesting eyes or pouty lips? Well, make them shine!

Consider having a color analysis done. Then you can weed out the makeup and the parts of your wardrobe that don't flatter you.

Professional makeup artists and beauty editors also offer these tips:

◆ Makeup brushes save time and apply makeup most evenly. Professionals recommend natural bristle brushes, such as sable, goat's hair, or human hair. The basics in your collection would be a blush brush, powder brush, eye shadow brush, and brow brush. Store upright in a glass, or invest in a brush roll. Wash often (every week to two weeks) with shampoo, use conditioner, and rinse thoroughly. Air dry, then store.

Resource Files

If you're looking for some extra tips on applying makeup or general grooming tips, here are some books that can help: *Making Faces* by Kevyn Aucoin; *Color Me Beautiful's Looking Your Best: Color, Make-up, and Style* by Mary Spillane and Christine Sherlock; and *Beyond Soap, Water and Comb: A Man's Guide to Good Grooming and Fitness* by Ed Marquand.

◆ Makeup sponges work best for applying liquid makeup. Wash and air dry.

◆ Get yourself a pair of good tweezers and a magnifying mirror. Store tweezers in a handy place such as the medicine chest, and always put them back. Some magnifying mirrors attach to the wall and pull out when you need them, saving counter space and time spent searching.

◆ Use a lip pencil in a nude shade (one that matches your lips) to outline and define lips, and then fill in with your favorite shade of lipstick.

◆ Have two sharpeners, one for lip pencil and one for eye pencils, to minimize the risk of bacterial cross-contamination.

◆ Cotton (not synthetic) swabs and pads are best for makeup removal. Store them in a pretty jar or clear plastic box with lid.

◆ Use a metal lash comb (professionals recommend them) to separate eyelashes. Sterilize regularly.

Don't let cosmetics or personal care salespeople load you down with more than you want or need. Find your own routine and stick to it, using the products you've determined work best for you.

If you keep what you use in a box, divided tray, or zippered bag, you won't have to hunt for what you need. Add duplicates of your major makeup products to your handbag, in smaller sizes if they're available.

Daily, Weekly, and Monthly Rituals

Standardize your regular beauty and grooming tasks as much as possible. If your habit is a morning shower and you share the bathroom with several other people, set up regular times for each person and have a caddy or shower shelf (the spring-loaded floor-to-ceiling ones work well for this purpose) for each person's daily care products.

For those longer, more involved beauty rituals such as manicures, hair coloring, hair treatments, masking, bleaching facial hair, and the like, why not make them an opportunity to pamper yourself? Make it a regular Friday night end-of-the-week treat or a midweek pick-me-up, if it's a weekly chore. A little imagination can turn it into a special occasion, when you can indulge yourself at the same time. Start with a good soak in a bubble bath, complete with relaxing music on the portable CD player and maybe a glass of wine, a mug of special tea, or a fruit juice cooler.

Key monthly tasks to a particular time of the month—say, the last day or the first day. Or get creative and schedule your magical beauty rituals for the full or new moon! You might even enjoy experimenting with the natural fragrances and health benefits of aromatherapy. On the market now are some excellent, easy-to-follow books and reasonably priced, high-quality oils, so that anyone can begin to experiment with some simple, mood-enhancing and healing scents. Make sure you know the safety indications for the oils you're using.

Give Your Handbag a Hand

I always marvel at those women who can carry a tiny purse. You know the kind—they barely hold a lipstick, $20, and a credit card. Heaven forbid you should need a tissue or a nail file!

I'm afraid I just can't pare down quite that much. But I do have a system for keeping my handbag from becoming a catchall for everything under the sun. I've used it for the last several years, and it's served me well.

I've developed what I call a "modular system" for handbag paraphernalia. Which module I use depends on where I'm going, for how long, and what I'll be doing. I choose the size of the handbag I carry according to what my needs are. The basic modules in my system are as follows:

Module 1: Makeup. This module just includes the basic neutral shades I use for my everyday makeup routine. It duplicates what I have at home on my vanity. In a tinier bag that goes inside this module I keep some bobby and hairpins, plus a couple of barrettes and a hair elastic. There's also a miniature tube of hand lotion; you could add a nail file or clippers, and some clear nail polish for pantyhose emergencies.

Module 2: Emergencies. A few simple first-aid or medical supplies (including aspirin, eye drops, a small tube of sunscreen, some lip balm, a small tube of antiseptic ointment, Band-Aids, and a couple of antacid tablets) are in this module, plus a small sewing kit.

> **Jump Starts**
>
> The basic modules are small, zippered cosmetic bags. Make your "module" cases clear or each a different color or pattern, so it will be easy to identify each one and its contents.

Module 3: Mini-office. Here I group a couple of pens, a marker, some Post-It notes, a few 3 × 5 cards, stamps, and a small roll of tape—anything I might need on a business call or if I expect to be waiting and might be catching up on my reading or correspondence. This is basically a companion to any clipped articles I might take with me to read, a book, or something I'm working on. By the way, I always carry some business cards in a holder in the small zippered pocket of my handbag, not in this module. You never know when you might meet a potential customer, client, or interview subject!

Module 4: The bank. This one has my cash, credit and membership cards, checkbook, and a credit card–size calculator. It's roomy enough to hold bank deposits as well.

By using these modules, I never have loose stuff floating around in my pocketbook. Most of the time I just have the bank in my handbag, because I'm probably running to the grocery store or dropping off a shipment at the post office. If I'm going out for a business meeting, I add the makeup module, the one for emergencies, and the mini-office. An evening out might mean just grabbing Module 1 and stuffing a little cash in it. If I'm going for a day trip in the mountains, I definitely take Modules 2 and 4.

Your modules may be made up of different elements, but at least give the modular system a try. Don't forget to periodically go through each module and restock or weed out.

Oh, and what to do with that age-old problem of finding the keys? One solution is to get a clip-on key chain that hooks to an outer ring on your handbag. Because I don't have any other loose things in my bag (the modular cases hold everything), I find just dropping them in one compartment isn't a problem. They're easy to find among the zippered modular cases.

Beauty Is Happiness and Good Health

To risk sounding like a cliché, beauty really does come from the inside out. I find if someone's relaxed, happy, and smiling, he or she is attractive, no matter what his or her actual facial characteristics. There's no remedy for a frown, a harried look, tiredness, or bad humor.

With your life organized and your most important goals being achieved on a daily basis, I bet by now you're absolutely shining, and people are asking you what's happened! I believe happiness comes from fulfilling your dreams, and there's nothing more beautiful than confidence and success.

Wise Words

"'Tis not a lip or eye we beauty call,
But the joint force and result of it all."

—Alexander Pope

Another element of beauty that comes from the inside out is health, and there's no substitute for that, either. You know the drill. If you drink plenty of water, eat a balanced diet, and get adequate rest and regular exercise, you're going to look your best. So keep these commitments you've made to yourself, put them on your schedule, and see to it that they become habits. You look better already!

The Least You Need to Know

◆ Weeding out cosmetics and personal-care products not only makes them easier to organize, it helps ensure products are fresh and free of bacteria.

◆ You can save time and keep bathroom and handbag clutter to a minimum by establishing a basic routine that you master and follow each morning.

◆ Weekly and monthly rituals can be important times to pamper yourself and slow down.

◆ A modular system using separate zippered bags is one way to keep confusion in your handbag to a minimum. It also makes it easier to switch handbags.

◆ The beauty that's generated from good health and a happy life is dazzling. No makeup can ever match it!

Chapter **11**

The Kitchen: Systems for Getting Your Daily Bread

In This Chapter

- ◆ Setting your food goals
- ◆ Making your kitchen your nutrition partner
- ◆ Creating a well-organized kitchen
- ◆ How to cut shopping time with lists and menus
- ◆ Cooking made simple
- ◆ Organizing cookbooks and recipes

Whether you're a gourmet cook or you eat "on-the-fly" most of the time, the kitchen is one of the most time-consuming spaces in your home to keep clean and organized. Clutter and chaos in the "heart of the home" is not a good thing. Having an efficient, well-laid-out kitchen can mean the difference between enjoying preparing a nourishing meal and dreading it. Before you start moving stuff around or giving away half your appliances, you first need to take an inventory of where you are now with regard to food, and decide what matters to you about the daily rituals that surround putting healthful, pleasing meals on the table.

You Are What You Eat

Take the time right now to ask yourself some questions before you start your kitchen reorganization. What we're looking for here is gaining some insight into the role food plays in your life and helping you decide whether there are some changes you'd like to make. Your answers will also become the basis for making decisions about what to keep and what to dispose of in what is the hub of most homes as you go. You will probably want to write them down to help you stay on track.

♦ What place does food occupy in your life? Do you just "eat to live" or is food preparation a major hobby and social event?

♦ Do you eat out or order in most of the time? Do you cook at home, but use a lot of prepared foods? Or do you cook largely from "scratch" using fresh ingredients? What, exactly, did you do for supper each night last week? If you can't remember, keep track for a week and the patterns you discover may surprise you.

♦ How would you assess the quality of the food you eat? Do you eat a lot of "junk" or fast food? Do you use a lot of prepared or frozen food? Do you consider your diet "healthful" or would you say you need some improvement in that area?

♦ Do you need to lose a few pounds? Are you battling a blood pressure, blood sugar, or cholesterol problem? Do you have food allergies? What other special dietary or nutritional needs do you have, if any?

♦ Do you usually eat alone, or with family, friends, or housemates?

♦ Are you expected to cook for your family or is meal preparation a shared activity?

♦ Do other people share your kitchen? What's their schedule? How is that working for you?

♦ Do you personally eat on a regular schedule or whenever you can grab a bite? Does your family have regularly scheduled mealtimes?

♦ What are some things about your cooking and/or eating habits you'd like to change?

How, when, where, and what you eat goes a long way toward setting you up to have a good or bad day. Food can affect your mood, your energy level, your general sense of well-being, and your health over the long term. This is a book about organization, not nutrition, but this isn't a bad time to consider the fuel your body depends on to help you accomplish all those things you plan to do now that you're on the road to organizing your life.

As you probably know by now, I strongly believe that before beginning any worth-while task it's good to see it in a larger context—to know its purpose and ask whether it supports you in what you want in your life. Now may be a good time to see a nutri-tionist or your doctor and take an honest inventory of your health and the role your eating habits have in keeping you healthy or making you sick. If everything's okay, you may only need to look at your kitchen layout, work flow, and convenience. If, how-ever, you want to make some major changes in the way you eat, you need to scrutinize these things, as well as which foods you have in your pantry and even the kinds of cooking equipment you use.

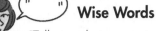

Wise Words

"Tell me what you eat and I will tell you who you are."
—Anthelme Brillat-Savarin

After examining the way you eat now and thinking about changes you'd like to make, write down two or three goals for the way you plan, shop for, prepare, eat, and clean up after your daily meals. Perhaps you'd like to begin eating at home a little more often. Maybe you'd like to get on a more sensible eating program that includes more fruits and vegetables. Are there some diet-related health problems you really need to face and take action to correct? Would you like to entertain more, but find yourself putting it off because cooking for company is such a hassle? Would you like to rein in your budget, and feel you could save money by changing your eating and cooking habits?

Whatever you decide your food goals are, write them down and keep them uppermost in your mind as you revamp your kitchen. Decide on specific actions to help you accom-plish those goals and add them to the Master List in your planner/organizer. You can confront the kitchen in an all-day session or work on it piecemeal, one small area at time. Whichever method you choose, you need to understand the design and layout of your kitchen as it is now, watch yourself work, and decide how to minimize your movement and maximize the space available to you.

Now let's take a look at your kitchen space. What works and what doesn't? Are you short on counter space? Cabinets? Where are the catchalls—places where clutter just loves to live? Are there certain things that "bug" you? Is it a one-person kitchen or can two or more people prepare a meal together? Do you find yourself making lots of steps to get a meal on the table?

Jump Starts

Not enough space in kitchen cabinets for food storage? Consider a free-standing cabi-net or piece of furniture. If you have wall space, you can install narrow wire racks designed espe-cially for canned goods and other food packages. There are even racks that fit over doors. Look for space in unconventional places!

Unstuff Your Kitchen

After analyzing your space and setting your goals, the next step is to go through your usual unstuffing routine, the one you learned how to do in Chapter 5. If you can, totally clear out the space in your kitchen you've decided to reorganize first. A good place to start is with any food you have stored in your kitchen cabinets, pantry, refrigerator, freezer, or any other food storage area using the following guidelines. Check them off as you accomplish each one.

◆ Toss out any food that has passed its expiration date. Separate foods that need to be used up shortly. These will go in the front of the cabinet or pantry shelf when you put them away.

◆ Give or throw away food that doesn't fit your nutrition objectives.

◆ If you have a lot of one item, evaluate whether you can use it up before it becomes dated. If not, pass some on to someone who can.

◆ If you tend to store a lot of canned goods, rotate by putting the oldest in the front, and when you shop again, put the newer cans in the back. Make a written inventory. Plan meals around what you already have.

◆ Clean out your refrigerator and freezer, throw out food that's bad or stale, and put remaining food back, grouping similar things together wherever possible. Freezer items not kept in original packaging should be labeled with name of food and date. Make a written inventory of what foods are in your refrigerator and freezer, so you can plan meals around them.

◆ Group your packaged and canned goods into categories: staples, baking ingredients, vegetables, fruits, meats, sauces, beverages, and so on.

◆ Store food using the same basic principles we've used for everything else: Put most-used items in *prime real estate*, least often used farther away; group like things together; consolidate and compress using different containers.

If you anticipate doing a major revamping of your cabinets and drawers, adding shelving or buying inserts and dividers, you may want to put your nonperishable foods into boxes according to category for a short while and put them back when you've got that project completed.

Now move on to the next area you want to subject to the "unstuffing" process. Use your sorting boxes: *Trash*, *Put Away* (for things that belong elsewhere in the house),

Pass On, and *Fix*. Go through cabinets, shelves, and drawers and look at dishes, pots and pans, appliances, and utensils. Ask yourself the following questions:

◆ When was the last time I used this?

◆ Do I have another tool that can do double duty in place of this one?

◆ Are there any duplicates? Which one works best?

◆ Does it need to be fixed?

If you come across kitchen tools that just don't do the job, get rid of them and replace them with ones that work well. Buy quality kitchen equipment and learn how to take care of it. A few excellent knives kept sharp are far more useful than a drawer full of the other kind, and take up less space. Learn how to use a steel and a whetstone properly so you can maintain your cutlery.

Have a few high-quality and easy-to-clean pots and pans in the most common and convenient sizes. When you buy new ones, don't keep the old. Seriously, how many frying pans do you really need if you're not running a restaurant?

The same is true with appliances. Buy quality, not quantity. Also don't overbuy. If a small chopper is all you ever need, don't buy a professional-size food processor with all the attachments.

Resource Files

There's a place you may be able to locate replacement parts for your small kitchen appliances, other than the manufacturer itself. Check with Culinary Parts Unlimited at 1-866-PART-HELP, or on the web at www.culinaryparts.com, before you toss something out for good.

Jump Starts

If you're having trouble deciding what kitchen equipment and utensils you really need, pack up everything as if you're getting ready to move except the bare essentials you need to prepare your daily meals. Locate the boxes somewhere else temporarily. As you need specialty items, go get them and find a home for them in your kitchen. Whatever is left after a month or so, you obviously don't use!

Now that you've pared down and have familiarized yourself with what you have to store, let's talk about how your kitchen is laid out and what you can do to make the most of its design.

Make Your Kitchen Do the Work

I'm not a contractor, so I'm not about to guide you through a major remodeling of your kitchen. If you have a chance to do extensive remodeling or build from scratch, and the money to boot, great. There are lots of good books on the market and plenty of experts to help you design your custom kitchen. I suggest you consult an organization expert *as well as* a contractor! However, we're going to work with what you already have, which probably has a number of design flaws, and make it the best it can be.

To plan how to use available space to its greatest advantage, a kitchen is best divided into activity areas or centers. There's a preparation center for cutting, chopping, and mixing ingredients, a cooking center that revolves around the stove, a serving center, and a cleanup center that basically involves the sink and dishwasher (if you have one). When you look at some kitchens, you can't help wondering if the designer ever tried boiling water in it, because none of these areas is clearly defined or efficiently located. So where do you generally do these activities now? Just make a note of it, and let's move on to see if you're currently using your kitchen space as efficiently as you might be.

The Preparation Center

In the preparation center, lack of counter space is the most common problem. You need adequate area to lay out your ingredients and use a variety of tools and small appliances at one time. This center includes the sink, to allow for rinsing foods and washing off utensils. Get as much off your counters as possible. Keep this area for work not display. Store appliances that aren't used every day in cabinets or on shelves, or consider the various appliance products available that mount under cabinets and out of the way. If you still don't have enough counter space, see whether you can make a fold-down one or add a kitchen island or movable cart with a butcher-block top. You want to locate items such as knives, bowls, cutting board, and food preparation appliances near this area.

> **Jump Starts**
>
> Short on storage for pots and pans? Look up! There are some beautiful racks on the market that hang from the ceiling for suspending cookware. If you have some wall space, you can hang them from a grid system or brackets instead. Check out the options in mail-order catalogs and culinary and decorating stores.

The Cooking Center

From the preparation center, you want to be able to move to the cooking area, which includes the stove and any nearby counter space. A triangular layout between preparation area, stove, and refrigerator works best. If you can rearrange your appliances so they give you that pattern of movement, try to do it. The items you use most should be located in the storage within that triangular area. If you can't arrange things in a triangle, then a rolling work cart may be the only solution. You can assemble items from the refrigerator and roll them to the work area, then take prepared ingredients to the cooking area the same way. This should save you some steps and spills along the way. Pots and pans, hot pads, spices, and other items used regularly during cooking should be located in the cooking center area.

The Serving Center

The serving center is best located near where you actually sit down to eat, and your dishes, eating utensils, and serving pieces should be located there if at all possible. I have a counter divider between my kitchen and dining area, so that's where I set things to be served. The silverware drawer and cabinets that hold the dishes are right next to it, which is also near the preparation center. Just notice how far away your dishes and serving bowls are from where you eat your meals. You may want to consolidate them and locate them closer to where you eat.

The Cleanup Center

The preparation center is usually best located next to the cleanup area. That way you can clean up as you go, while you're preparing a meal, to save work at the end. When you finish a meal, have a designated place to put dishes. To one side of the sink is usually a good location. If you're making too many trips from the eating area to the kitchen during the clearing process, that may indicate that you need to rethink how you're doing things. You may want to have a tray handy or a rolling cart for stacking dishes and taking them to the kitchen to be washed and put away. It helps if others in the household know where to put dirty dishes as well. There's no sense having them move dishes to one spot, and then you have to move them to another.

 Jump Starts

Make a list of storage problems you've identified in your kitchen. Then make a series of field trips to organizing, hardware, discount, and decorating stores. Be sure to take measurements of your cabinet spaces with you, and bring a tape measure. Take notes and check what you find against mail-order options. Find solutions to maximize your cabinet and shelf space. Look for options that make items easy to reach and easy to put away.

Keep one side of a double sink or a dishpan full of hot, soapy water ready to put dirty utensils in as you cook. This avoids clutter and makes them easier to clean later on. If you keep up with dishes, they'll be less of a problem. Unwashed dishes that have been sitting require more elbow grease, more water, and, if you're using a dishwasher, they sometimes won't even come clean without prescrubbing. If you can't get to them immediately, at least rinse them or put them in water to soak.

Marla Cilley, the Flylady (see Chapter 4), believes that a clean sink is the "magic bullet" for keeping a clean, organized house. She encourages her mail list subscribers and readers to always start here when things begin to get out of control. So clean your sink and see if it doesn't work wonders!

Advanced Kitchen Storage

Now that you've figured out where to locate the main areas of activity in your kitchen, the next thing to tackle is the storage located in each. You want to create storage solutions that save you steps and make the most of the time you spend in the kitchen. After all, we have other things to do, right?

Some cabinets have adjustable shelves. If yours do, you've got a lot more options. If not, there are still all kinds of racks, step shelves, and slide-out drawer units on the market that can make them more efficient and flexible. Check out the resources at the back of this book for products, organizing-supply and container stores, websites, and mail-order catalogs to help you plan. If your cabinets are very deep and things tend to get lost in the back, a step shelf along the back, a Lazy Susan, or a slide-out unit should help.

Don't overlook walls and ceilings or the backs of doors as possible storage components. There are grid systems for wall storage (or you might consider pegboard, which can be painted), racks that fit along the backsplash, over- and on-the-door racks, and various fixtures for hanging pots and pans from the ceiling. Just make sure you don't hang anything where you'll bonk your head! Also consider hooks under cabinets or shelves for cups or one of those racks that hold stemmed glasses upside down. There will need to be adequate space, however, to work underneath without hitting them.

Even a small space above a door between the doorjamb and ceiling might be used for cookbooks or other smaller, uniform items, just by installing a shelf.

One thing you'll probably want to have out on the counter is your collection of kitchen utensils you use all the time. Consider getting a large crock that will hold the spatulas, slotted spoons, and what have you, right there next to the stove or preparation area. You may need two—one for cooking utensils and one for mixing and preparation utensils. I find this solution is easier than having them in a drawer, but with drawer dividers and lots of drawer space, you may prefer storing them there.

When choosing decorating materials, appliances, fixtures, and equipment, think about functionality and ease of cleaning. Keep hardware such as faucets, knobs, handles, or pulls simple. The fewer nooks and crannies there are to get dirty, the better. Keep in mind that paint or wall coverings should stand up to kitchen grease and grime, and avoid fancy curtains or other decorating elements that can give you cleaning headaches. Don't forget to put up backsplashes where they're most needed—behind the stove and your work area.

Don't let your plastic food containers sit in a drawer—use them. You only need so many pieces for leftover food storage. If you bought your plastic storage containers at a Tupperware party, you may be able to replace those missing lids. Call your nearest representative (consult the phone book or their website at www.tupperware.com) and find out.

Get rid of containers you never use or have too many of in one particular size. Ditch those without lids, or use them under plants to catch water or to sort similar items in drawers if they're low enough to fit. They also make great storage for crafts and office supplies, among other things. Just get them out of the kitchen if you're not using them. Relocate and reuse them and they're no longer clutter!

If space is at a premium, keep little-used and seasonal items in the high, hard-to-reach cabinets above the stove and refrigerator or out of the kitchen altogether. You may need a step stool to reach them. Cleaning products can be kept under the sink in a portable caddy.

> **CAUTION Pileups!**
>
> Be careful what you store in the cabinet under the sink and in all low cabinets, especially if you have small children or entertain folks with little ones. Many cleaning products are highly toxic or, at least, can create a nasty spill. Get a child-proof locking device if you must store questionable items there.

Speaking of that dreaded under-the-sink area, make sure you do a thorough unstuffing job of that catchall, as well. There are probably cleaning products lurking there you haven't seen in years! Get rid of those you don't use, consolidate wherever possible (can three partly used spray window cleaner bottles be poured into one?), and keep your cleaning products and tools to a minimum.

When you're done unstuffing and relocating, make sure anyone else who uses the kitchen knows where stuff is and will be kept from now on. You might even consider making up lists in large type and taping them to the inside of cabinet doors or on drawer faces until everyone gets with the new system. At least once a year, do a thorough cleaning of your kitchen storage areas. Make sure you get rid of unused items just as you did in this first session. Reevaluate your work flow from time to time, and move things that don't seem to be in the best place.

When your kitchen is done, you will have pared down to only those things you use regularly and that work best for you, and each will have a home. You will have located everything so that you don't need to make a lot of unnecessary steps to prepare a meal. Survey your domain and smile!

Paper in the Kitchen

I said earlier that the kitchen is the heart or hub of the home. Not only do we prepare our daily meals there, but it's often the place that family and friends congregate. Especially with today's open floor plans, the kitchen is very much connected to the rest of the activity centers in the home.

Many people complain that the paper monster lives in the kitchen! Kids come home from school and drop their papers on the counter. The newspaper ends up there, too. So does the mail. Pretty soon there are piles of paper everywhere.

If you located your Life Management Center in the kitchen, you already have places for all of that. If it's located somewhere else, you may need to set up systems for handling paper that either doesn't belong there or is on it's way there.

The important thing is that all the categories of paper have a home and a system for handling them. Sort what's in the kitchen and see what categories *you* have. Maybe you'll want to set up a simple vertical mail tray labeled for each family member where their mail and telephone messages go. Have a place for the newspaper and only let a few days' worth pile up before they go into the recycling bin.

You need a place to display children's school papers and artwork as it comes in, replacing the old with the new. A magnetic strip or board might work well for this purpose, or a line with clothes pins suspended from it located along a wall. When work is taken down, give each child a chance to save what he or she wants in a box kept in a bedroom closet or on a shelf. At the end of the year, help your child purge for the next year.

Just remember that setting up systems for controlling and handling paper is just as important in the kitchen as anywhere else.

The Junk Plop Rock

Ever notice how much stuff that doesn't have anything to do with cooking ends up in the kitchen? It's all those flat surfaces just begging to be covered with clutter. The kids' backpacks, Dad's keys, packages from the store, tools, toys—you name it—somehow they find their way onto the kitchen counters.

The solution is to find all these things a home. Anticipate what's going to end up on the counters and head that plopping action off at the pass! Have a place for Dad to hang his keys when he comes in the door. Create a launching pad for kids to keep their school stuff for the next day. A cubby system, cupboard, or series of hooks (make them strong) should solve the problem.

When you see the accumulation begin, stop it in its tracks! Do a quick "put away" of these countertop hot spots before they get out of control!

Shop but Don't Drop

Now that you've pared down and unstuffed your kitchen, what's the best way to keep the necessary things on hand? Is there a way to make shopping easier?

I believe there is, and the way to do it is to standardize. Don't you find that there are a few basic meals that you and your family enjoy eating on a regular basis? Maybe it's chicken and dumplings or pot roast. Maybe you just love a particular pasta dish, soup, or stew. Or perhaps you grill regularly. I'll bet you could make a list of 15 to 20 meals you prepare over and over again, probably on a monthly basis. I call these my "rotation meals," and I keep the recipes for them all in my household binder, plus a list of them in my planner/organizer. I know them so well that I can pretty much name the ingredients from memory. What would your "rotation meals" be?

In addition to your personal list of rotation recipes, you need an ingredients list. This is a list of all the major ingredients you use in your everyday cooking, including those rotation meals, a kind of Master Shopping List. That way, if you're out running errands, you can just scan your list and see whether you've forgotten anything. Keep a running list for other items that come up in a prominent place where the whole family can add their shopping reminders. A dry-erase board is handy for this.

Another help is to plan your week's menus ahead of time. You may even want to do it for two weeks, to cut down on trips to the grocery store. You may not cook exactly what you'd planned on the day you planned it, but you'll have a pretty good idea of what you'll be doing for the next two weeks. Writing up weekly menus may seem like a chore at first, but once you get in the habit it will save you time, both in the kitchen and shopping, plus it takes the guesswork out of answering the question "What's for dinner?"

Buy in bulk when it's practical. If you're cooking for only one person, you obviously can't eat a bushel of apples before they go bad, but you could make applesauce for yourself and can or freeze it. But will you? Know what you're really capable of using and don't overbuy. Also be sure you have storage space for it. Buying in bulk cuts down on the time you spend shopping and can save you money, but it's no bargain if you can't find what you bought or it goes bad before you get to use it. In the next section, you learn about a cooking method that makes the most of bulk shopping and saves time and work.

Jump Starts

I suggest you do your menu planning with your calendar at your side, so you can figure on easy dishes for busy evenings and skip planning meals altogether for evenings you'll be out.

Items it truly make sense to buy in bulk are paper goods, cleaning products, nonperishable staples such as vinegar and baking soda, personal-care products, canned and bottled foods, and some dry foods, such as legumes and pastas, that keep well. You can store up to a six-month's supply in a fairly compact area, and you'll save time, effort, and money. Make an inventory and post it near your bulk storage area. Cross off items as you use them up and add them to your shopping list.

Crafty Cooking Strategies

Too busy to create yummy home-cooked meals? Nonsense! I'm going to give you three strategies that'll make it easy to put tasty, nutritional homemade meals on the table with the least amount of effort. They'll each save you money, too! Pick the one that's best for you and give it a try.

Cook Once, Eat for a Month

A couple of years ago, I made a fabulous discovery. It wasn't a totally new idea to me, because I had done a scaled-down version when I was a single parent, working full time and going to school, but I had never seen it systematized and explained quite the same way before. The method goes by many names—once-a-month cooking, freezer cooking, bulk cooking, frozen assets, investment cooking—but they all use the same strategy of bulk buying, marathon cooking, and freezing ahead. If you're serious about using this method, it helps to have a separate chest or upright freezer, but it's possible to do a scaled-down version with just the freezer compartment of an average-size refrigerator.

The basic idea is that you plan your menus for a month, do all the shopping in one day, then do all the cooking in another day or two, and forget about it for 30 days. I especially find this method helpful when I'm heavily embroiled in a book project and don't want to be burdened with thinking about "What's for supper?" It's also great when I have visitors. My mental and physical energy can go toward other things, because I took the time to think out our eating plan ahead of time, and all the work is done.

CAUTION

Pileups!

Why clean your kitchen every day? With bulk cooking, you only make a major kitchen mess once a month. One good scrubbing after your monthly marathon session and it stays clean until the next time, except for daily touch-ups and dishes.

Some of the benefits of bulk cooking are …

- Major shopping is only necessary once a month. You cut down on trips to the supermarket and the extra hidden cost of impulse buys and children asking "Why can't I have this, Mommy?" The fewer number of trips, the less you spend.

- You can take advantage of restaurant-size cans and quantity buys on fresh fruits and vegetables from wholesale clubs or food cooperatives. This saves lots of money and often means higher quality.

- Bulk cooking is environmentally friendly, because bulk buying usually means less packaging.

- Because you're cooking ahead and freezing, you can make the most of seasonal foods and buy ingredients when they're the freshest and least expensive.

- Meals are all planned and prepared, so you don't have to think about it. You can concentrate on other things!

- Because you're cooking several meals all at once, there's less waste. After cooking whole chickens for several meals, for example, the remaining carcasses and defatted drippings become the base for a soup or sauce. Trimmings from fresh vegetables can be used to make vegetable stock. More dollar savings!

Resource Files

In Appendix A, I list several good books explaining various versions of the bulk cooking method. One that gives you a total plan you can adapt to your own nutrition goals is *Once-a-Month Cooking* by Mimi Wilson and Mary Beth Lagerborg. Check out the OAMC website, too, at members.aol.com/oamcloop.

- Because the main meal is already prepared, you can concentrate on tasty and nutritious side dishes, like fresh salads or vegetable dishes, if you have the time and energy. You can also whip up a special treat for dessert.

- With dinner in the freezer, you're less likely to order pizza or stop for fast food. So you not only save money when you go to the grocery store, you also save money throughout the month.

- You save energy, because you're using appliances for large batches rather than many small batches. In warmer weather, you heat up the house less, especially if you use your slow cooker to thaw and heat up your dish earlier in the day.

- You'll actually *use* appliances such as food processors, mixers, grinders, slicers, blenders, and slow cookers on a monthly basis, and it will be worth your while to pull them out of cabinets and off shelves, *and* clean them!

- You can get the whole family involved in the various tasks associated with bulk cooking, such as chopping and slicing.

- Dinner is always in the freezer when you're caught with unexpected guests or a neighbor is ill and could use a home-cooked meal. In fact, you might actually find yourself asking more often, "Why don't you stay for dinner?"

- Having your meals planned and prepared means you're less likely to "throw something together" and eat foods you're trying to avoid.

- With the main meal taken care of, you actually have time to get creative about the side dishes, concentrating on making healthful salads and fresh vegetables or making a special dessert.

The only disadvantage I've found to this method is that we sometimes get tired of frozen foods, even if they are yummy and homemade from scratch, so we just extend our freezer stash with grilling and "quick-cook" meals from fresh bought ingredients. You learn more about this method in a moment.

It might be easiest for you to get a picture of how bulk cooking works if I describe a typical month's cooking. You can adapt my method to your own circumstances. At the beginning of the month, I go through my recipes (we have several favorites I make every month, then others we use less often) and plan the meals for the month. Then I write up a list of all the ingredients I need to purchase, grouping like things together. So if a recipe calls for two bell peppers, sliced, and another recipe calls for one pepper, chopped, I know I need three peppers total.

I spend almost an entire day shopping. You can break this up if you want. I just like to get it done all at once. First I go to the wholesale club, then my regular supermarket, and last I might have certain things to buy at the health-food market. That same night, before I go to bed, I put two whole chickens in the slow cooker to cook overnight. The meat from these will go into chicken casseroles, Mexican dishes, chicken soup, and chicken salad. I use the bones to make stock the next morning. I also fill a second slow cooker with a double recipe of one of our favorite dishes, or I use it to cook ahead some beans or grains. In the morning, I clean out the cookers and start another double recipe in each one. This creates four meals, and I still have several meals from the night before. I haven't even begun my main cooking day!

The rest of the second day is reserved for cooking. I make sure to take several breaks and to eat lunch. I group processes together (for example, chopping all the onions for all the month's recipes in the food processor). I then package each meal in a freezer container or plastic freezer bag, label it with contents and date, and add it to my meal inventory list, which I post on the refrigerator. I make sure that anything I need to complete the dish when I'm going to serve it to the family is attached to the dish in the freezer (such as a topping or cheese). If it can't be placed along with the dish in the freezer it resides in, I put it in the pantry with a big "X" on the can so no one uses it for anything else.

If I need to, I cook another large-batch recipe in the slow cookers overnight and package those meals the next morning. After I have finished with everything, I wipe down all my appliances, put them away, clean the kitchen thoroughly, and the rest of the month I thaw and reheat, keeping kitchen mess to a minimum. Many times, a month's worth of meals lasts considerably longer. Meals unexpectedly eaten out or quick meals made from fresh ingredients that become available during the month stretch my cooking "investment" still further.

You don't have to cook for an entire month, if that sounds too daunting. Try a week or two to start. Or you can just begin by doubling or tripling every recipe that lends itself to freezing, and start building up your freezer stash on the installment plan, a little at a time. Working folks can plan their bulk cooking sessions around a weekend or break up the tasks over a longer period. You also don't have to do this method using slow cookers. Some people do it all using top-of-the-stove and oven methods for cooking. I just find that having at least one slow cooker makes the job easier.

Quick Cooking, Easy Cleanup

Another way to get control of meal preparation is to learn quick-cooking methods. Quick-cooked meals involve a minimum of ingredients that can be easily assembled, are often cooked in one pan or dish, and usually take less than 20 minutes from start to finish. There are several quick-cook cookbooks out that should give you plenty of ideas. I've listed some in Appendix A for you.

Supper on the table in 20 minutes? Impossible, you say? Not at all! Especially if you have some of the ingredients prepared and waiting on hand in the refrigerator. Here's another use for that slow cooker you've got on a shelf in the garage! Put a batch of a whole grain such as brown rice in the pot, add the appropriate amount of water, and let it slow cook while you do other things. Use part of the batch for supper and save the rest for another meal or two during the week. It can be frozen, too. One dish might be a sauté, another a casserole, yet a third a cold vegetable and grain salad. Having some precooked grains makes quick cooking even easier.

Put some carrots, onion, summer squash, and zucchini through the food processor using the shredding disk and store the mixture in a plastic bag in the fridge. Then when you get home from work, you can toss some of your "vegetable medley" in a wok with a little oil, slice up some chicken breast or throw in a few shrimps or scallops, add some cooked noodles or brown rice, season, and you'll be sitting down to eat in seconds, not minutes. For a meatless meal, leave out the chicken breast or fish and substitute some tofu. If you don't feel like cooking, just toss the vegetable ingredients with some salad dressing and some canned chicken, tuna, or shrimp and eat it cold.

You can probably come up with lots more easy combinations such as this on your own. Scan cookbooks and magazines for ideas to add to your collection. You don't even have to follow the exact recipes—just gather combinations of simple ingredients for a quick, healthful meal. Add these to your "rotation meals" file or binder.

Apply a similar strategy to breakfast and lunch. Use leftover rice, some raisins or other dried fruit, a splash of milk, a little cinnamon, and honey, and you've got a nutritious and *fast* breakfast. Toss leftover noodles with a bit of soy sauce, some toasted sesame seeds, and green onions for a quick, healthful, and inexpensive lunch. Add an orange or apple on the side, or a handful of dried fruits and nuts, and you're all set. Simple food takes less time, costs less, and is almost always better for you.

For this cooking method, you want to have in your pantry certain easy-to-add ingredients that require little preparation. Stock up on items such as chopped canned tomatoes and cans of mushrooms, soups and broths, corn, bamboo shoots, water chestnuts, beans, and chili peppers. It would be handy to have items such as salsa, corn or flour tortillas, prebaked pizza shells, and quick-cooking frozen vegetables that can be added direct from the freezer, such as peas, chopped broccoli, or spinach on hand.

The advantages of the quick-cooking method include the following:

◆ You are cooking with the freshest ingredients on a regular basis.

◆ You have ultra-fast preparation time.

◆ Food storage space required is at a minimum. If you have a very small refrigerator/freezer and very little pantry space, this is a great option.

Jump Starts

If refrigerator and freezer space is at a premium, the quick-cooking method works especially well. Plan out your week's menus, chop or precook as many components as possible, and shop two or three times a week for fresh ingredients as needed. Just be sure to stick to your list and avoid those impulse buys.

The main disadvantages are that this method requires more frequent trips to the grocery store for fresh ingredients and it doesn't take advantage of the cost savings of bulk buying.

Resource Files

There are lots of Crock-Pot cookery books around. One of the best comes with your appliance, or I recommend the *Fix-It and Forget-It Cookbook: Feasting with Your Slow Cooker* by Dawn Ranck and Phyllis Good. The authors also have versions for entertaining, light cooking, and cooking for diabetics. If you don't want to add to your cookbook collection, there are several excellent sites on the Internet for slow-cooker recipes. Try www.crockerykitchen.com and www.ebicom.net/kitchen/page/cpidx.htm. Type "crock pot" or "slow cooker" into your favorite search engine and you'll find lots more!

Slow Cooking: Ready-and-Waiting Meals

Another great way to cut down on cooking time and preparation is to make skillful use of your slow cooker. I own three and I use them all the time. As I already mentioned, a slow cooker can be a very helpful tool if you're following the bulk cooking strategy, but you can use it to simplify meals day-to-day, even if you don't choose this method.

Wouldn't it be great if the moment you came home, the splendid smell of a complete, nutritious, home-cooked meal wafted from your kitchen—without your ever having to light the stove? How do sweet-and-sour beef, chicken Polynesian, or three-bean chili sound to you? Again, planning is the key, but in this case you're planning your meals around your kitchen powerhouse, the slow cooker.

Use your Crock-Pot for entertaining, making delicious gifts such as chutneys, jams, and jellies, and for concocting scrumptious desserts. You can even bake in your Crock-Pot with the right accessories and instructions from the recipe book that probably came with your appliance. Make it your business to learn how to use this marvelously versatile piece of kitchen equipment, and if you don't have one, you might want to whisper in someone's ear!

When I was working outside the home, I used my slow cooker to make our weeknight meals, and then cooked more elaborate meals on the weekends. The advantages of using the slow cooker include the following:

- A hot meal is ready and waiting for you when you get home.

- The slow cooking method makes the best of less-expensive cuts of meat.

- The slow cooking method keeps all the juices and nutrients in.

- Cleanup is minimal.

- Slow cookers take very little energy to run and they don't give off a lot of heat, which is a real plus in the summertime.

As with frozen meals, sometimes you want a break from slow-cooked ones. Just plan on having some variety and this method will hold you in good stead.

Constantly be on the lookout for systems, strategies, and methods that save time, use your resources to their best advantage, and support you in your nutrition and health goals. You won't regret it, because mastering this important part of everyday life will reward you in more ways than you might imagine. Experiment with these strategies and perhaps rotate or combine them. Do whatever works for you!

When you find yourself cooking for parties, holidays, or other special events, you'll find that having an organization plan will take away a lot of stress, plus your new cooking strategies will help you. There are some great stuffing recipes for the slow cooker, by the way. Organization and planning will stand by you every time!

Freezer Science and "Refrigology"

Your refrigerator and freezer are like any other cabinet or closet. Treat the shelves, drawers, and various compartments as ways of grouping like things together. You can add additional storage tools to make finding things even easier. Covered plastic containers, open plastic baskets, and resealable plastic bags all help organize your refrigerator and freezer. Use a Lazy Susan to help reach small bottles and jars like jellies and condiments. If storage items are going in the freezer, make sure they're "freezer-safe" and won't break, crack, or shatter in the extreme cold.

Group like things together on the same fridge shelf. Keep all leftovers in the same place, for example. Use the refrigerator door for storing the things you use most often. That way, you won't be digging in the back all the time, and you'll save time and effort.

Take advantage of individual cooling zones in your refrigerator so that, for instance, meat and vegetables are kept at their ideal temperatures, and butter can be kept soft enough to spread.

Group similar things together in the freezer, as well. Use baskets or boxes, if necessary, to keep them tidy. Put all frozen vegetables in one box, juices in another, and frozen meals in a third. This is absolutely crucial if your freezer is a chest type, where foods will be layered from the bottom up. Having boxes or bins that can be lifted out with the contents intact makes it much easier to get to the food at the bottom without upsetting everything.

Pileups! _____

A full refrigerator or freezer doesn't work as hard to keep cool, but you don't want to stuff it so much that you can't see what's in there or have to play "catch" every time you open the door.

Food Storage for Emergencies

There's a saying that goes something like this: "There are no emergencies for someone who's prepared." The Boy Scouts teach it, and experience bears it out. Whether it's a natural or man-made disaster or something personal, such as a financial setback, illness, or finding yourself unemployed, having a store of food and water, and planning for self-sufficiency in an emergency, gives you peace of mind and can actually save your life!

If you're without power, the Red Cross recommends you first eat up the food in the refrigerator, then the freezer, and finally turn to food in your long-term storage.

You'll want a small camp stove or gas-fueled burner to heat things up, but make sure to exercise caution about operating these with proper ventilation. If you have a wood stove, this might be an option in a cold weather emergency.

No long-term food storage? Well, perhaps you should consider building some. Having three to six months of food and water for your family buys an incredible amount of peace of mind and security. It's a lesson our ancestors knew well. They canned and dried food, dug a root cellar to over-winter vegetables, stored grains, and always had a "rain barrel." In our fast-food society, we've all but forgotten what it means to "put food by," but with recent hurricanes, tornadoes, floods, and even terrorist threats, people are rediscovering its wisdom.

You want to set up and locate your system based on the particular circumstances that relate to your region. Are you in a tornado region? A flood plain? An earthquake area? Are there alternative sources of water, or is water a problem where you live?

Resource Files

If you want to learn how to create an effective emergency food-storage system, a good place to start is *Making the Best of Basics: Family Preparedness Handbook* by James Talmage Stevens.

You don't need a lot of expensive provisions, but can handle just about any crisis with forethought, planning, skills, and knowledge. Just remember to "store what you eat and eat what you store," rotating your provisions regularly. A fun family project is to throw the breaker for a whole day and night or two and see how well you're able to cope with the lack of electricity. No fair hopping in the car and going to the local fast-food restaurant!

Handy Recipe Rationale

Recipes come from a variety of sources: cookbooks, magazines, newspapers, television shows, friends—maybe even from your computer online service. Of all the recipes that come into your hands, how many do you think you'll ever actually try? This is another time to do some soul-searching and examine your true ambitions as a cook. I'll bet right now you could eliminate two thirds of your recipe collection, if not more. And, hey, if you really need another cheesecake recipe in the future, I'm sure you can find one in the library, in a magazine, or on the Internet!

I already mentioned rotation recipes. These are the tried-and-true dishes that everybody in your family loves. If you have recipes you use regularly, and especially if you're trying one of the cooking methods described in this chapter, you want easy access to them. There are several ways to store your recipes to make them easy to find and less bulky.

Recipe Binder

One way to keep track of recipes is to use binders with plastic sheet protectors, "magnetic" sheets (used for holding photos), or just paper for pasting onto, as in a scrapbook. You may want to have several smaller binders, with each covering a particular food category, such as one for meats, poultry, and fish, another for desserts, a third for appetizers, and so on. Using sheet protectors or magnetic albums allows you to rearrange or take out recipes, which is an advantage over a more permanent scrapbook. If you're saving tried-and-true recipes in a scrapbook, however, this might be less of a problem. I personally have two recipe binders. One is strictly for holiday and special-occasion dishes. The other is part of my Family User Manual and contains my "rotation meal" recipes. Find a system that makes the most sense to you for the way you cook and entertain.

Recipe Box

This is the old-fashioned method for keeping frequently used recipes, and it works as well as ever. A new twist might be to laminate the recipe cards so they hold up better and can just be wiped clean. If you find the recipe in a magazine, just cut it out, paste it on a file card, and laminate it. If it's from a cookbook, photocopy it, cut it down to size, paste, and laminate. Simple and efficient, and it doesn't take a lot of time to keep up.

Recipe File

A filing folder system is another way to keep track. But remember to purge it regularly, as you should any file drawer, and only save those recipes you honestly think you'll use. Depending on how much you cook and like to experiment, you may set aside part of the household filing cabinet for this purpose.

Recipe Database

Proponents of the computer school of recipe-keeping have a point. Why struggle with cumbersome cookbooks, cards that get dirty, binders, or file boxes when you can put everything on the computer? The powerful cookbook software available today comes with several digital cookbooks that even allow you to add your own recipes. You can create menus and shopping lists and keep track of cholesterol, fat, and calories. Best of all, they're searchable, so you can find that recipe in a flash. If you want a fresh copy, just print it out. If you have a laptop computer, you can just bring it along to the kitchen. Just keep it away from the sink and the stove!

Typing in recipes can be time-consuming, which is a disadvantage. However, with so many mail lists and websites on the Internet, where recipes are exchanged in common recipe software formats, there are a great many more options.

Organizing Your Cookbooks

Most people have many more cookbooks than they ever use. It's honesty time! Unstuff your cookbooks! Gather all your cookbooks together and quiz yourself about when you referred to each one last. If it's been more than a year, you can probably live without it.

Keep the ones you use the most; if you have some cookbooks you refer to regularly, but only for a couple of recipes, why not copy the recipes and ditch the cookbook? You can also get so many recipes online now, that if you're looking for something new to fix, you'll never be at a loss. Consider paring down your cookbooks to only a few and you'll gain some breathing room and shelf space.

Now arrange your cookbooks in a way that makes the most sense to you. It can be alphabetically by author or by type of cooking or by title. Just be sure it will make it easy to find what you want, when you want it.

When culling recipes from cookbooks, magazines, or your recipe files, apply the "quality not quantity" principle. Why have 60 recipes for brownies when you always go the Aunt Fanny's recipe because it's the best? Maybe there are a couple of brownie variations you want to try, but save Aunt Fanny's recipe and let most of the others go.

The Least You Need to Know

◆ A good time to look at your eating habits and see whether you need to make any changes is when you decide to reorganize your kitchen.

◆ The first step toward putting your kitchen on the right track is paring down food, utensils, dishes, appliances, and equipment.

◆ Simplify shopping and meal planning using a Master Shopping List and rotation recipes.

◆ Cooking ahead and freezing saves time shopping and cleaning, and is a boon when entertaining. Other time-saving methods are quick cooking and slow cooking.

◆ Purge your recipe files and cookbook shelf of recipes you will never use. Organize what you have left onto index cards, into binders or file folders, or in your computer.

The Bedroom: Making a Haven for Your Spirit and a Home for Your Clothes

In This Chapter

- Applying your unstuffing skills to make your bedroom a relaxing retreat
- How to determine your clothing style and design your wardrobe
- Smart shopping tips
- Unstuffing your closet and making it work for you
- Clothing care and laundry tips to keep your clothes looking great

Although this chapter is about the bedroom, in most homes we're actually talking about organizing more than one. There's usually a master bedroom, an adult space, then perhaps a guest bedroom, and as many other bedrooms as there are occupants needing a place to sleep. In this chapter, we focus mainly on the master bedroom, but the principles can be applied to any bedroom in the house. We also tackle that "other little room," the closet.

Bedroom Savvy for Masters

Let's start with the master bedroom. Walk into yours and tell me how you feel. Is it truly an adult space? If you have children, do they respect this space or is it filled with their things? Do they feel they can come in anytime or do you have rules about privacy? Does it feel serene and inviting? Is it comfortable? Is it peaceful? Does it invite sleep? If you were ill, is this a place you would want to go to heal? When you need to renew your spirit, is this a haven where you can spend some private time and relax? Is it quiet?

Envisionings

Close your eyes; take a long, deep breath; and imagine your ideal bedroom. What color or colors would it be? What would the furnishings look like? What kind of sheets and other bedding would dress the bed? Would there be lots of pillows or only a few? Would it have a reading nook with a comfortable chair and a good reading lamp? How about the lighting overall—what would you like that to be? What personal things would be there to look at? What mood would your ideal bedroom evoke? Add as much detail to this picture as you can. How do you feel when you open the door to this imaginary room?

Try not to censor yourself. Don't think right now about cost, just about what you'd ideally like to create in this special room. Start collecting pictures from magazines and catalogs that remind you of the room you've created in your mind's eye.

What is a bedroom? Stripped down to basics, it's a place to sleep and dress. But when you consider that you spend at least one third of your life in this room and it's the place of intimacy and dreams in your life, it's so much more.

For many people the bedroom is also a place they go for entertainment. They may watch TV there or read. Maybe they knit or sew in their bedroom or even do bills or other kinds of household paperwork.

Personally, I like to limit a bedroom to sleeping, dressing, and intimacy, with a corner for quiet relaxation, if at all possible. I strongly recommend against having a TV in the bedroom, but in some households this is the only place where busy parents can get away to watch their own programs and relax.

If you must have a TV in your bedroom, try to house it behind closed doors when it's not in use. There are many beautiful armoires and entertainment centers with doors that work well for this purpose, or you can build a unit to hide the "one-eyed monster."

I also recommend that you not have a phone in the bedroom. In our busy world, there should be someplace we can go and escape the ringing and clatter of everyday life. The bedroom seems to me to be the perfect place if we set limits and create that space.

So what are the functions for the bedroom space you're trying to organize? This is the first thing you have to decide. If it's a room that has to do double duty, you have to include all the tasks going on there in your organization plan.

If you currently do work in your bedroom, is there anyplace else you can set up to do bills or computer work? If not, you need to create a separate zone for "the office" and make sure it stays contained and organized and doesn't spill over into the rest of the room. After you organize the room as a whole, give some serious thought to creating a separate area for these other tasks that doesn't intrude on the most important purpose of the room—rest, relaxation, and romance.

But before we can create your perfect bedroom, we have to get out the clutter and take back the space.

Back to Basics, Bedroom Style

Remember the "unstuffing" method you learned in Chapter 5? Well, here we go again! This is the skill you'll be using over and over to organize every area of your life. The more you practice, the easier it gets.

First, let's do a quick sort. I suggest you start with the areas you can see from the bed and the fastest route to the bathroom. If the floor is strewn with stuff, start there and work up. You should be able to move around your bedroom without tripping over stuff, even in the dark!

Get the timer from the kitchen and grab your sorting boxes. Challenge yourself to work fast and make decisions immediately. Ask yourself the questions from Chapter 5. Keep in mind the vision you have for this room. You're going to decide what to *Toss*, what to *Pass On* (to charity or someone else you know who can use it), what to *Put Away* (in another room), and what to *Fix*. What's left is what you *Keep*. Anything you're not sure of goes in the *Keep* pile (for now).

Ready, set the timer to 30 minutes, and go!

Now get rid of what you can from the first sort. Empty the trash box or bin, take the stuff that needs to be put away to the appropriate places, and then bag or box up the stuff you've earmarked for charity and put it in the car. How does that feel? Better, I'll bet.

If you feel you can keep going, give it a try. If you can devote a day or a half a day to this project, all the better. If having a buddy by your side will help, then arrange it.

The rewards of an uncluttered, organized, inviting bedroom are worth whatever you have to do to make it happen.

We're going to treat the closet as a separate room, so for now just determine what you're going to keep that belongs in there and we'll handle it later.

After you've gone through stints of quick sorting what's on the floor, in the night-stands, on shelves, and in dresser drawers, what you have left is your initial Keep pile. As you do a deeper sort of that pile, separate what you're finally going to keep into two piles—one for items that need to find a home in the bedroom on shelves or in drawers, and one for items that normally belong in the closet. As you do a more detailed sort, put like things together. If you need additional containers to do this, then find some bags, boxes, or baskets that will help. Make sure that what's going back in the closet is sorted together by like things as well (shoes, shirts, hats, etc.).

Adding Furniture

Now put away what you've decided to keep, making sure that everything has a defi-nite home. If you need to add a piece of furniture, make a plan for that. Look for solutions that are both attractive and functional. A nightstand with at least one drawer will help contain bedside items you use often. Or you might consider one of those "sidekick" organizers, which are made of fabric and fit between your box spring and mattress. There are pockets for your glasses, some tissues, a magazine or paperback, and a few other odds and ends so everything is right by your side when you're in bed.

Perhaps a small shelf for pictures needs to be added. There are several kinds of under-the-bed storage containers, including ones that are on wheels to make them easy to move. I like to keep the space under my bed open and airy, but if you need space to store things that would otherwise clutter the room, then go for it.

Organize your dresser drawers as you would containers, putting like things together. If you need to further subdivide drawers, look for dividers or containers to fit. There are some great diamond-shaped drawer organizers for individual pairs of socks, for instance, that you can just cut to size.

There are also headboards that provide storage space. But if you pare down your clut-ter and choose your other furniture wisely, you may not need one of these, because they tend to be somewhat large and bulky and can give a heavy feeling to the room. Do whatever you can to maintain a light and airy look and feel in your bedroom for a relaxing atmosphere.

If you read in bed, have a basket nearby for magazines or a book, but don't let any more paper build up than what the basket can hold. Use the size of the container to contain the clutter and set limits for what you allow in the room and your life.

If your bathroom is small, you might want to consider adding a dressing table or vanity to your bedroom, if you have room for it. Just make sure that it has adequate storage space for things such as cosmetics and hair-care items so they're not spilling out onto other surfaces.

If you need drawer dividers, baskets, or anything else to contain your final items, put what you need on a list and make sure you get them right away. Remember, what you have left should be things you use and things you love. This is not a storage locker—it's your *bedroom!*

Behind Closed Doors

The single greatest source of clutter in a bedroom is usually our clothes. Somehow they end up on the bed, on the floor, over a chair—everywhere but in the closet. But why? Are we just lazy? Well, I can't speak for you (ahem), but more often it's the "domino effect." The closet is so stuffed full of clothes it takes too much effort to hang them up! Many of the clothes taking up that valuable *prime real estate* are hardly (if ever) worn because they're outdated, they don't fit, you don't like them, or they need repairs. For one reason or another, these clothes just don't make you feel good when you put them on, but still, there they hang.

Imagine getting dressed on any given morning when you can walk into your closet and everything in it is ready to wear. Everything fits, it's clean, it's in season, and when you put it on you look and feel your best. Not quite the current picture at your house? There's no reason why it can't be, if you commit now to making some decisions about what kind of clothes really work for you, to doing some serious weeding of your wardrobe, and possibly to investing in some new hardware or storage units for your closet. Add to that an easy plan for doing laundry and keeping up with mending and ironing, and voilà! You're ready for anything.

What's Your Style?

Before you can unstuff your closets and dresser drawers, you have to have some sort of criteria by which to judge what to toss and what to keep. Think of the people you know who always seem poised and well dressed. They don't necessarily look like they just walked out of the board room or the pages of *Vogue* or *GQ* magazines—maybe their look is quite casual—but their clothes suit their personality and their activities. They're well groomed and their clothes look that way, too. They seem comfortable and natural in whatever they're wearing. They have a personal style.

In addition to understanding your own personal style and how you like to dress, you also need to consider the activities you engage in. If you're a jeans and T-shirt type, but your job demands a three-piece suit, you're obviously going to have to make some compromises.

Your off-hours wardrobe might be more of an expression of your real clothing personality, and maybe you can add touches to your otherwise staid work outfits that hint at the other side of your life.

Envisionings

If you had unlimited funds and could start from scratch, what would your wardrobe look like? Think about the colors you like. Textures. Cut. Fabrics. If you were to pick one word to label your ideal dressing style, what would it be? Classy? Casual? Sporty? Ethnic? Romantic? Dramatic? Nonconformist? Keep the picture you just made in your mind (or better, jot it down on paper) and refer to it as you begin to design a wardrobe and organize your closet. When you see pictures in magazines that fit your style, tear them out and keep them with your wardrobe design ideas.

Take out your organization notebook, planner/organizer, or just a sheet of paper, and make a list of the activities you engage in during a typical week. You'll probably have things on your list such as "work," "play tennis," "jog," "garden," "houseclean," "work outdoors," "hike," "date," "go out to dinner"—whatever. Add to this any special occasions or seasonal activities you might expect to come up in a given year. These might include a formal dinner/dance, holiday parties, skiing, or swimming—anything that isn't part of your regular routine.

Now go into your closet and group your wardrobe into four categories: *Work*, *Play*, *Dress Up*, and *Specialty*. Don't forget the piles of clothes on the floor from our purge and sort of the rest of the bedroom. The first three categories are self-explanatory. The last category would include seasonal items (the sweater with the big Santa Claus design, for instance), Halloween costumes, formal wear, and clothing that's especially for a particular sport or other activity, such as a ski jacket or hiking boots.

Unlike some of the other organization projects you've done so far, I don't recommend you break this one up into small sessions. Allow at least two or three hours for your clothing/closet blitz with a couple of smaller follow-up sessions to accomplish some of the actual redesign projects you choose to implement. Tackling this task all at once will give you a good overall picture of your wardrobe, and investing this time now to get your closet in shape will have a huge impact on your everyday life.

Clothes, Clothes Everywhere and Not a Thing to Wear!

The next process is repeated for each part of your wardrobe. You're going to "unstuff" your closet and later your dresser drawers or anywhere else you keep your clothes. After this process, everything you have in your closet will be clean and ready to wear, and will make you feel good when you put it on. You'll also be weeding out what no longer fits your "personal style."

Ask these questions as you look at each item:

◆ Does this fit you *now?* If you plan to lose 30 pounds and are actually on a weight-loss program, you may want to put aside one favorite outfit that doesn't fit you now, but will when you're done dieting. However, don't fall into the trap of having different wardrobes for different weights. Keeping "fat" clothes gives you permission to get fat again. Keeping "thin" clothes mocks your efforts and erodes your confidence.

> **Jump Starts**
>
> Think of ways to express yourself without compromising your career objectives. One woman who likes lacy, romantic, vintage-style clothes, but needs to dress in a more conservative, corporate style at work, wears a variety of antique lace handkerchiefs tucked in her jacket pocket, secured with a vintage pin to express her inner style.

◆ Does this go with anything else? Is it an odd color or style?

◆ How long has it been since you wore this? Why?

◆ Is this too complicated to wear? Is it too fragile (silk, sequins, fur) or does it require too much special care?

◆ Does this need to be ironed? Mended? Washed? Dry-cleaned?

◆ Is this in season *now?*

◆ Does this flatter you? You may want to get a buddy to work with you on this. Sometimes we think certain things look good on us, when they simply don't. Pick a friend who'll tell you the truth, and be open to what your buddy says.

◆ Is this comfortable? Does it pinch, ride up, or bind?

◆ Is this a duplicate? How many other items like this do you have? Of the similar items you have, which do you like best or wear most often?

◆ Does this sock have a mate? Do these hose have a run? Underwear stretched out? Stains? Tears? You know what to do with them!

◆ Do you have clothes hanging in the closet that still have dry-cleaning plastic over them? If you're protecting them from dust, you're probably not wearing them often enough to keep them!

As you go through your closet, take out the things that don't fit or flatter you and put them in one pile. If you have four black blazers, decide whether you really need them all and put the least attractive or lower-quality ones in this pile, as well. This is the Pass On pile.

If an item needs to be mended or ironed put it in a Fix pile. Decide first whether it's really worth the effort. One reason you may not have gotten around to it could be you didn't really miss it. If that's the case, put it in the Pass On pile. Set aside things that need to go to the dry cleaners.

> **Pileups!**
>
> Be careful of the "If-I-keep-it-long-enough-it'll-come-back-in-style" trap. Even if it does (sort of), the trend won't be quite the same or it won't really fit by then. Get rid of it! Besides, if your wardrobe is full of classic, high-quality pieces, you'll always be "in style."

If you're not sure about a piece of clothing, put that in a separate pile. This may include items there's nothing wrong with—you like them, they fit you well, are of good quality, and don't need fixing—but for whatever reason you just haven't worn them in a long time. Ask yourself whether the reason you don't wear a particular item is that you don't have anything that goes with it. If that's the case, you may want to set it aside and purchase something that will bring it back into your regular wardrobe. Whatever's left, put it in a bag or box and try living without it for a week or two. If you don't miss it, transfer it to the Pass On pile. At the end of our session, we're going to go back to this pile.

A good time to seriously reevaluate your wardrobe is any time you experience a change in lifestyle. I went from being a corporate professional, wearing high heels, suits, and pantyhose every day, to a work-at-home entrepreneur. I don't wear high heels anymore, ever! Guess what you won't find in my closet! I also moved from New England to the Southwest, so I don't need a down jacket or heavy snow boots either. Have you experienced a lifestyle change, but your closet hasn't caught up yet? Look at what you've hung on to from old activities, locations, and lifestyles. Think about the way you live now, and get rid of clothes that no longer make sense.

Put off-season clothes in the least-accessible part of your closet or in another closet altogether if possible. Make sure what's upfront in your closet is right for *now*.

Do this for each type of clothing we've identified—work, play, dress-up, and specialty. Put a limit on clothes you keep as "grubbies" for grungy jobs. One or two sets of clothes for outdoor work or painting should be enough.

Now all you should have hanging in your closet are items that make you look and feel good and are in good condition and ready to wear. Continue this process with your shoes and accessories and anything else in your wardrobe.

Now back to that last pile of clothes that seem right in every way except you just don't wear them. The question here is "Do I *love* this?" This should be the final criterion for your clothes. Having a closet full of well-fitting clothes in good condition that you only feel so-so about isn't where it's at. The final goal is to have a closet full of clothes you love and that you feel great in.

I challenge you to live with only two weeks of outfits or less in your closet. Make them all things you love, that interchange, and that can be classified as the "cream of the crop." Put the rest away in a safe place, but give yourself some time to try this pared-down system. See whether it doesn't make your life a lot simpler. You may actually need fewer clothes than you think.

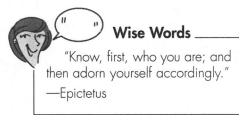

Wise Words

"Know, first, who you are; and then adorn yourself accordingly."

—Epictetus

Take the Pass On pile and give the clothes to charity or whomever you think can use them. Box them up. Do it now! Do the same with the Fix pile if you're taking these items to the tailor. Put them directly in your car so you can drop them off the next time you're out and about. If you leave them around the house, they just may creep back into your closet. If you're going to do the mending yourself, schedule time in your planner/organizer this week and just do it.

Take a look at what's left in your wardrobe and notice the colors and styles. Does this match the earlier picture you came up with of your dressing style? Make a list of a very few quality purchases that would make better use of what you have and add a little more of your personal style to your wardrobe. Something as simple as a new blouse or shirt or some color-coordinated accessories might pull together several elements and make them more versatile. If you have a lot of neutral colors, you might want to add something with more color pizzazz. Or perhaps you need some more basic pieces to enhance the usefulness of what you already have.

Now that you've organized your closet space, reward yourself with some extra touches. Make the inside of your closet even more pleasant by adding sachets between clothes, lining walls with attractive postcards or art posters, and using scented shelf papers. Colorful hatboxes or baskets work well as organizers. Have an attractive box, basket, or hanging bag in the closet to keep clothes that need to be dry-cleaned, and another for mending.

A-Shopping We Will Go

When you go shopping for new things for your wardrobe, keep these basic points in mind:

♦ Don't buy anything just because it's "on sale." Have a list of things you need to make your wardrobe more complete, and stick to your list.

♦ Fashion = waste. Stay away from clothes that are too trendy. Generally, fads disappear after a short time, and you're left with clothing "junk." The classic styles never change much because they're flattering, easy to wear, and go with everything. If you must keep up with the latest trend, try to limit your purchases to accessories, not major wardrobe items.

♦ Invest in quality. With your wardrobe basics, buy the best you can afford. They'll last and look good for a long time. Plus you get more than your money's worth.

♦ Buy clothes that are easy to wear and easy to care for.

♦ Buy any needed accessories when you buy the outfit. That way, a new item won't sit in the closet waiting for the right pair of shoes, a complementary tie, or the right scarf or pin. You have something ready to put on the moment you bring it home.

♦ Keep an inventory of your wardrobe in your planner, and refer to it any time you see something and consider making an "impulse purchase." Ask yourself what it will go with or whether it's a duplication of something you already have.

◆ Wear clothes that are easy to remove when you go shopping and, if possible, have on the same shoes and undergarments you intend to wear with the item you're buying. Don't wear much makeup or jewelry.

◆ If there's enough of a seam allowance, clip a small amount of fabric from the item you're trying to coordinate accessories with, or bring the item with you so you get a perfect match.

◆ Use thrift stores for around-the-house clothes. Who says everything you buy has to be brand new? Second-hand is fine for painting or gardening, and you may even find some items for your other wardrobe needs.

◆ Check over new garments when you get them home. Reaffix buttons that appear loose and reinforce seams in problem areas like the back seam in pants or underarm seams of blouses or shirts. Make sure hems are secure and cut off all loose threads. This will save you lots of mending time down the road.

◆ Sew extra buttons on an inside seam allowance and you always have an extra if you need it. Lord knows, you'll never find it in the button box!

> **CAUTION**
>
> **Pileups!**
>
> If you buy something that needs to be dry-cleaned after only a few wearings, you'd better love it. It's going to cost you a bundle! Avoid clothes that need ironing or special washing. Read the label!

> **Jump Starts**
>
> Stick with solid colors for basics. That's where your biggest dollars will go, and you want them to mix with as many things as possible. Add variety with accessories—think texture, print, color accents, jewelry, scarves, hats, ties, and handkerchiefs for the pocket, belts, and sashes.

The idea is to end up with a wardrobe full of clothes you love that work well together, flatter your figure, suit your lifestyle, express your personality, and are ready to wear right now. Don't let a wardrobe just happen. Plan it. By using these guidelines, you're less likely to end up again with a closet stuffed with clothes you don't wear.

When there's a change of seasons, go through what you're about to put away and apply the same process. No sense in saving a lot of useless garments until next year. Do any laundering and mending so they're ready for next year with only a little touch-up pressing. Dry-clean woolens before putting them away to avoid moth damage.

When you pull out the current season's wardrobe, decide, sort, toss, and fix again. If you do this every six months, when you make your seasonal wardrobe change, you maintain your clothing organization system without really trying.

The Great Hang-Up: Closet Design Basics

Now that you've got your wardrobe pared down and in working order, the next thing on our list is taking a hard look at your closet itself. Follow this checklist and then concentrate on those areas you've checked off as needing attention.

Yes	No	
❏	❏	Does your closet make the best use of space?
❏	❏	Are there areas for hanging long garments as well as short ones such as shirts and jackets?
❏	❏	Can you double up on certain areas with a second rod placed halfway down? Can you add additional shelving at the top?
❏	❏	Is your shoe storage effective? (If there are piles of shoes all over the floor, check No!)
❏	❏	Do all special items (such as pocketbooks, ties, jewelry, and hats) already have their own storage solutions?
❏	❏	Can nonclothing items such as sports equipment or luggage be stored in the garage or attic, if appropriate? If No, decide where these items are going and remove them from the closet. Put them away when you're done organizing.
❏	❏	Are your hangers well used? Good-quality plastic hangers are far better than wire ones. Even better are those hefty wooden ones. Even though they take up more space, they give better shape to your clothes and keep you from cramming your closet. Do you have special pants and skirt hangers? If No, put these items on the shopping list in your planner.
❏	❏	Can you clearly see what's contained in boxes or other storage containers? If No, consider labeling and/or transferring to clear containers. Another way to know what's inside is to affix an instant snapshot to the outside of the box or container. Add any containers or supplies you need to your to-do list and shopping list, if necessary.

A number of companies offer custom closet makeovers, and others allow you to design your own closet. If you choose either of these options, you want to completely empty your closet and start from scratch.

Closet design systems can double or even triple your closet capacity. If you decide to go this route, be sure to get several estimates. Ask the closet company the following questions to help you evaluate:

◆ Do you remove old rods and repair any wall damage?

◆ Are special hangers needed for your system?

◆ How do hangers fit into the system? Don't opt for a system where each hanger sits in its own groove or grid section and clothes can't be slid along a rod. This is very limiting and very annoying when you're looking for something.

> **Jump Starts**
>
> Put a towel bar or two on the back of your closet door. Hang flat things such as scarves on them. Look for places to put up hooks for things such as nightclothes, hats, belts, handbags, or a drawstring bag to hold delicate items for hand-washing.

◆ Are the shelves and any slide-out units they provide sturdy? Put some weight in drawers and be sure they still slide out easily when full. You want to see an in-store sample.

◆ Will the system you design work with each season's wardrobe? Don't go ahead unless you're sure.

◆ Are there ways to add flexibility to the system with free-standing units that roll out or adjustable shelves? Can it be changed?

If you don't have the money to go the total redesign route, start out by completely measuring your closet and doing a layout on your own before you buy any additional shelving or organization aids. Measure the length of your longest jacket, skirt, shirt, or blouse before you install double rods. That will ensure they're the right distance apart to accommodate all your tops and bottoms. Stores such as the Container Store, which sells do-it-yourself storage systems, will do a free consultation. Don't hesitate to ask. Check Appendix A of this book for companies that offer closet design products and services.

There are also solutions you can simply add to your existing closet configuration. A rod that hangs from the existing upper rod in your closet, for instance, can be used to create two shorter hanging areas for shirts and jackets. Make a field trip to your local do-it-yourself, hardware, and department stores to see what's available, and then take a trip through the online closet world for comparisons and more options. Keep your closet and clothing measurements with you and don't be afraid to ask questions.

Look also for various specialty hangers if you have the space. (Now that you've purged your closet of all the things you don't love, you probably do!) There are special hangers for scarves and ties, plus multiple-skirt and -pants hangers that might increase your closet space still more.

Slide-on shelf dividers help keep sweaters and other folded items in their place on closet shelves. These come in clear plastic or wire and are designed to work on wood shelves.

Even with your pared-down wardrobe, are you still hurting for closet space? Then consider an armoire. Especially in older homes with smaller closets, this versatile piece of furniture can be a lifesaver.

Jump Starts

A great way to keep stacks of folded clothes from toppling over is a product called Fold 'N Stax. These flat dividers are smooth on one side and have a gripping surface on the other, allowing you to stack your clothes neatly and keep them upright. Use the divider as a template when folding to create uniform stacks of folded clothes. These are sold in sets of six at www.organize-everything.com.

It All Comes Out in the Wash

What's it like at your house on laundry day? Do you even have a regular system for getting your clothes cleaned, ironed, and mended? If you don't, we simply can't leave this chapter without getting that part of your life organized, too.

Jump Starts

If it isn't dirty, don't wash it! Sounds simple, doesn't it? And yet many of us automatically throw whatever we've worn in the hamper at the end of the day. Stop and look first! A simple airing might be enough. Carefully fold or hang the article of clothing and save yourself some work. Train family members to do the same.

My mother and her mother always did their laundry on Mondays. Monday was Laundry day. Try as I might to emulate them, it just never worked for me. The system I later devised is a simple one, and the reason it works so well for us is that it's visual—even a child can use it. In fact, I devised it to teach my daughters to do their own laundry.

The first thing we did was get in the habit of sorting as we went along. I bought three kitchen-size plastic garbage cans. These each held just about one washing machine load of clothes. One was labeled Darks, one Lights, and one Whites. A separate mesh bag or basket was sufficient for hand-washable items. As the kids undressed at night, we sorted the clothes together. Soon they did it automatically, peeling off their clothes and putting them in the appropriate bin. I taught them to look at labels for dry-clean or special-care items. When a bin was full, it was time to do a load. Come washing time, they helped in the laundry room, so they could see how the machine worked and how to measure soap powder and pretreat stains.

As they got older, they had been doing the sorting for so long and had seen the washing procedure enough times they just grew into doing a load when the garbage bin got to the top. The next step was teaching them to sort out their own clean clothes, fold them, and put them away. They were more motivated to do this because they had a limited number of clothes in the first place and needed what was in the load.

The last step was teaching them how to mend and iron, which took a little more of my attention. Basically, my children were doing their own laundry by age seven or eight. If young children can be taught this system, why not use it yourself? My daughters are now grown and long since out of the house, but my husband and I still use "the garbage can system." It may not be pretty, but it works!

There are some great three-bin laundry systems available now. The girls are grown with families of their own, and my husband and I still use this system, but instead we have a streamlined rolling cart with three removable canvas bags for this purpose. It fits nicely on one side of our closet. When a bag is full, we do a load of laundry.

If you don't adopt my system, come up with your own routine and make it a habit. If a once-a-week system makes more sense in your life, then do it that way. Especially if you live in an apartment building and don't have your own washer and dryer, this may be the only logical solution. But presorting such as I'm suggesting will still save you time, even at the Laundromat.

Stain-Busters

Even if you never took Chemistry 101, you can still be a stain-removal expert. All it takes is a few basic principles, a "stain-busting kit" containing a few important ingredients, and fast action. (Stains are harder to remove when they're "set.")

Treat stains as soon as you notice them. Learn something about the chemistry of stain removal. It will save you lots of money and time. Get yourself a plastic container. (A shoebox-size one is what we have in our house.) Label it and put it in your laundry area. Have on hand the following products for fighting stains and learn how to use them:

- ◆ **Acetone.** Get at your local hardware store; don't use nail polish remover. Good for taking out glue or nail polish.

◆ **Bleach.** Both the kind for whites and for colors. Removes the stain's color, but not the actual stain.

◆ **Club soda.** Excellent for removing pet stains and odors. Just saturate and blot up.

◆ **Color remover.** Get at the fabric dye section of your supermarket.

◆ **Enzyme presoak.** Biz, for example. This "digests" the stain with powerful enzymes. Use on protein stains such as blood and chocolate.

Jump Starts

Too stained to use or even pass on? Cut it up in handy wipe-size squares and use in place of disposable paper towels. Start a "rag-bag" today!

Resource Files

Get yourself a copy of Don Aslett's *Stainbuster's Bible: The Complete Guide to Spot Removal.* It tells you how to remove just about any kind of stain from any kind of surface, explains all the household chemistry involved, and even gives advice on how to avoid making stains in the first place.

◆ **Glycerine.** Get at a pharmacy. Used to soften and dissolve "set" stains, especially on wool and fabrics that don't take kindly to water.

◆ **Hydrogen peroxide.** Another bleaching agent.

◆ **Lemon juice.** Use as a very gentle bleaching agent on delicate fabrics. The effect is intensified by exposing the fabric to sunlight while saturated with lemon juice.

◆ **Low-alkali soap bar.** For example, Woolite or Ivory. For delicate fabrics and wool.

◆ **Oil solvent.** For example, Carbona or K2r. Use for oil and grease stains.

◆ **Oxalic acid solution.** For example, Zud. Used to remove rust stains.

◆ **Paint remover.** Make sure to store this safely.

◆ **Petroleum jelly.** For softening up hardened grease and oil stains.

◆ **White vinegar.** For removing hard-water stains and any other alkaline deposits.

Ironing, Mending, and Other Unfamiliar Subjects

To have a closet full of useful, ready-to-wear clothes, you have to maintain them. This is one of those tasks that takes only a little effort each week, but can become daunting if left to pile up. Part of the problem can be handled upfront during the buying process and immediately after taking your purchase home. Take time to read the labels *before* you buy. Ask yourself whether you really want to iron that cotton shirt or wash that silk blouse by hand. Consider the dry-cleaning bill if that's what it takes to keep it clean. Look the garment over carefully and reinforce any buttons, seams, or hems *before* they come apart.

You'll still have to do some ironing and mending. Here are some ways to save yourself time and effort, while keeping your wardrobe in tip-top shape:

♦ Learn how to use your washing and drying appliances. Read the manuals and follow directions. Select the right cleaning products for your appliance and water type. (You might want to have your water tested and may need to purchase a water softener if it's especially hard.)

♦ Dampen a washcloth with liquid fabric softener and toss in the dryer. It's cheaper than disposable fabric-softener sheets and works just as well.

♦ If you go to a Laundromat, set up a caddy with all the products you need, including a stain-treatment kit.

♦ Sort ironing by the temperature required. Dampen as you go.

♦ Have a basic mending kit handy. If you do your laundry at a Laundromat, be sure you take your kit with you to do small mending jobs while you wait.

♦ Kids mean more repairs and more laundry. Look for shortcuts. Use fusible bonding fabric, iron-on patches, a button puncher, and anything else that'll save time and effort.

♦ If the laundry has really piled up, you can go to the Laundromat and get it all done at once to get on top of it (even if you have laundry facilities at home). If you've got 10 loads to do, you can fill up 10 washers and dryers and do all 10 loads in the time it takes to do one. Go at off-peak hours so you don't have to wait for a free appliance. You go home with everything washed and folded and only a few things to iron or mend. Then implement your system and keep up.

Jump Starts

Take clothes out of the dryer immediately and fold or hang them. You may hardly ever have to iron if you observe this simple rule, and you won't pile up laundry waiting to be ironed. If you forget to take your clothes out of the dryer, throw in a damp towel and dry 5 to 10 minutes to remove wrinkles.

◆ Limit the purchase of items that take special care and make sure you really enjoy the extra work it takes to keep them. I like collecting old linens and hand-made items. They take careful washing and ironing. I use them regularly and, for me, the extra effort is worth it when I see them out on the table.

Dry Cleaning Made Simple

Did you know a lot of the clothes labeled "Dry-Clean Only" don't have to be dry-cleaned? It takes some confidence and maybe a few mistakes before you get the hang of it, but over time you'll find you can really save on the dry cleaning bill with just a few pointers. Items with linings or inserts of a different fabric aren't good candidates, but simply constructed garments of all the same material can often be hand-washed rather than chemically dry-cleaned.

Here are the basics:

◆ Before putting your clothes in the closet, air them out—outside or in a covered porch if possible. They may not even need cleaning, just some deodorizing.

◆ Use a mild liquid, flaked, or powdered soap, not detergent. Dissolve whatever you decide to use completely in a basin or sink before putting in the garment.

◆ Wash one item at a time, so if colors do run you haven't ruined anything else. Things tend to wash better in plenty of water, anyway.

◆ Rinse thoroughly—several times if needed.

◆ Don't wring the garment—gently squeeze. Roll in a towel or several towels until fairly dry, then lay flat or iron to dry. You won't have to dampen a second time when you iron.

If an item does need dry cleaning, make sure you don't roll it in a ball until you take it to the cleaners. Hang or fold neatly. Tell the dry cleaner any stains you know of and what they're composed of. Check buttons and seams. Repair yourself or ask whether the dry cleaner has someone who can do it and what it will cost.

Finishing Touches

Survey your domain! Is it beginning to look more like the picture you created at the beginning of this chapter? As you look around, the floor should be free of clothes, shoes, and papers. The only accessories should be those that truly give you pleasure and create beauty for you in this important space. When you walk into your closet, only your favorite clothes should be hanging there, all ready to wear. You now have a working system for handling all aspects of your laundry.

So reward yourself with some of the elements in your dream bedroom. If you imagined a reading area, find a chair and a lamp and an ottoman. Add a comfortable throw and a small pillow and presto! Instant comfort. Little things such as a small pitcher and glass to set on your night table for fresh water each night, a vase with some fresh flowers, some artwork that evokes the mood you wanted to create, can be added now. Continue to create your personal haven. This is one of the most vital rooms in your home!

Allow the other members of the family to create their own dream bedrooms as much as possible. Children need space for doing homework and studying, so take this into consideration, but it's also where they go for privacy and respite, and it should reflect their tastes as well.

If you have a guest bedroom, spend a night in it yourself and see how comfortable it really is. Pretending to be a guest in your own home can be an enlightening experience. Add whatever amenities you think would make it a cozier, more inviting place to stay.

The Least You Need to Know

- The bedroom is one of the most important rooms in your home. By unstuffing and organizing it, you can create a haven where you sleep better and renew your spirit.

- You can make dressing, shopping, and clothing care simpler by planning your wardrobe and weeding out what you have to conform to that plan.

- A professional closet job or a do-it-yourself plan that's well thought out can at least double your clothing storage space.

- Ensure you don't make any more clothing goofs by having a clothing inventory and shopping list, and taking with you samples of what you want to match.

- A carefully planned laundry system will keep your clothes ready to wear and take less time. Even a child can be taught a simple system.

- Regular maintenance as clothes need it saves time in the long run and keeps your wardrobe ready to wear.

- Spending a night in your guest bedroom will give you insight into how comfortable it actually is. You may need to make some improvements!

Chapter 13

Rooms for Living

In This Chapter

- ◆ Strategies for decluttering the living room, family room, or den
- ◆ Setting up your family spaces for multitasking
- ◆ Problems and solutions for shared living spaces
- ◆ A word about the dining room
- ◆ The fine art of preventive maintenance

Whether you call it the living room, the family room, or the den, there's always a room in the house where the family congregates on a daily basis. Even if you live alone, there's usually one location where you watch TV, read, maybe eat a snack or even most of your meals. Along with the dining room or eat-in area of the kitchen, these are the "common" rooms, meaning they are shared by all the people living in the house and often are where visitors spend time.

If you have both a living room and a family room or den, the information covered in this chapter will generally apply to both, but I want you to tackle the room you spend the most time in first because it will have the biggest impact on how you feel and function.

The "Living" Room

Let's concentrate on whatever room in your house is the true "living" room. That's the room where you and your family spend the most time every day. Take a minute to analyze the layout of your living room. Is it a separate room that's closed off from the rest of the house or is it part of a larger, more open living area? How does traffic generally flow into and out of that room? Survey the room. What clues are there to the activities taking place there?

The living or family room is generally the true "multitasking" room in the house. Some of the duties this room is expected to perform are as follows:

> Entertainment area/media center
>
> Playroom
>
> Study/homework/computer room
>
> Home office
>
> Hobbies and crafts room
>
> Game room
>
> Entertaining area

Envisionings
Create a vision of what you want this room to say. How do you want it to feel? What would it take to make it more that way? How do you want your family and guests to feel in this room? Can you make it the way you see it with what you have now or would you need to purchase some new things? Let your imagination go and write down your idea of the perfect living room.

Which of these activities is your living room handling (either by design or by default)? It's easy to see why this area can get cluttered and chaotic. Keeping it clean is a challenge, too, because it takes a beating from hard, everyday use.

Setting Up Zones

One of the best ways to begin to get a handle on organizing the living room is to set up zones in different parts of the room determined by the various uses of the space. You need to be realistic about whether the room you have, given its size and configuration, can actually manage all these activities or whether you need to rethink the space and move some of them elsewhere.

If the kids' rooms were more organized, would they be doing their homework there instead of in the living room? We work more on the kids' rooms in Chapter 14, but tuck that idea away in your mind for now. If you created your Command Center when you read Chapter 7, perhaps there are papers and other items in the living room space that now have a home in your household management area. Remove any obvious things that now make more sense relocated to newly organized spaces in other areas of the house. Do this now.

If you're doing crafts in the living room, could you store the majority of your materials somewhere else and make a space for your current project only? Just think about whether there's simply too much going on in this room for it to function well and see whether you can relieve some of the burden by relocating stuff to a more logical place elsewhere in the house.

Also remove any stuff that can be thrown out or just doesn't serve a purpose in your life anymore. Especially pay attention to the flat surfaces around the room. These include the coffee table, side tables, shelves, top of the television and entertainment center, the mantle, and, of course, the floor! See whether you can fill a garbage bag with stuff that can go in the trash or to charity right away. Pay particular attention to knick-knacks and memorabilia.

Now that you can breathe a little, let's consider those zones again. There could be a media area, a kids' area, a home office or computer area, a hobby or crafts area, a place to read—make a list of your zones and decide where in the room they most logically belong.

Contain and Control: Furniture That Works

The furniture in this room is a key piece of the organizing puzzle. You need adequate storage space so you can put away the things you take out each time you use them. It needs to be easy not only for adults but for the kids sharing the space as well. Think about height of shelves and cabinets as you rethink how you use this room. Generally, you want to have the kids' stuff on the lower shelves and the adult stuff at a higher level.

Now let's get more specific about the stuff you're likely to have in this space. Below is a list. Add to it anything unique to your life that I might have overlooked. Subtract what isn't true of your living room.

Media: CDs, DVDs, tapes, computer games

TV

Stereo equipment

Playstation or similar computer gaming equipment

Board games and puzzles

Toys

Computer and accessories

Books, magazines, and newspapers

Mail and other paper

Photos

Craft projects and supplies

Entertainment center

Shelving and cabinets

Seating

Coffee table

Toy box/storage

End tables

Lighting

Table for playing games or doing crafts

Computer furniture or desk

How well do the pieces of furniture you have in this room function? Do they allow for storage or are they more decorative than functional? Are there enough shelves or storage units for the things you regularly use in this space? Is there a designated place to store electronic media and printed material?

I'm not asking you to go out and buy all new furniture, but make a note of any pieces you feel could be replaced with items that would help you more in your efforts to get organized. After you have purged and sorted what you're keeping, you'll have a better idea of whether you really need to replace some furniture items in this room. Perhaps you even have pieces elsewhere in the house that could be repurposed for this room.

A Room of Another Sort

By now you know the routine. The first step to getting organized is as always to unstuff the room or area you want to bring order to. Get out your sorting boxes, grab your timer, and start your engines! Get the whole family into the act, because the clutter likely belongs to everyone. Set aside a weekend day and plan a reward for the whole family when you've finished.

After you've done the first purge of clutter and removed the stuff going to the trash and charity, and have put away what belongs in other rooms, go back to the pile of things you decided to keep initially and see whether you can't pare that down by a third or half. Do a more detailed sort by type of item (CDs, magazines, etc.), keeping in mind the zones we talked about earlier.

As you create piles of stuff you want to keep, start envisioning some storage solutions. Do you have a "home" for everything or do you need to add some organizational tools to your list? Let's look at some clutter traps for the living room and some solutions for keeping them neat and easy to use, then simple to put away when you're done.

High-Tech Horror Show: Wires and Cords

Whatever your electronic poison—a personal computer, stereo system, home theater, or just a TV and VCR or DVD player (or both)—you'll inevitably have a tangle of cords and shared electrical outlets to deal with.

There are basically two types of products on the market for managing cords and wires. One type is a flexible tube, slit down one side. You open it up and insert each cord or wire individually, snaking it along shelves to catch each set from individual pieces of equipment, then guide down to where the electrical outlet is.

The second type of cord and wire management system is basically a Velcro strap that either gathers cords into bundles or "catches" them and sticks to various surfaces to hide them along baseboards, shelves, racks, or desks.

Another decision you have to make is how you want to display your electronic equipment. Do you want it out in the open or do you want it discreetly hidden behind closed doors?

Resource Files

Rip-Tie manufactures Velcro cord management products. Write them at P.O. Box 549, San Leandro, CA 94577; call 1-800-7-RIPTIE; e-mail (info@riptie. com); or visit their website at www.riptie.com. Look for their CableCatch and CableWrap products.

If your equipment is somewhat smaller in scale, you might want to hide it in a sideboard, armoire, or cupboard. You can have a unit custom-made or you can adapt an existing one. Check out unpainted furniture places and used furniture shops, as well.

Don't overlook yard sales and newspaper classifieds. Entertainment centers specifically designed for audio equipment, TVs, VCRs, and DVD players can work. The better ones are quite pricey, however, and the less expensive ones can be flimsy. When shopping, don't forget to consider the weight of your components, size (take measurements and bring them with you), air circulation, and ease of access for use and cleaning.

Composing Your Music and Video Collection

There are many options for camouflaging or completely hiding your musical and film media. You need to decide whether you want to store them so you can see them (some people feel it's part of their décor) or get them out of sight.

There are lots of racks and towers for storing these items in plain sight. But if you opt for getting them behind closed doors or drawers, look for pieces of furniture originally intended for other uses and retrofit them for music and movie storage.

Don't overlook the storage possibilities of drawers. If they're the right height you can store your media so that the spine is easily read. Drawers also keep your collection at a lower height, so they're easier to see and you don't have to reach up to get them.

Because tapes and CDs are fairly narrow, you can build custom shelving that makes use of shallow hidden spaces. Look behind doors or along walls. We made storage shelves that just fit the depth of our largest video cases. They line the wall in the guest room. Often overnight guests appear from their room with a video request in hand! If a piece of furniture doesn't fit the bill, consider stacking boxes. Narrow plastic shoe boxes are just about right for CDs. Larger ones might fit videos. There are also sturdy, attractive file boxes created just for CD, DVD, and video storage.

If you're really challenged for space, consider ditching the jewel cases that CDs come in and moving to a scratchproof plastic sleeve system that holds both CD and liner notes. These come in flip-through album styles and individual sleeves designed for a file drawer unit. One caution on this design is to be careful of transporting CDs in these plastic sleeves where they're going to be exposed to heat or dirt. The plastic can melt more easily than the hard plastic of jewel cases and ruin your CDs.

Old-fashioned vinyl is fast becoming replaced by the new forms of digital media, but there are those who feel vinyl is still technically superior, or for sentimental reasons have a few LPs they want to hang on to. Always store vinyl albums vertically, never flat, because they're easy to warp. Keep them upright (use bookends, if needed).

Acid-free and polyethylene sleeves are available to replace the inferior paper ones that often came with the original album.

Consider temperature and humidity when storing your electronic media. Ideally your air temperature will be constant, with a steady 40 percent to 60 percent humidity—which, by the way, is also ideal for musical instruments.

Most audiophiles consider audiotapes a more temporary medium. Tapes are subject to stretching, and audio quality just isn't up to CDs or even vinyl in good condition. Now that most of us have CD burners, we can make custom CDs from our tapes and LPs or copy those we want to preserve. It's also fun to make specialized collections for certain themes, occasions, or moods.

You need a labeling and filing system for your music and movie collection. We have our videos organized by general categories and then alphabetically within those categories. This proves especially helpful if you have a large collection, which we do. DVDs take up less room, but you may not be up to replacing all your favorite videotapes with DVDs. Before you do that, consider whether you really watch them as often as you thought you would anyway.

Most of us have both tape and disk technology and need to store both videotapes and DVDs. Periodically purge your collection and carefully consider how likely you are to watch them before you purchase more. If you tape something and decide later you've seen it enough times or it's not a favorite, tape over it or pass it on. Give away music you no longer listen to. Or make a tape of the few cuts on the albums, tapes, or CDs you truly enjoy, and let the individual volumes go.

Jump Starts

When shopping for media storage options, take a few CDs, DVDs, and audiotapes and videotapes along with you to see how many will fit, and estimate what materials might be needed to adapt your flea market or unpainted furniture find. Or write down the measurements of each.

Pileups!

The enemies of all electronic media are dust, fingerprints, dirt, moisture, and extremes in temperature. Think carefully about where you choose to store CDs, DVDs, tapes, and LPs, and use the right cleaning systems to maintain them. Don't forget to keep your electronic equipment clean as well.

Racks created just for the purpose of storing CDs are fine, but they do have some disadvantages, especially individually slotted racks. If you're trying to set up an alphabetic filing system, every time you get a new CD you have to move each CD and reinsert it into a new slot. Kind of a pain.

If you have an especially large music and/or movie collection, you may need to go to a more complex filing system. You can use index cards if you want to go low tech, or check into some of the computer programs designed for the purpose. These are essentially databases, and their advantage is that they allow you to search for titles based on key words, artists, labels, or even individual song titles, if you want to get that detailed.

Try to stick to the "new one in, old one out" rule for your media. If for some reason you suddenly missed a movie or some music you passed on, could you rent it, borrow it, or download it (hey, now there's iTunes!)?

Consider replacing an older stereo system with a more compact newer model. These components have come down in size and price. You create space immediately when you get rid of those gorilla-size speakers! Now create a media center with a limited amount of storage space and keep your collection confined to that space. With new technology such as digital video recorders you can save a movie or show, watch it a couple of times, and then get rid of it. We have one of these, and I'm a big fan. There are very few television programs or movies we're likely to watch more than two or three times. If it's something we really love and are sure we will want to see again, we can purchase the DVD or record the movie or program to tape.

Another good thing about digital video recorders is that when they're full, you can't record any more! You have to dump some to keep recording. Think how much space you'd save (and time) if you just limited yourself to the 35 hours or so that your DVR can hold. If you don't watch what's on it in a day or two, get in the habit of deleting it.

Toys in Tow

If your living room is also a playroom for younger children, start by paring down and getting rid of toys that are broken, toys they've outgrown, and items they've simply lost interest in. Sort by category: large toys, smaller items, stuffed animals, games, art supplies, etc.

If the children have other areas to store toys, you might want to get the bulk of them out of the common family area and allow them to bring in one at a time or create a cabinet or toy box for those items they're most interested in now. Toys can be rotated from storage to this limited space.

Make sure that, whatever device you use to contain toys, it's easy to reach and safe for small fingers. Divide toys into categories with smaller boxes, bins, or baskets and label them. If a child is too young to read, use color or pictures to help them remember what goes where. See whether some storage options on wheels might be appropriate.

That way they can either be removed from the room to create an adult space after the little ones are in bed or when entertaining or at least pushed out of the way.

Make it a fun daily routine to put a toy back in its place when a child is done playing with it and before another item comes out into the room. At the end of the day, the toys can be "put to bed" along with your little one as part of his bedtime routine. If permanent toy storage is in another part of the house, keep a bin or basket (a laundry basket works well) for your child to put things in to cart them to where they belong. Have toys sorted there in bins as we mentioned before and have your child put them in their proper "homes" before bed or before moving on to another activity.

Impose the "new one in, old one out" rule on toys, too. Kids will learn at an early age that space is finite and clutter destroys peace and tranquility. Let them experience the enjoyment of giving a no-longer-used toy to a child who can really use it by passing it on to charity.

Life's a Game and a Puzzle!

Sort through all the board games you have and get rid of any you don't play or that have missing pieces. Pass on the ones you're bored with and trash the incomplete ones (so you don't frustrate anyone else!).

Game and puzzle boxes tend to sit in a pile and when one is removed the others fall down. Boxes can become crushed or worn. If the box is coming apart replace it with a plastic box large enough to hold the board and all the pieces. Another solution is to get smaller boxes for each game's pieces and group all the boards together. Label both the boards and the boxes. (Don't forget to include the instructions and rules, too.)

Replace puzzle boxes with rigid plastic ones if needed. Photocopy the cover of the puzzle so you can see what it looks like finished. After you've done the puzzle, pass it on unless you truly think you will assemble it again.

If your coffee table or side tables don't allow for storage, you may want to think about purchasing ones that do. These are great places to store games and puzzles. If you make them easy to retrieve and put away, you may actually find the family will want a weekly game night!

Gaming Goes Digital

Pass on the electronic games that no one plays anymore. Do the same with outdated equipment. Consolidate equipment and games in one place.

Consider renting rather than buying. Kids can also exchange games until they're tired of them, and then return them. Those games that are favorites need to have a consistent place for storage (see "Composing Your Music and Video Collection" in this chapter). There are plastic systems that attach to conventional shelves and slide out for easy viewing of CDs and DVDs. These fit Sega, GameCube, XBox, and Playstation games.

Pick your favorite Internet search engine and type in "video game station." You'll find a number of storage options for the whole kit and caboodle, games and equipment.

Computer Time

If your living room must double as a computer area for the family or a home office, you need to think carefully about how much space to give it and how to keep it contained and clutter-free.

Give some thought to your computer equipment before you buy. If a laptop will do for your needs, maybe that's the best choice. You can use a laptop for a main computer with just the addition of a printer and maybe an extended keyboard and a more ergonomic mouse. The laptop allows the family to move the computer to other places when working there makes the most sense.

Choose computer furniture that's space efficient and easy to keep organized. It helps to have storage for discs and accessories, paper, and manuals. Closed cabinets will help keep things dust-free and look neater in the room.

Look for multipurpose equipment, such as fax, scanner, copier, and printer combinations. Make sure you have adequate space to write as well. If you're going to be doing bills in this area or kids are going to be doing homework, you need to set up a system for handling the paper. Use stacked boxes or upright slotted systems. Sort the mail and take bills directly to this area. If this is your Command Center, go back to Chapter 7 and reread how to organize that area for yourself.

If several people are going to be using this area, make sure each one knows the rules and how things are organized so they can follow the system, too. You may need to set up individual cubbies nearby for each user.

Dealing with Books

To book lovers like my husband and me, a house is not a home without a substantial reading and reference library. When we married, between us we had thousands of books. We've pared down to old favorites and the most useful reference works, but we have a tendency to acquire new books on a regular basis. Managing our library is a major organization issue, as it is for lots of other readers and book aficionados.

The system that seems to work best for us is to organize our nonfiction books according to subjects, and then alphabetize within each. Fiction has its own section. Like most people, we don't have the space for a separate library room, so our books are spread throughout the house in logical groupings. Books related to movies and TV, cooking, gardening, and travel live in the guestroom, where the videos, CDs, and DVDs are stored. Guests seem to enjoy perusing these volumes the most, and the shelf of local history and travel books makes a practical addition to this location.

My husband's Civil War, World War II, and American Western history collection is downstairs where he spends a lot of time. Books related to my profession as a writer are on bookshelves in my office. Fiction, poetry, and craft-related books have their own home in a series of bookcases in my hobby area. We regularly purge our books as our interests change, better books come along, or books become outdated.

Try to categorize your own library and see where the most logical places might be to store particular groupings. Look for spaces that best suit the number of volumes in a particular category. If you're not sure what you have or suspect you have quite a few books you could pass on, do a major overhaul and gather all your books together into categorized stacks for redistribution.

> **Jump Starts**
>
> Books can be a decorative feature, as long as they don't become clutter. If you have an especially attractive leather-bound set, display it in a living room or study. A neat pile of splendid picture books looks attractive on a coffee table or occasional table. Small volumes of poetry can grace a small nook almost anywhere.

If you sometimes have visitors who need to wait in a foyer or living room, or if you have a client waiting room for your home business, have a stack of interesting books and magazines available to keep them occupied. Don't put any special favorites there, though, just in case one decides to walk away!

Don't forget to keep a list of books you've borrowed from others and books you've lent. A bulletin board is a good place for this, or you may want to have a sheet in your planner/organizer. I've lost many treasured volumes through my habit of loaning favorites to others. I'm sure they don't intend to keep them, but over time they forget, and so do I. Put your name inside your books so the borrower has no excuse for not returning them, like forgetting who he borrowed them from!

Keep books borrowed from someone else's library in one place, so they don't somehow get absorbed into your own library and become lost forever. Put a sticky note on the inside front cover with the name of the person you borrowed it from, and you'll remember where to return it.

> **Wise Words**
>
> "I have never known any distress that an hour's reading did not relieve."
>
> —Baron de Montesquieu

Dust books and bookshelves regularly. Once a year, take them all off the shelves, dust, and vacuum. Make sure wherever you're storing them is free of dampness. If there's any chance they might get mildewed, put a dehumidifier in the room and monitor it. Don't squash books into shelves—you'll damage them. Most books like to be stored upright, but very large books are best stored on their sides individually.

Photo Finish

Photographs capture the past for future generations. But in piles with no rhyme or reason, they are simply clutter. Group all your photos together. This includes framed photos as well as snapshots and negatives. Maybe you have trays of slides as well. The living room is a likely place to display your favorite family photos, but have they taken over? Be selective and pare down to those you most treasure and what you have room for.

Now sort through the photos you've gathered. Get rid of only the best shots. If you have duplicates, either pass them on or throw them away. Now group them chronologically or, at the very least, in general categories. You may want to do all your Christmas photos in one box or album or all your summer vacations or you may want to group by person. You can probably ditch the negatives, because digital technology will now allow you to scan photos and make as many copies as you desire. If you feel you must hold on to negatives, label them with the subject and date and put them in a safe place.

> **Pileups!**
>
> If you have photos in magnetic albums, boxes or envelopes that are not acid-free or are in their original developing envelopes, you need to take them out and get them in the appropriate (acid-free, archival) albums or boxes or else they will be damaged in time.

Photos are only valuable if they are put in some context and if they can be viewed easily. Get in the habit of trashing "out-takes" or poor quality photos, be they prints or digital. Display a select few that have real meaning in quality frames. If you keep every photograph, then the really special ones will be lost in the clutter of junk photographs. Keep only those photos that inspire and "tickle" you, and let go of the rest.

Put what's left in photo albums (make sure to use archival quality albums or your prints will deteriorate over time) or in sectioned, labeled archival-quality photo boxes. Date everything and note anything important about the event they commemorate that might be forgotten years from now.

If you have a lot of photos to organize, work backward so you don't get too over-whelmed. Start with the current year and then the previous year and so on. Label photos to the best of your memory using a pen or pencil that's safe for photographs. (Check your art-supply or photo store.) Even if you can't remember the exact date, a close approximation will be helpful years from now.

Unless scrapbooking is a bona-fide hobby of yours, skip the elaborate layouts, cute stickers, and frames. You can add captions later. If you have time to do something more with your photos in the future and you really want to, fine. At least this way, you'll be way ahead of the game when you do.

If you're working with digital photos, the organizing process is similar to that of print photos. Delete the out-takes and set up labeled folders with event names and dates. Burn images to a CD when you have a few hundred. Make sure you label the disc with the dates and events it covers. If the photos are very important to you, make a copy of the CD and keep it in a safe place. Share photos with family and friends by sending them via e-mail, or mail them a disc.

Several photo organization programs are on the market. Check out the ones for your operating system and read reviews before you buy. Adobe Photoshop Album and Microsoft Picture It! Digital Image Suite are two popular ones.

Another great way to share photos is online through a service such as Snapfish. Go to www.snapfish.com and set up albums, and then e-mail folks to tell them there are photos up for them to view.

Consider having old slides and photos scanned onto CDs or DVDs (or do it yourself). They are far less likely to be damaged by moisture, light, or age, plus you can make up copies for other family members to use as they wish.

Pileups!

Don't be a shutterbug. Think before you click! Be selective about the photos you take and you'll have less to do later.

Resource Files

Looking for archival photo storage supplies? Log on to www.gaylord.com for the same ones that library archivists use. Another good sources is www.exposuresline.com.

Make sure you label these as well. Create digital slide shows. Again be realistic about your photos, and for those you decide to keep, honor and preserve them for the future.

Crafty Solutions

If your living room is a place where you do needlework, scrapbooking, beading, or other crafts, you need to corral your equipment and supplies so you can make the most of your hobby time.

But there are hobbies and then, well, there are good intentions. Sometimes projects seem like something we'll enjoy and then we lose interest. Some so-called hobbies are simply excuses for accumulating and cluttering.

Make an honest assessment of your favorite pastimes—the ones you always turn to when you have some free time. Be honest, too, about the passing fancies that you haven't touched in years. Pass unfinished projects, supplies, and tools on to someone who will really enjoy them (and finish them). Concentrate on the ones you truly enjoy.

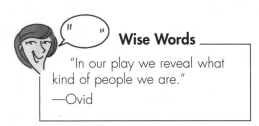

Wise Words

"In our play we reveal what kind of people we are."
—Ovid

One reason hobbies may not be completed is because they're so inaccessible they'd take too much trouble to dig out. Ferret out all those orphaned projects and gather them in one place. If finding them again piques your interest, put them where you'll be able to take them out at a moment's notice and see whether they strike your fancy again. If not, pass them on.

Because a craft or hobby isn't necessarily something you're likely to do every day, you may not want it lying out where it can get soiled, pieces can get lost, or where supplies might be chewed by the dog. Have a space in your living room for projects you're currently working on and store the rest elsewhere. Here are some general solutions to storing projects, tools, and supplies:

- See whether there's a carry-all, case, or box that can house all you need to do your hobby. This can be grabbed any time and keeps everything together. My main hobby is beading. I have a rolling tool box with several compartments that holds just about everything I need in a very small space. I roll it out into the living room when I want to work on it and roll it back into a closet when we entertain or I'm busy with other things.

- Try a rolling cart with drawers in various sizes. These come in a variety of sizes and can be found in the closet department of your favorite Kmart, Wal-Mart, Target, or art-supply store. Roll it away into a corner when it's not in use.

◆ Some projects lend themselves to a box or bin for storage. You'll usually want a lid to keep light, moisture, and inquisitive hands out, and pieces in. This works well for hobbies such as embroidery and hand-sewing. You may want a special keeper for threads and needles that fits neatly in the box.

◆ If your hobby involves many small pieces (such as beading, for example), you probably want compartmentalized storage boxes that close tightly.

Check hardware stores before you buy specialized boxes and chests from craft stores. The hardware variety is usually less expensive. So what if it's battleship gray or military green instead of pink, mauve, or turquoise?

◆ Use binders to keep instructions and printed directions for projects. Rip what you want out of craft magazines, three-hole punch, and throw the rest away. Like recipes, there are only so many projects you can make, so be selective and realistic.

◆ Sewing patterns never fit back in their envelopes once they've been unfolded. If you use patterns more than once, set aside space in a file cabinet, put patterns in manila folders, large resealable plastic bags, or large envelopes, label, and file. Be sure to include instructions and the original envelope in the file, plus any notes you'd like to add.

Jump Starts _____
Try marine, office, kitchen, closet, and scientific supply catalogs, and peruse them from a new vantage point—storage solutions! Also request catalogs for your particular hobby to find storage solutions specifically tailored to its tools and materials.

Pileups! _____
There's nothing worse than a space hog. I know one couple where the man dominates the whole house with his hobbies, and the woman, a seamstress, has to use the kitchen table and pack up her projects every time they eat. No fair! Be sure you check with the other residents of your abode before you appropriate space for your hobby. And share! Didn't they teach you *anything* in kindergarten?

If your hobby is portable, keep your supplies in a living-room drawer, next to your favorite chair, or beside the bed—wherever you're most likely to spend time and think to pick up the project. I have my embroidery in an attractive hatbox that sits in the living room under the coffee table. While the family watches TV (something I don't really do much of), I can grab my project and still be a part of the action.

Sometimes your choice of hobbies or the extent to which you can pursue them, is decided by the space you have available. I mean, if you live in a two-room apartment, is it really practical to start building model airplanes as a hobby?

Use basic organizing principles once you get the containers, shelves, and carrying cases you need:

- **Group like things together.** Group by type, subject, color, texture, or purpose—whatever makes sense.

- **Consolidate and compress.** Use smaller, compartmentalized containers if possible. Stack and layer. Keep things from spreading out.

- **Label it!** If it's not in a see-through container, make sure you label your supplies so you don't have to go through a dozen boxes before you find the right one.

- **Set limits on your crafts and hobbies.** Let your containers or shelves be your limiting factor. Use the "new one in, old one out" rule.

Collection or Clutter?

Whatever your favorite collecting hobby, be it baseball cards or art glass, find some sort of special container or cabinet to house it in and use that container as a limit-setting device. My Depression glass has its own cabinet, and when that's full, the size of the collection is determined. If I see something else I'd like to have, I need to make a decision to retire one to make room for it or hang on to what I already have and pass it by.

CAUTION

Pileups!

Beware of collections becoming just another Acquisition Trap. You know you're in trouble when your collection starts taking over the house and pushing other activities out of the way. Be aware of changes in your interests, as well. When a collection no longer gives you any pleasure and just collects dust, it's time to let it go.

If you've got a really special or rare collection, why not donate it to a museum related to your particular interest so other collectors can enjoy it? There's a museum for almost anything. Check with your reference librarian if you're not sure where there is one.

Why not use your collection? Although I wouldn't be pleased if I broke a piece of my Depression glass, I gain the greatest pleasure from setting a table with it, not from keeping it in my china cabinet. If your collection is not substantially growing in value or you don't use it or gain pleasure from it regularly, consider giving it away.

Another suggestion is simply to pare down your collection. How about keeping only the rarest or most interesting examples? Narrow your collection to only one category or color. Or use the "trade up" principle. Keep only a certain number, and when you find something that's better than what you have, trade up—get rid of the lesser example and replace it with the better quality or more special one. Display your collection and make it a part of your décor.

Dining in (Organized) Style

Wherever there's a flat horizontal surface, that's where clutter lands. Whether you eat most often in your kitchen or your dining room, take a look now at the flat surfaces and see whether I'm not telling the truth.

In many households, the dining room or kitchen table often doubles as a work table, homework table, or crafts table. With today's open floor plans the kitchen, dining area, and living area or family room are often all one large space. This is both a help and a problem, because stuff tends to spread out all over the place.

Think of your dining area as having zones, just like your living room area. You may need to store dishes and serving pieces there. Possibly linens need to live there as well. First consider function, and then make an assessment of the furniture and existing storage in the room.

Do you have room for a hutch, china cabinet, buffet, or sideboard? This can be both for typical items used in the dining room as well as for storage related to other activities that are regularly done there.

If the dining room table is a space for children to do homework or artwork, consider a rolling cart with drawers that can be put out of the way at meal times. This will encourage putting things away and make it easy to keep things contained. Look for places to add storage cabinets or shelves. (Look up!) Make them a part of preparing the table for the family meal.

Because the dining area is one that needs to be cleaned two to three times a day after each meal, keeping it as clutter-free as possible is a priority. The materials used on furniture and other surfaces and their ease of cleaning is very important, so consider this when making any future purchases for this room.

Keeping Your Cool

Maintaining spaces where everyone spends so much time is a daily job. Let it go for a day and pretty soon you have chaos! These rooms usually have particular areas that are prone to clutter. I call them *danger zones*. Determine your danger zones and police them regularly.

Get the family (and yourself) into the habit of picking up the living room each day before retiring and the dining room before and after every meal. Make it into a ritual, and everyone will be more likely to remember. Make it fun for children and you'll be creating an important lifelong habit. Maybe you can come up with a "pick up" song!

The Least You Need to Know

- The living room is the true multitasking room that sees hard use and lots of activities. Keeping it clean and organized will have a huge impact on how you feel and function.

- Decluttering is the first step toward organizing your living area. Start by sorting and purging, and then organize the rest.

- Be realistic about how many tasks your living space can be asked to perform. Try to relocate whatever you can, and then organize the room into zones.

- Finding storage solutions for what you decide to keep in the living room will help keep it organized.

- If the dining room table has to do "double duty" for homework or other tasks, having a cart, caddy, or cabinet to contain supplies is a must.

- Making a daily ritual of picking up the common living spaces will help keep it orderly and teach valuable lessons to children.

Kids' Stuff: Organizing with Little Ones in Mind

In This Chapter

◆ Helping kids sort, purge, and organize so they can play happily in their own space

◆ Motivating children to learn new organization habits

◆ How to travel trouble-free with your kids

◆ Organizing kids' parties they'll always remember

You probably picked up this book because you felt your life was in some way out of control. Somewhere along the line things got out of hand or perhaps you've never really been able to organize your life and you needed to be taught how.

So how would your life have been different if you'd learned how to handle this stuff when you were a kid? How much distress, anger, and frustration would it have saved you?

You now have the extraordinary opportunity to give your children the gift of organization that you perhaps never had. Believe me, they've been watching you these past few weeks or months. Ever since you bought this book and started changing your life they've been keeping an eye on you. They may have looked dazed and confused or even made some unflattering remarks, but in the end they *noticed*.

There's no greater teacher than example. By taking the steps we've made together so far, you've taken the biggest step toward giving your children a brighter future.

Taking the Time Will Save Everyone Time

I won't lie. When you begin teaching organization skills to your children, at first it will be time-consuming. It takes time to raise happy, successful, responsible adults. Chores that you could do alone in minutes will take longer when you do them with your child. It takes time to explain concepts and principles that may be new to them. But minutes spent now will save countless hours in the future.

You didn't get into chaos overnight, and neither did they. You can't expect them to change overnight either. Be patient. Have an honest talk about the way things have been for you, how you're trying to change them for yourself and the rest of the family, why it's important to you and how they can help. Explain what you want for them and how keeping the junk out of their lives and honoring what they have by keeping it organized will make their lives easier, too.

Too much stuff in a kid's daily environment is over-stimulating and stressful. Things get lost in the chaos and become difficult to see or distinguish. If your child tends to be a little "over-active" you may find that helping him get organized may make a huge difference.

Don't try to do too much at once. Gear your organizing sessions to a child's age and attention span. Work on teaching them organization skills as you go along. You might want to play the "Clean Sweep" game (after the television show of the same name) and clear out their entire room except for a few things they'll need for the week and start sorting with them a little at a time. Leave only the essentials and work through one category at a time. Seeing the room empty can help everyone spot opportunities for storage and organization solutions they might not have been able to see amidst the clutter. You can begin to do a broad sort as you remove the debris, putting all the clothes in one box or area, all the toys in another, and so on. The breath of fresh air your child will experience by removing the clutter in one fell swoop may just have an immediate effect.

Or work more slowly and use the box system you've already learned on one area at a time. *Trash*, *Pass On*, *Put Away*, and *Keep* are easy for a child to understand.

If your children are young, you're way ahead of the game. Sometimes all it takes is providing the tools and creating a routine together. By setting up his or her environment so it's easy to put things away and find what they need when they want it, they'll naturally gravitate toward "doing the right thing."

If you're dealing with teenagers, you may meet with a little more resistance. You need to be patient (just like you've had to be patient with yourself), take a little more time, and think of rewards that will provide motivation.

When your child is ready to go off to college, think of what he'll be taking with him (besides your hard-earned cash). He'll know how to clean a house, fix a meal, look good at a job interview, organize his schoolwork, and make friends and influence people. Those things may prove just as valuable as his college education.

By teaching kids how to organize themselves and getting them in the habit of helping around the house, they will appreciate the things others do for them much more. Besides, while he's learning and you're teaching, you get to spend some great times together. When your child begins to help and becomes more independent, everyone will have more time to have fun.

The skills you'll be teaching them now and the self-confidence having these skills will engender can be a powerful tool for success in adulthood. These are the building blocks for acquiring habits that will serve them for the rest of their lives in having the life they really want and deserve. We're doing noble work, my friend!

Babes in Toyland

We talked a bit about organizing toys in shared areas of the house in Chapter 13, but now we're going to talk about the toys that live in the kids' rooms.

The first thing you need to do with their help is pare down. There's only so much space and so much time. Teach them to use both wisely. Using the same basic procedure we've been going back to throughout this book, do a quick or rough sort and purge what you can right away. Next do a more detailed sort based on definite principles and criteria you decide on together, and finally find a home for what you're keeping that's easy to reach and that makes it easy to return the object to its designated address every time.

Putting some things away into storage and rotating toys is a way to keep the clutter down, but if it's really something they've lost interest in help them let it go. It may help to visit a charity so they can see where their surrendered toys will be going. If you use a rotation system, maybe you can give kids a way to "check out" a toy and return one to storage they find boring for now. They can even sign toys in and out to add to the game.

Grouping like things together is a concept that can be taught at a very young age. Make a game of it! Then show your children how to consolidate and compress (instead of scattering things everywhere), label *everything*, alphabetize where they can, and if there are duplicates, help them make decisions based on quality so they can let the lesser one go. And an added bonus: you hammer these concepts home in your own mind as you give your kids the organization power tools you wish you'd had as a kid. Teaching is a great way to reinforce your own learning.

Jump Starts

Stop toy clutter at its source! Ask Grandma, Aunt Fanny, and whoever else can't resist a new toy for the kids to ask you first. At holiday time and birthdays, set limits and ask relatives to contribute toward one large item that you know will enrich your child's playtime or to pay for an important trip or activity. My grandson gets way more out of his toddler gymnastics than any number of BPTs (translation: "big plastic things") he'll lose interest in a couple of months down the road. And stay away from the toy department yourself!

Toy boxes can be like a black hole. Things get crushed and broken as other things are thrown on top. If you're using a toy box, make it fairly shallow and subdivide it with sturdy bins or baskets that can be removed for play and put back.

Sturdy shelves at child height with bins or baskets for toys work well. If you make them adjustable and expandable, you can raise and add shelves as the child grows. If there are things you want to display or keep in a child's room, but they're not old enough to touch them yet, put them on higher shelves out of reach. Use color, shape, and size to help children remember where things go (doll clothes go in the bin with the pink triangle on it, trucks go in the big green bin, tinker toys go in the little green bin, etc.). Add pictures taped on the front of boxes to help, but label them anyway so your child begins to recognize the words. See? Teaching organization can be used to teach other skills as well!

Use smaller plastic bins with lids for things with small pieces that can fall out. Make sure the lids stay on but are easy for a child to remove. Label everything!

You may also want to create a small box or tray for stray items that pop up in and under couches, behind doors, or under rugs while you do your weekly cleaning. Simply gather them up in one place and let your child match them up with the game or toy they came with.

We talked about how to store games in Chapter 13. If they're going to be kept in your child's room, you want to consolidate and compress the boxes by taking out the boards and putting the pieces along with instructions into smaller boxes, plastic containers, or resealable plastic bags.

Resource Files

Tuffyland makes attractive, sturdy bin systems for kids. Take a look at all their great options at www.tuffyland.com. And when the kids outgrow their bins? I'd co-opt them for my craft studio in a heartbeat!

Clothes

Use the same procedure on clothes that you did for toys. Sort, purge, sort again, and then find a permanent home that's easy to return the item to every time.

You may need to rethink the clothing storage you're asking your child to use. Look at the closet and the dresser. Do you need to lower closet rungs to make it easier? You want to make the closet work for the child, not the other way around. As your child grows, you need to make adjustments.

Resource Files

Check out the "closet doubler" at www.organize-everything.com. For less than $15, you can double the capacity of the closet and bring a rod down to child level. Use the top part of the rod for out-of-season clothes or ones that are worn less often.

There are also rod extenders that suspend from the high rod to create a lower, second tier. This might just be at the right height for your child. Taking the doors off closets can also make it easier to put clothes away. Add a curtain that can be slid back to reveal the contents and add color to the room.

Perhaps a wardrobe or armoire scaled to your child's size would be less daunting. A chiffarobe is an old-fashioned piece of furniture for children with a small closet on one side and shelves and/or drawers on the other. We've had one in our family for generations, and it's still in use. If you search for one, you'll find both antique ones and some still being made by woodworkers who know their value and usefulness.

Hooks work better for some things. Backpacks, nightclothes, coats, and jackets are just some of the things you might want to provide hooks for, either in your child's room or at the morning launching pad, which we talk about in "We Have Liftoff!" later in the chapter.

Resource Files

I found a lovely chiffarobe online made in the traditional configuration in both oak and cherry wood from a company called Amish Traditions at 3233 State Route 39, P.O. Box 339, Nashville, OH 44661. Their phone number is 330-378-2791, and they have a website at amishtraditions.com. Maybe you'll want to be the first to have one in your family to pass down to future "little folks" in generations to come.

If you decide to use a dresser in a child's room, the drawers need to be light enough and low enough for your child to maneuver them. Make sure the hardware is child-size as well and that the drawers aren't so deep he has to dig down to get to the bottom. Tape pictures to the drawers so your younger child knows what goes in which one. If clothes are falling out of the drawers and your child can't close them, he has too many clothes!

I'm a big fan of bins for almost all of a child's things. Use bins for things such as socks, underwear, and any other multiples of smaller things. I also like shelves for clothes better than drawers, but you should experiment and find what works best for your child. Use plastic containers or baskets to sort clothes and keep them from falling over on shelves. You can also purchase wire dividers to help keep stacks in shape.

Get a shoe rack that sits at the bottom of the closet or one with little cubbies for each pair and "put shoes to bed" when they're not out playing.

Encourage good grooming habits by putting a mirror at child level either in their room or in their bathroom. Have the things they need to brush their hair and teeth easy to get to. Make sure there's a hamper in their room and encourage your children to use it. Make this part of their nightly ritual. Or perhaps you have a spot where you can set up a shared family laundry system and can teach them the sorting method we talked about earlier. By the ages of six and eight, my two daughters were sorting their laundry and helping to wash, dry, fold, and put away their own clothes. It's not rocket science!

Little Paper Monsters Soon Become Big Ones!

Even before kids go to school, they'll be creating works of art and "notes to Mommy" at an alarming rate. What do you do with all those papers? When they set foot into kindergarten, the real paper blitz begins.

First, realize that you can't (and they can't) keep everything. Second, realize that everything is not of equal value. Third, understand that time both increases and decreases the value of things. I still have both of my daughters' first "drawings." They are precious and have definitely grown in value both to me and to them over the years. But the second, third, and fourth drawings are long gone and aren't missed. We must learn to identify milestones and commemorate them. Then we must learn that over time we do new work and create better things and we can let the old things go.

Talk over with your child what matters to him. What things does he think he'll like to look at a year from now? Try to honor to some degree these desires, but also set limits with him about what can be retained in a designated space for a designated time. Have one large box of long-term storage for childhood and school papers and at the end of each year sort through the current pile and pick out the most important ones to both of you.

Have two places in your child's room to keep papers that are easy for him to maintain. One is a folder for the week's papers and might sit on his desk or worktable. The other is a box that might be on a shelf that can hold a year's worth of papers that are selected out of each week's pile and stored. This is the box you'll go through together at the end of year to find the gems you want to keep for posterity. Again the lessons here are setting limits and learning what's important and valuable. Just respect your child's wishes as much as you can and allow him to decide what he's ready to let go of and when.

If there's space in your child's room for a filing cabinet (you may want to work this into their desk arrangement), you can teach the filing habit early. You can have separate folders for artwork, test papers, reports, and so on and purge them at the end of each school year together. What was exciting at the beginning of the school year will likely have a different cast to it as summer fun begs for their attention.

You probably want to keep important test scores and report cards in your own family files along with medical files for each member of the family.

Artwork poses a different challenge. Your child will be proud of what she made and will want to display it, at least for a time. Be sure to date artwork so what you finally end up keeping for posterity will have added meaning. Make comments on the back that might be especially meaningful in years to come.

A great display idea for artwork is to attach a cord or clothesline to the wall on both ends using inexpensive plant or picture hooks and adding clothespins along the cord. Your child now has a removable, ever-changing art show the she can direct by herself. An indication that a work of art has lost its luster is when your child removes it in favor of something new she's proud of to take its place. This may be the time to suggest throwing it away.

If Johnny or Janey makes a large picture or project that's really difficult to store or display, take a picture of the child holding their treasure and keep or display that instead. You may want to have a special shelf in the living room or family room that's a temporary place for the "honorary object of the week." At the end of the week, it gets recorded on film or pixels for posterity and tossed.

Speaking of pixels, if you're handy with a computer there are all sorts of digital applications for your child's artwork. Scan in some of the best and create a slide show or collage and send it to grandparents, aunts and uncles, and whoever else would love to see your budding artist's talents take shape.

Artwork that your child is especially enchanted with can be laminated and turned into a place mat or framed as a permanent piece of artwork for his room or a common family area. Another great idea I've heard for kids who just love to draw is to get a roll of butcher paper and let them color and draw to their heart's content. Roll the paper up as they go and use it at holiday time for wrapping paper. What a super idea that supports recycling, too!

Notices from school should be handed to you when the kids come home each day, or there should be a designated place for them that you check each day. Put important deadlines and dates on the family calendar and in your planner/organizer. If your child is old enough to have a planner/organizer of his own, make sure he's done the same.

Form letters and checklists are great! Why reinvent the wheel every time you need to send in a permission slip or release form or a note justifying an absence? Make up a checklist for school trips or family outings or even for morning routines. Post ones that would be helpful where the family is most likely to see it. Perhaps a good spot is by the door or at your Command Center.

Make sure there's a trash can in each child's room for papers and other garbage. No food allowed, though! Just like adults, kids need a place for storing books and magazines. Teach them the principle you learned in Chapter 6. When there are more than three months' worth of magazines, something has to go. Using containers to set limits with children is an awesome idea! Don't throw away anything without asking first though. That's a no-no.

We Have Liftoff!

Everybody in the family can benefit from a launching pad in the morning. This is where everyone gets to put the things they need each day to get them out the door. You know yourself, if the morning goes off in a smooth and orderly way, that's how you're set up for the rest of the day. Why not create a place and a routine that makes every morning a "fresh start?"

Mom and Dad need a place to put their keys, coats, wallet, and purse. Kids need somewhere to store their backpacks and lunch sacks. Is there a place near the door, perhaps in a foyer or corner of whatever room the door opens up into, where you can create a morning liftoff center? Ideally it would have cubbies for each person, a hook for each family member, and maybe one for the dog's leash while you're at it.

Label or color-coordinate hooks and cubbies (bins under a bench for sitting on as you put on and remove shoes might be another solution) so there's no mistake about whose is whose. This might also be a good place to hang a message board if you haven't already found a better place for it. A dry erase board works well or a well-tended bulletin board with a pad and pencil attached. The family calendar might be located here as well, although having it at your Command Center is also a good idea. See which works best for you and your family.

Under the hooks, you want to locate that shoe rack I mentioned earlier. If it's winter and there are likely to be muddy boots, have a boot tray there as well.

If you're having trouble finding space for your launching pad, look up! Is there a way to create shelves with bins or a cubbyhole unit on the wall? If you're afraid the entryway will look cluttered put it behind closed doors. But remember when designing your morning madness solution to keep short people (children) in mind.

If older kids have a lot of different activities on different days during the school week, have a duffel bag or tote bag for each activity ready and organized ahead of time so all they have to do is grab that day's "activity bag." Keep these in a designated place and make sure they clean or restock anything they might need for the activity the following week. Different colored bags will make grabbing the right one easier.

Chores and To-Dos

The best way to raise responsible, caring kids is to give them responsibilities and things to take care of. Very young children can have household chores to do, even if they're as simple as pushing in their chair when they get up from the table and tucking their dolly in at night to start.

Charts are a super way to get kids interested in doing chores. Start with a chart of the chores related to where he lives—his room! By age three or four, a child can begin to take responsibility for picking up her room every night before bed and putting away pajamas every morning. She can even help with making her bed or dusting. After a good system for sorting and putting away clothes has been put into place, there's no reason why a small child can't help put underwear, socks, shoes, and other clothes in their appropriate spots.

You can make a master chart with chores illustrated along the top and days of the week along the left side. Use pictures or drawings with words underneath to show what each chore is to be. You can photocopy your chart and reuse it every week. We used to use gum-backed silver and gold stars when chores were completed in the "old days." Now there are lots of colorful stickers and rubber stamps to spice things up.

Make doing chores a positive time where you get to spend time together and wherever possible add poems, slogans, stories, games, and songs to make it more fun. If he's having a bad day and feels like rebelling, just pick up where you left off tomorrow. But no fair doing it *for* him!

As your child becomes ready to take on more responsibility, make a new chart and celebrate "stepping up" to a new level. Add a reward to the celebration to mark their accomplishment, such as a special day trip, activity, item, or even some money to spend as he wishes and a shopping trip. If you opt for the shopping trip, use this as an opportunity to teach yet another lesson. The name of this lesson is "Where Will it Go?" If it doesn't have a home, you'll have to make one or something old will have to go.

Provide the right tools for children to do their chores. If you want to teach them to do housework, why not provide them with their own equipment scaled to their tiny hands and height so they don't have to struggle? How well could you dust with a

Resource Files

A bright, colorful chore chart that hangs on the wall with hooks and hanging cards that are color-coded for different times of the day and personalized for your child is available online at www.onlineorganizing.com. It's called "I Did My Chores" and is personalized for your child. Cards are placed in the "I Did It!" pocket when they're done, and there are reward tokens parents can give out.

Wise Words

"Train up a child the way he should go, and when he is old he will not turn from it."
—Proverbs 22:6

giant's duster, anyhow? It may be as simple as cutting down a handle. Use mild cleaning solutions such as vinegar and baking soda that are safe for even a very young child to handle.

To make beds easier to make, use a comforter or "bed sack" instead of sheets and blankets. Forget the bedspread! To make it easier for kids to dress themselves, buy clothes that have fasteners that are easy to open and close.

You need to teach children how to do their chores before you can expect them to do what you're asking. Don't assume they know how or that they can just learn by watching. Break tasks down into smaller steps and explain them clearly, and then show them how the steps are done. Then let your child try it on his own with your guidance and heap on the praise when he's done.

Jump Starts

Bissell makes a fully functional Barbie vacuum for kids. It has a removable filter and is just the right size for toddlers learning how to keep their rooms clean. You can also find small dustpan and brush sets. Sur La Table (www.surlatable.com) has a nice broom and pan set for kids. Look for other tools that are pint-size to give children a jump on their chores. How about a work apron that's just their size?

Also give them guidelines, including the time of day jobs need to be done. If feeding pets is one of their chores, they need to have a specific time to do it. But don't watch their every move. After you've done a task with them a couple of times, give them a chance to perform it on their own and check the results. Don't be overly critical or set standards that are too high. Know what to expect from a child of a particular age and take into account your child's specific talents and limitations. Don't redo a task after a child has done it. That's a sure way to discourage cooperation and create low self-esteem.

Having a specific time and place where homework is done each day is a good rule. This creates consistency and makes it easier to get started. Provide a desk in your child's room for doing homework. At our house homework was usually done as a family at the kitchen table. For some reason that worked well for us. Wherever the "homework habit" takes place, make sure there's a caddy or set of drawers for keeping supplies and reference books. This way you can create a "homework zone," even if it is used for another activity at dinnertime.

Divide larger jobs into smaller definable tasks. Expect boys and girls to do the same chores. Use a timer to challenge them. Let's see who can make their bed in 15 minutes! Ten! Five! And be consistent. Don't just "let it go" because you're tired or preoccupied. Consistency is the mother of habit.

When children rebel against picking up after themselves and doing other chores, there is usually a good reason. You may be coming down too hard or may be too rigid. Or it may be you've fallen down on the job yourself, and they're taking their clues from you. Or maybe they're simply tired or cranky. Give them some slack, but don't fall back into your old ways (and theirs). Just start over again tomorrow. As Marla Cilley reminds her Flybabies, you are not behind and you don't need to catch up. This is another valuable lesson a child can learn from you.

Older children present different challenges. After all, they've lived all these years with you. What do you expect? Again, the best tool is your own example. When they see you enjoying life more, less stressed out, and more fun to be with, they'll wonder what happened. They may even say something. What a great opportunity to tell them what you've just learned about yourself!

Try not to change your teenager all at once. Put yourself in their shoes. How would it feel if someone suddenly got on a new kick and tried to turn *your* life upside down? Pick the issues that will make the most dramatic difference in *their* lives. And sometimes it's as simple as *asking*. Ask how they feel when they go in their rooms at night. Ask what they think could be done to improve the situation. Maybe a room makeover could be an incentive for taking on more responsibility and picking up after themselves. They get to pick the color (grit your teeth) and decorate they way they want (within reason) after a reasonable amount of time and effort put in toward mending their ways.

Older children can benefit from the same organizing tools you've provided for yourself. They need a Command Center, an organizer/planner, and a filing system just like you! If you create it, they will (maybe) come. The more input they have into creating it, however, the more likely they are to sign on.

One professional organizer suggests using a teacher's planning book (available in office-supply or educator stores) as a planner/organizer for kids. It has big squares for writing and can be set up for subjects and days of the week. There are also other great systems on the market that have been mentioned before in this book. There's sure to be one that will fit your child's needs.

As a parent, it's important to keep the lines of communication open between you, the child, the teacher, and the school so that you can work together to help your child do his best. You can ask the teacher for copies of upcoming assignments, and some teachers even put up this kind of information on the school's website. Let the important "players" know that you're interested, you're watching, and you want to help.

And sometimes you just have to be willing to disengage. If your teenager is keeping up with her homework and getting good grades, doing her household chores, and behaving like a decent human being, maybe you should just make it a rule that the disorder stops at her door and let it go at that. In time, when she gets tired of the tornado she lives in and experiences how the order in the rest of the house makes her feel, she may come around. I can tell you as a grandmother that the one daughter who was so sloppy I thought her room might need to be condemned (and her car definitely needed to) is now an impeccable housekeeper and an efficient, loving mother. So there's hope. Take heart! I can't wait to see whether her son turns out to be a "messy" and how she deals with it!

Rewards

One author told of using a sticker in her family as a way of rewarding children for being responsible and caring on their own. She called it a "Caught Being Good" sticker. Besides heaping praise on a child for what he or she just did, the child got to show off the exemplary behavior with a special visible reward. Recognition is often the best reward.

I have mixed feelings about paying children to do chores. It seems to me that getting an allowance is a separate issue. It might be something you withhold from a child for especially bad behavior, but it shouldn't be a bribe for doing things they should be doing anyway. I especially have a problem with paying children for things they should be doing for their own benefit. If you want to pay your kids to do extra chores around the house, that's up to you, but everyone in the family needs to have responsibilities they're expected to do regardless. The job done is its own reward, and that's a lesson that needs to be learned as well.

Share and Share Dislike!

If kids have to share a room, bunk beds are a great space saver, but make sure each child has a space all his or her own. Some great loft beds have built-in desks and shelves underneath. If the room is small, this may be the best option, and it clearly defines the space for each child.

You want to make sure there's some open space for play and surfaces to write and draw on. If space is really tight, consider a portable table that folds down when not in use. Also look for solutions with a writing surface on top and storage underneath, to make the most of the space, preferably on wheels.

If there's a way to create a partition or curtain or to place the furniture in such a way as to create privacy for each of the room's occupants, give this some serious effort. You'll reap the rewards in peace and quiet, and they'll thank you for it.

Child's Play: Planning Great Parties for Kids

Children's parties can be fun for everyone, including parents, but it takes preparation and planning, with lots of emphasis on the children's participation. Whether it's a birthday celebration, a Halloween party, or a Valentine tea party, children at just about any age can be a part of the decision making, decorating, food preparing, and activity planning. Parties give your child a chance to develop organization and planning skills, as well as to try out social skills, such as how to be a good host, take turns, introduce friends, and observe the house rules while having a good time.

Children can make the invitations with construction paper and crayons or on a computer. There are simple programs just for this purpose. After they're printed out, your child can color and fold them and help address the envelopes. It's best to mail them, rather than have your child give them out at school and run the risk of their not reaching their destination. Kids have a knack for forgetting to tell their parents important things! You want to follow up with a phone call to the children's parents.

Jump Starts

After the party, put all your notes and the recipes that worked best into a file folder or party-planning notebook for the future. Note what worked and what didn't for the next time. Keeping track of quantities per person and costs will help you budget, as well.

Themes help make parties even more fun. Try dinosaurs, "tea," outer space, jungle animals, dressing up, angels, race cars, a time in history (medieval, Renaissance, Western, or Victorian are always fun)—anything that strikes your child's fancy—for his or her next party. If it's a seasonal party or your child enjoys certain activities associated with the season, build them into the party. Make it an apple festival (complete with a trip to the local orchard to pick apples) or a spring nature celebration, winter carnival, or summer pool party.

Be careful to gear the number of guests, the difficulty of the activities, and the duration of the party to the child's age. If you're not sure, ask the child's teacher for suggestions. One idea is to invite as many children as the child's age. Two guests for a two-year-old's party is just about right, and so on. If you're planning a party around an outing, be sure to have enough adults to help for the number of kids in your charge. One adult for every three or four children is a good minimum. If you're going on an outing and bringing food, choose food that's easy to transport and handle, such as juices and cupcakes.

The food can become part of the party's activities. Make cupcakes, for example, and ice them with plain butter-cream icing. Then let children decorate with sprinkles, candy dots, and tubes of decorative icing. This gives them a fun thing to do and saves you time to boot. Children can create their own place mats as a party activity. Give them sheets of construction paper, stickers, magazine cutouts, and crayons, then cover with clear self-stick shelf paper. These mats can be wiped off and taken home when the party's over. For an outer space theme party, for example, have plenty of astronomical stickers, stars, and science magazines to cut up—maybe glue and glitter, too.

Helping your kids get organized means lots more time for fun for everyone, a more peaceful household, and the satisfaction of knowing you're helping them develop skills for living that will serve them well.

Resource Files

If you're looking for more party ideas, here are some books to help you: *The Kids' Pick-a-Party Book: 50 Fun Party Themes for Kids, Ages 2 to 16* by Peggy Warner; *Einstein's Science Parties: Easy Parties for Curious Kids* by Shar Levine and Allison Grafton; and *The Ultimate Sleep-Over Book* by Kayte Kuch.

The Least You Need to Know

- Helping your child get rid of clutter will mean everyone breathes easier. Clutter can affect a child's mood and temperament.

- You need to teach your child how to sort, purge, and organize his things. Just as you had to learn these skills, so will he.

- Charts, consistency, and rewards are good ways of teaching kids to take responsibility in the household and do daily chores.

- Planning and organizing for travel with kids will help everyone have a smooth ride.

- Themes give children's parties a natural sense of organization and cohesiveness.

Part 5

Money and All That Stuff

Money isn't everything, but when there isn't enough to pay the bills, it can certainly seem that way. And then there's the question of what's in store for the future, from as little as a year away when the IRS comes knocking, all the way to retirement.

The next two chapters guide you through an organization plan for the financial side of your life. First, in Chapter 15, you take stock of where you are now and find out how to get control over your current finances. Then in Chapter 16, you prepare to meet the future with financial confidence.

Winning the Money Wars: Guerrilla Budgeting

In This Chapter

- ◆ Assessing your current financial condition and preparing a realistic budget
- ◆ Repairing damaged credit and staying out of debt
- ◆ Getting help out of financial chaos
- ◆ Avoiding credit card fraud
- ◆ Surviving the holidays without plunging into debt
- ◆ Discovering the benefits of frugal living

Organizing your financial life is worthwhile both from a cost/benefit standpoint and as a boon to your sense of well-being and control. In fact, after you get your finances organized, many other areas of your life will seem to skyrocket to new heights overnight. I can't emphasize enough how important this is.

In this chapter, I guide you through the first steps: taking stock, setting up a budget, cutting costs, and repairing credit. You may not need to do all of these, but if you're like many Americans, you've neglected most of them.

Afraid to find out the truth? Don't worry, there's help here even if you're in serious debt or suspect you may have a compulsive spending problem.

Facing Facts About Finances

Let me ask you a question. What are your financial goals, and are you meeting them right now? If your answer is something like, "To be able to find the checkbook," then it's time to take serious action. Whether you're dodging creditors and trying to stretch a paycheck, or wondering how you're going to put the kids through college, the first step is to find out where you are now and make a plan for where you want to be.

Budgeting Baby Steps

Here are the first steps you need to take to set up a budget:

♦ Gather together your monthly bills (*all* of them) and put them in a pile. Weed out any duplicates and be sure you have the very latest statements.

♦ On a piece of paper, write down each payee on a separate line with the amount owed next to it. Add up your total amount of debt. Don't just include minimum payments on your credit cards, but the entire balance. Include the entire balance of any loan you have, including a mortgage. If you're not sure of the balances on your loans, call the lender and find out.

Resource Files

If you're looking for a step-by-step financial management system that's integrated into your overall life organization plan, I highly recommend the book *Your Money or Your Life: Transforming Your Relationship with Money and Achieving Financial Independence* by Joe Dominguez and Vicki Robin. This book can change your life!

♦ Write down any other debts not represented by your monthly bills (for example, a loan from a friend or family member).

♦ In another column, write down the amounts of the fixed bills again, but this time, only include the minimum payments on your credit cards and your regular monthly loan and mortgage payments. Add this column up. You should have now two figures, one representing your total debt and the other representing your debt for the current month. If you're behind on any payments, add those back payments to the second figure.

♦ Now add up all your assets, with one line for each item and the amount written next to it. Include bank account balances, cash, and any paychecks or other payments that haven't yet been deposited, plus any investments, CDs, savings bonds, IRAs, 401(k) plans, life insurance policies, and the like. Add to this the estimated current value of your home, cars, and any other major asset, such as a boat, second home, or valuables. Do *not* include any future payments, such as bonuses or commissions that are not definite or that have not yet been earned. Look only at net income (after taxes) not gross.

♦ Do a second calculation of only your liquid assets—all the cash you could easily lay your hands on without any penalties or fees.

♦ Do a third calculation, this time of your total yearly income. You can do a gross income statement or a net income statement. I prefer to use a gross figure and include in the budget all deductions that might come out of a paycheck (401[k], automatic savings, FICA, Social Security, etc.) in a budget. That way you see where all your money is coming from and where it's going. The gross income system would also work best if you're self-employed. Also include in your year's income statement any anticipated bonuses or commissions.

♦ Arrange to get a copy of your credit report. As we discussed in an earlier chapter, the three major credit bureaus are Equifax, Experian, and TransUnion. To order your credit report, use the following contact information:

Equifax; Equifax Credit Information Services, Inc., P.O. Box 740241, Atlanta, GA 30374; 1-800-685-1111; www.econsumer.equifax.com

Experian; 1-888-397-3742; www.experian.com

TransUnion Corporation, P.O. Box 2000, Chester, PA 19022; 1-800-888-4213; www.transunion.com

All three have online ordering capability. Just follow instructions on their websites.

Looking at your cash on hand and immediate monthly debt, you obviously need to have more in the plus column than the minus column. If that's not the case, you need to look at some of your other assets and see what you can access to pay your bills for this month. If that's not possible, you somehow have to generate enough cash to cover your bills.

> **Pileups!**
>
> While you are preparing a profile of your financial status, it is absolutely *key* not to withdraw and try to ignore the situation. As difficult as it may be to face reality, this is your chance to get valuable information and use it to improve your financial outlook.

Difficult Decisions

You *must* make an honest assessment of exactly where you are and find a way to work your way out of your immediate debt. If you're not standing on the financial precipice, you can skip this section and move on to the budgeting section. But if you're in a financial crisis, consider the following:

♦ Work a second job for a short time to get yourself on a more even keel, while at the same time reducing spending (with a clear budget you can follow)? Do you have a skill you can temporarily use to create some income?

♦ Sell something of value that will take care of the immediate crisis?

♦ Consolidate your debt into one payment at a lower interest rate? Make sure you can afford one lump payment a month as opposed to making smaller payments spread throughout the month.

♦ Declare a moratorium on spending (other than fixed expenses) until you get yourself on track? Try using up the food you have in the house, cutting out all entertainment (read a book), packing a lunch instead of eating out, and walking to work. Challenge yourself to be a tightwad.

♦ Is there any temporary assistance you might qualify for? You know what has to be done if you have more bills than income. It's really pretty simple. You either need to increase your income or reduce your spending. And while we're on the subject of spending, what kind of spender are you?

♦ Do you continue spending on credit, even though you're unable to pay off your current credit card debt?

♦ Do you spend inordinate amounts of time shopping or thinking about shopping?

♦ Do you shop to avoid pressure, to escape or fantasize, to increase your self-esteem, or to feel more secure?

♦ Do others regularly make comments about your excessive spending, or do you spend money you don't have on things you don't need?

> **Jump Starts**
>
> While you are getting your finances in order, separate essential from nonessential expenses and see how many nonessentials you can do completely without—at least until you get yourself out of the woods.

If you answered yes to any of these questions, you may need some help. Go back to Chapter 4 for resources to help get control of your spending.

Back on Track: Creating a Household Budget

After you're out of the fire and back in the frying pan, you need to figure out how you got into the heat in the first place. Go through your checkbook, your credit card statements, and any receipts you have, to gather a picture of what you've spent over the last few months. Include no fewer than three months; six would is even better.

What Are the Details?

Down the left side of a piece of lined paper, write out the following categories:

- **Housing,** which should be broken down into mortgage (or rent), maintenance, homeowner insurance, and utilities.

- **Auto,** which should be broken down into car payments, maintenance, fuel, and auto insurance.

- **Medical and dental** (include each member of the family), with a separate category for medical expenses and insurance.

- **Clothing,** broken down for each member of the family, including dry cleaning.

- **Food,** which includes both groceries and meals out (broken down separately).

- **Child care,** if applicable.

- **Education,** if applicable.

- **Interest** on credit cards and other debt, as well as regular monthly credit card and loan payments.

- **Life and disability insurance payments.** If these are already deducted from your paycheck, look at your pay stubs for the correct amounts and put them in the appropriate category.

- **Taxes,** including federal withholding, Social Security, and state income taxes. Make a separate category for real estate taxes.

- **Entertainment,** including cable or satellite TV bills and video rentals.

> **Jump Starts**
>
> Keeping your finances simple cuts down on clutter and paperwork. Set up a financial center where you manage your other household affairs (your Command Center would be a good place—see Chapter 7), keep bill-paying supplies and financial files handy, give yourself a comfortable chair, and turn on some soothing music. Make your weekly financial chores as pleasant as possible!

- **Gifts,** including holidays.

- **Miscellaneous,** which might include cash expenditures such as lunches, newspapers, cigarettes, and so on.

- **Charitable contributions.** Keep thorough records of your charitable giving. You just might find yourself eligible for a tax break based on your generosity.

- **Savings,** including any automatically deducted 401(k) savings plans.

Across the top of the paper, put each month you're going to be calculating and draw lines down to make a grid. Now write down the total you spent in each category during each month. Be consistent about putting expenses in the same category each time.

Now calculate the monthly average for these categories. In some categories, you can make projections for the year just by multiplying the average by the number of months left in the year. Some categories may need to be adjusted, however, for seasonal variations. For instance, you may find most of your gift category spending is concentrated in the months before Christmas. So if you've calculated a 6-month picture that includes the holiday months, you probably don't need to double that amount to get a 12-month projection. You might only need to add another third or less of that figure for the remaining six months of the year.

Add up all your expenses for a grand total, and as a final part of the process, compare your expenditures with your total income.

What Do the Details Tell You?

Where do you stand? Are some areas, such as food or entertainment, way out of whack? Are you paying higher mortgage or rent payments than you can afford? Are utility bills, especially phone bills, too high?

Pileups!

Don't get caught short! Overestimate your expenses and underestimate your income. If you make more or spend less than you figured, rejoice and use it to pay off debt or deposit the windfall into savings.

If facing the facts means you can see that you're living too high on the hog for your income, you have some decisions to make. Again, it's a matter of "stuff" versus "time." Some people would rather work more hours or find a better job so they can make more money and enjoy the lifestyle they want. Others would rather have more time for themselves and choose voluntary simplicity, either saving money for the things they want or simply doing without.

But the facts are clear—you need to either cut expenses or increase income. Otherwise, you're headed for disaster.

In addition to the obvious areas where expenditures are too high, take a look at the less obvious areas where you can save money. Have you done some comparison shopping for insurance rates lately? Perhaps you can lower your monthly payments. Have you looked at mortgage or car loan rates lately? Would a refinance at a lower rate help your situation?

If you've done your assessment and realize you should have more money than you do, then you probably have a spending leak you're not aware of. The cure for this problem is to keep a spending diary for a few weeks. In your planner/organizer, write down every penny you spend, recording the date, what was bought, and how much was spent. Look for patterns and categories you may have missed.

From this exercise, you can now develop a budget. Transfer your categories to another sheet and transfer fixed expenses. Next, decide on cost control measures and come up with realistic figures you can adhere to each month for variable expenses, and put down those amounts on your budget sheet.

If after a couple of months you still can't seem to control your budget, make yourself stick to a cash system. If you haven't done so already, do away with all credit cards (you may want to consider a debit card, however, only for emergencies), and even stop using your checking account for a while. Put all money into a savings account and pay all your fixed expenses with cash or money orders. Whatever's left is what you have to live on. This takes discipline, but it can really help get you on the right track. If a cash system is the only way you can make ends meet, stick to it for a while. In the meantime, you may want to take emotional stock, too. What is it about you and money, anyway?

This is your chance to figure out your relationship with money and get it right. You may find that when you begin organizing your life you end up changing your life in deeper, more meaningful ways than you ever imagined. Who ever thought that getting organized could help get you out of debt and raise your standard of living?

Resource Files

If you're looking for ways to cut costs, join the ranks of the tightwads and frugal-living advocates. Check out *Living More with Less* by Doris Janzen Longacre (Herald Press, 1980); and Mary Hunt's *The Cheapskate Monthly* at www.cheapskatemonthly.com.

Budget Review

In the beginning, it's probably a good idea to review your budget each month after you pay your bills (more often, if necessary). This holds you to a monthly standard and you'll know immediately whether you're going over or under what you estimated. If you decided you needed to cut costs in certain areas, you'll see how your efforts have panned out—and if you succeeded, you'll be motivated to continue the trend.

When you achieve some monthly financial discipline, I recommend building a quarterly review into your schedule. Make sure to put the date in your planner/organizer so you don't forget. It's a good idea to hold yourself accountable on a regular basis. You can correct any problems before they turn into disasters, and if you're ahead of the game, you can channel resources into savings and investments.

When you get out of debt and tame your financial tigers, you'll be amazed at the energy you'll regain and the extra time you'll have. The more you owe, the more enslaved you are, and the more time you spend trying to catch up. Free yourself of the burden and worry of debt.

Computer Finance Tactics

Several good computer software programs can help you manage your finances. For fifteen years, I have used Quicken from Intuit, which is one of the most popular. The best packages are set up in checkbook format. You can either hand-write checks and simply record deposits and withdrawals in your computer, print checks directly from the program, or pay bills electronically online.

There are many benefits of using a computer program for managing your finances, including the following:

- Balancing the checkbook takes less time.

- All accounts are searchable and integrated, so you can find things faster when you need to track an item down.

- Online paying of bills is cheaper per transaction than the cost of a stamp and envelope, and it eliminates having to write a check.

- You can set up, modify, and monitor your budget, right in your computer program.

- Tracking investments is easier.

- ◆ Online banking, featured in the top programs, allows you to make funds transfers and get up-to-date balances without leaving home, any time of the night or day.

- ◆ When tax time rolls around, you can pull things together faster by assigning categories to all your transactions as you enter them.

Some additional features, depending on the program, are the ability to set up a debt-reduction program, do mortgage comparisons, develop overall family financial plans, keep a home inventory, and get online stock quotes.

You do need to enter the information, however, and that takes time. The initial setup, where you enter all your financial information to get started, can take many hours, but the benefits in terms of knowing where your money goes and saving time in the long run make the effort worth it. I suggest setting aside time once a week to enter your information so it doesn't pile up. Some credit card companies and banks that are online are now integrated with financial software, so you can shortcut a lot of the hand entering. See whether yours are.

> **CAUTION**
>
> **Pileups!**
>
> A computer program can do certain things efficiently—for example, it will catch mathematical mistakes you might otherwise miss. But remember that it is only as good as the information you give it. Take care that the information you type in is accurate and complete.

It's a good idea to choose a regular day to do your financial record keeping. Fridays are my time in the office to do paperwork, file, catch up on correspondence, and handle various odds and ends. I add to that paying the week's bills and entering my deposits and the checks I've written into my personal finance software. My son-in-law does his every day after work. He pays bills as they come in and enters the day's checks and statements. This way he's on top of his finances all the time.

Don't forget to back up your computer data periodically, as well. I do this on Fridays, along with all my other maintenance chores; but whenever you do it, do it *regularly*.

You'll need to decide whether using personal finance software is for you. Ask someone to give you a demonstration. Talk to people who use it and get their feedback. If you decide to use a manual system, do just that—use a *system*, and use it faithfully. The important thing is to keep track of where your money goes and stick to your budget. Whatever tools best help you do that are the ones to use.

Don't Let Santa Blow Your Budget!

Every year when the holidays roll around, families brace themselves for the ensuing debt. And they often spend much of the following year climbing out. This doesn't have to be the case ever again, if you make a pact with yourself and your family *right now!*

The vast majority of families don't make a holiday budget. Without a plan, disaster is far more likely. When you make up your overall family budget, don't forget to include holiday spending.

There are at least two good strategies for handling holiday spending so that it doesn't put you into debt. One is to put a portion in savings just for the holidays each month, and use only that money when shopping time comes. This means *no* credit. What you've saved is what you can spend.

A second strategy is to budget a small amount for gift buying throughout the year and do your shopping a little at a time, taking advantage of sales and the less-frenzied shopping environment. Catalogs and online stores can also help, and although shipping can add to the overall cost of the item, keeping you out of the stores may mean less money spent in the end.

Some families set up a gift exchange early in the year, drawing names so each family member only needs to shop for one person. The benefits are obvious—there's only one person to shop for, so you can get just the right gift, and the financial pressure is removed. Or you can set a cap on spending for each gift—not to exceed, say, $25. This can present a fun challenge, as each person tries to outdo the other for less. It also makes it easy to budget.

> **Pileups!**
>
> Beware of "pay later" or "skip a payment" offers from credit companies. The interest still accumulates, so read the fine print. The same warning applies to "checks" you may be sent in the mail. These are actually loan applications, often with very high interest rates.

Or consider alternatives to traditional store-bought gifts. Make something instead. I like to make what I call "consumables," which are items that are used up and don't remain as clutter after the holidays. Food items, bath salts, potpourri, and homemade toiletries are a few suggestions. We also give holiday coupons, which entitle the bearer to any one of a number of services to be redeemed at a later date. These could be for baby-sitting, a massage, a car wash, a day running errands, preparing a meal, cleaning—use your imagination! Or how about a pair of tickets and your time? One year we gave contributions to a worthy cause in each relative's name. This works well for the people on your list who have *everything*. Throughout the year, they usually received a newsletter or regular updates, and nothing had to be returned because it was the wrong size or a duplicate!

Credit CPR

Even though you may now have a handle on your budget and you've got your expenses down, what do you do if you've ruined your credit?

You can take some definite steps to repair damaged credit. You've already taken the most important one—you've done an honest inventory of your financial situation, set up a budget, and begun to get yourself out of debt.

Here are the next basic steps for repairing your credit:

- ◆ Find out how bad it is. You should have already requested your credit report from the major credit bureaus mentioned earlier in this chapter. If you haven't, do it now. You can't see what has to be done until you know where you stand.

- ◆ Contact your local credit bureau, which is basically a credit-reporting agency that may cover only a single state or county. If you're not sure whom to call, check your local Yellow Pages under "Credit-Reporting Agencies." Call them all.

- ◆ Look for any inaccuracies or missing accounts on your report after you receive it. You may request an investigation of anything that's incorrect or incomplete. You can also have out-of-date information removed by writing a letter to the credit bureau. You are also entitled to tell your side of the story in any credit dispute that is on your record by sending a letter to be added to your file.

> **Jump Starts**
>
> Ordinarily you have to pay for copies of your credit reports. If you have recently been turned down for a loan or credit card, however, you can get a free copy from the agency that reported your credit, as long as you act quickly. Send the agency a copy of the credit denial letter with your written request to see your report.

- ◆ Make sure you follow up on any changes and request a copy of your updated file to make sure the changes were made.

- ◆ Reduce the number of credit cards you carry. One is usually enough. Two might be helpful if you own your own business, to keep expenses separate.

◆ Return all unwanted credit cards to the issuing company. Just cutting them up means they're still on your credit file. Ask the company to close the account and send you a letter of verification stating you requested the account to be closed.

◆ Leave credit cards at home unless you're making a planned and budgeted purchase.

◆ Only charge items you're able to pay cash for. Remember to calculate into the cost the interest charges if you don't pay your credit card bill right away. Imagine what that interest money would earn you if it were invested at an 8 percent return. Investing $250 a month at that rate would grow to almost $600,000 in 35 years.

◆ Buy yourself a copy of Robin Leonard's *Money Troubles: Legal Strategies to Cope with Your Debts*, and read it! There are probably things you can do to help yourself you didn't even know were possible.

◆ Make sure your credit file includes any positive account histories that might be missing. Try to build a positive credit history when you're financially healthy by borrowing small amounts using a secured credit card or bank passbook as collateral, or by finding a cosigner. Be diligent about making payments in full and on time.

How to Avoid Credit Fraud and Identity Theft

Credit fraud costs everybody money, even if it never happens to you. Credit card companies cover the cost of fraud through higher fees and interest rates, and it's a growing problem. And identity theft is one of the fastest growing crimes in America today.

Types of Credit Fraud

There are different kinds of credit fraud, some more easily detected than others. The most common is the lost or stolen credit card, which can be stopped simply by reporting the loss or theft to the issuing company. But some fraud can occur even when you have possession of your card. Criminals steal account numbers through a variety of methods, including telephone or Internet scams, looking over your shoulder and copying the information from your card when you're not looking, or "dumpster diving"—taking information from receipts or account statements you've thrown in the trash.

A more serious form of fraud is "identity theft," where a criminal uses your name and Social Security number to take over existing credit accounts and/or start new ones in your name.

Avoiding Fraud

How do you prevent this kind of fraud? Well, getting yourself organized as you have, following the steps in this chapter, will go a long way toward keeping you out of harm's way. You're more aware of what's happening with your accounts, you've gotten your credit reports, and you've cut down the number of credit cards you have. These are all steps to preventing credit fraud. Some other tips are the following:

- Treat your credit cards the same way you would cash.

- Don't carry your Social Security card, birth certificate, or passport with you on a regular basis. That way, if your purse or wallet is stolen, you minimize the information a criminal has.

- Sign your credit cards as soon as you get them. (As an added safeguard, next to your signature on your credit card write with a permanent maker "Ask for photo ID.")

- Know the billing dates of your credit cards and call the issuing company if the bill is late. It may mean someone has diverted your bill to a different address.

- Read your statements carefully each month and check for charges you didn't make. Report them immediately. Each month I enter my credit card purchases under individual categories in my finance software for tax purposes, so I'm on top of my statements and can detect any irregularities.

- Don't give anyone credit card or any other personal information over the phone or online, unless you initiated the communication.

- Get a shredder and use it. Shred all pre-approved credit card offers, receipts, and any other documents that indicate your credit card number.

- Get a credit report once a year and check it for errors.

Wise Words

"Through want of enterprise and faith men are where they are, buying and selling, and spending their lives like serfs."
—Henry David Thoreau

Another credit ploy to be avoided is so-called "credit doctors" or "credit-repair" companies. They charge a fee for something you can easily do yourself, and some are actually conducting scams, promising to expunge negative but accurate credit information from your record. (This is not legally possible.) Instead, contact the National Foundation for Credit Counseling at 1-800-388-2227 (or at their website at www.nfcc.org/) and get the name of the local member agency near you.

If you suspect identity theft, contact the fraud departments of all three credit bureaus listed in this chapter and log on to the Federal Trade Commission's Identity Theft Resource Center at www.consumer.gov/idtheft for step-by-step instructions and to file a complaint.

Frugal Living Is Fun!

Getting your financial life in order is crucial to organizing the rest of your life. You now know where you stand, you know where you're going, and you have a plan. One benefit to having a financial reckoning may be less noticeable. You may actually have embarked on a lifestyle change, a frugal way of living, and you may find you like it much better that way.

The frugal living/simple living movement (yes, I think we can call it a movement—just look at the number of websites and books on the subject!) is here to stay, and is a logical reaction to the "buy-more, do-more, enjoy-less" direction of much of today's consumerist society. As Joe Dominguez and Vicki Robin put it so well in their book *Your Money or Your Life:* "If you live for having it all, what you have is never enough. In an environment of more is better, 'enough' is like the horizon, always receding." So create financial freedom by living within your means and wanting what you have.

The Least You Need to Know

- ◆ To organize your finances, start by determining exactly what your assets and liabilities are.

- ◆ Designing a realistic budget will keep you on track.

- ◆ If your credit is damaged, you can take some simple steps to repair it on your own.

- ◆ Nonprofit agencies can help you with debt counseling or financial planning; beware of quick-fix "credit doctors."

- ◆ Debt elimination can be the beginning of a healthier (and happier) financial lifestyle.

Chapter 16

Tax Tactics and Advanced Money Maneuvers

In This Chapter

♦ Getting a head start on April 15

♦ What records to keep and for how long

♦ Organizing your insurance information

♦ Preparing your will

♦ Tricks to organize yourself into saving

♦ Choosing a financial planner and accountant

If your tax, insurance, will, and investment records are in a jumble, you're playing a high-stakes procrastination game. As you saw in the preceding chapter, a little sober reflection and a solid plan can get your household budget straightened out. In this chapter, you're going for the longer view and looking at your future. How well you prepare for it will determine whether it's rosy or not. You'll also put your affairs in order so if anything happens to you the people you care about won't be burdened by any lack of preparation or disorganization on your part. Think of it as a gift, both to yourself and to those who survive you.

There are benefits to financial planning in the here and now, as well. Because you're on top of things, you'll be able to sleep well at night. Moreover, you'll have the information you need to take advantage of financial opportunities and adjust your plan if the winds of change dictate. The disorganized person doesn't know what's happening and leaves everything to luck or providence. You, of course, know better than that!

The Tax Man Cometh

Are you one of those people who file for an extension every year because you just can't get your records together or even face preparing your forms? Do you always have that nagging feeling you might have been able to pay less or get back more if you'd been more together?

Well, you're going to fix that right now. First of all, let's review a bit. In Chapter 6, we organized your household financial records. If you haven't done that already, go back to Chapter 6, reread that section, and *do it now!* This is the first step in getting ready for tax time, this year and in years to come. If you're thinking of buying a personal finance software program, do it now and take the time to enter your information.

Resource Files

If you're a computer maven, consider getting a program called Personal RecordKeeper, available for Windows from Nolo Press at www.nolo.com. Personal RecordKeeper is a predesigned database program that tells you everything you need to keep and even where to store it!

It will take longer to prepare your tax return if your financial records are incomplete or scattered hither and yon. If you have a professional prepare your taxes, it'll cost you more, the more he has to pull together. So I'll say it again: get your regular financial files complete wherever your Command Center is set up, and keep them up-to-date. Doing a little bit each week or month (however often you pay bills) will make tax preparation relatively simple. Now that you're on a budget, you should have an idea of what's ahead. When tax time arrives, it's a good time to evaluate your budget and see whether you're on target.

The Not-So-Tender Tax Traps

Here are some common mistakes taxpayers make that can be the indirect result of keeping poor records.

◆ **Forgetting or not budgeting for a tax-deferred retirement plan contribution.** According to the Institute of Certified Financial Planners, 34 percent of eligible workers don't participate in 401(k) plans offered at the workplace. If you're self-employed, you need to look into an individual retirement account (IRA) or a simplified employee pension (SEP) plan and see whether you should make a contribution to one of these. If you're not sure, you may need to talk to a financial planner or accountant.

◆ **Having too much withholding deducted from your paycheck.** Why make a tax-free loan to the government when you could be saving or investing that money (or paying off your debt)? If you get a large refund each year, go to your employer and fill out a new W-4.

◆ **Overlooking deductions.** Again, this is where good records can save you money. Did you take all your medical deductions? How about mileage, phone calls, parking, and postage relating to charitable activities? The best way to find these hidden deductions is by going over your planner/organizer. If it's well kept, it will be a record of your day-to-day life over the past year and will tell you where you went, whom you saw, and what phone calls you made.

Pileups!

Don't forget to claim deductions carried over from previous years. Have your previous years' tax returns handy and make sure you've included all losses, depreciations, and so on.

Tax Records Demystified

After you've filed your return, what do you keep and what do you toss? Good question. Here's a simple list of what you should keep:

◆ Receipts for deductible expenses

◆ Canceled checks or bank photocopies for deductible expenses

◆ Canceled checks or bank photocopies for any estimated tax payments, if you're self-employed

◆ Automobile mileage logs

◆ Any other proof of deductible expenses such as your daily planner/organizer sheets with notations of business appointments, and so on

◆ W-2 forms

Jump Starts

Instead of keeping canceled checks in a box, organized by month, you may find it handier to staple them to the invoices of deductible expenses. Because fewer and fewer banks are actually returning canceled checks, it's probably easiest to save your bank statements in one place.

- Interest income statements

- Investment income statements

- 1099 statements

- Records of charitable contributions

- Records of all medical expenses, as well as any medical insurance payments you may have received

- Records of any other deductions, such as mortgage interest, real-estate taxes, or tax preparation fees

- A copy of your annual tax-return form

The only time I was audited, my detailed daily records proved my case. The IRS auditor, after seeing how thorough I was, told me to "just go home." Keep your planner/organizer pages for the year with that year's tax information. They can help you re-create events in case of an audit.

These items all go in whatever container you use to store each year's tax information. There are corrugated cardboard boxes available from local office-supply stores such as Staples or Office Depot or from mail-order and online office-supply houses such as Quill. (You can reach them at 1-800-789-1331 or www.quillcorp.com.) I find the ones made for checks and vouchers to be just the right size to keep a year's worth of tax information, but you may need something bigger, or perhaps can manage with something more compact. Whatever you use, make sure the containers are uniform so they can be stacked easily. If you store your tax records in a location that's prone to dampness, use plastic containers that are tightly sealed. And, of course, *label them!*

CAUTION

Pileups! _____

Don't rely on your memory! If you had anything unusual on a return, such as a discrepancy between your declared income and the sum of your 1099 forms, write a note to include in that year's file box about how you came up with your calculations. You'll never remember three years down the road.

Remember, tax time isn't just another excuse to start piling up all that *stuff* again! Use the same criteria you used for all your paper in Chapter 6. If it's a duplicate of information you have or could easily obtain elsewhere, if it isn't truly related to taxes, and you wouldn't need it in an audit, toss it!

These tossable items include the following:

- Loan books for loans you've already repaid

- Tax-related receipts that are more than seven years old

◆ Canceled checks or receipts for non-tax-related items such as food, spare cash, dry-cleaning, or haircuts

Keep all your statements, receipts, and paid bills until you've had a chance to tally them for the month and check the totals against your budget. If you do this each month, you'll have a handle on where the money's going and be able to decide quickly if you need to adjust your spending, bring in some more cash, or put some money in savings or investments.

How Long Is Long Enough?

How long do you keep your boxes full of tax information? The common wisdom is that you should keep your current year's return plus those from the six previous years. Generally speaking, the IRS can audit up to three years from your due date or the date you finally filed if you were late. However, if auditors suspect a problem with a return, they can go back six more years.

Laws on tax audits vary from state to state, so you must also check with your local tax authorities. And, by the way, the "records" that you keep include electronic records, if you do your cash management or taxes on computer. I recommend keeping a backup disk off-site and updating it regularly.

After you're clear on both federal and state requirements, go back and weed out the previous year's records so you have the essentials, transfer them all to uniform boxes, and label them. Get rid of anything older than six years, except the documents you should keep longer, which are listed next.

Jump Starts

Toss the oldest year's records when you store the newest ones. Just empty the oldest box, relabel (use pencil, so you can erase), and put in the newest information. Hang on to just the tax forms longer than six years. They take up little space and give you an ongoing record of your financial history.

And While You're at It: More Records to Keep

Besides backup information for taxes, there are additional financial records you should have files for and keep. These should be stored in your regular file cabinet, the one you have at your Command Center, or at least somewhere you can easily get at them. First, there are medical records. Keep a file for each person for each year and put in receipts for treatment and prescriptions chronologically, as well as statements from the insurance company. At the very least, keep indefinitely a record of illnesses and injuries, and the doctors who treated them.

In files you store separate from your individual year's tax returns, you should keep the following:

◆ **Profit-and-loss statements,** if you own your own business. These you should probably keep indefinitely. You may need them to apply for a loan, analyze your business direction, or appraise the market value of your business should you decide to sell.

◆ **Personnel records.** Again, this one's for business owners. You need to keep employee records for seven years after an individual has left the company.

Resource Files

To get the skinny on what federal tax information to keep and how long, log on to www.irs.gov, and download the PDF file for IRS Publication 552, "Recordkeeping for Individuals." It's *free* and no long waits on the telephone!

◆ **Payment records** for all equipment you depreciate on your return. You should keep these for seven years after the last return on which the equipment (such as a computer or fax machine) is listed.

◆ **Pension records.** Keep your 401(k), IRA, or SEP records in a separate file and hang on to them until you retire and are happily spending the money. Keep both the plan documents and the statements, at least the annual ones.

◆ **Investment records.** If you're investing money that's not tax-deferred in stocks or mutual funds, keep records of all your transactions so you can create a basis for those assets when you sell them. If your annual statement shows all your transactions for the past 12 months, you can keep that and toss the monthly or quarterly statements. If not, you need to keep them all.

◆ **Data about your home,** if you own one. This includes bills, canceled checks, and invoices for any improvements you make. When you sell, you can reduce the tax due on your profit by deducting the cost of permanent home improvements.

◆ **Receipts for high-ticket purchases** such as expensive jewelry, antiques, and artwork. You may need these as proof of value in case they're lost or stolen and you need to file a claim. The best place for these might be with your Home Inventory file (we discuss this in the following section on insurance), in a separate Valuables file or, if you have a lot of valuables, in separate files by category.

Hard-to-replace original documents, such as birth certificates, cemetery deeds, marriage papers, and the like should be kept in a safety deposit box, but only if your state law doesn't require the box to be sealed upon the owner's death. In that case, you may want to consider keeping a fireproof safe on your own premises or having your lawyer keep them.

Get the Most from Your Insurance

Being disorganized can cost you money when you need to file insurance claims. When you did your budget, you may have found you were short on cash. Did you overlook medical insurance claims you may have failed to file? If someone broke into your house, could you document what was taken and its value? Do you know whether your auto insurance covers a cracked windshield?

Setting Up

If you haven't already done it, set up files for each of the different types of insurance you have. For most people that'll be four files: Health, Auto, Life, and Homeowner or Renter insurance. If you're self-employed, you might need to add a file for business disability income and/or liability insurance.

Some people recommend storing life insurance policies in a safety deposit box. I think, however, that if they aren't stored in the home, they can easily be forgotten in case of emergency: out of sight, out of mind. Besides, you can get replacement copies of your policy from your insurance company, and if you have an emergency, you'll probably need it to refer to right away. If you have a fireproof box or safe, keep your policies there rather than in your safety deposit box.

I suggest putting basic policy information for all types of insurance you carry in your planner/organizer on one sheet. Include the type of insurance, the insurer, the policy number, deductible amount, agent information or number to call to make a claim, the dates the policy is in force, the key provisions of the policy, and anything you might find useful in an emergency.

Resource Files

For a comprehensive glossary of insurance terms, check out the list online at www.insweb.com/learningcenter/glossary/general-a.htm.

Always Read the Fine Print

Now gather up your policies and read them. I don't want to hear all that moaning and groaning! This is for your own good. Just go through each policy and make some quick notes on what your coverage includes, plus any exceptions. How big a deductible do you have? Does your homeowner policy cover water or wind damage? How about vandalism? If your home is completely destroyed, does your coverage provide for guaranteed replacement cost? Ask similar questions for your auto, health, and other insurance policies.

Be critical. Ask questions about what the policy says and means. Imagine different scenarios that could occur and whether you'd be covered. If you're confused and need something explained, call your insurance agent and go over the information until you're satisfied you understand it. You need to know what you have before you can evaluate it. Even if you decide you can't afford better coverage, at least you know where you stand, and you may want to plan on upgrading in the future. An annual insurance review with your agent is a good idea in any event.

If you haven't evaluated your insurance coverage lately, you want to make sure it meets your current needs. If there have been any substantial changes, such as the birth of a child or a marriage, you need to revamp your coverage. Now that you know what you have, make a few phone calls and see whether you can get better rates or increased coverage for the same rate. Be sure to ask whether you're entitled to any discounts. Some homeowner policies have discounts for nonsmokers and seniors. Health insurance discounts vary from company to company. Auto policies have discounts for safe drivers with no accidents or tickets over an extended period of time.

> **Pileups!**
>
> If you're self-employed, don't overlook disability income coverage, business insurance, and liability coverage. If you have a home office, you may be able to extend your homeowner or renter insurance to cover your business equipment and inventory, but more often than not, you need a separate business policy.

Opinions vary on how much life insurance you should buy, and what kind. I'm not an insurance specialist, so I can't advise you. When you go over your total insurance situation, you should inform yourself about life insurance and assess whether you ought to carry it, how much, and what type.

Stake Your Claim!

The next thing you need to review is the claims procedure. Do you have all the forms you need? Do you have all the information you might need to make a claim? For homeowner insurance claims, this means knowing what you have (or had before it was stolen or damaged). Aha! Now you understand why we talked about doing a home inventory in Chapter 13. If you haven't done it yet, put it on your schedule and do it as soon as possible.

Pull out your medical bills and see whether you've neglected to file any claims. Find in your policy (or ask your agent) how far back you can make claims, and submit as far back as you're allowed. Even if you don't get any money back, you at least have everything applied toward your deductible for future medical expenses that you're entitled to. If your doctor or hospital doesn't file claims for you, make sure from now on that you place claims to be made in your Action file, kept at your Command Center. That way, you won't forget.

The basic message I'm trying to get across is this: know where you stand, take advantage of everything you're entitled to, and be prepared to document any future claims you could conceivably have to make. By having your insurance materials filed so you can find them, reading your policies, making any claims you've failed to make, and completing your home inventory, you have made the most important steps toward getting that part of your life organized.

Having a Will Gives You a Way

Experts estimate that 70 percent of Americans die with no will. So let me ask you—do you have one? If your answer is no, chances are you have your reasons. Which one of these has the ring of truth for you?

- ◆ I'm too young.

- ◆ I don't own enough.

- ◆ Everyone knows who gets what.

- ◆ It costs too much.

- ◆ I don't have the time.

- ◆ It's hard to find a good lawyer.

- ◆ I don't like making these kinds of decisions.

Resource Files

Good books and software programs available for writing your own will include *Nolo's Simple Will Book* and their *Quick & Legal Will Book;* and Quicken WillMaker Plus (Nolo for Windows; call 1-800-728-3555 or visit www.nolo.com).

Guess what? None of these excuses cuts it. As long as you're an adult and have some assets that would need to be divided up if you died, you need a will.

Be advised that if you don't have a will, the state decides what happens to your assets and belongings, and it may decide in a way you wouldn't want. By the way, if you're married, don't assume that everything goes to your spouse. It may end up being divided equally between your spouse and your children, and maybe even your parents!

Initial Considerations

In organizing your thoughts to write your will, you need to ask yourself some questions beforehand:

♦ What specific property do you have that you would like to go to certain individuals and who are they? If those people die before you do, would you like your bequest to go to their heirs, to someone else, or to an organization or charity?

This is another good reason to do your home inventory, as recommended in Chapter 13. You can refer to it now and select those items of value, monetary or sentimental, that you'd like specific people to have.

♦ Do you need to name a guardian to care for your children? If you have someone in mind, have you discussed it with him or her? Would that person also manage your children's money and property? If not, who would?

♦ Who will be the personal representative (called an *executor* in some states) for your estate? Have you discussed it with them?

♦ Are there any debts that would need to be paid off, and are there specific assets you would like used to make those payments?

♦ Are there assets your personal representative should use to pay off estate and inheritance taxes and probate expenses?

♦ Is there anyone (person or organization) you'd like to have whatever's left from your estate after specific instructions have been carried out?

> **CAUTION**
>
> **Pileups!**
>
> Will-writing software, books, or kits may be adequate if your needs are simple. If you have considerable assets, children under the age of 18, or other special conditions, you should probably seek the advice of a lawyer who specializes in estate planning. It couldn't hurt to do a draft first, though.

These are just a few things you should think over (and discuss with your spouse, if you're married) before meeting with an estate lawyer or sitting down to write your own will. You may want to consider transferring property by means other than a will. This saves on probate fees and taxes. Some of these ways are as follows:

- ◆ Gifts

- ◆ Living trusts

- ◆ Joint tenancy

- ◆ Pay-on-death bank accounts

- ◆ Marital trusts

- ◆ Life insurance

You should discuss these options with a knowledgeable estate planner and find out whether any of them would benefit you in your current situation.

A word about where to store the original copy of your will—some people recommend storing it in your safety deposit box, but that may be a problem if, as mentioned earlier, your state law requires your box to be sealed upon your death. Find out, and if your state does seal upon death, have your lawyer or a close member of the family or your executor keep it.

Other Issues

While we're on the subject of wills, you might want to consider preparing a living will. This is another document that explains what you want done about life-prolonging medical care in the event you have a terminal illness and you can't speak for yourself. This can be coupled with a durable health-care power of attorney, also known as a

health-care proxy, which gives someone you choose the ability to make all health-care decisions for you. Together, these are called your advance directives. Laws concerning living wills vary from state to state, especially with regard to state proxy requirements, health care during pregnancy, and witnessing and notarizing requirements.

Another document you may want to prepare is a durable power of attorney, which gives someone you choose the power to make financial decisions for you in case you become mentally incapacitated. You can make this power fairly limited or very broad in scope. That's up to you.

Resource Files

You can get help writing many of the documents referred to here by using your favorite search engine to locate sample documents and regulations from your state. You can also order prepared forms online at a fairly low cost. Check out www.legalzoom.com and www.findlegalforms.com for some choices.

When preparing your will, either by yourself or with an attorney, the question that should be uppermost in your mind is "what if?" When dealing with money, be careful of giving fixed amounts. Rather, work with percentages. Who knows how much you'll be worth when you die?

Figure on reviewing your will every three years after you work it out. It probably wouldn't hurt to read it over once a year, when you do all your other year-end tasks such as taxes. You're less likely to forget if you make it part of a yearly ritual.

Other times you want to review your will include the following:

- If you get married or remarried
- If you have a child
- Whenever your financial situation changes markedly, as in the case of an inheritance or winning the lottery (lucky you!)
- If you get a divorce
- If you retire
- If your spouse dies

Saving for a Rainy Day

Besides a will, you should give some thought to developing a general financial plan. You may feel you don't have enough assets right now to even think about such a thing, but as soon as you start to accumulate even a little in savings, you want to put those funds where they'll earn the highest returns. That immediately puts you in need of some financial planning.

Plenty of reputable firms can help you set up a plan, and you can start yourself on a simple stock investment plan. There are even investment clubs around the country (or online, for that matter) through which you can invest small amounts each month and learn about investing together. You can also join the National Association of Investors Corporation (NAIC) as an individual (most investment clubs belong to this organization as well) and learn all about investing in stocks on your own. Just call the NAIC at 1-877-275-6242 for more information, or check out their website at www.better-investing.org.

Whether you're working with a financial adviser or making investments on your own, you need to have both short-term and long-term goals clearly in mind. A short-term goal might be a vacation or a new car; more long-term goals are children's education and your retirement. After you determine these, you can better choose investments that will help you achieve your goals.

Another factor to consider is your tolerance for risk. If you tend to be very conservative and tolerate very little risk, it may take you longer to reach your goals. This takes some soul searching and an honest evaluation of your temperament. Usually a mixture of conservative and more aggressive investments is recommended.

Because you did a household budget in Chapter 15, you know where your money is going and how much you can realistically set aside for saving and investment. This should be done before you pay bills. Either have your savings automatically deducted from your paycheck or "pay yourself first," meaning write yourself a check and deposit it in your savings or investment account the very first thing. This becomes your "do not touch" fund and can either help you make a major purchase down the road or protect you from a disaster.

The next step is making sure what you put away is earning money for you, not merely keeping pace with inflation or, worse, losing value over time. If you have an investment plan at work, you want to go over it with your financial adviser and compare it with what you can do on your own. You may be able to get a better rate of return on something other than what your company offers. Sometimes 401(k) or 403(b) savings plans allow (or require) you to make one or more investment choices within your account. You want to base these choices on sound fundamental principles and make sure they're compatible with your financial goals.

If you decide to work with a professional planner, you want to use his or her time to your best advantage. Having your financial records in order and your budget in place, as you've done in previous chapters, will help you do that. A good financial planner will help you put all of this into an overall plan for the future, and will review it with you annually.

Do You Need a Financial Planner?

How do you know whether you need a financial planner? Well, if you're achieving your financial goals, have no money worries, are rarely confused about investing, and have plenty of time to manage your investments, you probably don't need one! Most of us don't fall into that category, however, including me. I tried planning my own finances for a while, but I decided later to hire Mike, a professional planner, and this was a good decision. Even if you *do* have time to manage your own investments, you still might want to consider a financial planner, if only to do a "tune-up" now and then, and to provide you with a second opinion on key decisions.

Studies show that, on average, people who work with a financial planner do considerably better than people who don't. I'm convinced! Since we started working with Mike six years ago, we've been able to move to a nicer home *and* increase our investment portfolio by well above average.

There are independent financial planners and those who work for financial services companies, and there are pros and cons to each. The independent isn't selling any particular product, so might be more objective in choosing investment vehicles for you. On the other hand, the planner who works for a financial services company has a lot of resources available that the independent might not. Mike works for one of the large corporations, but he frequently recommends investments outside his company's offerings. He wants us to make money. If *we* make money, *he* makes money.

A good financial planner analyzes how changes in financial conditions affect you personally. He or she understands your goals and knows how to diversify your investments to protect you from changing market conditions.

But how do you choose a financial planner? Here are some things to look for and ask about:

- Is the planner with a reputable company?
- Have you heard recommendations from others concerning his or her performance?
- What kind of background and credentials does the planner have? How long has he or she been in the business?
- What degrees, licenses, certificates, and registrations does the planner have?
- What services does the company provide?
- What is the overall financial management philosophy?
- What fees can you expect and what do you get for them?
- How often will your portfolio be reviewed?

Interview several financial planners and make your decision based on how they answer these questions and whether you feel comfortable with them. Mike is like a partner; he's someone we share our hopes, dreams, and fears with. We feel free to ask questions of him when we're confused. He listens and has answers that make sense to us.

We liked the services Mike performed for us so much that we got referrals for planners from the same company for our children where they lived. The financial plan included helping them each put together a budget and evaluate their current job benefits. Some began while they were in debt and had no savings. Happily, none of them are still in that position today, and we believe working with a financial planner got them on the road to getting out of debt and starting to save and invest.

Do You Need an Accountant?

Whether you need an accountant is based on a different set of factors. If your tax returns are simple and you don't own your own business, you may be able to handle things yourself, or simply use a tax preparer. But if you feel your tax-related tasks are too complicated to handle on your own, hiring an accountant is probably the solution. And don't think of an accountant simply as a glorified tax preparer. Think of her as a tax planner as well. She is part of your financial-planning team. And don't wait until just before taxes are due to hire an accountant. You need time to get to know each other and to devise a tax strategy for the future.

Besides tax planning and preparation, an accountant can help you evaluate and install accounting systems for a new business, decide on a structure for a new business, help improve profitability of an existing business, help get financing or restructure existing financing, give advice on mergers and acquisitions, design employee compensation and benefits plans, and make sure your business is in compliance with government regulations.

How do you choose an accountant? If you know little about accounting, you need someone who can get down to basics and explain things so you understand. Be aware that the more you learn on your own and the more organized you are, the more money you save. Some things you want to know are:

- How much experience does she have? How about experience in your particular type of business? In your initial conversation, does she seem to understand *your* business? If you have a home-based business, how well does she understand the home-office deduction?

- What billing procedures are used? Can you get an estimate?

- Will the accountant you're interviewing be doing the work, or will a staff member be doing it instead?

◆ Can you get a list of references? Are any of those references for businesses such as yours or related to yours?

◆ Is the accountant willing to seek outside expert services, if necessary?

Even if you're not in your own business, you may want to consider an accountant, especially if you're managing an estate, own rental properties, or simply have fairly complicated finances. Your financial planner can help you decide whether you need an accountant, as well.

The Least You Need to Know

◆ You'll save time and money by keeping accurate and complete financial records.

◆ Most tax-related documents should be saved for six years; some should be saved indefinitely.

◆ A thorough review of your insurance policies may mean found money, either in unfiled claims or by finding better coverage for less money.

◆ Keeping a summary of your insurance policies in your planner/organizer can prove invaluable in an emergency.

◆ Everyone needs a will, even if it's a simple one you prepare yourself using will-preparation software or a published kit.

◆ It's never too early to think about financial planning and investing. There are many resources for investing intelligently on your own, but hiring a professional financial planner is also worth looking into.

Part 6

Getting People Involved

By now you might be experiencing some resistance or downright hostility from the people around you. After all, you've been a lovable slob all this time and people have gotten used to you that way. Now all of a sudden you're on this organization kick, and your family and co-workers might not know what to make of it.

Be patient. Help is on the way. In this part, you learn how to make your transition from messy to marvelous easier for the people around you, and even get them to be part of the team. You also learn when and how to call in the cavalry and get some outside help.

Nobody Said This Would Be Easy

In This Chapter

- Listening to what other people want and need
- Communicating your organization systems to others
- Identifying problem areas and negotiating solutions
- Accepting limitations and resolving issues of control

What kind of reaction are you getting at home to the changes you've been making? At work? How have you been behaving? Have you become an evangelical organizer, pointing out other people's lack of order? Are you keeping these changes to yourself, leaving everyone unable to figure out where you put things that aren't where they used to be? Are you beginning to see some chronic problems in your household or workplace that you didn't see before? Is there someone at home or at work whose habits conflict with your desire to get organized? Or, now that you're getting organized, do people suddenly want you to organize *them?*

If some of these challenges are cropping up, believe me, you're on the right track. It means you're making progress. Any time you move out of your comfort zone and start taking action, challenges will appear. You may even meet serious resistance. All that's as it should be. You may just need to stand back and take a longer view of your behavior right now and make some minor adjustments. Maybe you need to take some time to communicate, negotiate, and enlist the people in your life in your mission.

If They Don't Know, They Can't Do It

The most common mistake newly converted unstuffers and organizers make is to fail to explain to people what they're doing. In your enthusiasm, you may simply have overlooked this. Maybe you weren't sure you'd succeed. Or maybe you thought they'd laugh at you, because you've tried this so many times before and your efforts never got off the ground.

In the very beginning, it may not be a bad idea to keep things to yourself. If you've attempted this many times before and failed, people just may not have the confidence that *this* time you mean it! No need to set yourself up to be undermined or criticized. Besides, you needed to prove to yourself that you could do it. But chances are, people have already noticed a change. They've watched you get on top of your paperwork, organize your time better, and keep your work flowing when it used to pile up. They see you managing things at home, getting control of your finances, and making plans for the future. Heck, your whole attitude has changed and nothing succeeds like success!

But they may not know *why* things have changed. They may not even trust the changes. They don't realize you've experienced a major shift in the way you see the world, a *paradigm shift*, and are committed to having your life be more directed, more effective, and more satisfying.

> **Pileups!**
>
> Just because your new orderly, more goal-centered life brings you happiness doesn't mean that everyone shares the feeling. Pay attention to the reactions of others, keep the lines of communication open, and beware of the "zealot syndrome." Besides, other people learn best by example, not from hearing others "preaching the gospel."

It is hoped you involved other people as you tackled individual organization projects outlined in this book. When you revamped the finances, you talked it over with your partner and your kids. If you found while taking stock that your financial picture was truly bleak, you called your creditors, explained that you intended to pay, and asked them to work with you. If you reorganized your filing system at work or changed the way you sorted your mail, you let your secretary or your boss know.

These are just basic courtesies, fundamental communication that goes a long way to having people in your court. If you haven't been communicating in these ways, start now.

For some, the change they see in you will be welcome. For others, it may not be. At one time I was a temporary office worker at an international corporation. As a long-term "temp," I had no axe to grind, no promotion or raise to seek; I was simply trying to make things work efficiently for my often-traveling boss, an executive vice president. I streamlined files, set up a better telephone-message system, and found that by computerizing some operations I could get through the work he left me in half the time it took the former secretary. Other secretaries in the department began to sabotage my efforts, and even pointedly told me to "cool it." After I convinced them I wasn't angling for a full-time job and would keep the improvements to myself, I got a lot less flack and I learned a lesson in team building.

Change causes all sorts of discomfort for people, for a variety of reasons in a variety of ways. Some may resent change because they feel it points out their own failings. It may mean they have to learn something new or adjust to a new system and they may resist. Don't worry about the reactions in other people too much. Expect them. Accept them. Be compassionate. And know that consistent behavior on your part can eventually change attitudes.

Listen Up!

When you explain what you're trying to do, make sure you allow a lot of room for feedback. Hear what other people have to say. Be conscious of other people's needs. When I started to get serious about organizing our home and home businesses, my husband stood in the doorway of his home shop/office with arms outstretched and said, "You're not getting in here!" I heard him, and to this day I don't touch that room. That's his "inner sanctum," and he arranges it however he wants. (But I don't dust or vacuum in there either. That's his job!) He was perfectly willing to make changes in the common areas of the house, and of course I could arrange my own office and affairs the way I wanted, but he needed some turf all his own that could be however he wanted it to be.

Listening doesn't mean patronizing. It means listening until you understand. It means giving someone your full attention. It means putting aside your point of view and fully experiencing another's. It means checking periodically to see whether you understand what the person is saying and not injecting your own insights and information. It's so easy to say something like "I know exactly what you mean! Why, when I ...." That's not listening—it's using what another person is trying to share with you as a spring-board for talking about yourself.

Instead, after the person stops speaking, rephrase what you think you heard and ask whether you understand correctly.

Some people talk about learning to compromise, but I prefer learning to *synergize*. This is a process where the sum of the parts is always greater than the whole. If you have worked it out that the laundry gets done on Tuesday and Friday nights, but the family just wants to collapse and watch TV on Friday night, then be with them Friday night and agree to do the laundry in the morning.

Work Within Your Sphere

Stephen Covey tells us to concentrate on our "circle of influence." The well-known Serenity Prayer suggests we ask for the wisdom to know the difference between what we can change and what we can't. The Beatles simply said, "Let it be."

The first place you can effect change is within yourself. Work with yourself and the things you have control over. Perhaps you were always late, unprepared, and constantly in an uproar, but now things have changed for the better. If you maintain these changes, making them habits, people will eventually come to trust them. Continue to work in the areas where you've begun to make strides. Remind yourself of your goals and work on your plan. Stick to the basic principles we've gone over. Continue to take small, regular steps toward fulfilling your mission in life. Use your new skills to improve your life and the lives of the people around you. People will most likely come around!

What About the Kids?

One of the greatest gifts you can give your kids is to teach them organization and time-management skills. You'll help them excel in school, accomplish their career goals, manage their own households, flourish financially, and even get the most out of their relationships. The fact that you're taking steps to get your own life in order means you're developing the greatest teaching tool of all, your own example.

We talked extensively about helping your kids get organized and teaching them organization skills in Chapter 14. Remind yourself that things didn't descend into chaos overnight and everyone needs time to adjust to change. Use your listening skills with your children, just as you would with your co-workers or your spouse.

Your Spouse Is Not Your Child—Really!

Beware of treating your spouse like one of your kids. He or she is your adult partner and deserves to be treated as such. If your partner seems to be sabotaging your efforts to get organized, you need to work out some control issues. Does he or she understand what you're trying to do? Have you consulted your partner before making changes? Was he or she a part of the important decisions?

You could say mine is a fairly traditional household. Most of the running of the household falls to me. My husband is perfectly willing to help, but he just likes to be told what to do. He's not one to take it upon himself to see something that needs doing and just do it. There are good and bad parts to that. The bad part is that I'm responsible for seeing that everything gets done. That's also the good part. By being responsible, I'm also in control. It gets done my way, and I can organize things the way I want. I just need to remember to ask for help and I get it.

Pileups!

Your partner may be threatened by the changes you're making. He or she may be afraid of losing you or fear the relationship will change. Reassure your partner by doing special things to remind him or her how much you care. Remember, you're partners, not adversaries!

What's the situation in your household? Does your spouse like to be the organizer? Does he or she prefer to leave that to you? Is it more of a team effort? Can you split tasks by preference? Can you focus together on certain problem areas? What changes would have the most immediate impact for both of you?

Don't forget to communicate clearly what's important to you. Make sure your spouse "gets" your commitment and understands your goals. Ask for cooperation and input.

What if your spouse is simply messy? Perhaps you can give the "offending" partner a place where he can be just that—as messy as he wants! The deal is, he keeps the mess confined to one area—preferably somewhere out of the way!

Jump Starts

Collect in a folder all the things you need to talk to a team member about. Add a sheet of paper to jot down ideas and share them on a regular basis, whether at meetings, through phone calls, e-mails or memos, or whenever you're in contact. This will keep you from forgetting to discuss important points or just remind you to say "well done!" Your spouse, child, or co-worker may accept your offer, decline, or make a counteroffer. If he accepts, great! You've got a partner and the support you need. If he declines, respect that, but let him know you're going to work on the things within your control. If he has a different plan, you can work to synergize and still move forward.

If you live with a packrat, the important thing is not to nag or take it personally. It's about him, not you, even if it sometimes seems like deliberate provocation. Recognize there's a deep psychological need at play here. It may be a need to feel thrifty and smart or a need for security spawned by an emotionally and/or financially deprived childhood. It may be a sentimental attachment to the past due to events that you may not know about.

Don't attack; just be an example and express the good feelings you experience as you make your way toward order and simplicity in your own life. Try to help your partner fulfill these needs in other ways. And most of all, be patient.

Caution: Work Zone!

Handling challenges at work isn't so different from handling those at home. Sure, you can't tell a colleague to clean up his room or brush his teeth (too bad), but the basic principles of delegating (that's what you were doing at home, didn't you know?) are the same. Many people think of "delegating" as "sloughing off" or passing the buck. But if it's done right it's more like building a team. At work, as at home, you have to work with the people around you, gain their cooperation, and depend on their input.

Here's a list of some basic steps to follow to delegate effectively:

♦ Meet regularly with the people you want as part of your team.

♦ Pay attention to the people you're working with. Make sure they hear you and understand what you expect from them. Leave *how* something gets done up to the individual. The more freedom they have to choose the method, the more they'll take ownership of the task.

- Identify resources. Make yourself one of them.

- Give a minimum of guidelines, but give advance warning of pitfalls.

- Agree on realistic deadlines and standards of performance. Have people evaluate *themselves* at the agreed-upon time.

- Be clear about what the rewards will be when the job is accomplished—and the consequences if it's not.

- Say "please" and "thank you." Pay attention to simple courtesy and manners.

Roommates and Other Strangers

When you decide to organize your life, sharing your space with someone who's not a family member or partner can pose some different challenges. I mean, when the two of you moved in together you were a slob, so what happened? Well, maybe the change hasn't been that dramatic, but still it's a change that you decided you wanted to make, and your roommate may be happy with things the way they were!

Again, communication is the key. Hopefully, you and your roommate respect each other's values, goals, and desires and can talk about your feelings. That's where to start. Just as you worked out how to handle visitors to the dorm room or apartment, who takes out the garbage, and how loud the music can be, you need to discuss your excitement about "getting organized." Recognize that this is a personal decision, something you've decided to do for yourself, and that your roommate may feel his or her level of organization is just fine.

Your roommate may want to work on this, too. But then again, maybe not. If that's the case, work on your own space, change your own habits, improve your own life. And refrain from being critical or acting superior as you make strides toward your goals. Things will go more smoothly if you respect differences and let your progress speak for itself.

There will probably be areas where you need to make compromises, especially where you share space. Concentrate first on the areas that are yours exclusively, and slowly work on enlisting your roommate's help and enthusiasm about unstuffing and organizing common areas. You may also find that, although the other person doesn't want to get involved, he or she doesn't mind if you want to do the work! If it will make things better for you, then why not "just do it"?

Don't Take Yourself Too Seriously

Lighten up! Admit you've been a slob or a ditz or both, but you're trying to do better. Don't become an ogre or a taskmaster. I don't care whether someone is a professional organizer or just someone like me who works hard at being organized—none of us is perfect. The idea is not to become a machine enforcing a completely orderly world where every spill is eradicated immediately, there's never a dirty dish in the sink, no piece of paper ever lands on any surface for longer than half a second, and no hair is ever out of place. If that's being organized, I wouldn't want it either!

What you're aiming for is more time, less stress, streamlined methods for the "must-do" tasks, and doing more of the things you really want to do in life. If you get the basics handled, you can concentrate on the really good stuff! "Organized" does not mean "neat." Organized is not necessarily pretty. Organized is not spotless. Organized is a level of order that allows you to function efficiently and be in control. That level of order is different for each of us. The object is to notice what's going on, change what's not working, make and implement a plan, then reevaluate it periodically, adjusting it according to what you've learned.

Envisionings

Go back and revisit the "ideal day" picture you created in Chapter 1. Knowing what you know now, imagine getting up in the morning in your newly organized bedroom; walking into your newly organized, pared-down, fully functioning closet; eating a leisurely breakfast with a quick cleanup in your newly organized kitchen; and climbing into your newly organized car.

Be more specific than you were the first time. Allow yourself to feel pleasure about the things you've accomplished. Make a mental note of things you'd still like to attend to. Pat yourself on the back. How does this picture differ from the first one?

I've made lots of suggestions to you so far. Some of them come from my own experience. Some of them were offered by others, I tried them, and they worked. Others I mentioned because I know they work for other people, although they've never been particularly useful to me. It's up to you to find the formula that works best for you. Muster up your creativity and come up with new ideas of your own. Remember it's your starship, and you're the captain! Make it so.

Keep in mind that, as we discuss in later chapters, what works at one stage of your life may need some major adjustments at others. When I was a single parent with two growing daughters, my life looked a lot different from what it does now that I'm remarried, my children are grown, and my husband and I both have home-based businesses. Sticking to the old ways wouldn't make sense. The principles don't change, but the methods and practice do. If you remember this and apply the basic principles, you can't go wrong. Getting and staying organized isn't "once and for all"—it's part of your life's work!

If You Organize It, They Will Come

One final thing to remember: When it all comes out in the wash (as my mother and grandmother used to say), the only person's behavior you can control is your own. You're the one who wanted to get organized! Just because you made this decision and are taking action doesn't mean anyone else has to. You can have many areas of your life the way you want them, even if other people aren't very cooperative. You're responsible for yourself. Don't use other people as an excuse for not following through.

Amazingly, if you just go along doing your thing, making the improvements that you want to for yourself, other people may start to make changes, too. They may see how much happier you seem—how you seem to be getting more done and enjoying life more. They may actually be reaping the benefits of your newfound organization. Maybe you have more time for things they've been wanting to do with you. As with so many things, the key ingredient is *time*. Give yourself time for this new way of life to become a part of you. Give other people time to adjust to the changes you're making. Just don't look back, and keep on keepin' on.

The Least You Need to Know

- If you want to gain cooperation and useful ideas from others, you need to *communicate*.
- Listening is an important part of communication. Give people your undivided attention when you listen, and don't try to inject your own experience or thoughts.
- Children need to be taught basic organization skills to succeed in life. You can play an important role in giving them the gift of these skills.
- Delegating well means you're building a team, rather than just someone passing the buck.
- People don't appreciate a "preacher" or "taskmaster." Having a sense of humor is extremely important, especially being able to laugh at yourself.
- In the end, the only person you can change is yourself. Accept people for what they are and go forward with your plan.

Chapter 18

Calling In the Cavalry: Hiring Others

In This Chapter

- ◆ When to consider hiring someone else to do a job
- ◆ How to hire the right people and keep them doing their best for you
- ◆ Pitfalls to avoid when hiring professional help
- ◆ Benefits of hiring a professional organizer and how to get the most out of the experience

There may come a time when you throw up your hands and say, "I quit!" Maybe you've organized yourself to the hilt and you still can't get caught up. Perhaps you've tried to get cooperation from others but somehow ended up doing everything yourself. Or maybe there are some tasks no one wants to do, ever!

Solving the problem may be as simple as picking up the phone and dialing "Dirtbusters," but before you do, here are a few things to consider.

When Do You Hire a Pro?

In some instances you should definitely consider calling in a professional, rather than trying to do it yourself:

◆ **When there's a disaster.** We once had a torrential rainstorm that separated a gutter pipe and caused water to wash into a window frame and behind the wall in our living room. It stained the wall and soaked the rug. This is an obvious instance when it's a bright idea to call a professional. Even though the damage didn't exceed the deductible on our homeowner insurance, we didn't have the equipment or the expertise to do the job right.

In a disaster, time is of the essence. You have to drop everything and tend to it or further damage could result. If you happen to be a professional carpet cleaner, plumber or carpenter, by all means feel free to handle the disaster cleanup yourself. But if you're not, this kind of work is best left to the experienced professional. Get a few estimates and get the job done quickly.

> **Pileups!**
>
> If you're behind on a regular basis, something's wrong. Look at how you spend your time, whether your methods are efficient, whether you have the proper tools, and whether you're expecting too much. You may need to hire someone on a regular basis if you have everything else covered. Analyze the situation and be honest about what's really going on.

◆ **When you get behind.** I'm all in favor of sending out the laundry or having a cleaning company come in occasionally to get caught up. The boon to your psyche is immediate. You're suddenly back on track and can start working your plan again. Seasonal shifts might also make hiring out a good idea. Some years I have had an outside cleaning service come in and help with spring cleaning. If I've kept up with washing windows and cleaning carpets, grand! But sometimes I don't get to those jobs, and bringing someone in to handle them makes me feel (and the house look) like a million bucks.

If you own your own business and generally handle most of the paperwork yourself, fine. But if it starts to pile up, consider hiring someone to get you back on solid ground again. Other chores you may occasionally want to consider hiring out are yard work, running errands, dog grooming, and home-maintenance chores such as cleaning gutters or raking leaves. Go over your Master List of things to do and decide which ones would have the greatest impact on your life if you paid someone else to do them. Then go back and see what your budget allows.

◆ **When you really don't know how to do it.** I'm not a plumber—never was, never will be. I have lots of better things to do and you probably do, too. Leave things you don't know how to do to the people who have the expertise, the tools, and the training. Measure, too, the time, effort, and money (tools are expensive!) it would take to learn how to do something yourself versus the cost of paying a professional.

There are also times when hiring a one-time consultant makes sense. If you're not particularly talented in the home decorating department, it may be worth it to hire an interior decorator to guide you. This can save you considerable money and time in the long run, as well as saving you from decorating mistakes that you would have to live with. A computer consultant can be another worthwhile investment. Paying an expert for a few hours of time can save you many hours of frustration and trial and error. Look again at your Master List and decide whether there are areas where professional help might move things along.

◆ **When you just don't have the time.** Work schedules coupled with long commutes may make hiring someone to do regular cleaning and other chores a must if you're going to have time for family, friends, or other things you enjoy. It's a matter of time versus money, and setting priorities. Some people find it's not worth it to spend their hard-earned money to pay someone else to do chores. For others, the time saved is worth the money spent.

Some possibilities: cleaning, laundry, landscaping and yard work, errands, gift-buying services, business paperwork, and household paperwork such as filling out insurance forms. Figure out what you make an hour and compare this with the cost of having a task done by someone else. It may make economic sense to hire the task out.

> **Jump Starts**
>
> If you decide to get a regular weekly cleaning service, find one that will let you work along with them. Once a week, while they do the heavy jobs, you can do your weekly chores. At least use the opportunity to get some things put away so you can get the most from your cleaning service while they're there.

◆ **When you're at an impasse.** My friend Marcia's husband, John, fancies himself a "do-it-yourselfer." He means well, but somehow things around the house just never get done. Secretly, I believe John wants to be rescued from himself, but he just won't call someone else to come in and do the job. His procrastination was driving Marcia up the wall until a friend said, "Why don't you just hire somebody to do it and see what happens?" It wasn't a matter of money. It seemed to be more a matter of pride.

Well, Marcia called a carpenter and got all those little unfinished jobs done. John heaved a sigh of relief. Now, when John suggests he'll do it himself, Marcia simply says, "Why don't I have someone come in and do it this time, and next time you can do it if you want to." John doesn't protest. It's a funny little game they play, but things get done and John still has his pride.

♦ **When a professional's advice will hold more weight than yours.** It's amazing how someone can come in from outside the office or the household and say the same thing you've said for years, and suddenly it's a "great idea." Don't throw a fit, just be glad it's finally sunk in—even if you don't get the credit.

Professional organizers repeatedly relate this phenomenon to me. They may say something their client has heard a thousand times; somehow, though, because it comes from the expert, it holds more weight. So what? It's results we're after, right?

A professional cleaning service can get away with things you'd never be able to. Try touching the stuff on top of your teenager's dresser and you'd get your head handed to you. When "the cleaning lady" does it, nobody complains; in fact, the kids may even put the stuff away *before* she comes!

Jump Starts

Look for free services to help you save time and get organized. Did you know that many large department stores have free wardrobe consultants? They'll tailor clothes to your size and color and style preferences. Ask about free home decorating consulting at furniture and home décor stores, too.

♦ **When it's a job you (and everyone else) simply hate to do.** Let's face it. There are some things you just don't like doing. That's why you procrastinate. You know they need to be done, but you just can't find a way to make them palatable. Long before I met my husband, he used to do all his own automotive maintenance. At the time, he couldn't afford to have someone else change the oil or tune up the motor. On bitterly cold New England winter mornings, he would get up early and tinker with the car so he could get to work. He swore that when he became more successful he would never work on a car again. Since I've known him, he's been pretty much true to his word. It's perfectly okay to choose not to do something you hate and hire someone else to do it for you.

♦ **When you want to reward yourself.** Earlier I told you to make up a Rewards List. Several things on my list involve hiring someone to do something for me.

Maybe it's a manicure or a facial. I sometimes treat myself by taking the car to a car wash, rather than washing it in my driveway. For more money, you can have your car detailed, where they do all the little extras and even give it that "new car" smell!

Make a list of tasks you'd truly enjoy getting done for yourself, tasks you'd consider a reward. Add them to the Rewards List you keep in your planner/organizer. Put some money in your regular budget for celebrations and rewards. Then give yourself a gift whenever you need a boost or want to say "well done!" This list can be helpful for thinking of gifts for others in your life, as well.

How to Hire Happily and Avoid Getting Ripped Off

One reason people put off hiring out certain jobs is they're afraid they might not pick the right professional to do it. There are a lot of unprofessional "professionals" out there who simply don't do a good job. How do you know you're getting the best one?

Here are five helpful hints for hiring anyone, from a key employee to the cleaning lady. Follow them, and 9 times out of 10 you'll hire the right person.

1. **Know the job you're hiring them for.** It helps if you actually know how to do the job you're hiring someone for or at least the basics of how it's done. If you don't, the person you're hiring should be able to explain exactly what the job entails and how they're going to accomplish it. If they can't or won't explain it, go on to the next person.

2. **Do your research.** Check the Yellow Pages and get a list of the people in your area specializing in a particular service. Then call your Better Business Bureau to see whether they've had any complaints lodged against them. Ask people you know and trust for recommendations. Ask for references and check them out.

   This is such an obvious step, and yet people often ignore it and choose a professional without getting any background information.

Jump Starts

Besides emergency repairs, some of the most common services people hire others to do are house cleaning, gardening, carpet cleaning, window washing, pet grooming, laundry, cooking, home maintenance, personal shopping, gift buying, reminder services, financial planning, and record keeping. Which ones make the most sense for you?

3. **Interview the prospective "employee."** Before you offer someone the job, make sure you interview him or her. Make a list of questions before you call to make the appointment. Ask whether they're bonded, if that's appropriate. Do they have the necessary licenses or insurance? How long have they been in business? What methods, equipment, or cleaning products do they use? What preparation will you have to do? Is there anything they won't do? Many smaller cleaning services do not do windows or carpet cleaning, for example. Do you get the feeling they want your business, or are they put off by your questions? If they don't want your business, find someone who does.

4. **Communicate clearly the results you want.** Make sure you're on the same wavelength and that the job you need done is the job you hire to be done. Get a contract or letter of agreement if at all possible.

Most cleaning services will want you to sign a contract at the outset. If yours doesn't, write a list of what you want done each week and give them a copy. Be sure to cover regular jobs and things you want done periodically, with a schedule for getting them done.

Pileups!

Don't hover over the cleaning staff. Be available to answer questions, of course, but don't stick your nose in where it's not needed. The next time the worker should see you is when the job is done and you're ready to evaluate it and hand over a check. If you don't trust someone to do the job right, why did you hire him in the first place?

5. **Don't accept shoddy work.** Hold the professional accountable and work with him or her until the job is done to your satisfaction. You have a right to get what you're paying for, so make sure you do. If necessary, withhold payment until the job is done properly. If, on the other hand, you're pleasantly surprised with more than you expected, let the person know, and perhaps even give him a bonus. Let him know you'll use him again and recommend him to your friends and neighbors. We all like to know when we've done well.

Don't Clean for the Cleaning Lady

When you hire someone, it's his job to perform the work. Let go. This can be especially hard if you hire out a job you've done yourself for a long time. Remember, you're the customer and you're not entering a popularity contest.

If you called in a cleaning service because the house is dirty and you don't have time (or the desire) to clean it, they expect the house to be dirty. Let people do their job.

Do make sure you know what the cleaning service is specifically going to do, and how much you're paying for individual tasks. Ask what their routine tasks (basic fee) include. Usually, included in a basic cleaning are dusting and polishing of furniture; dusting open shelves, ceiling fans, air vents, baseboards, window sills, and mini-blinds; cleaning mirrors and picture glass, cleaning and towel drying of bathroom tile, shower doors, commodes, sinks, countertops, and open shelves; cleaning the top, burners, and front of the stove; cleaning the top, front, and sides of the refrigerator; damp mopping floors; and vacuuming all carpeted areas.

Don't assume, however! Most dissatisfaction comes from the customer not communicating properly what they expect and the service not explaining clearly what their basic fee includes. Make a list and check it before handing them the check.

Many tasks are usually not included in the basic deal, including cleaning inside the refrigerator; cleaning the oven and under the stove top; damp wiping baseboards, window sills, door facings, and frames; cleaning up the fireplace; oiling and polishing kitchen cabinets; and vacuuming or cleaning upholstered furniture. Of course, you can still get them done—for a price. If you want carpets cleaned, windows washed, floors stripped and waxed, and outside decks, porches, or furniture cleaned, you need to make this clear and find out what each task will cost.

If you decide you don't want to pay to have these specialized jobs done, doing some of them yourself either before or right after a commercial cleaning job will add value to what you've just had done. For instance, you may want to vacuum, shampoo, and rotate the cushions on upholstered furniture just before the cleaning service comes in and steam clean the carpets. Schedule outside services at a time when you can make the most of them.

Resource Files

If you're considering simplifying your yard work, hiring a landscaper might make sense, if only for a consultation on how you can change your yard from high maintenance to easy care. For suggestions on how to reduce the work in your yard, consult *The Free-Spirited Garden: Gorgeous Gardens That Flourish Naturally* by Susan McClure. You'll know what you're talking about when you speak with the landscaper!

Maybe You Just Need to Move!

"Maybe you need to move." Shocking idea, isn't it? But don't dismiss it too quickly. Are you still living in a four-bedroom house even though the kids are grown? Do you have a lawn you hate to keep and a big garden even though you don't like gardening? Maybe you just need to wise up, dump the old homestead, and move to a place that's easier to take care of.

What kind of maintenance does your home require? Do you live in a climate that requires a lot of extra work to keep up a house? Do you have to live there? Could you move to a planned community or condominium where much of the outside work is done as part of the regular monthly fee? Give it some thought. It's not for everyone, but it could be for you.

If not a move, how about making some changes to cut down the work? Aluminum siding and simpler landscaping might be just the ticket. Just getting rid of certain plants might cut your garden maintenance in half. When a neighbor of mine moved in, she had all the rosebushes torn out and replaced with low-maintenance shrubbery. Although she enjoyed roses, she wasn't willing to fertilize, prune, feed, spray, and clip them each year.

How about replacing plants that take a lot of care with native plants that are adapted to the environment you live in? These usually require less watering, fertilizing, and general care than plants that aren't naturally suited to a particular climate or soil. I've seen people replace a lawn with a field of wildflowers that doesn't need to be mowed, or simply let part of their property overgrow to merge back into the surrounding woodland. Simplify, and you'll save time (and money, too).

You're Hired, Kid

Should you hire your kids? This is a sticky question. Only you can tell whether this is a worthwhile arrangement. First of all, I don't believe in paying kids for things they should do anyway. After all, they live there, too! However, if there are bigger jobs that older kids could handle and you want to offer to pay them, that's up to you. *Offer* is the operative word here. If they don't want to do it, then that's the end of it.

By the way, I don't consider mowing the lawn a job worthy of extra pay. If you give your children a regular allowance, fine, but I've never liked the idea of tying that allowance to specific jobs. The subject of an allowance is separate from the chores a child or teenager is expected to do to maintain the house.

Now if we're talking major work like rototilling, washing windows, or digging a ditch, then compensation makes sense. And all the principles of good hiring apply!

The Benefits of Bartering

The barter system is ancient. Before we used currency, humans bartered or traded for everything. The concept has made a comeback in recent years, and it can be a creative, inexpensive way to get things done. For example, my husband is a leather craftsman. He paid for his eye exam and pair of glasses with a beautifully hand-carved leather item, custom-made for our eye doctor. Not a single cent changed hands. For him, it was a matter of time and some inexpensive materials, but it reflected a skill the eye doctor doesn't have. In exchange, my husband received a service that requires a special skill. An even trade.

This may be an excellent solution in many areas. You can exchange child care for cleaning services, sewing for home repairs—whatever you can think of. Just make sure you exchange products or services of equal value. It's also advisable that you get an agreement in writing and work out the tax consequences.

It's common when bartering to trade for full value. So even if you would normally give your friend Sue a discount on your hourly accounting fee, if you barter with her, swap your full amount for her full amount.

> **CAUTION**
>
> **Pileups!**
>
> Don't try to hide the dollar value of what you receive as part of a barter arrangement. You must report it as income on your federal income tax. Be sure you know what your state income tax requirements are, as well. Order IRS Publication 525, "Taxable and Non-Taxable Income," for details on federal tax requirements at www.irs.gov.

When Do You Need a Professional to Organize You?

No matter how organized you are (or think you are) now, you can almost always benefit from at least a few hours with a professional organizer. Why? Because a professional organizer does this day in and day out. Believe me, they've seen just about everything, and they've solved problems in ways you and I haven't even dreamed of.

I see several good reasons for hiring a professional:

◆ **You can't solve a particular problem no matter what you do.** I already told you about my problem with missing papers and messages. I thought I'd tried everything, yet I overlooked two simple solutions that were inexpensive and easy to implement. My professional organizer solved the problem in a minute.

If you can, get the lion's share of the work done yourself and bring in a professional for the few things you just can't seem to get a handle on; that's the ideal situation.

Resource Files

To get in touch with the National Association of Professional Organizers (NAPO), call (847-375-4746847-375-4746; or write to 4700 W. Lake Ave., Glenview, IL 60025. Their website is www.napo.net. NAPO publishes an annual membership directory and has an online "organizer finder."

- **You're almost a hopeless case.** Okay, you've read this book (and many others, I'd wager) and you just can't seem to get it together. You can always hire a professional to work with until you get your problem licked. This won't be cheap, mind you, but it may be the only way to go—you're desperate! A good professional will work with you on one area at a time—just as we did in this book. You'll get a list of things to do before the next session and then pick up where you left off. You can concentrate on one area or keep going until you've done it all. That depends on you and your pocketbook. Consider this "organization therapy."

- **You need to nudge others and haven't been able to do it yourself.** As I mentioned earlier, sometimes people take direction from an outsider better than from someone they know. You may see the problem clearly, but a professional will know all the tricks for getting cooperation and getting the job done. Besides, when someone's paying for the advice, sometimes they're more likely to use it!

- **You need a "jump-start."** If getting organized seems overwhelming and you aren't able to get going, a professional can be just the push you need. A professional organizer can sit down with you and help you break the whole up into manageable chunks, setting priorities and following up with you over time.

- **You need help to stay on track.** It could be you've done a mammoth job of unstuffing, organizing the heck out of your life, but things seem to be going back to the "old way." Maybe what you need is a periodic checkup! Share your goals with your professional organizer and ask to be called for a quarterly checkup session (or more often if needed). You and your organizer can refine your systems, pull you back to your goals and priorities when you get sidetracked, and set up better maintenance schedules.

- **You've experienced a major lifestyle change.** Perhaps you've gone out on your own and have moved your office into your home. Or maybe you've been a stay-at-home mother and have just reentered the workforce. Any time you experience a major lifestyle shift, organization systems that worked before may suddenly not fit anymore. A professional organizer can help you adapt and revamp for the way you live now.

How do you find a professional organizer? Follow the same procedures for hiring someone that I outlined earlier in this chapter. As a jumping-off point, I recommend contacting the National Association of Professional Organizers (NAPO). This non-profit organization has annual meetings for organization professionals where they exchange innovative ideas and solutions for problems. They also have many local chapters located around the country.

You can hire a professional organizer to help you with your home, your business, or both. Some specialize in one or the other, so be sure to ask. If you are computer-based, you'll probably want a professional with computer expertise.

Don't be afraid to ask about qualifications or experience. If you're doing some heavy-duty revamping of complicated business systems in your organization, you want someone with the ability to handle such an in-depth project.

> **Jump Starts**
>
> One effective way to use this book along with a professional organizer is to take one unstuffing or organization project I've outlined and tackle it yourself. If you feel you need additional help, bring in a professional to augment that particular project. You'll save money and get the best from your organizer!

Ask upfront about pay schedules. Many organizers charge by the hour, but some charge by the project and will give you an estimate. They may even have a "frequent visitor's plan," whereby you get a discount for a longer-term arrangement. Be sure to ask about travel pay as well. This may be a considerable expense if your organizer is traveling some distance.

A good professional organizer will call after a session to see how you're coming along, and you'll probably want to schedule a checkup after you have a chance to work with the new system.

Another thing to ask about is whether you or your organizer will provide supplies. You have to pay for them either way, but your organizer may mark them up—or they may get them for you at a discount. Ask about his or her policy and compare prices.

Some professional organizers do a lot more than just organize you. Some have personal shopping services, where they get your sizes and shop for clothes then bring them to your home where you try them on. You pay for what you keep and your organizer returns the rest.

Others have gift-reminder and -buying services. You give your organizer information about birthdays, anniversaries, and anything else you want to be reminded of and they'll even send a gift and a card for you at the appropriate time. This is too impersonal for my taste, but may be just what you've been looking for.

Still other professional organizers are image consultants. They work with businessmen and -women to improve their professional images, helping them choose clothing, accessories, hairstyle, and makeup to create the best impression. They may even work with people in the public eye and coach them on public speaking or for radio and television appearances.

There's no shame in admitting something is over your head or you just could use some help. Whether it's a specific task that a professional could remove from your to-do list or an organization overhaul, weigh the pros and cons. Then farm out whatever your budget (and psyche) can handle.

Envisionings

Close your eyes and imagine you had unlimited time and money to work with a professional to help you organize your life. What areas would you tackle that you haven't dared to so far? If you didn't have to do the work, what would give you the most pleasure to just snap your fingers and have it all "handled"? Can you take a piece of that fantasy, perhaps just one phase or step, and give it to a professional to help you with it?

The Least You Need to Know

- There are many good reasons to bring in an outside service or expert to help you.

- If you follow some specific steps before making the final decision to hire someone, you can maximize your chances of having a mutually beneficial experience.

- It's common for people to have trouble letting someone else do tasks they've normally done. Let the person do his job, then sit back and enjoy the results.

- You may not need to hire professionals to help with the work; you may simply need to cut back on the work. Moving into less-demanding quarters or making some time- and work-saving home improvements could be a solution.

- Alternatives to hiring an outside contractor may be to hire your kids or to barter services.

- There are many benefits to hiring a professional organizer, and one of the best ways to use one is to do as much as you can on your own and then consult a professional for specific areas where you need help.

Part 7

Now That You're Organized, Let's Keep It That Way!

Congratulations! You've come a long way. You've got the essentials in your life unstuffed and organized. Now you need to know how to maintain your new systems, figure out how to fix them if they start breaking down, and be able to adjust what you've learned for your particular lifestyle and the different stages of your life. What works today may need some tweaking or even total revamping tomorrow. The next two chapters address these issues and help you kick yourself up another notch.

Chapter 19

Maintaining and Managing Your Progress

In This Chapter

- ◆ Strategies for keeping your life-management machinery in optimum working order
- ◆ Moving to the next level and putting your life in high gear
- ◆ Avoiding pitfalls that cause backsliding
- ◆ Dealing with system breakdowns

After you do the major reorganizing projects outlined in this book, all that's left is to maintain the systems you adapted for yourself and enjoy your newfound free time. The key to maintenance is simple—do a little each day, *every* day.

This chapter will help you solidify the progress you've made and look for ways to move to an even higher level. Don't panic if your efforts seem to erode or even come unraveled. You'll learn some practical ways to get back on track and keep it from happening in the future. Don't worry if you're not there yet. You're not behind and you don't need to catch up! Just keep on working from where you are and if you've stalled you can always start again.

Here's the Bottom Line

We've covered a lot of ground together, so you may feel a little overwhelmed. Ask yourself, "Have I tried to do everything at once?"

If the answer is yes, stop! Take stock! There's an easy remedy: Remember my advice on setting priorities. Focus your time and resources on the areas that cause you the most grief, confusion, money, time, or stress. That's where the dividends will be the greatest. What's *your* bottom line? Do you desperately need to get your finances on an even keel or everything else will soon fall apart? Then do that first. Are your disorganization and inefficiency in certain areas causing real problems with your significant other, housemates, or co-workers? Then working on those areas may be your first priority.

Decide on the basics that make your life work (or not), and do them no matter what. The basics for most people would be:

- Getting bills paid on time. Getting out of debt.

- Having the dishes done every day.

- Doing the weekly grocery shopping.

- Making sure you get adequate rest, nutrition, and exercise.

- Having your house tolerably clean, so you feel comfortable coming home to it.

- Doing the weekly wash.

- Getting to work on time and keeping up with your assignments.

- Keeping track of appointments.

- Maintaining your automobile (if that's your main mode of transportation).

> **CAUTION**
>
> **Pileups!**
>
> Taking care of yourself isn't for later. It's definitely a part of "minimum maintenance." Without the captain, the ship loses direction. Make sure you're part of the "bottom line."

The systems I've outlined for these areas should handle them for you in a hurry. Have in mind an absolute minimum level of order that you won't go below, and stick to it. That's your *bottom line*. You can always do better, but maintaining this bottom-line organization will give you a good foundation on which to build.

Get Regular Tune-Ups for a Smoother Ride

Just like maintaining your automobile, maintaining your organization systems takes regular checkups and even periodic replacement of parts. Here are some regular maintenance tasks to keep everything humming:

◆ Add to your Master List the projects you didn't get to while you were working with this book. You've been concentrating on high-priority tasks and major life systems, but you probably came across tasks and projects you know need to get done at some time. Get them in front of you so you can schedule them for the future.

◆ Schedule regular maintenance days. Have a closet-maintenance day, a file-maintenance day, a car-maintenance day, a food-and-kitchen-maintenance day, and a financial-maintenance day. If it only takes half a day, treat yourself to an afternoon off.

◆ Make up checklists for maintaining various areas of your life, and make copies. For example, a food and household-supplies inventory list. Or how about a spring cleanup list for the outdoors? Why reinvent the wheel each time when you can save the time and energy for other things?

When you set out on your maintenance mission, look carefully at the new systems you've created and ask yourself these questions:

◆ How's my system working?

◆ If it's not working well, where and how is it breaking down?

◆ If it's working pretty well is there anything I can do to improve it?

◆ Have I learned any new tips, methods, or ideas to try? Have I found any new storage solutions or organization products that might work better than what I have in place now?

◆ Are there any ways I can streamline this system, make it more efficient, or save additional time?

Jump Starts

New products are constantly being developed as more people take organizing their lives seriously. Browse hardware, business-supply, craft, and department stores for new space-saving ideas. Check out the many new organizing products stores, catalogs, and websites for new solutions. Write down the measurements of problem areas in your planner/organizer in case you see something that might work.

◆ Is there any way I can make my system more aesthetically pleasing? For example, I have some cardboard organizers that I know do the trick. My next step is to find or make something more durable and nicer to look at. The idea is working, but I can still improve on the way it looks.

Making and keeping appointments with yourself for evaluating and planning is essential to maintaining your organization systems. If you pick a regular time slot it will become a habit—something you actually look forward to. For me, planning time is Sunday evenings. I curl up with the three Cs (a cat, a comforter, and a cup of tea), get out my planner/organizer, and do everything from reminding myself of my mission statement, goals, and plans, to deciding on the week's menus and making out a shopping list. Find a time that works for you and make an enjoyable event of it. Consistency is the mother of habit, and pleasant rituals help make it easier to be consistent.

Continue to reward yourself for the strides you're making. Praise yourself. You'll discover that the rewards of the changes themselves are self-reinforcing. Cooking in a kitchen that's efficient, orderly, and clean makes it more fun to cook. Opening the garage door and seeing everything in its place, in working order, and well maintained is a reward in itself. Every time it takes me one step and five seconds to retrieve an account number or balance, I get this smug, self-satisfied grin on my face. It works that way—honest!

Taking It a Step Further

Here are some more "tune-up" ideas:

◆ Make a list of self-improvement or inspirational books to read, seminars you'd like to attend, or audiotapes or videotapes you'd like to purchase or borrow. Use them regularly. Reinforce your new habits and build on them by feeding your conscious and unconscious mind with positive messages.

◆ Set up a "brain trust" or resource network of positive, organized, motivated achievers. When you "unstuffed" your relationships, you eliminated those that dragged you down. Build new ones with people whose goals are to constantly improve themselves and make their lives and the lives of those around them better. Tap this network when you're looking for new ideas and share ones you've found that work.

◆ Keep writing down your goals. In fact, try keeping a journal as well, so you can express your thoughts on your self-improvement journey and, later, look back and see how far you've come.

◆ Ask "Why not?" instead of "Why?"

◆ Continue to develop yourself and look for ways to contribute to the lives of other people. If you need something, give it away. In other words, if you need understanding, give understanding. If you need love, give love. There's more power in this than you may realize.

◆ If you're having a problem with something, study people who have solved the problem effectively. Find models for success.

◆ Meet regularly with the people in your life. Make sure you listen.

◆ If you find a system that works, see whether you can apply it to some other area of your life. You may need to adapt it somewhat, but see whether you can standardize it in some way.

Jump Starts

Make a list of resources that you know you can count on and keep it in your planner/ organizer. Include companies that sell supplies you use most often and their toll-free numbers or websites, dependable people you can call to hire for various tasks, organized friends you can brainstorm with, books you refer to regularly. Whenever you're stumped or things don't seem to be working quite right, turn to your resource list for help.

If you pay attention every day to honing your life-management skills, the results will be enormous. Organization and simplification give you a feeling of control and self-confidence. From there, you can accomplish anything.

Lists, Schedules, and Files Revisited

You're probably tired of hearing it, but I'm going to say these three things one more time. If you missed them before or they didn't sink in, now you have no excuse!

1. **Lists are your friends.** Your Master List is one of your most powerful tools. It keeps you from forgetting things you must do and helps you get in touch with your real desires. Lists hold you accountable, and they let you see all you accomplish as you check off the items. Eventually, some things will become automatic and you may not need a list (such as your daily cleaning list, for example). But keep it handy in your planner/organizer anyway, so you can check up on yourself periodically and see whether you're beginning to slide. If you are, you can use the checklist again for accountability.

2. **Schedule, schedule, schedule!** Make appointments to do things on your list. Make appointments with the key people in your life. Make appointments with yourself. Don't just put it on the list, set a time to *do it*.

3. **Set up efficient files and purge them regularly.** A good filing system keeps the mounds of paper in your life moving. When it's filed, it's out of the way and you can retrieve it when you need it. By purging regularly, you keep those files fresh and useful.

> **Wise Words**
>
> "Our remedies oft in ourselves do lie, / which we ascribe to heaven."
>
> —William Shakespeare

If you haven't finished setting up or revamping your files, this should probably be a high priority. If they need purging, do it promptly. You'll create space and you'll be on top of what's there.

If Things Start Breaking Down

It's not unusual to experience some amount of breakdown even if you worked hard to get things in order and you thought you had it licked. Don't despair, and don't pack it in. Just step back. Ask yourself, "What's happening here?"

You may be trying to do too much at once. Do one thing well and completely. After you master that, move on to the next. Choose the problem area that came up during some of our visualization exercises and work on that first. You'll see an immediate impact.

Envisionings

Review your day yesterday. Close your eyes and see it in as much detail as you can, exactly as it happened, from morning until you laid your head down at night. Where did problems come up? Is there a pattern? How could you have solved or prevented those problems with what you now know about organization? Write down what you discover, and set aside time this week to concentrate on these areas.

The area that kept coming up for me when I first committed to getting myself organized was our household finances and records. It loomed over me, aggravated me daily, and caused resentment. When I finally said, "Look, I'm going to make this work, and I'm going to make it as easy on myself as possible," things immediately got better.

I organized our financial files, got on a regular bill-paying schedule, computerized with financial-management software and electronic bill paying, and rounded up all our back tax information and transferred it to uniform boxes. Then I hired a financial planner to help me develop an investment plan and set up a flow system for incoming bills, checks, and financial statements.

Concentrating on this one area had an enormous effect on my disposition, sense of control, and ability to lay my hands on anything financial in seconds; it actually made tasks I dreaded—such as bill paying—almost enjoyable. After my success in that one huge problem area (yours might be a totally different one), I was so charged with energy I was almost self-propelled. Choose what most annoys you or gets in your way. The rewards you'll experience will get you moving again.

Don't forget to delegate, either by getting people to take more responsibility at home or at work, or by hiring out some work. The latter solution may only be temporary, until you get organized in that area. Or you may find that you'd rather concentrate on other things, so it's worth it to pay someone else to do it. If things are breaking down, it may mean other people aren't pulling their weight.

Remember it takes 21 days to make a habit. Are you giving yourself enough time? You may be expecting too much, too soon. You didn't get disorganized overnight, and it will take longer than one day to fix it.

Here are a few tricks I use to get back on track when things seem to be slipping:

◆ Make appointments that will force you to focus. If you're losing control of your finances, call up your financial planner to do a portfolio or budget review. If the house looks like a pigpen, make an appointment for a cleaning service to come in. You'll have to straighten up at least a little bit before the service can do their work.

> **CAUTION**
>
> **Pileups!**
>
> When obstacles appear, you may be tempted to give up and go back to the old way. Resist the urge to abandon what you're doing altogether just because some of it isn't working right now. Rewrite the plan; don't scrap it!

◆ Entertain. Really, this works! Invite your mother-in-law or your boss (or just imagine you have). Imagine them going through every room in your house. Imagine them going through your closets, your files, your kitchen, and your garage. If you're single, invite a date over. Before that special someone gets there, the floor and countertops will be clean enough to eat off of!

◆ Get an estimate for a cross-country move. When you get the estimated cost of moving all that junk, you'll start unstuffing your house like you wouldn't believe. Just imagine packing it all, too!

Terminating Time-Wasters, Overcoming Organization Ogres

If you're not getting where you want to be as fast as you expected, you may be the victim of one of these adversaries:

Falling into the television trap. Analyze your TV-watching habits. It's easy to mindlessly sit in front of the tube to "relax," but it will rob you of precious time with very little return. Choose your TV programs carefully and put them on your schedule. Don't just sit down in your easy chair and zap the remote. Use your VCR or DVR (adding TiVo is a definite bonus) to record programs to watch *what* you want *when* you want. And you'll save time by zipping through all those ads besides.

Succumbing to interruptions. You may undermine yourself by allowing too many interruptions. Of course, not all interruptions can be avoided, but many can. Don't just accept them—control them. Set aside a period of time that you don't take any phone calls. Let the answering machine or voicemail do its job. If people drop in, tell them you have an appointment (you do—with yourself) or that you're on a deadline and will see them when you're done.

Procrastinating. Do a procrastination checkup. Go back to Chapter 3 and review the section on procrastination. Keep giving yourself the message, "Do it now!" Make that your new mantra.

Not having a plan. You may have done a great job of identifying your goals, but failed to work out a manageable plan, breaking things into smaller chunks and adding them to your schedule. Goal setting is an important step, but it doesn't go far enough. Set aside time to plan if that's what's hanging you up.

Re-accumulating stuff. Keeping your life from becoming overrun by "stuff" is an ongoing process. If your system worked great for a while and then started to bog down, you may have fallen into the Acquisition Trap again. Do a clutter inventory and pare down right away. Stop allowing junk to come into your life (including junk relationships), and get rid of what already has. Remember, too, if you buy something that's better than what you have, don't keep the old one.

Making things too complicated. Simple is better. You may have packed away umpteen widgets in neat little boxes with color-coded cards to tell you where everything is, cross-referenced and dated. The chances you'll keep up such a complicated system are slim. If you stick with the KISS system (Keep It Simple, Sweetie), it'll be less likely to break down.

Giving up too soon. If your system doesn't work the first time you try it, you may be tempted to scrap it entirely and give it up. Not so fast! It may just need some fine-tuning or some simple repetition to get it up and running.

> **Jump Starts**
>
> Ask your friends and family to stop giving you stuff. Tell them you'd rather they spend time with you, contribute to a worthy cause in your name, or create an experience for you. Share with them how hard you've worked to unstuff your life and how much you're enjoying your newfound space.

Resting on your laurels. I said to reward yourself, but I didn't say you could stop there! Enjoy your successes, do something nice for yourself, and move on. Continually ask, "What's next?" This is your other new mantra.

Being too much of a perfectionist. Have you become an organization zealot? Are you spending too much time doing everything perfectly instead of just getting it done? Somewhere between a neatnik and a slob is a functional, comfortable level of order we can all strive for. You can always go back and do it better, if and when you have the time, but personally, I'd rather be out walking in the sunshine or spending time with my husband! Organization is a tool to master, not our master.

Failing to include yourself in your maintenance plan. If you leave yourself out, everything will break down. Make sure you renew yourself in the four basic areas: physical (exercise, rest, nutrition), mental (reading, learning, organizing, and planning), social/emotional (relationships), and spiritual (prayer, meditation, nature, creative expression). Make sure you include activities each week to fine-tune, maintain, and improve all four areas. Seek a balance.

Can Your Computer Keep You Organized?

If you have a home computer, you may be underestimating it as a tool to help you maintain your organization systems. One of the best ways a computer can help is as a reminder tool. There are plenty of software packages out there for scheduling appointments. Even if you don't use a program for your day-to-day ones, program it for major maintenance reminders. Some organization software has the ability to create audio reminders. These are little alarms that sound when it's time to do something important. You can use this feature to reinforce maintenance chores that may be easy to forget, such as quarterly file purging, early tax preparation, or regular oil changes; use it as a reminder for birthdays and anniversaries. Maybe this can work for you!

If a paper-based system you're currently using for some task doesn't seem to be working well, maybe there's a computer program that does it better. Stay on the lookout for any tools that might help keep you on track. There are new ways of accomplishing things via computer being developed all the time. You can now vote on stock proxies, buy and send gifts, track packages, look up phone numbers and addresses, send greeting cards, and even file your tax returns online. Many of these services are free. Why not take advantage of them?

> **CAUTION**
>
> **Pileups!**
>
> Computer-based solutions are not *always* the most time- or cost-efficient. They're also not always the most mobile or adaptable. Before you make a major changeover to a computer program, consider the low-tech solutions as well as the high-tech.

Some programs require some heavy setup—such as recipe, personal record-keeping, or financial software—but after the initial data is entered, they're quick and easy to maintain. Weigh the investment in time and money needed for setting up a program against the time, money, and/or clutter savings in the long term.

Aesthetics Essentials

My first aim in writing this book was to help you get things functioning more smoothly in your life. When that happens, you can move to the next step, which is making what already works more beautiful. Order in itself is beautiful, in my opinion, and after you have a basic level of order and simplicity in your life, you can then turn your attention to making it even more aesthetically pleasing.

You can use the free time that results from being organized to pay more attention to details, including aesthetics. I have two rules, however. First, if something looks nice but fails to do the job I created it for, I opt for the less-attractive tool that works. And, second, if it isn't functional, it goes—unless it truly adds pleasure and beauty to my life.

I've tried lots of household paper-sorting systems, including ones made of wicker and other decorative materials, but the one that works best for me is a horizontal cardboard cubby system that fits on a shelf. Someday I may have a more attractive wooden one made, but until then, I'll take my ugly organizer over the decorator ones anytime!

There are lots of little ways, however, to add some beauty to otherwise mundane aspects of daily existence. Here are a few:

♦ After you get your closet organized, decorate the inside with colored hangers, attractive boxes, and picture postcards or posters on the unobstructed wall space. Change them periodically when the spirit moves you.

♦ Put fresh flowers on the breakfast table regularly and maybe a single bloom on your nightstand next to your bed.

♦ Cover recipe binders with wallpaper scraps or coated gift paper.

Resource Files

Alexandra Stoddard has made a study of adding beauty to everyday rituals and spaces. For some inspiring ideas, try reading her books *Living a Beautiful Life: 500 Ways to Add Elegance, Order, Beauty, and Joy to Every Day of Your Life* and *Living Beautiful Together.*

♦ Add scented sachets to your closet and drawers.

♦ Have a pretty, well-stocked basket of stationery within easy reach, and postcards, note cards, stamps, and an elegant letter opener that you can grab when you have a few minutes to do your personal correspondence.

Think of additional ways to make your personal world a more beautiful place!

You Have a Dream!

Being organized doesn't mean becoming a drudge. On the contrary, it should mean you're pounds lighter, experiencing a freedom you've probably never known.

If you find yourself burdened, a slave to your schedule, then you've lost sight of the purpose of getting organized—to fulfill the mission you said you wanted in life! Go back to the beginning and take another look. Review Chapter 2. Redo some of the exercises. If you need to, get some additional help with developing a mission statement and formulating your goals.

As I've mentioned before, I strongly recommend Stephen Covey's book *The 7 Habits of Effective People* and any of Anthony Robbins's books or self-improvement tapes. Many other excellent books, audiotapes, and videotapes are on the market, as well as seminars, that cover these topics. Doing this groundwork will make the difference between being a drudge and a dynamo! Tapping into your real desires and passions can't help but infuse your efforts with zest and energy.

Make sure you allow yourself time and space to wish and dream. Exercise your visualization muscles. There are good books and tapes on developing and using visualization techniques, as well. These techniques are enjoyable because they activate the unconscious, invigorate the imagination, and teach you how to employ your fantasies to help you identify what you really care about in life. I've listed several tools and how to obtain them in the resource guide at the back of this book.

Getting organized around your true desires for a fulfilled and joyous life is fun. If it's not, you're doing something wrong! Give yourself the time and space to embark on this important exploration—it will fuel everything you do.

Let the Seasons Tell the Time

Since first developing my own organization plans and implementing them, I've learned a trick that has added a new dimension to tasks that need doing every year: Key them to the seasons. This is how our ancestors made sure things got done on time! I find it adds a wonderful rhythm to life, when what I do works along with the changes in nature.

Winter is a time for turning inward. There's not much that can be done outside, so I can focus more on the house's inner workings. This is when my life centers more around the hearth and my own goals and dreams. It's a time for taking stock and planning. Chores such as cleaning out drawers and closets seem perfect for this time of year. Detail work, such as mending and sewing, takes precedence.

Spring means clearing out. There's a reason why our mothers and grandmothers called it "spring cleaning." That's the season when the earth is waking up and activity will begin to heighten and move outdoors. What better time to unstuff, have a yard sale, and get the family car in shape?

In summer, we can shed our heavy clothes, live more in the fresh air, and schedule tasks such as painting and refurbishing for a time when windows can remain open and cleanup is easier.

The fall, harvest time, is a time for reaping the rewards of our industry, making preparations for the coming cold weather. This is a good time to survey your disaster preparedness, food storage, and batteries.

Make Maintenance a Celebration

I can't encourage you enough to make organizing your life and maintaining your organization systems joyous and celebratory. Growing a happy life is something to celebrate! Add silly rituals, songs, rhymes, readings, music, and dance to your celebrations. Add whatever trappings make them fun. Make up your own holidays to both celebrate and serve as a reminder, or key them to our mysterious past, if you like.

Each February, for example, I celebrate Candlemas (or Imbolc, if you prefer its Celtic name), an ancient holiday that has since been transmuted into Groundhog Day, which reminds us of the longer days to come with the spring. I air out the house (whatever the temperature), imagine any stale influences taking flight out the windows, take an inventory of my spices and pantry staples, light every candle we own, and welcome the coming of the light and green of spring. All winter holiday decorations and seasonal cooking utensils are carefully put away in long-term storage. I begin collecting all the statements, documents, and receipts for taxes. I drool over seed catalogs. The actual celebration of this event when the date appears on the calendar adds a depth and a richness to it that grows in meaning each year.

Whatever your nationality or religious faith, look for ways to integrate daily tasks into larger events and celebrations. Find out what seasonal tasks were associated with these dates and adapt them to your own. At least try it. You may like it!

Resource Files

Want to learn more about seasonal celebrations? Find a copy of *Mrs. Sharp's Traditions: Nostalgic Suggestions for Re-Creating the Family Celebrations and Seasonal Pastimes of the Victorian Home* by Sarah Ban Breathnach for a perspective on the old-fashioned way of observing seasonal changes.

The Least You Need to Know

- Finding your "bottom line" and maintaining it is the best foundation for keeping your life organized.
- Lists, schedules, and an efficient filing system are the fundamental tools for maintaining an organized life.
- If your organization plan starts to break down, you can take specific steps to identify problem areas and get yourself back on track.

◆ If your system is functioning well, you can add beauty to everyday spaces and rituals.

◆ Giving yourself time and space to fantasize, visualize, wish, and dream is crucial to successfully building and perpetuating order and high performance.

Chapter 20

Organization Styles for Different Lifestyles

In This Chapter

- How to adapt your basic organization plan to your current lifestyle
- The importance of changing your plan for changes in lifestyle
- Resources for the special needs of frequent travelers
- Tips for single parents, caregivers, singles, widows, and widowers

The basic organization principles I've given you in this book apply regardless of your age, living situation, or financial status. Whether you're a student or a retiree, live alone or have a large family, getting organized will make your life better.

In this chapter, however, we look at how you can adapt these basic principles to your specific lifestyle and status, concentrating on the areas of food, clothing, shelter, people, money, and work.

All by Yourself

According to the latest U.S. census information, men and women are marrying later than ever before, and one in every nine adults lives alone.

If you have the house or apartment all to yourself, it's easier to implement an organization plan that works for you. You don't have other people to mess it up! You may live alone by choice; you may be a student living on your own for the first time, or a professional seriously pursuing a career; you may be divorced or widowed. Whatever your situation, being single presents its own organization challenges, whether you're beginning your adult life or are well into adulthood.

Young and Single

If you're young and single, chances are you have a fairly social lifestyle at this stage of your life. You may not eat at home very often. You're more likely to rent a house or apartment than own your own home, and you may move several times before settling in one place.

Although you may not yet be building equity in a home, it's important that you begin budgeting now, so you can keep a close watch on where your money goes and plan for emergencies. Now is also a good time to think about the future with a small investment fund. If you're not sure of the best way to begin investing, speak to a financial planner or educate yourself through an investment club or seminar.

Start organizing your work records now. Keep employment information and reviews in your files. Think ahead about references for future employment. If you're a student, your professors will be among your first references, so keep them in mind. Organizing to find a job might be a top issue soon, if it's not already. Now is the time to think about that resumé and begin collecting the information you need to write a good one.

Resource Files

For helpful tips on cooking for one, you can head for your computer, the bookstore, the TV, or the video store. Check out *Going Solo in the Kitchen* by Jane Doerfer, and *Serves One: Super Meals for Solo Cooks* by Toni Lydecker. You can join the Cooking for One or Two Recipe Club online at www.kitchenlink.com.

Although you may be inclined to eat out a lot, with some simple kitchen tools and basic ingredients you can create meals that are more nourishing and easier on the budget than eating out or "ordering in." It's easy to get into the junk food habit when you live alone, but it's expensive and doesn't promote good health. Even if you only cook for one, treat yourself like a guest. Sit at the table, not in front of the TV. Put on some dinner music and set the table. Enjoy a good, wholesome meal you prepared yourself.

Go back to Chapter 11 and review the information on bulk cooking, quick cooking, and Crock-Pot cooking. Experiment to see which methods work best for you. If you're simply not in the mood to cook after a hard day at work or school, try cooking only a couple of times a week and freezing single portions for other days. Soups and stews work well, as do many pasta sauces and casseroles.

You can often find good used cookware at garage sales and thrift stores if you're on a tight budget. Whatever you can't find there, purchase from reputable companies and try to buy the best quality you can afford. Here's a short list of the basics:

- 10- or 12-inch nonstick skillet
- 1- and 2-quart saucepans with lids
- 5-quart Dutch oven with lid
- 8- or 10-inch high-carbon, stainless-steel chef's knife
- 3-inch paring knife
- Sharpening steel and whetstone for sharpening knives
- Large cutting board (plastic or wood)
- Wooden spoons of various sizes
- Slotted spoon
- Ladle
- Plastic spatula for nonstick cookware
- Rubber spatulas, large and small, for scraping out bowls
- Tongs
- Set of measuring spoons and measuring cups
- 2-cup glass measuring cup
- Mixing bowls in various sizes
- Grater
- Baking/roaster pan
- Large strainer or colander
- Can opener
- Corkscrew and bottle opener
- Oven mitts and trivets
- Kitchen towels

CAUTION **Pileups!**

Not only do manual can openers work better than electric ones and take up less space, they come in handy when the electricity is out or you don't have an outlet handy.

> **Resource Files**
>
> There's a great book called *Where's Mom Now That I Need Her? Surviving Away from Home* by Betty Rae Frandsen, Kathryn J. Frandsen, and Kent P. Frandsen. It explains basic food preparation, simple first aid, laundry and clothing repair, stain removal, and lots more basic survival information for starting out on your own. A second volume, *Where's Dad Now That I Need Him? Surviving Away From Home*, handles the "guy" stuff such as money, home and car maintenance, and safety.

- Kitchen shears
- Vegetable peeler
- Microwave-safe storage containers
- Jar and bottle opener

Of course, you'll add to your collection as you cook more or if you decide to bake, but these are the basics. Add one good, basic cookbook such as *Joy of Cooking*, the *Fanny Farmer Cookbook*, or the *Better Homes and Gardens New Cookbook*, and you're all set.

You're probably doing your laundry out, but because you're only one person, the weekly trip to the Laundromat shouldn't be too taxing. Take advantage of off-peak hours, but don't compromise your safety. Dinnertime is usually a good time for doing laundry and grocery shopping.

Because you're just starting out, you can unstuff and avoid the Acquisition Trap now. Make careful selections, and buy quality things. It's better to buy quality used things than new, cheaper ones of inferior quality. When selecting furniture, remember that you'll likely be moving it several times. Stay away from massive pieces that need special handling or may not fit through the door or up the stairs of your next apartment.

Older and Single

If you're older and single, you also have control of your environment and destiny, but you're at a different stage in life than the "young single." You may be living alone as an intentional lifestyle, or you may be divorced or widowed and have no children at home.

One great challenge for you could be balancing alone time with social activities. It may mean forcing yourself to get out and be with other people. If you have a career, you'll have more opportunities to socialize, but if you're no longer in the work force, you may have to make a conscious effort to involve yourself outside the home.

Add some activities to explore to your Master List. Using your planner/organizer to schedule specific activities will remind you of your social needs. Join a discussion group, take up a hobby, volunteer, or get involved in your community. There are lots of opportunities to meet new people and contribute your skills and experience.

Statistics show that women make up the largest number of those surviving a spouse. Many women haven't had responsibility for the finances during their married years, so developing money-management skills becomes crucial once they're on their own. If you're in this situation and haven't done so yet, taking stock of your finances should be your number one priority. If you and your husband had a financial plan, it needs to be revised for your new circumstances.

Jump Starts

If you're alone due to the death of a spouse, one delicate issue is getting rid of things belonging to your departed loved one. It's hard to say when is the best time to pack up your spouse's belongings and pass them on, but at some point it will make sense. If you need support, have someone go through the process with you.

A book specifically aimed at widows and divorcees that can get you on the right track is *After He's Gone: A Guide for Widowed and Divorced Women* by Barbara Tom Jowell and Donnette Schwisow.

Now that you're cooking for only one person, you can cut down the ingredients for your favorite recipes or make the same amount you did for two and freeze the rest for a later meal. Make sure you don't give in to the "why bother?" syndrome when contemplating a meal just for yourself.

My recently widowed friend Edith, who loves to cook, decided she missed cooking for other people more than she realized. She now regularly invites friends over for dinner. Everyone pitches in with ingredients, but she does the cooking. Guests help with the cleanup, too. This gives Edith great pleasure and stimulating evening conversation. She eats more nutritious meals than she would if she were only preparing food for herself. And her guests don't have to cook that night! A good deal all around. Don't be afraid to try offbeat ideas. They're often the ones that work the best.

Single-Income, Dual-Parent Families

Some couples feel the sacrifices they must make to have one parent home at all times are worth it. One partner may give up his or her income altogether, or each may have a part-time arrangement so they can share child-care responsibilities. I think that this trend will grow even more in the coming years.

Resource Files _____

Subscribe to "The Dollar Stretcher," a free online newsletter that's delivered to your e-mail address, by sending an e-mail message to gary@stretcher.com with "subscribe" in the subject and your e-mail address in the body of the message. This cybernewsletter is filled with useful suggestions for those trying to get by with less.

Pileups! _____

Because they tend to be very career-oriented, DINKS (dual-income, no kids) can sometimes forget how important it is to pay attention to their primary relationship. Over time, they may grow apart. Make sure if you fall into this lifestyle category, you see to it there's adequate focus on your significant other, not just your own personal ambitions.

For couples embracing this lifestyle, organization issues focus around thrift and scheduling child care. Time-management issues are different. With reduced income, the family is choosing a quality of emotional life over material things. Careful budgeting, cooking from scratch, and even having a vegetable garden and sewing some of the family's clothes might be part of the plan. Children can be brought into these activities and, in fact, taught valuable self-reliance skills. If children understand the reasons for the tradeoffs and are made a part of the process, they'll be more willing to cooperate.

Steve, a writer friend of mine, and his wife, Leslie, decided they both wanted to be highly involved in the daily life of their new baby. Leslie is a schoolteacher, and Steve was a technical writer. Steve left his job to become a home-based freelance writer, while Leslie kept her teaching job. Together their two present incomes equal roughly half of what they were making when both worked full time.

During the summer, Leslie takes over the child-care duties so Steve can develop his writing business. During the school year, Steve has to juggle caring for the baby with getting his work done. He can handle some of it at night and on weekends, but when deadlines loom, he sometimes needs help.

One solution is in-home childcare, where the parent is still available, and the babysitter tends to the child's needs while the at-home parent works. Another is a trade situation, where several at-home parents trade off caring for each other's children one day a week.

If one parent takes on the role of at-home child-care provider, it's important that the other spends time with the children and gives the at-home parent some private time. Negotiating these times, as well as the cleaning duties, are key issues. It's all too easy to assume that the at-home parent is responsible for cooking, childcare, and keeping the house clean. No fair! Those duties should be shared. How they're divided up needs to be negotiated and jobs scheduled.

Dual-Income Couples

For DINKS, meshing schedules and sharing housework are the key organization issues.

The only time available for maintaining both the house and the relationship is evenings, weekends, and vacation time, so it's important that both partners share their schedules and commit to certain chores around the house. This group can often benefit from hiring outside help, and they're more likely to have the income to do it. Doing housework chores together is another solution, building some fun and communication into what needs to be done anyway.

Another time for sharing and reconnecting is during the preparation and enjoyment of the evening meal. Make these times special by planning menus and perhaps doing some food preparation ahead of time (refer to Chapter 11 for meal preparation strategies), so you can concentrate on making mealtime unhassled and relaxing. Light some candles, use those fancy cloth napkins, hold hands, and talk!

> **Jump Starts**
>
> Like other families, dual-income families need to look at accumulating money for college tuition, so financial planning and careful budgeting are high priorities. Because time for managing investments is most likely hard to come by, finding a good financial planner is crucial. Review Chapters 15 and 16 to get your finances in shape for now and the future.

Dual-Income Families

Organization issues for families where both parents work are likely to revolve around child-care and work-related topics. The working couple knows that spending time with the children needs to be one of the highest priorities, but it can be tricky. Balancing the personal need for renewal and "downtime" against the needs of the children isn't easy. And, again, who does the housework? All too often it's the working woman who ends up trying to do it all. No fair, guys!

Planning and scheduling come to the rescue here. So does finding ways to get things done and spend time with the kids at the same time. Who says washing the car has to mean time away from the family? It can mean a fantastic water fight and a cleaning session at the same time. Even the dog may get a bath.

If you're clear about your mission in life and you write down your goals, develop a plan, and work on it each day, you'll raise great kids (a worthy life mission) and get ahead in your career. It doesn't just happen by accident.

Single Parents

The adult of a single-parent family has to do it all. There simply is no one else (or so it seems). It's a tough place to be. I know—I've been there. If you become a single parent through divorce, besides all the challenges you face, you may hear from outsiders and the media that your home is "broken." Well, I never accepted that, and neither should you!

Sure, it's best for kids to grow up in a healthy two-parent household, but when you're going it alone there's no reason not to have a great family! Just recently I read a list of ways that single-parent families have unique strengths. I thought I'd paraphrase some of them for you:

- Just because a family has two parents doesn't mean it's healthy or happy. If there was an unhealthy situation before, a single-parent situation is vastly superior. Now the children may have an opportunity to bond with both parents separately, without the discord that existed before.

- Single parents have more flexibility in planning time with their children. They don't have the regular demands and distractions of another adult. When the children are with each parent, they can have exclusive attention and the individual parent may be more attuned to their emotional needs.

- Single-parent households can be more interdependent. Single parents depend more heavily on cooperation from each family member, and children are more likely to pitch in voluntarily. I'm convinced my children are the responsible adults they are today largely because they learned responsibility early. They felt needed and rose to the occasion.

- Children in single-parent households are often exposed to a wider range of experiences. Rather than getting a baby-sitter (which I couldn't afford), I took my children to college classes with me, to work on my college newspaper, to the library, and on field trips. When I organized the company Christmas party, they were the elves.

◆ In divorced families, children can experience two totally different spheres. They get a wider view of life, and besides, they get two birthday parties and two Christmases!

Jump Starts

Although it's not something we naturally want to discuss, it would be a good idea to feel your children out about what they would want if you couldn't be there to take care of them. Choose a time carefully to broach the subject, reassure them that nothing's wrong, but tell them you want to make certain that no matter what the future brings, they're always taken care of. Take their wishes into consideration when choosing a guardian.

Of course, single parents have their work cut out for them, as well. Certain standards may have to be lowered, especially those surrounding housework. But order and organization are even more important in a single-parent household. Because there's so little time, things need to be streamlined to operate as efficiently as possible.

The once-a-week food preparation method worked best for me when I was a single parent with young children. I shopped and cleaned on Saturday while the children were with their father, and cooked the week's meals on Sunday afternoon. The children knew what was scheduled for when, so even if I got home late they could get things started. If the meal was frozen, I took it out to thaw in the morning before I went to work. We had good, wholesome, home-cooked meals that were within my budget, without having to cook after a long day at the office. The Crock-Pot came in handy, too.

Resource Files

The National Organization of Single Mothers can be reached at www.singlemothers. org. This award-winning organization helps new members form or join local support groups and publishes "SingleMOTHER," a bimonthly newsletter offering information and advice, plus tips that can save single mothers time and money.

Two of the biggest issues for the single parent are making sure that children aren't alone when they come home from school and that there's always someone available in an emergency. Some school systems have after-school programs for "latchkey kids." If you don't live in an area with support programs for single parents, you may want to consider relocating. You can't do this alone, and it helps to live in a community where you can get some help. Look to church groups and single-parent organizations as well.

For emergencies, the best system is to have several people who can cover for you in case you can't be reached. Line up relatives, friends, or neighbors you can trust in advance. You also need to cover the times the children are sick and you have to go to work. A redundant system with several backups is the way to keep things covered no matter what.

It helps to work for a company that is pro-family. You should never have to choose between your job and the well-being of your child. There are organizations that rate companies in these areas. Do some research. (Start with your local research librarian.) When you go job hunting, have this objective clear in your mind. You're more likely to find what you want if you firmly plant the idea in your mind before you start looking.

On the financial front, you need to provide for your children in case something happens to you. Get all the benefits you're entitled to at your workplace and through the local, state, and federal governments, whether you're divorced or widowed. Think through what you want done with and for your children if you die or become seriously ill. Name a guardian who will have immediate access to all your financial information. Organize it the way I outlined in Chapters 15 and 16, and show the person you choose how you have it set up. Be sure to include any special information about the children that this person may need to know, such as medical history or special needs.

The Empty Nest

I can personally address the empty-nest change in lifestyle, because I'm smack dab in the middle of it! When the fledglings fly from the nest, Mom and Dad can be anywhere from their 40s (if they started a family early) to well into their 70s. The issues for empty-nesters are somewhat different depending on age and financial status, but certain things crop up regardless of when your little birdies fly the coop.

One such issue is deciding when to take over the kids' rooms. This can be more trouble than you might think. When my oldest daughter left for college, I immediately moved my office into her bedroom. I had been using the dining room, but there was too much activity there for me to work effectively and I couldn't keep my papers in order. Rachel was crushed. I was looking at it from a

> **Jump Starts**
>
> It's sometimes difficult to be balanced in our approach to our children. On the one hand, we want to make them feel that they're loved and can always come home if they need to. On the other hand, we want them to be independent and self-sufficient, solving their own problems and forging their own future. Strive to create this balance—both offering support and letting go.

totally practical standpoint; her reaction was purely emotional. I never intended to make her feel she wasn't welcome (I had a bed fixed up in the family room downstairs), but that's how she felt. What can I say? I goofed! It's a good idea to find out from your kids how they feel about using their old space *before* you make changes.

On the other hand, don't become a storage facility for your grown kids. As soon as they're on their own and settled semi-permanently, they need to decide what to take, what to toss, and what they'd like you to hang on to. Keep the last category to a minimum. Strike a balance between keeping a place for your grown children and moving on to the next stage in your lives.

Make sure you reevaluate your finances. Most likely your children will have their own benefits at work, and you'll be able to make some changes there. As a gift to each child, one year we arranged for them to have a professional financial planner where they live draw up a complete financial plan for them, while we did the same for ourselves. Rather than contributing more clutter to your children's lives, why not give them something they can really use?

Caregivers and Extended Families

Having an ill, disabled, or aged family member in a household creates several crucial organization issues. Laying out the home in an efficient manner is essential to saving steps for caregivers and making it easier for a loved one to care for him- or herself as much as possible.

Much has been written on this topic, and contacting one of the various organizations that addresses your particular situation would be an excellent idea.

You may need to rethink how you store things and how you shop. Perhaps smaller sizes would make it easier for a disabled or aged family member to prepare meals. Many ingredients come prechopped or semi-prepared now, making it less labor-intensive to put together a dish. Lower shelving might help or simply relocating essentials to an area within easy reach. Some simple aids might contribute to independence.

Resource Files

To find a caregiver support group, contact the American Self-Help Clearinghouse at www.mentalhelp.net/selfhelp. They'll give you information on self-help organization chapters in your area, or send you to the headquarters of a national organization that addresses your needs.

In some cases, you may need a home health-care aide to assist you, even if only temporarily. Contact your local social-services agency and ask for referrals. A professional might know simple techniques to make things easier or be able to point you toward helpful equipment and tools.

The role of caregiver needn't fall to one member of the family alone. Everyone can be involved, sharing scheduled time and responsibilities. Even small children can give the primary caregiver a hand, and older children can provide much-needed relief.

These days, extended families often include adult children living at home. If older children come back home to live, it shouldn't be on the same basis as it was when they were children. They are now housemates, and they need to understand that right from the get-go. Negotiate their household share of the cooking, shopping, cleaning, and financial requirements. Expect them to behave like adults, and resist the temptation to treat them like they're young children again. It's also a good idea to have a defined period of time for this arrangement. Is it for six months? A year? Don't wait until they've moved in to discuss these things. Get things out in the open from the start.

> **Jump Starts**
>
> Ideally, in a dual-custody situation, chores assigned to a child in one household should also be assigned in the other. This will reduce the feeling of disruption in a child's life and will also help both households keep working efficiently. Both parents need to work together to create consistency and see that one doesn't undermine the discipline efforts of the other.

You need to work out storage arrangements, too. If they have furniture, where will you put it? You have to make room, they'll have to find a solution, or someone will have to pay for rental of a storage facility. Will you be eating together, or will your adult child be responsible for his or her own meals? If the latter, will they be shopping for their own groceries? Do they understand they'll be cleaning up after themselves? What about laundry? Discuss these issues upfront, to avoid misunderstandings and hurt feelings later.

Blended Families and Dual-Custody Arrangements

With more than half of all marriages ending in divorce and many divorced partners remarrying, new solutions have evolved to handle parenting by more than one set of adults. These arrangements can work if everyone involved keeps their main priority in mind: the welfare of the children. Beyond this, organizing for smooth transitions from one residence to the other is imperative.

In some cases, there are as many as five sets of children involved in the blending of families: the divorced couple's, each of their new spouse's kids, and children from the two new unions. The challenges are enormous, but are being met by real people every day.

My friend Katie and her husband have a dual-custody arrangement with Katie's children. Both she and her ex-husband live in the same area, so the kids attend the same activities, they just go home to a different house every other week. Certain basics are duplicated in each household, and personal areas are designated for each child to call his or her own. Certainly, this arrangement would not work for everyone, but when adults put their efforts into cooperating and promoting their children's welfare, it's amazing how well children adapt.

Scheduling regular "family conferences" is crucial to keeping communication flowing and resolving logistical issues before they get out of hand. If a child is being disciplined in one household for unacceptable behavior, the adults in the second household need to know what's going on and, hopefully, support those efforts.

The Road Warrior

I covered the needs of the home-based worker at length in Chapter 9, but one lifestyle we only touched on was that of the "road warrior" or frequent traveler.

Whether you're self-employed or working for someone else, your job may involve a great deal of travel. This lifestyle brings up a whole host of special organization issues. To name a few …

> **CAUTION**
>
> **Pileups!**
>
> Don't forget to designate someone to keep extra keys if you live alone, so that person can get into your home or apartment in an emergency, and so *you* can get in your home if you lose your keys. Trusted neighbors are ideal, especially if they're home during the day.

Who handles things while you're away? If someone is holding down the fort at home and/or at work, you may naturally be tempted to dump everything on him or her. How fair is that? You need to be organized to handle your daily tasks on the road. If you normally pay the bills, consider an electronic bill-paying service and computer cash-management program on your laptop (with built-in modem, of course), which makes handling this stuff on the road pretty easy. If this won't work, see whether your bank has an automatic bill-paying service. If it doesn't, you may want to look for a new bank. Look for other ways you can take care of the same responsibilities while you're traveling that you do when you're at home.

Resource Files

Three good books to help you learn the ropes of serious business travel are *The Unofficial Business Traveler's Pocket Guide* by Christopher J. McGinnis; *The Business Traveler's Survival Guide, How to Get Work Done While on the Road* by June Langhoff; and *Keeping Your Family Close: When Frequent Travel Pulls You Apart* by Elizabeth M. Hoekstra.

What happens in an emergency? Have people and services lined up for everything that might go wrong, from a flooded basement to a sick pet.

What if people need to get in touch? A detailed itinerary with accurate information about where you'll be at all times is crucial. Be sure to include phone numbers. If things change en route, be sure to amend the itinerary as soon as you know. Leave this information with all the key people back on the home front.

I've been a "road warrior" myself at various times, and I know many other writers and business people who spend a lot of time in planes, trains, and automobiles. Here are a few tips I've put together from my own "road show":

Portable everything! Consider bulk, weight, and durability in things such as luggage, clothing, computer equipment, and personal appliances. Look for small-sized toiletries, too, and small containers you can transfer things into. Make frequent use of resealable plastic bags for individual items that can leak.

Exercise. Select accommodations where you can walk safely, or ones that have exercise facilities indoors. Schedule time in your planner/organizer just as if you were at home. You'll feel better, and it's a great stress reliever!

Eat a balanced diet. Stay away from fast-food places and try to eat balanced meals that aren't too rich. Ask the locals to recommend places that fit the bill. Take your vitamins! If I'm going to be in one place for a few days, I often get meals from my favorite take-out: the grocery store! Fruits and vegetables can be kept on ice from the hotel or motel ice-maker. Some cooked chilled shrimp with cocktail sauce and a salad add up to a delicious, light meal that's easy to put together in a hotel room. My husband and I, tiring of rich restaurant food, have often made a repast of fruit, cheese, and hearty bread.

Pack light. Most experienced, heavy-duty travelers recommend packing everything into your carry-on luggage. If you can't get it into two manageable bags, don't take it. That way you don't have to wait in line for your baggage or run the risk of losing it between stops. If you're away for a long time, you can use hotel laundry services or a Laundromat. If you know you'll accumulate stuff on the road, such as brochures or conference materials, pack it up and ship it home.

Stay in touch. Make regular calls if someone at home is taking care of things. Tell them how much you appreciate their help and support. If you're maintaining a relationship, communication is essential. Most people I know with heavy travel schedules who are in a relationship call home at least once a day. This gives the one at home base the opportunity to involve you in important decisions, and gives you a feeling of "connectedness," even if you can't remember which city you woke up in this morning. Cell phones make this all the more simple, but there will be times when you simply can't be reached, so make sure you "check in."

Dress for travel success. Invest in lightweight, easy-to-care-for, mix-and-match separates. Women actually have it easier in this area, because male business travelers generally have to cope with bulky suits. Many clothes travel best rolled rather than laid flat. Make sure to wear only comfortable shoes.

Don't bring it home. Restrain yourself from bringing home clutter from your travels, either for yourself or as souvenirs for those who stayed behind. E-mail often. Write long, love-filled letters. Share your feelings. Tell them you miss them and what you love about them. Those things are better than souvenirs any day!

Envisionings

Take some time to think about your present lifestyle. Has it changed recently? What are the positive things about your particular situation? What are the unique challenges that might be helped with planning and organizing? Are finances the greatest area of concern? Or does finding time for intimacy need more of your attention? If you could change one thing about your current lifestyle, what would that be?

Be sure to detox from your trip as soon as you can. Listen first to what's gone on at home, and then tell your tales from the hinterlands.

Whatever your particular circumstances, an organization plan can be adapted to suit them. It's not a "one-size-fits-all" world. Know the specific challenges and advantages of your lifestyle, and create a plan that works best for you.

The Least You Need to Know

◆ You can adapt the basic principles of organization to every lifestyle.

◆ You can organize for the way you live now and for future changes by changing emphasis and priorities.

◆ Key activities for adapting your organization plan are negotiating, scheduling, and planning.

◆ Whatever your situation, strive for balance between the physical, mental, emotional, and spiritual.

Part  8

You're Ready for Prime Time

You've worked hard and you deserve some fun. You also deserve a rosy future, filled with good health and vigor. These last chapters are for flexing your organization muscles and moving on to the big leagues. Here you learn how to sail through the holidays with aplomb and even improve your health. From here you'll think of lots more ways to apply your clutter- and time-busting tools to make every day a great day.

Chapter 21

Healing Trends: Organizing for Health and Fitness

In This Chapter

◆ Using your organizing skills to get and stay fit and healthy

◆ Making sure you don't forget doctor and dentist appointments

◆ Getting your sports and exercise equipment ready for anything

◆ Organizing health information to prepare for emergencies

We've all heard the saying "If you don't have your health, you don't have anything." Well, it's true. Ask most anyone who's suffering from a chronic disease, and she'll tell you she'd give up anything to be healthy. So what's the most important thing we can do to stay "in the pink"? Use preventative medicine! Although there are some things we can't control or foresee, there's so much we can do to ensure our health and well-being. And now that you have some basic organization and time-management skills under your belt, there's no excuse for putting your health on the back burner.

A Healthy Dose of Organization

"Can my health really benefit from being organized?" My answer is that your health *depends* on your being organized! I read somewhere that "if you're too busy to stay in shape, you're too busy," and I agree. How you manage your time, what you allow to take priority, and how much stress you have in your life could help determine how fit and healthy you are.

Not sure where you stand with regard to your health? Well, let's apply the basic principles and processes of organization to your health and see what happens.

Take Stock of Where You Are

Taking stock of your health is pretty easy. You know what to do. Step on the scale and consult a weight chart if you're not sure what you should weigh. If you know you need to lose weight, admit it here and now. Get your blood pressure checked, and while you're at it, get a complete physical. (Throw in a visit to the eye doctor and the dentist, too, if it's been a while.) Learn how to check your heart rate and what it should be. (Your doctor can help you with this, and you can find the information in any number of books on health and fitness or online.) Decide whether you're getting enough sleep and eating the right foods. Take a look at the amount of exercise you're getting, and be honest about whether you're really taking care of your body.

> **CAUTION**
>
> **Pileups!**
>
> Don't let your family be caught without the information they need in case of an emergency or when a question arises. Keep a good medical reference guide handy. Several good ones are available; one popular one is the *Harvard Medical School Family Health Guide* edited by Anthony L. Komaroff, M.D.

Set Realistic Goals

If your doctor tells you your blood pressure is high, the goal is clear. You need to make whatever lifestyle changes are necessary to bring it down a little at a time. If you know you need to lose a few pounds, that's one of your goals. If you need to lose a lot of weight, take a manageable amount and make that your first goal. If you don't get enough exercise, make building regular exercise into your daily life a priority. Write your goals down, and make them as specific as possible. Wherever possible, make them *measurable* so you can hold yourself accountable!

Decide on Actions to Achieve Your Goals

Actions are the things you're willing to do to get what you say you want. They reflect the big picture. If you need to bring your blood pressure down, for example, some of your actions might be lose weight, get more exercise, and learn to manage stress. In the next stage, you decide what steps you need to take to support those actions.

Divide Major Actions into Manageable Steps

After you've figured out what major actions to take, wherever you can, subdivide activities into daily and weekly steps you can take right now. What changes do you need to make to meet your goals? How can you make those changes as satisfying and fun as possible?

If you need to get more exercise, for instance, what activities really give you pleasure? Which ones are you most likely to stick with? Why decide you're going to take up running when it's martial arts you really enjoy? What kind of support would you need to lose weight? Would having a buddy or group to work with be the most enjoyable to you? If you're eating unhealthful snacks, what healthful foods could you substitute that you enjoy? Make one of your actions a purge of those unhealthful foods from your pantry, and add to your to-do list a shopping trip to replace them with yummy and healthful goodies.

Resource Files

To determine the ideal weight for your height, check out the weight charts at www. changingshape.com/resources/ references/idealbodyweight.asp.

Put These Steps into Your Overall Plan

Write down the specific steps you've decided to take in your planner/organizer. Make appointments with yourself to exercise. Make an appointment at a future date to have your blood pressure rechecked. Make an appointment to attend the next weight-loss program meeting, if that's what you've determined you need. Or keep a daily food diary to get a handle on where you're spending unnecessary calories. Tell the people who care about you to be supportive and even "in your face" about your goals, if that's effective for you. Get whatever help you need. Commit to having what you say you want.

Evaluate Your Progress

Regularly measure your success. Take your physical measurements once a month to evaluate the effects of your weight-loss and/or exercise program. Get regular checkups if there's a medical problem you're working on. Check off on your calendar the times you exercised this week and for how long. Keep track of this information so you can chart your progress. Make a fanfare of doing this if it engages your spirit. Play the Olympic theme as you disrobe and step onto the scale. Have a progress chart on the bathroom mirror or in your planner/organizer if you're too shy to publish the results just yet. Whatever works! Have fun with it.

Reward Yourself and Move On

When you complete each step toward a goal, give yourself a pat on the back, but also give yourself a tangible reward. Consult your rewards list for ideas. If you haven't made one yet, do it now! Make sure you have both large- and small-scale rewards. Having a major reward in mind for when you reach your final goal is great, but you need smaller incentives to keep going. Buying a bottle of special bath oil to commemorate a 10-pound weight loss, or treating yourself to some new exercise clothes as a reward for sticking to your routine for a month, will spur you on to greater successes. Enjoy, then quickly pick a new goal and move forward.

If you believe you're fit and healthy, if you get regular exercise and have regular medical checkups with a "clean bill of health," and then move on to the next topic in this book. But if you can't honestly say you fall in that category, if there's room for improvement, and then get organized to support your new goals regarding your health.

Finding Time to Get Fit

One of the most common excuses offered for failing to get in shape is "I don't have the time." Well, you *know* you're not going to get away with that here! If you're committed to being fit and healthy, there are no valid excuses. Even with disabilities and various physical limitations, you can always do *something*. Something leads to more and more "somethings," and pretty soon you're getting fit.

You've learned that the only reason to "get organized" is so you can have the things in your life that you most want. So the first thing to do is evaluate your motives and honestly decide whether you want a healthier lifestyle.

Sometimes all it takes is a new approach—some ideas for making it easier to create new habits. Here's a list of ideas to help you set up a healthier lifestyle. Take what most applies to the things you need to change, and add them to your master list in your planner/organizer, or schedule them *now*.

- Decide on the form of aerobic exercise you find most pleasurable, make sure the tools you need are functional and easily available, and schedule at least 30 minutes three times a week. For example, if you like using an exercise machine, put it next to your home office or in front of the TV. If you enjoy exercise tapes, make sure there's ample space to exercise by the TV, and store the tapes right next to it. Ease the way to sticking to your schedule.

- Consider joining a convenient gym or a nearby aerobics class. Perhaps you find you get a better workout when you do a class than when you're by yourself. Some people find that taking a class gets them started, and then they can take off on their own. Plus they get the added bonus of learning how to do the moves correctly.

- Get your bicycle, or any other equipment you plan to use for your fitness program, in tip-top shape. You've been going through the house sorting things into categories, including things that need to be fixed. Put your exercise equipment at the top of that list, if it needs repair. Make sure you have the necessary tools to begin and stick to your program, and put them in a convenient place. We talk about sports storage later on in this chapter. Get ready to organize the garage!

- The form of aerobic exercise that most turns you on is the one you're most likely to stick to. Don't let the lack of clothing or functional equipment stop you. Consider used equipment if finances are tight. (Just make sure it's in good working order. You don't need another thing to fix.)

Envisionings

Close your eyes and visualize what a healthier "you" might look and feel like. What can you do in your fantasy that you can't do now? Notice what resistant feelings come up about it. What obstacles do you think you might have to surmount? After you settle the issues with yourself and make a commitment, you'll find the time and the will.

Resource Files

Looking for exercise videos? The best catalog I've seen is from Collage Video. You can call them at 1-800-433-6769; write to 5390 Main St. NE, Minneapolis, MN 55421; or visit their website at www.collagevideo.com. For everything imaginable to do with fitness and nutrition, check out the Internet Fitness Resource website at www.netsweat.com.

◆ Fitness can help you in your relationships, too. How? One way to find more time for someone you care about is to exercise together! Besides, when you have a fitness buddy, you're far more likely to stick to your plan.

◆ Choose a lifetime pursuit that gives you that satisfied feeling and holds your interest. If you prefer exercise that's built in to a something that gives you an additional benefit, consider gardening or marital arts.

Jump Starts

Even people with super-busy schedules can fit exercise into their routine. Walk or ride a bike to work. Walk to lunch. Take the stairs instead of the elevator. Park a good distance away from the office, allow some extra time, and walk. Use this same trick at shopping malls or any time you run errands.

Pileups!

Do you have a tendency to forget doctor appointments? Then take advantage of office reminders, if your doctor or dentist provides them. Ask to be called the day before. If you have computer software with an audible reminder feature, put it in there, too. Wherever you can build in redundancy, do it.

◆ Don't overlook organizing for exercise at work. Would having an extra pair of walking shoes, a Walkman, and a fitness audiotape (or motivational tape or upbeat music) in your desk drawer make you more likely to go walking on your lunch hour? Chances are it would!

◆ Before you begin any exercise program, consult a doctor. With your planner/organizer in hand, schedule doctor, dentist, eye doctor, and any other health-related appointments you've been putting off. Then decide on a yearly event to tie your visits to every year.

I find that scheduling appointments around my birthday ensures I never forget. If finances require you to spread them out over the year, picking special days of the year still isn't a bad idea. Be creative—such as choosing the week of Valentine's day to have your yearly physical and heart check.

◆ Check in with yourself regularly. Weigh yourself weekly or monthly. Take your measurements. Calculate your heart rate. Get a home blood pressure machine and take your blood pressure if that's something you need to watch. Take responsibility for your health, and give yourself the tools and information you need to track your progress.

♦ Decide on a food plan that's balanced and based on sound scientific research, and adapt it to your lifestyle. Consult your doctor first, if you're not sure which one to choose.

♦ Get foods out of the house that don't support your eating program, and stock up on those that do. Purge your pantry, your refrigerator, and other places you store food. Set yourself up for success.

Jump Starts

When you reward yourself, try to make your reward something that won't sabotage your health objectives (*not* a hot fudge sundae, for example) and won't add clutter to your life. How about a self-nurturing experience instead? Treat yourself to a massage or a visit to a favorite place.

♦ Pull out the recipes (or find some new ones) that are in sync with your eating plan. Make up menus for a week or two using them. You'll be less tempted to go off your program if you already have meals planned. Make up batches of healthful soups, grains, and cut-up veggies, so when you're hungry they're easy to fix in a hurry. You can use any of the three methods discussed in Chapter 11 to work with your goals—bulk cooking, quick cooking, and slow cooking in a Crock Pot are all adaptable to whatever food program you need to create for your health.

♦ Photocopy suggestions for healthful eating out at restaurants, and keep them in your planner/organizer, wallet, or purse. When you're looking at the menu and are overwhelmed with temptation, having a list might keep you in check.

♦ Reward yourself regularly for sticking to your eating and exercise program.

The simple principle I've been hammering home since we started our Organizing Your Life journey—*the fundamental purpose of organizing is to support you in your goals*—can help you move toward a healthier lifestyle. Use all the tricks you've learned so far and make them work "to your health!"

Be a Sport!

You need some storage space for the equipment and supplies for whatever lifetime sports or exercise programs you and your family members choose. You need to store your equipment where you can get to it easily and near where you'll be using it.

If you've chosen to do indoor exercise with videos, you need a place to store your videos and exercise mat, yoga blocks, stepper, or whatever else you might need. Find a regular space that's pleasant and available, have all your stuff right there, and schedule a regular time. Make sure to have some water at hand so you can stay hydrated as you work out.

If walking is your thing, put a small backpack by the door with a water bottle and anything else you might need to keep you comfortable (sunscreen, sweater, lip balm, umbrella, etc.). If the temperature rises and you need to shed a jacket or sweater, you can put it in your backpack, keeping your hands free for upper-body exercise. Walking is one of the safest forms of exercise for almost anyone and it's free!

If a gym or fitness center is your choice, have a gym bag packed and keep it near the door.

If you've decided on a lifetime sport with a lot of equipment, most likely you're going to turn to the garage for storage. Add a couple of more family members' "sports stuff" and you've got another clutter disaster! If you rotate between several sports or turn to different kinds of exercise depending on the seasons, the clutter can be compounded.

Sooner or later you're going to have to turn to the garage, clean it out, and make it work for you. A typical garage might house a portable basketball hoop, baseball paraphernalia, soccer balls, skis and poles, bicycles, exercise equipment, and more. Weed out stuff from activities you or your family members no longer engage in. If junior doesn't play baseball anymore, but is heavy into soccer, ditch the former slugger's gear.

Jump Starts

If there really isn't any room in your garage, consider whether you can add a shed or small outbuilding on your property to store large equipment such as the lawnmower, snow blower, and wheelbarrow, as well as flammable substances. Make sure it can be locked and is thoroughly protected from the elements.

You've got the unstuffing routine down pretty well by now. Get rid of junk that is broken, no longer used, or used so infrequently you can probably share it with someone else. You can use the box system or simply make piles, but the categories are the same: *Trash*, *Pass On*, *Put Away*, and *Keep*. You want someplace to group recyclables and things that need to be fixed as well.

Storage Shopping List for the Garage

After you've thrown away what you no longer need, and fixed and sorted what equipment is left, the next step is to make a list of the storage products and hardware you need to store it. Consider these garage storage solutions:

- **Plastic boxes in various sizes and shapes.** Uniform box sizes help make the most of shelf space because you can space shelves closer together.

- **Shelving.** Design shelves around what you store most often. Consider products that allow you to change shelving configurations as needs change.

- **Hooks and clamps** for hanging things overhead or on the walls. Heavier hooks, such as those made to hold ladders, can also be used to hang up bicycles. Hooks or racks suspended from the ceiling need to be put into the joists.

- **Pegboard.** A pegboard system is extremely flexible. You can get hardware for shelves and move them when your needs change. Make sure the pegboard is screwed into the studs, so it doesn't pull down with heavier items. Go from floor to ceiling in at least one area.

- **Plastic and metal trash cans.** These can be used to store materials and keep them dry. If wall space is at a premium, you can use them to store things vertically.

- **Netting.** An old hammock or flexible netting made specifically for storage is useful for suspending things such as sports equipment, beach balls, and pool toys.

Resource Files

For ideas on storage to build or buy for your garage, attic, or basement, check out *Creating Storage: Hidden Storage and Rescued Space in the Garage, Attic, or Basement* from the editors of Sunset Publishing Corporation, and *Complete Home Storage* from the same publisher. Both books are excellent home-storage primers.

Resource Files

There's a highly flexible and strong storage system for garages called the storeWall system. It's a panel with slots that allows use of a variety of baskets, shelves, cabinets and hooks for all manner of sports equipment and accessories, as well as garden and other tools, cleaning supplies, paints, and just about anything else you need to store in a garage. Check out their online catalog at www.theaccessoriesgroup.com or call 866-404-8570.

- **Floor-standing racks** made just for storing sports equipment are also available. I found one called the All Sports Organizer at store.greatgolfmemories.com/ allspor.html. Look for other versions at your local department store or sports and outdoor-equipment store.

◆ **The Trunk Sports Organizer** is a canvas storage box that keeps everything in one place rather than rolling around with every turn. It has a breathable, mesh closet for smelly shoes and separate compartments for balls, mitts, and other paraphernalia. It's lightweight, collapses flat for easy storage, and is available exclusively from www.redenvelope.com.

Another inexpensive solution I've seen is reconditioned lockers. This may be an option for you if you can locate a company that offers this service. Or you may simply be able to find used lockers and recondition them yourself. You can assign a locker for each person or for each sport.

There are special storage systems for specific sports gear—ski racks, fishing gear, netting to hold balls and gloves, and bicycle brackets, but most can be adapted from inexpensive hardware for general use. Fishing poles lie nicely, horizontally suspended from two pegs or hooks. A fishnet hangs from pegboard on a hook. Ladder hooks screwed into studs hold up bicycles off the floor. Skis can be put with bottoms together and tips turned upward, then suspended between two pegs put close together. Ski poles can each rest between two pegs. Look around at commercial storage solutions and see how they can be imitated.

Whatever storage option you choose, organize by activity and put like things together. Even just putting things in labeled boxes that are easy to get to is better than having them scattered all over the place.

Periodically revisit your sports-equipment storage center and honestly evaluate whether you're still "into" each activity. If not, pass the equipment on. There are now outlets for secondhand sports equipment that might be eager to have yours—they might even give you cash or a trade-in discount for new equipment for your current sports passion. Just make it as easy as possible to keep up with your exercise routine or sport and meet your health and fitness goals.

Grow Smart: Setting Up a Garden Center

Gardening is another super way to add exercise to your life, accomplish something satisfying, get lots of fresh air, and even beautify your home. If you're an avid gardener as I am, you need lots of room for supplies and tools. But even if all you do is maintain a simple, low-maintenance yard, you need some basic things to do the job, and a place to store them.

Most garden implements can be stored in the garage, but certain substances may be best stored in a shed that's not attached to the house, and should be under lock and key. I try to use only nontoxic fertilizers and insect-control methods, but once in a while the only solution is a mild poison. Weed out old sprays, powders, and poisons, and dispose of outdated ones properly.

Most long-handled garden tools hang nicely on the wall. You can stagger them up and down (like shoes in a shoe box—one with handle up, the next with handle down) to fit them closer together and make the best use of available space. Pegboard is a good storage solution, or there are several rack systems you can buy that hold tools with clamps, pegs, or brackets. If you don't have enough wall space to hang tools, use a heavy, metal garbage can and set them in the can, handles down. Use a garden caddy for smaller tools or sort by type in boxes and label.

> **CAUTION**
>
> **Pileups!** _____
>
> Proper disposal of hazardous household products and chemicals is extremely important to protect your local water supply. To find out how and where to take them in your area, contact your city or town, your garbage disposal company, or your cooperative extension service. Excellent guidelines are available through the North Carolina Cooperative Extension Service at www.ces. ncsu.edu/disaster/ent/st-chem.htm.

Have an area set aside for caring for your garden tools and equipment. At the end of each day you garden, wipe off dirt and moisture. Every couple of months, sharpen, grease hinges, repair or replace split or broken handles, and replace missing parts.

When fall cleanup or spring planting comes around, we consider the garage our "staging area." All the appropriate tools for cleaning gutters, touching up paint, planting bulbs, cleaning up debris, or whatever, are assembled and either laid out on the floor or arranged on a large folding table we keep in the garage after we've moved out one of the cars. We make a list of what's needed to complete the job and then do our shopping, and when we return home we're ready to roll.

So now there are no excuses. Find the thing you love to do to stay fit and fit it into your space and your schedule!

Managing the Medical Morass

There's more to organizing to take care of your health than finding time and space for fitness. Are you deluged with receipts, insurance forms, and other medical records that never seem to be there when you need them? Do you neglect making insurance claims because the paperwork is just too much of a hassle? Let's tackle organizing your family's health records next. Devoting one good weekend's worth of time is probably all you need to get this area "rosy."

Gathering Information

Keeping accurate medical records is an important part of taking care of the health of you and your family. I suggest having a family health center, where you keep a well-stocked first-aid kit, any prescription medicines (out of children's reach and locked up, if necessary), over-the-counter medications used most often, and a complete record of everything about your family's health. This is a logical part of the Family User Manual that we set up in Chapter 7. Your Command Center is the best place for this so that anyone caring for your family will have it at his or her fingertips. Here are some of the lists you should have in your binder:

Resource Files

If you want to use a pre-designed medical records book for your child's history, consider *Childhood Medical Journal* by Cathleen Gasper.

◆ Emergency contacts. Doctor's names, specialties, and phone numbers, as well as phone numbers of relatives and friends you might call in an emergency.

◆ Prescribed medication being taken categorized by family member. Include purpose, dose, instructions, counter-indications, doctor, and date prescribed.

◆ Over-the-counter medication taken regularly, categorized by family member.

◆ Any allergies to medication, foods, insects, and pollens.

◆ All diagnosed illnesses.

◆ Surgeries for each family member, including dates, doctor, and hospital where the surgery was performed. Include the same information for any hospitalizations.

◆ History of any pregnancies.

◆ Insurance information, including phone and ID numbers. Include a copy of your insurance form, which can be photocopied, if necessary.

◆ Blood work and x-rays. Include when and where they were taken and what type. Know and record everyone's blood type.

◆ The name of your preferred hospital along with emergency information.

- All your family doctors, including dentist and eye doctor, along with their address and phone number. Also list their specialty.

- A record of your last eye exam, along with a copy of your prescription if you wear glasses or contact lenses.

- A record of your last dental exam.

- Immunization records, including last flu shot, most recent tetanus, pneumonia, and hormone injections.

- Dates of childhood diseases for each member of the family.

- Family medical history. If you have a relative who has or had diabetes, epilepsy, stroke, heart disease, glaucoma, cancer, asthma, or a genetic disorder, include that in your family's history.

Wise Words

"The first wealth is health."
—Ralph Waldo Emerson

- Manuals and information on any special devices such as a pacemaker or hearing aid.

If you don't have all of this information, make an effort to get it from the appropriate health-care professionals. You may need to write some letters or make some phone calls if you've moved or changed doctors over the years. Do your best to fill in everything you can to give a complete medical history of each person in your family. If you kept a baby book for your children, some of the information may be there.

Update your family medical records each time you have an appointment. When you go on vacation, take your family medical records binder with you, or at least have most of the significant information in your planner/organizer and take that. If you leave your kids with a baby-sitter or send your child off on vacation with another family, make it available to them. At least copy the child's information so the temporary caregiver knows everything he or she needs to know about your child's health in case of an emergency. Whenever you move or change doctors, having this information is invaluable for remembering the details you need to pass on to your new physician. In an emergency, when you're flustered or too ill to communicate well, having everything written down can mean the difference between life and death.

Other Considerations

There are several computer programs on the market for keeping these records, but keeping your records in a simple database or word processing program will enable you to update them easily each time you or a family member makes a doctor or dentist visit. You want to have a scaled-down version of this information (the most pertinent in an emergency) in your planner/organizer and in each family member's wallet. You also want a current printout in your binder, regardless, so anyone can access this important lifesaving information.

If you're caring for someone with an acute illness, you want to have separate records to track the progress of the disease. A friend of mine provides home care for her husband, who has multiple sclerosis. Her doctor keeps a copy of her reports each time they make a visit, because they're so thorough and helpful. I know she gets the highest quality care for her husband, because she's so involved in seeing that he gets it!

Look over your insurance forms carefully, and make sure you understand how to fill them out and where to send them. Keep them in the folder with your medical insurance information and bills. If you're not sure how the claims process works, make an appointment with your agent and have him or her explain it to you until you understand. This is part of what they should do to earn their commission.

To make the most of your health-care professionals, it helps to be an informed consumer, just as you would strive to be in any other area of your life. Today there are many resources to help consumers be aware, including reference books and free online databases on prescription and over-the-counter medications, disease prevention, and general medical knowledge. Know the drugs you're taking and their side effects. Look up terminology, if you're not sure. Ask questions and do your homework. You're responsible for your own health and well-being, as well as your own health care.

The Least You Need to Know

- By including your health in your overall life plan, you'll be more likely to become and stay healthy.

- Organizing your home (and office) and having the right tools to support you in your health and fitness goals is another important step to achieving them.

- Making time and setting realistic goals with immediate rewards will help keep you on track.

- To make the most of the professionals who care for your health, and to protect yourself and your family in an emergency, having complete and organized family medical records is a must.

Chapter 22

Wrap It Up: Holiday Planning Made Easy

In This Chapter

- ◆ Making your holiday schedule less hectic
- ◆ Creating a holiday season that's less about "stuff" and more about "fun"
- ◆ Tips on holiday gift giving that save you time and keep you out of debt
- ◆ Conquering holiday storage problems

We all know the recipe for ruining the holiday season: start with unreasonably high expectations, heap on a good dose of guilt and a dash of procrastination, let simmer with family differences and distances, try to do too much, and then garnish with a little flu bug. No wonder you'd rather spend the holidays alone in Timbuktu!

If you've become a Grinch, why not turn things around? Make this the year you truly look forward to the holidays with wide-eyed enthusiasm and delight.

Goal Setting, Holiday Style

There are those words again: *goal setting* and *planning*. Do the holidays have a way of just "happening" to you? When you don't focus early on how you want things to be, they can take on an unintended life of their own. But if you start out with clear intentions, you're more likely to create what you intend.

Granted, getting in touch with your inner desires when it comes to the holidays may not be as simple as it sounds. Holidays are fraught with emotional triggers and baggage that are often very complicated and not wholly clear. I think you'll agree, however, that it's easier to navigate a minefield when you know where the bombs are buried.

Creating a great holiday is a lot like orchestrating a great party. Imagine you're putting on a play or making a movie. There's a script, props, scenery, various players, and a director. Everyone's the director in their own holiday pageant, whether they know it or not. Why not accept the role and make the production your own?

Envisionings

Close your eyes and imagine your ideal holiday. Imagine it the absolute best it could be. Start with Thanksgiving and make your "movie" go all the way through New Year's Day. Who would be there? What kind of food would be served? How are things decorated? What is your mood? Be free in your imaginings. This doesn't have to be like any holiday season you've ever known.

Write down the major elements of your "movie." If you imagined going out into the woods and cutting down your own Christmas tree, put that down. Keep your list close by. We're going to use it later.

Write Yourself a Book: Your Personal Holiday Planner

Some years ago I made a holiday binder that I now rely on every year to make our holidays bright. It's a standard-size loose-leaf notebook, with colored dividers and lined three-hole-punched paper. My categories are Cards, Crafts, Décor, Food, and Gifts. I use it for Thanksgiving, Christmas, and New Year's planning each year. Other possible categories you might want to add are Parties, Menus, Lists, Songs, Traditions, Budget, or anything else you want to keep track of.

I have our Christmas card mailing list on a label program. Each year I revise it, making any necessary changes, additions, and deletions, then print it out on regular paper and add to my planner behind the Cards divider. I use that printout each year to make notations and then to revise my label program when card-sending time arrives.

Under Crafts, I keep directions for making decorations or ornaments that we especially liked that year or ones I want to try next year. I add notes that might be helpful. If I make ornaments to give away, I sometimes take photos and add them.

The Décor section contains ideas for decorations, inside and out. If I see something in a book or magazine, I photocopy it or tear it out and add it to my binder. I do the same for printouts from my Internet wanderings. If you create a decorating scheme you're especially pleased with, take a picture and put it in your binder so you can duplicate it the following year.

The Food category contains copies of our traditional family recipes, plus some new ones to try. I also have these recipes elsewhere, but I find that during the holiday rush it's nice to have them all in one place—a sort of personalized family holiday cookbook. I also keep menus and shopping lists. (You can use plastic sheet protectors as "envelopes" to store these.)

Under Gifts, I keep gift lists and any notes on what people might mention during the year that they'd like for Christmas or "someday." If you see an item in a catalog, you may want to make a note of it here. Having gift lists from the past reminds me what I've already given, so I don't duplicate.

You may want to have a shopping list page and a to-do list for next year. When the season begins to draw near, that can become your head start. You may want to make a copy of the shopping list and keep it in your planner/organizer so you can buy stocking stuffers or even major gift items when you see exactly what you want, or when items are on sale.

The holiday book is your book and can be as elaborate or as simple as you want or need. You can have several volumes for various family celebrations. I believe that once you begin to "write" it, your holiday book will fast become as indispensable at your house as it is at ours.

CAUTION

Pileups!

One cause of holiday disappointment is family members having different priorities or emotional attachments to different traditions. Try the "ideal holiday" visualization (see the "Envisionings" earlier in this chapter) with your family. Look for ways to fulfill some of each person's fantasy. Compromise on the rest.

Making a List and Checking It (at Least) Twice!

Referring to the "Envisionings" earlier in this chapter, use your visualization list to decide which holiday activities mean the most to you. It might be baking cookies, making Hanukkah goodies such as donuts or latkes, having a tree-trimming party, going out caroling, or doing an extravagant job of decorating the house. What activities would give you the most pleasure? The greatest kick? Which would cause you the most pain or disappointment if you didn't do them?

Now decide on the top three or four and break them down into the main tasks needed to make them happen. Caroling might be as simple as finding a group that organizes such an event, getting the music together, practicing a few times, and putting the date on your calendar. The best time for advance planning is a couple of months before Thanksgiving, so you have time to really play with your ideas, reserve time on your schedule, and prepare ahead.

Jump Starts

Remember, when you delegate, things may not be done exactly the way you would do them. Especially at holiday time, standards and expectations can be impossibly high. Decide on the desired results and let whomever does the job do it his way. This will probably yield the best results, too.

Be realistic about your schedule, your budget, and your skills. Look for ways to get others involved and committed to helping with cooking, cleaning, decorating, and shopping. Whatever events or activities you choose as your holiday centerpieces, make plans and throw yourself into them. The more energy and focus you give the things you care about, the more fulfilling the holidays will be.

Make up menus and gather recipes early. If your family is like mine, certain traditional favorites must be on the table, but it's fun to experiment with vegetables, appetizers, or desserts from year to year. By planning ahead, you may be able to stock up on some ingredients at bargain prices.

The same goes for your gift list. By having in mind what you're giving each person well in advance, you can shop here and there instead of putting in a few grueling days close to the holidays. I know you've heard this advice many times before, but it really does make the season much more enjoyable if you shop ahead. And it's easier on the budget to spread out holiday buying over as wide a period as possible.

Some years I've had a "signature" gift that I bought or made for everyone on my list. One year it was bath and body products I made myself, another year it was gourmet coffee and spice blends, and this past year it was a crocheted scarf from some really beautiful imported yarns. This makes it easy to plan, and you can get started early, because you know what you're giving. And you can use the same wrapping method for everything!

Finding Time to Get It All Done

First and foremost, realize that you *can't* get it all done! Just accept there will be things on your list that won't make it into reality. If you put your list in priority order, so what if the items on the bottom bite the dust? You did the things you wanted to do most.

Here are a few more tips for getting the important things done and having a top-notch holiday season this year and every year:

- ◆ Remind yourself who the most important people in your life are and commit to pleasing them first. And remember the most important person on that list is *you*.

- ◆ Sit down with your family and negotiate their share of the work. Make a list of holiday chores and let them choose those they'd most like to do. You won't get help if you don't ask.

- ◆ Hire some help. Sure, you want to do the good stuff yourself, but who says you can't hire someone to do the stuff nobody wants to do? My friend June has a cleaning service come in before the holidays and has her carpets done as well. She throws a big bash on Christmas Eve, and has the wine and champagne delivered. She always makes a few dishes herself, but she supplements her favorites with others from a caterer. This allows her to concentrate on the things she enjoys most.

> **Resource Files**
>
> Watch *National Lampoon's Christmas Vacation* on video or TV at least once this holiday season. Sure, you can get teary-eyed over *It's a Wonderful Life* or *Miracle on 34th Street*, but when you need to come back to Earth, let Chevy Chase's disastrous attempt to create the "ideal" holiday add some humor to your holiday cheer.

- ◆ Consider hiring a baby-sitter while you do your shopping or, better yet, trade off a couple of days with other parents.

- ◆ Hit the mall as a family, with one parent taking the kids for the morning while the other shops solo. The whole family meets for lunch at the food court, then the kids switch and shop with the other parent.

◆ Learn to combat "the perfects." Instead of aiming for the perfect meal, the perfect tree, or the perfect gift, be present in the moment and make it wonderful as only you can.

◆ Don't beat yourself up. Don't tell yourself you've somehow failed because you didn't make cranberry relish. Don't berate yourself because you couldn't afford all the gifts the kids asked for. Don't whip yourself because Aunt Jane asks why you're still single this holiday season and tries to fix you up with the deliveryman. Decide not to accept the guilt!

◆ Remember, a holiday isn't any one moment. It's larger than that.

Christmas in July (and Other Time-Savers)

For most of us, the holidays seem to creep up on us, and suddenly there's only a few weeks left to do everything. Well, get a real head start—in July! When the kids are home from school and that familiar chorus "I'm bored!" starts ringing through the house, tell them to get ready to celebrate the winter holidays. Put on Christmas music, don your Santa hat, and get out your Christmas planning binder. (This works for any holiday, by the way!) Assemble craft materials, go through old magazines and holiday craft books, try out new cookie recipes, or make up the family's gift lists. Are there any decorations that need repairs, spiffing up, or even replacement?

Dust off the holiday sheet music and make copies. Make a nice cover, bind them, and you're all ready for a musical gathering or caroling. Talk over party possibilities and begin planning decorations and menus. If you don't use them this year, they'll probably come in handy some other holiday season.

When you have "Christmas in July," there's time to experiment and an opportunity to perfect new skills so that gift making can be relaxed and creative. It's like having a buried treasure put away for just the right moment!

You Shouldn't Have! Giving Great Gifts

For some people, the holiday season is one enormous Acquisition Trap. They spend too much, enjoy too little, and pay for it for the next six months. The holidays aren't about getting or having, they're about doing and being. This year, give things that won't add clutter to the lives of the people you love and won't bury you in debt.

Consider these ideas for greater gift giving:

◆ Give something really useful that you know an individual wants or needs (even if it isn't what *you* want to get for them). You can even ask directly. If your favorite crafter really wants a glue gun or a band saw, then make that her gift.

◆ Give something consumable—a special liqueur, a monthly fruit or flower club, bath salts, or a homemade cheesecake. Make it yourself if you have the time.

◆ Make a donation to someone's favorite charity. If you don't know which one it is, but know he likes animals, adopt a wolf, a dolphin, or a manatee in his name.

◆ Give gifts that emphasize the tradition of the holiday, not the commercialism, such as homemade holiday treats and decorations. Don't put the focus only on the children, but also on the elders in your family and community.

◆ If you don't subscribe to the religious part of the holiday, but love the seasonal associations, make your gifts reflect the season and its symbols, with decorated evergreen arrangements or ivy topiaries for the winter holidays.

◆ Give something only you can give. Make a collection of meaningful photographs. Record an audiotape of you reading your favorite poems or a videotape of your locale if you're far away. Write a song. Draw a picture. How about compiling a family cookbook? Solicit contributions from everyone, type in the recipes on your computer, lay out the book, and then have it photocopied and bound. From now on, no one will be calling at the last minute for your famous crab dip recipe. *It'll be in the book!*

Resource Files

You can adopt a wolf through Wolf Haven International in Tenino, Washington. Their phone number is 360-264-4695, and their website is www. wolfhaven.org. Your gift will include a photo of your chosen wolf and a subscription to Wolf Haven's newsletter for the year.

◆ Give something that grows. Start bulbs that will come up during the dark winter months—an amaryllis, paperwhites, maybe a crocus. Include watering and planting instructions. Start some houseplants from cuttings of your own. Include care instructions.

◆ Give experiences instead of things: a balloon ride, a Jeep tour, a picnic, a massage, a day at the movies, a trip to a museum, tickets to the ballet, a concert, or sporting event—whatever will tickle the recipient's fancy.

◆ Give gift certificates to favorite stores, restaurants, or service providers. Or make your own gift certificates, customized for the people you're giving them to. You can offer baby-sitting, cleaning, hugs, afternoons together, foot massages, or a weekend getaway.

◆ Divide the giving. In some families, each buys for one person by drawing his or her name from a grab bag. That way, the recipient can get something more substantial, and the giver only has one person to worry about.

◆ Set a limit on spending. One way is to use cash only—no credit cards. When you lavish gifts on your children and put yourself in debt, think: "Are these the lessons I really want to instill in my kids?"

◆ Use mail-order catalogs or Internet shopping sites. They allow you to avoid the crowds, and make it easier to map out your spending. You can also use your computer to help map out local shopping trips to maximize your time and gas mileage. For specific items, go to www.switchboard.com to find phone numbers of stores in your area. Call ahead and see whether they have the item in stock or have extended holiday hours.

Pileups!

Some people hate practical gifts such as appliances or tools. For the practical-present-hater, give something that's pure indulgence, such as some sinfully rich chocolate or sumptuous bath oil. Note, too, the people on your list who thrive on practicality!

◆ Put aside a few small gifts for serendipitous giving. Include a couple of items for adults and some for children. A book of holiday verses, a pretty box, some stationery, some crayons with a holiday coloring book, or some homemade gourmet coffee or hot chocolate mixes (I make these up in big batches) are all good things to stash away "just in case."

◆ Let the store (or mail-order company) do the gift wrapping and shipping. It's worth the extra couple of dollars so you won't be running to the post office at the last minute trying to make the deadline if you have gifts to mail.

◆ Give yourself a present! That's right. You deserve it. Wrap it up and put it under the tree.

Most of all, give of yourself. Give your attention, your listening ear, your love.

Stellar Strategies for Holiday Entertaining

Because the holidays are more hectic than most times of the year, if you throw a party, you need to give it extra thought and planning.

You'll probably have to be creative with the calendar, because so many events are competing with each other at this time of year. Consider throwing a party just before or right after Thanksgiving—a sort of "launch-the-holidays" party. Combine Hanukkah and Christmas in an interfaith household, or celebrate Twelfth Night, a medieval tradition that falls after Christmas. Or how about having your party the week after Christmas, but before New Year's? Or perhaps the weekend after New Year's?

Open houses work well because people have more flexibility to fit them into their schedules. It's often easier to merge your professional and personal worlds in this less-formal setting. An open house works well for a tree-trimming party. Make sure to have the lights already strung before guests arrive. A potluck might work better for a menorah lighting, with guests arriving at a set time.

If you're just starting out on your own, have guests bring an ornament for the tree. It's a great way to start your own collection, and what your friends bring can be amazingly revealing. You can also provide a few simple materials for making ornaments.

> **Jump Starts**
>
> Don't forget to pay attention to presentation. It can turn the mundane into the spectacular. Sprinkle gold glitter or "confetti" over tablecloths before you lay down the silverware or serving dishes. Make use of greenery and seasonal fruits, berries, and nuts. Enhance candlelight with mirrors and inventive candleholders. Scan magazines and books for creative presentation ideas.

Don't be afraid to do something different with your holiday entertaining. How about a cookie-exchange party? Everyone brings a couple of dozen of his or her specialties, there's a quick sampling, and each guest ends up with an enticing array of goodies.

How about an ornament- and decoration-making workshop? I've done this for the past several years, and it's always a hit. I provide lots of craft materials, a big newspaper-covered table, some craft books and magazines, and plenty of finger foods and refreshments. Then we play!

Do a historically oriented Christmas party. You might try a medieval, colonial, or Victorian theme. Slant the decorations, foods, music, and customs toward whatever historic direction you choose. If you have a costume that reflects the era, wear it to set the mood.

Cocktail parties work well, because they can be held early in the evening and guests can still fit in another engagement that night. Or consider a party for the other end of the meal. Dessert and champagne is elegant and relatively easy to do.

How about a Day-After-Christmas brunch? I'll bet you have enough leftovers to pull this one off without even hitting the supermarket!

Decorations can be traditional or modern, fussy or uncomplicated, depending on your taste. Take pictures of your most effective ones so you can duplicate them.

Finessing the Family Tug-of-War

"Whose house do we go to for Christmas (or Hanukkah) this year?" Is that a familiar question at your house around Thanksgiving? Or how about this variation: "Who gets the kids this year?"

Conflicts over who gets to host the family holiday celebration or, if you're divorced, who gets the kids on what days, can wreck even well-laid plans. If you're newly married or newly separated, I can understand this being an issue, but if it's a problem every November, this year I suggest you come up with an enduring solution.

Some couples spend Thanksgiving with one set of parents and Christmas with the other. Others alternate each year. Because Hanukkah is eight days long, there's plenty of opportunity for equal time. The same arrangement can be worked out between divorced couples. My ex-husband and I used to alternate Thanksgiving, and split Christmas Eve and Christmas Day. The kids and I made our celebration on Christmas Eve, and he usually took them for Christmas Day. As long as the children know what the plan is and all the kinks have been ironed out ahead of time, this can work quite smoothly.

The important thing is not to let it ride each year—come to an agreement as to how it's going to be on a regular basis. Then there are no surprises, and the one who's going to be without the children can make alternative plans. If you're going to be alone on Thanksgiving, Hanukkah, or Christmas, why not invite someone else who's going it solo to spend the holiday with you? Other singles are bound to be in the same boat, and if you're feeling a little self-pity, they're sure to understand.

If you'd rather not be with other people, plan a special trip. Book a room at an inn or B&B, sign up for a cruise, or stay in a rustic cabin and get away from it all. Whatever you do, prepare yourself and do something. Don't let it sneak up on you.

Just because the family is not together on a particular holiday doesn't mean you can't celebrate the spirit of the season together at a different time. Institute some creative family traditions that aren't just for a particular day. Make tree-trimming a regular event with specific rituals you repeat each year. Have an annual light-gazing tour or go window-shopping. Volunteer each year to work at a soup kitchen or to go caroling at a local nursing home.

> **CAUTION**
>
> **Pileups!**
>
> Trying to accommodate everyone's wishes will leave you angry and exhausted. You can't be everywhere and please everyone. Decide with your own family what's most important to each of you, and honor those things first. Even extended family and friends are less important. Gently make changes and assert your wishes, and don't back down.

If You Must Travel

With extended families spread out from coast to coast, someone will probably have to travel at holiday times. Sometimes it's worth bringing the family to you (tickets become presents), but sometimes this just isn't possible. If you're going to travel for the holidays, here are some ways to make it easier:

- Book flights and accommodations well ahead of time.

- Travel at odd hours to beat the rush.

- Ship gifts ahead so you don't have to carry them with you. Do the same thing on the return trip with the gifts you've received.

- Travel light, and prepare for changes in climate. We live in the Southwest, and if we're traveling back East in the winter, we need to arrange to borrow warmer clothing to wear while we're there. (I got rid of my down jacket years ago!)

> **Jump Starts**
>
> Now that our children are spread far apart across the country and don't usually visit until Christmas, we've begun a tradition for Thanksgiving. We call it Orphan's Thanksgiving. Anyone in our circle of friends or neighbors who doesn't have a place to go for Thanksgiving can come to ours. We do it as a potluck, and move or add furniture as needed. One year we had 21 "orphans" for a sit-down Thanksgiving dinner! Everyone had a ball, hosts included.

◆ If you're driving, prepare for bad weather. Make sure you have emergency supplies such as a flashlight, blankets, and flares, and watch the weather reports.

Travel happily and be safe!

Holiday Storage Snags

What to do with all those bows, lights, ornaments, gift-wrap, and boxes? Well, first of all, if you have some you haven't used for the past three years, you know where they go! After you unstuff, the next thing is to gather the proper storage materials so you don't end up having to replace things because they're crushed or broken.

I've used one of those divided ornament boxes for umpteen years now, and have never unpacked a broken or damaged ornament. They work great for those of a fairly uniform size, but some of the larger or unusually shaped ones need to be wrapped in tissue and put in a separate box.

Group all your holiday decorations and ornaments together, and label them clearly so they'll be easier to retrieve next year. They can be stored in less-valuable *deep-freeze* storage space, because it will be a whole year before you'll need them again.

Try to buy just enough wrapping paper so you won't store it a whole year. I use colored tissue for everything throughout the year and customize it with colored ribbon and stickers for the occasion. With the popularity of angels, you can use angel paper for a variety of special events. Glossy plain white, red, gold, or silver paper lends itself to any gift-giving purpose.

If you use all-occasion paper, make sure you don't store it with the holiday stuff, but somewhere more accessible, because you'll be using it throughout the year. Gift-wrap organizers available from mail-order catalogs or in stores work quite well. You can also stand up rolls of paper in a wastebasket or deep bucket in the bottom of a closet. Ribbon, flat paper, gift cards, stickers, and rubber stamps (another way to customize gift wrap) can be stored in a flat box on a shelf, clearly marked. Another idea is to use one of those large, flat sweater storage boxes and store everything under a bed.

Other decorations such as artificial wreaths, garlands, menorahs, figurines, and banners should be put away carefully, protected with tissue or newspaper and a sturdy box, labeled, and put in a clean, dry place. Consider the effects that extreme temperatures, dampness, and dryness might have. I once stored a beautiful tree-top angel in the attic, not thinking about how hot it got up there in the summer. The next Christmas, our beautiful angel was a melted mess.

Special corrugated boxes for storing wreaths of various sizes work very well, or you can construct your own. Untangle lights before you put them away, and wrap them around stiff cardboard. Boxes designed especially for storing lights are also available through mail-order catalogs.

Don't get carried away keeping packing materials. Unless you ship regularly throughout the year, get rid of this stuff and buy (or start accumulating) new a couple of months before the holidays. Storing bubble wrap or Styrofoam peanuts for 12 months usually means it's unfit to use when you need it anyway. The same is true of boxes for shipping. Figure out how many you need and in what sizes for the gifts you have to ship, and be on the look-out closer to the holidays.

> **Jump Starts**
>
> If you find you've acquired more ornaments and decorations than you can use each year, share the ones you no longer use with a young person just starting out on her own or someone who's lost his belongings in a divorce or disaster. You'll lighten your load and help put the "happy" back into someone's holiday.

Finally, It's All Up to You

What I like most about the holiday season is the time it allows for reflection. It's a time of renewal and excitement about the year ahead. When else do we get to sip a glass of brandy, sit in front of a crackling fire, and contemplate the meaning of family? Whether it's a deeply religious holiday for you or more of a seasonal festival, why not make it a time to be thankful for the abundance and natural beauty around us? Force the hubbub into submission and insist on a holiday filled with fellowship, appreciation, and joy. The holiday spirit is, after all, *your* spirit!

The Least You Need to Know

- Planning and scheduling are the keys to turning your holidays from madness to merriment.

- Sensible gift giving means less clutter for the recipient and more enjoyment for the giver. Keep a careful watch for signs of the Acquisition Trap hidden in your holiday celebrations.

- Holiday entertaining requires choosing a date early or picking one that has less competition. Creative party ideas can forge new holiday traditions.

◆ Preparing for family issues ahead of time and negotiating standing arrangements can reduce holiday anxiety and conflict.

◆ Basic organization principles make storing holiday paraphernalia a simple chore.

◆ By controlling your focus and state of mind, you can make any holiday a happy one.

Appendix A

Resource Guide

Here, all in one place, is a list of resources to help you develop your own personal organization program. To make it even easier to find what you're looking for, I've grouped them by chapter. In some cases, I have repeated sources that were mentioned in various chapters, just so you could have them where you need them as you work through various areas in your life.

Chapter 1: The Big Picture: Setting Goals

Books

The 7 Habits of Highly Effective People: Powerful Lessons in Personal Change by Stephen Covey, Simon & Schuster, 1990; ISBN 0671708635.

The Magic Lamp: Goal Setting for People Who Hate Setting Goals by Keith Ellis, Three Rivers Press, 1998; ISBN 060980166X.

Wishcraft: How to Get What You Really Want by Barbara Sher and Annie Gottlieb, Ballentine Books, 1986; ISBN 0345340892.

I Could Do Anything If I Only Knew What It Was: How to Discover What You Really Want and How to Get It by Barbara Sher, Dell, 1995; ISBN 0440505003.

Software

GoalPro 6.0 is a product of Success Studios Corporation, and you can download a free trial of the software at www.goalpro.com/trial.

Chapter 2: It's All About "Stuff" and "Time"

Books

How Much Is Enough?: The Consumer Society and the Future of the Earth by Alan Durning, W.W. Norton & Co., 1992; ISBN 039330891X.

Voluntary Simplicity: Toward a Way of Life That Is Outwardly Simple, Inwardly Rich by Duane Elgin, Quill, 1993; ISBN 0688121195.

The Complete Idiot's Guide to Simple Living by Georgene Lockwood, Alpha Books, 2000; ISBN 0028639073.

Newsletters

Creative Downscaling, Box 1884, Jonesboro, GA 30237-1884; 770-471-9048; e-mail: kilgo@mindspring.com; $20/yr. for 10 issues.

Audiotapes, Videotapes, CDs, and DVDs

Affluenza and *Escape from Affluenza*, PBS programs available on VHS or DVD from The Simple Living Network, www.simpleliving.net/.

Chapter 3: Excuses! Excuses!

Books

First Things First: To Live, To Love, To Learn, To Leave a Legacy by Stephen R. Covey, A. Roger Merrill, and Rebecca R. Merrill, Fireside, 1996; ISBN 0684802031.

How to Get Control of Your Time and Your Life by Alan Lakein, New American Library, 1996; ISBN 0451167724.

Time Management from the Inside Out: The Foolproof System for Taking Control of Your Schedule and Your Life by Julie Morgenstern, Henry Holt, 2000; ISBN 0805064699.

Chapter 4: When Stuff Rules Your Life

Books

A Brilliant Madness: Living with Manic-Depressive Illness by Patty Duke with Gloria Hochman, Bantam, 1993; ISBN 0553560727.

Currency of Hope by Debtors Anonymous, General Service Board of Trustees, Inc. 1999; ISBN 0970323808.

An Unquiet Mind: A Memoir of Moods and Madness by Kay Redfield Jameson, Random House, 1993; ISBN 0679763309.

Born to Spend: How to Overcome Compulsive Spending by Gloria Arenson, Human Services Institute, 1991; ISBN 0830621555.

Credit, Cash and Co-Dependency: How the Way You Were Raised Affects Your Decisions About Money by Yvonne Kaye, Islewest Publishing, 1998; ISBN 1888461063.

Sink Reflections: Flylady's Babystep Guide to Overcoming CHAOS by Marla Cilley, Flylady Press, Inc., 2002; ISBN 0971855110.

The New Messies Manual: The Procrastinator's Guide to Good Housekeeping by Sandra Felton, Fleming H. Revell Co., 2000; ISBN 0800757262.

Organizations

Clutterers Anonymous
P.O. Box 91413
Los Angeles, CA 90009-1413
clawso@hotmail.comwww.clutterersanonymous.net

Clutterless Recovery Groups Inc.
Mike Nelson
13121 South Madrone Trail
Austin, TX 78737-4431
512-351-4058
clutterless.org

ADDA
P.O. Box 543
Pottstown, PA 19464
484-945-2101
mail@add.org
www.add.org

Debtors Anonymous
General Service Office
P.O. Box 920888
Needham, MA 02492-0009
781-453-2743
www.debtorsanonymous.org

Emotions Anonymous International
P.O. Box 4245
St. Paul, MN 55104-0245
651-647-9712
info@EmotionsAnonymous.org
www.emotionsanonymous.org

Messies Anonymous
5025 SW 114th Avenue
Miami, FL 33165
786-243-2793
www.messies.com

National Association of Professional Organizers
4700 W. Lake Avenue
Glenview, IL 60025
847-375-4746
e-mail: hq@napo.netwww.napo.net

National Depressive and Manic-Depressive Association
730 N. Franklin Street, Suite 501
Chicago, IL 60610-7224
1-800-826-3632
www.ndmda.org

Obsessive-Compulsive Anonymous
P.O. Box 215
New Hyde Park, NY 11040
516-739-0662
hometown.aol.com/west24th/index.html

Obsessive-Compulsive Foundation
676 State StreetNew Haven, CT 06511
203-401-2070
info@ocfoundation.org
www.ocfoundation.org

The American Association for Chronic Fatigue Syndrome
27 N. Wacker Drive, Suite 416
Chicago, IL 60606
847-748-8288
Admin@aacfs.org
www.AACFS.org

Online E-Mail Lists

Decluttr mailing list

Decluttr@MAELSTROM.STJOHNS.EDU

The Flylady mailing list and website

To subscribe, go to the Flylady website at www.flylady.net.

Compulsive Spenders mailing lists

There are several mailing lists for people with compulsive-spending disorder. To sign up, register at group.yahoo.com and type in "compulsive spending" to get a list.

Bipolar Disorders Information Center

Their main website is www.mhsource.com/bipolar/index.html.

Subscribe to the bipolar mailing list at www.mhsource.com/bipolar/mailinglist.html.

Roses and Thorns

A mail list for diagnosed mood and personality disorders, such as depression, bipolar disorder, and seasonal affective disorder (SAD). To subscribe, go to health.groups.yahoo.com/group/rosesandthorns.

Newsgroups

alt.recovery.clutter

alt.support.depression.manic

soc.support.depression.manic

soc.support.depression.misc

soc.support.depression.treatment

Other Online Resources

www.pendulum.org

Bipolar Disorders Portal at Pendulum Resources.

www.cdc.gov/ncidod/diseases/cfs/index.htm

Chronic Fatigue Syndrome home page from the Centers for Disease Control and Prevention.

Chapter 7: Creating a Command Center

Books

How to Do Everything with Your Palm Handheld by Dave Johnson and Rick Broida, McGraw Hill/Osborne, 2003; ISBN 0072230827.

How to Do Everything with Your BlackBerry by Curt Simmons, McGraw Hill/Osborne, 2004; ISBN 0072255870.

Products

Day-Timer
Day-Timers, Inc.
One Willow Lane
East Texas, PA 18046
1-800-452-7398
www.daytimer.com

DayRunner
DayRunner, Inc.
2760 W. Moore Avenue
Fullerton, CA 92833
1-800-643-9923
www.dayrunner.com

The Family Facts Family Life Organizer
info@family-facts.com
www.family-facts.com

FranklinCovey
2200 West Parkway Boulevard
Salt Lake City, UT 84119
1-800-819-1812
www.franklincovey.com

palmOne Zire, Tungsten, and Treo
palmOne, Inc. Corporate Headquarters
400 N. McCarthy Blvd.
Milpitas, CA 95035
408-503-7000 (main phone)
408-503-2750 (main fax)
www.palmOne.com/us

BlackBerry
www.blackberry.com

Chapter 8: People Who Need People: Interpersonal Systems

Books

Quick & Easy Scrapbook Pages: 100 Scrapbook Pages You Can Make in One Hour or Less by Memory Makers, Memory Makers Books, 2003; ISBN 1892127202.

1001 Ways to Be Romantic by Gregory Godek, Casablanca Press, 1995; ISBN 1883518059.

Chapter 9: Work Systems: Getting Ahead Without Getting a Headache

Books

How to Take the Fog Out of Business Writing by Robert Gunning, Dartnell Corp., 1994; ISBN 0850132320.

The 30-Second Commute: The Ultimate Guide to Starting and Operating a Home-Based Business by Beverley Williams and Don Cooper, McGraw-Hill, 2004; ISBN 0071424067.

The Three Boxes of Life and How to Get Out of Them: An Introduction to Life-Work Planning by Richard Nelson Bolles, Ten Speed Press, 1978; ISBN 0913668583.

What Color Is Your Parachute? by Richard Nelson Bolles, Ten Speed Press, 1998; ISBN 1580080081.

Working from Home: Everything You Need to Know About Living and Working Under the Same Roof by Paul and Sarah Edwards, J.P. Tarcher Inc., 1999; ISBN 0874779766.

Products

For office supplies online (and locations of stores near you):

www.officemax.com

www.staples.com

www.radioshack.com

www.quillcorp.com

For all kinds of headset phones, add-on headsets, and accessories gathered in one place:

www.headsets.com

Organize-It
2079 25 Mile Rd.
Shelby Twp., MI 48316
1-800-210-7712
www.organizes-it.com

Organize Your World
15 Commerce Boulevard/Suite 309
Succasunna, NJ 07876
973-927-7684
www.organizeyourworld.com

Restoring Order
P.O. Box 1204
Sherwood, OR 97140
Organizing Services: 1-888-625-5774; Products: 877-625-5774
E-mail: Info@RestoringOrder.com

www.thecontainerstore.com
By going to their website, you can find a store near you or shop online.

Online

www.junkbusters.com

Organizations

The International Association of Business Communicators
One Hallidie Plaza, Suite 600
San Francisco, CA 94102
415-544.4700
www.iabc.org

Chapter 10: Bathroom Organization: Methods for Your Morning Madness

Books

Beyond Soap, Water and Comb: A Man's Guide to Good Grooming and Fitness by Ed Marquand, Abbeville Press, 1999; ISBN 0789204452.

Color Me Beautiful's Looking Your Best: Color, Makeup, and Style by Mary Spillane and Christine Sherlock, Madison Books, 1995; ISBN 1568330375.

For Men Only: The Secrets of a Successful Image by Richard Derwald and Anthony Chiappone, Promethueus Books, 1995; ISBN 0879759100.

Making Faces by Kevyn Aucoin, Little, Brown, 1999; ISBN 0316286850.

Chapter 11: The Kitchen: Systems for Getting Your Daily Bread

Books

Fix-It and Forget-It Cookbook: Feasting with Your Slow Cooker by Dawn Ranck and Phyllis Good, Good Books, 2001; ISBN 1561483176.

Frozen Assets: How to Cook for a Day and Eat for a Month by Deborah Taylor-Hough, Champion Press, 1998; ISBN 1891400614.

Making the Best of Basics: Family Preparedness Handbook by James Talmage Stevens, Gold Leaf Press, 1997; ISBN 1882723252.

Rachael Ray's 30-Minute Get Real Meals: Eat Healthy Without Going to Extremes by Rachael Ray, Clarkson Potter, 2005; ISBN 1400082536.

Once-a-Month Cooking: A Proven System for Spending Less Time in the Kitchen and Enjoying Delicious Homemade Meals Everyday by Mimi Wilson and Mary Beth Lagerborg, Broadman & Holman Publishers, 1999; ISBN 0805418350.

Online

Frozen Assets: Cook for a Day. Eat for a Month: members.aol.com/oamcloop

Busy Cooks: busycooks.about.com

Products

Search for Rubbermaid products online at www.rubbermaid.com. The company's more than 1,000 products are also available in many department and hardware stores.

Go to www.closetmaid.com for an online guide and locator service that can tell you which retailers carry ClosetMaid products. These include a paper rack, cup racks, wine glass racks, towel bars, plate and lid racks, slide-out cabinet, and over-the-door organizer.

Chapter 12: The Bedroom: Making a Haven for Your Spirit and a Home for Your Clothes

Books

Don Aslett's Stainbuster's Bible: The Complete Guide to Spot Removal by Don Aslett, Penguin USA, 1990; ISBN 0452263859.

Short Kutz by Melanie Graham, Whitecap Books, 1992; ISBN 0801983525. This book tells you everything you want to know about repairing and maintaining your clothes.

Products

The Closet Factory. For information about the franchise nearest you and a free in-home consultation, log on to their website and fill out an appointment request form. This company not only designs custom closet solutions, but also pantries. Website: www.closetfactory.com.

ClosetMaid, "The Storage Authority," has an online 3D Visual Storage Planner you can use to design your own storage solutions. Their website: www.closetmaid.com.

The Container Store has catalogs for just about every room in your house. Call 1-888-CONTAIN (266-8246) to request yours. Their website is www.containerstore.com, where you can shop online or locate a store near you.

The Hold Everything catalog can be obtained by calling 1-888-922-4117, or pointing your browser to www.holdeverything.com.

Organize Everything products are at www.organize-everything.com, including those dividers we mentioned.

InterMetro Industries Corporation. Call 1-800-441-2714 or log on to their website for a local dealer that sells these versatile modular shelving systems. Website: www.metro.com.

Chapter 13: Rooms for Living

Products

Rip-Tie manufactures Velcro cord management products. Write them at P.O. Box 549, San Leandro, CA 94577; call 1-800-7-RIPTIE; e-mail (info@riptie. com); or visit their website at www.riptie.com. Look for their CableCatch and CableWrap products.

Chapter 14: Kids' Stuff: Organizing with Little Ones in Mind

Books

Einstein's Science Parties: Easy Parties for Curious Kids by Shar Levine and Allison Grafton, John Wiley & Sons, 1994; ISBN 0471596469.

The Kids' Pick-a-Party Book: 50 Fun Party Themes for Kids, Ages 2 to 16 by Peggy Warner, Meadowbrook Press, 1998; ISBN 0671579665.

The Ultimate Sleep-Over Book by Kayte Kuch, Lowell House, 1996; ISBN 1565653254.

Products

Tuffyland bins and organizers: www.tuffyland.com

Closet Doubler: www.organize-everything.com

Chiffarobe: Amish Traditions, 3233 State Route 39, P.O. Box 339, Nashville, OH 44661. Their phone number is 330-378-2791. Website: www.amishtraditions.com.

"I Did My Chores" wall chart: www.onlineorganizing.com.

Chapter 15: Winning the Money Wars: Guerrilla Budgeting

Books

Cut Your Bills in Half: Thousands of Tips to Save Thousands of Dollars by Rodale Press Editors, Rodale Press, 1993; ISBN 0831718927.

Everyone's Money Book by Jordan E. Goodman and Sonny Bloch, Dearborn Financial Publishing, 1993; ISBN 0793107210.

How to Get Out of Debt, Stay Out of Debt and Live Prosperously by Jerrold Mundis, Bantam Books, 1990; ISBN 0553283960.

How to Want What You Have: Discovering the Magic and Grandeur of Ordinary Existence by Timothy Ray Miller, Avon Books, 1996; ISBN 0380726823.

Living More with Less by Doris Janzen Longacre, Herald Press, 1980; ISBN 0836119304.

Money Troubles: Legal Strategies to Cope with Your Debts by Robin Leonard, Nolo Press, 2001; ISBN 0873376404.

The Best of Cheapskate Monthly: Simple Tips for Living Lean in the '90s by Mary Hunt, St. Martin's Press, 1993; ISBN 0312950934.

The Cheapskate Monthly Money Makeover by Mary Hunt, St. Martin's Press, 1995; ISBN 0312954115.

The Complete Tightwad Gazette: Promoting Thrift as a Viable Alternative Lifestyle by Amy Dacyczyn, Random House, 1999; ISBN 0375752250.

The Tightwad Gazette II: Promoting Thrift as a Viable Alternative Lifestyle by Amy Dacyczyn, Villard Books, 1995; ISBN 0679750789.

The Tightwad Gazette III: Promoting Thrift as a Viable Alternative Lifestyle by Amy Dacyczyn, Villard Books, 1997; ISBN 0679777660.

Your Money or Your Life: Transforming Your Relationship with Money and Achieving Financial Independence by Joe Dominguez and Vicki Robin, Penguin USA, 1999; ISBN 0140286780.

Audio and Video Tapes

"Transforming Your Relationship with Money and Achieving Financial Independence," an audiocassette/workbook course by Joe Dominguez of the book *Your Money or Your Life*. It includes four 70-minute audiocassettes and a 132-page workbook and is available from The Simple Living Network, P.O. Box 233, Trout Lake, WA 98650; 1-800-318-5725; Website: www.simpleliving.net.

Chapter 16: Tax Tactics and Advanced Money Maneuvers

Books

Nolo's Simple Will Book, 5th edition by Denis Clifford, Nolo Press, 2003; ISBN 087337939X.

Quick and Legal Will Book, 3rd edition by Denis Clifford, Nolo Press, 2003; ISBN 0873379489.

The American Bar Association Guide to Wills and Estates: Everything You Need to Know About Wills, Estates, Trusts, and Taxes, Random House Reference, 2004; ISBN 0609809342.

Software

Personal Recordkeeper and Quicken WillMaker Plus (for Windows) available at Nolo; call 1-800-728-3555 or visit www.nolo.com.

Booklets

There are many useful tax-related booklets available *free* from the Internal Revenue Service. Just log on to www.irs.gov, and then download the PDF files, or call 1-800-829-3676 to request the print versions. Some titles you may want to ask for include the following:

Publication 525, "Taxable and Nontaxable Income," which includes information on reporting bartering transactions

Publication 463, "Travel, Entertainment, Gift, and Car Expenses"

Publication 334, "Tax Guide for Small Business"

Publication 552, "Recordkeeping for Individuals," which includes information on what you need to keep for the IRS and for how long

Chapter 18: Calling In the Cavalry: Hiring Others

Books

The Free-Spirited Garden: Gorgeous Gardens That Flourish Naturally by Susan McClure, Chronicle Books, 1999; ISBN 0811821129.

Organizations

National Association of Professional Organizers
4700 W. Lake Ave.
Glenview, IL 60025
847-375-4746
www.napo.net

Chapter 19: Maintaining and Managing Your Progress

Books

Alexandra Stoddard's Living Beautiful Together by Alexandra Stoddard, Avon Books, 1991; ISBN 0380709082.

Living a Beautiful Life: 500 Ways to Add Elegance, Order, Beauty, and Joy to Every Day of Your Life by Alexandra Stoddard, Avon Books, 1988; ISBN 0380705117.

Mrs. Sharp's Traditions: Nostalgic Suggestions for Re-Creating the Family Celebrations and Seasonal Pastimes of the Victorian Home by Sarah Ban Breathnach, Scribner, 2001; ISBN 074321076X.

Chapter 20: Organization Styles for Different Lifestyles

Books

After He's Gone: A Guide for Widowed and Divorced Women by Barbara Tom Jowell and Donnette Schwisow, Birch Lane Press, 1997; ISBN 1559724331.

Better Homes and Gardens New Cookbook, Meredith Books, 1996; ISBN 0696201887.

Fannie Farmer Cookbook by Marion Cunningham and Fannie Merritt Farmer, Knopf, 1996; ISBN 0679450815.

Going Solo in the Kitchen by Jane Doerfer, Knopf, 1998; ISBN 0375703934.

Keeping Your Family Close: When Frequent Travel Pulls You Apart by Elizabeth M. Hoekstra, Crossway Books, 1998; ISBN 0891079750.

Serves One: Super Meals for Solo Cooks by Toni Lydecker, Lake Isle Press, 1998; ISBN 1891105019.

The Business Traveler's Survival Guide: How to Get Work Done While on the Road by June Langhoff, Aegis Publishing Group, 1997; ISBN 1890154032.

The Family Puzzle; Putting the Pieces Together: A Guide to Parenting the Blended Family by Nancy Palmer, William D. Palmer, and Kay Marshall, Strom Pinon Press, 1996; ISBN 0891099492.

The New Joy of Cooking by Irma S. Rombauer, Marion Rombauer Becker, and Ethan Becker, Scribner, 1997; ISBN 0684818701.

The Unofficial Business Traveler's Pocket Guide: 165 Tips Even the Best Business Travelers May Not Know by Christopher J. McGinnis, McGraw-Hill, 1998; ISBN 0070453802.

Where's Dad Now That I Need Him? Surviving Away From Home by Kent Frandsen, Aspen West Publishing and Distribution, 2003; ISBN 1885348169.

Where's Mom Now That I Need Her? Surviving Away from Home by Kent P. Frandsen, Aspen West Publishing and Distribution, 2003; ISBN 0961539011.

Online

American Self-Help Group Clearinghouse: www.mentalhelp.net/selfhelp

Organizations

The National Organization of Single Mothers: www.singlemother.org

This organization helps new members form or join local support groups and publishes "SingleMOTHER," a bimonthly newsletter offering information and advice, plus tips that can save single mothers time and money.

Newsletters

For the two million dads staying home and raising kids, there's "At-Home Dad," an online newsletter edited by Peter Baylies. For a free subscription, go to www.athomedad.com. There's even information on forming at-home dad playgroups and an at-home dad convention.

Also check out The Dollar Stretcher at www.thedollarstretcher.com.

Chapter 21: Healing Trends: Organizing for Health and Fitness

Books

Childhood Medical Journal by Cathleen Gasper, 3G Publishing Inc., 2004; ISBN 0615121667.

Complete Home Storage from the editors of Sunset Publishing Corporation, 1997; ISBN 0376017651.

Creating Storage: Hidden Storage and Rescued Space in the Garage, Attic or Basement from the editors of Sunset Publishing Corporation, 1995; ISBN 0376017686.

Bibliography

Aslett, Don. *Clutter's Last Stand*. Cincinnati: Writer's Digest Books, 1984.

———. *Is There Life After Housework?* Cincinnati: Writer's Digest Books, 1981.

———. *Make Your House Do the Housework*. Cincinnati: Writer's Digest Books, 1986.

———. *Pet Clean-Up Made Easy*. Cincinnati: Writer's Digest Books, 1988.

Berthold-Bond, Annie. *Better Basics for the Home*. New York: Three Rivers Press, 1999.

Breathnach, Sarah Ban. *Simple Abundance: A Daybook of Comfort and Joy*. New York: Warner Books, 1995.

Cilley, Marla. *Sink Reflections: FlyLady's BabyStep Guide to Overcoming CHAOS*. Brevard, North Carolina: FlyLady Press Inc., 2002.

Covey, Stephen R. *The 7 Habits of Highly Effective People: Powerful Lessons in Personal Change*. New York: Fireside/Simon & Schuster, 1989.

Dominguez, Joe, and Vicki Robin. *Your Money or Your Life*. New York: Viking Press, 1992.

Duncan, Peggy. *Conquer Email Overload with Better Habits, Etiquette, and Outlook Tips and Tricks.* Atlanta: PSC Press, 2004.

Edwards, Paul and Sarah. *Working from Home: Everything You Need to Know About Living and Working Under the Same Roof.* Los Angeles: Jeremy P. Tarcher, Inc., 1999, 5th edition.

Elgin, Duane. *Voluntary Simplicity: Toward a Way of Life That Is Outwardly Simple, Inwardly Rich.* New York: William Morrow, 1993.

Gawain, Shakti. *Creative Visualization.* San Rafael, CA: New World Library, 1978.

Gawain, Shakti, with Laurel King. *Living in the Light: A Guide to Personal and Planetary Transformation.* Mill Valley, CA: Whatever Publishing, 1986.

Hunt, Mary. *Debt-Proof Living.* Nashville: Broadman & Holman Publishers, 1999.

Kiechel, Walter III. "Getting organized … the secret is, gulp, making decisions." *Fortune.* March 3, 1986, v. 113, 123.

Kolberg, Judith. *Conquering Chronic Disorganization.* Decatur, Georgia: Squall Press, Inc., 1998.

Linn, Denise. *Sacred Space: Clearing and Enhancing the Energy of Your Home.* New York: Ballantine, 1995.

Longacre, Doris Janzen. *Living More with Less.* Scottsdale, PA: Herald Press, 1980.

Marcelis, Nicole. *Home Sanctuary: Practical Ways to Create a Spiritually Fulfilling Environment.* Chicago: Contemporary Books, 2001.

Mendelson, Cheryl. *Home Comforts: The Art & Science of Keeping House.* New York: Scribner, 1999.

Miller, Timothy. *How to Want What You Have: Discovering the Magic and Grandeur of Ordinary Existence.* New York: Avon, 1995.

Moran, Victoria. *Shelter for the Spirit: Create Your Own Haven in a Hectic World*. New York: HarperCollins, 1997.

Nearing, Helen and Scott. *The Good Life*. New York: Schocken Books, 1989.

Nelson, Mike. *Clutter-Proof Your Business: Turn Your Mess Into Success*. Franklin Lakes, New Jersey: Career Press, 2002.

Nelson, Mike. *Stop Clutter From Stealing Your Life: Discover Why You Clutter and How You Can Stop*. Franklin Lakes, New Jersey: New Page Books, 2001.

Pratkanis, Anthony, and Elliot Aronson. *Age of Propaganda: The Everyday Use and Abuse of Persuasion*. New York: W.H. Freeman and Company, 1992.

The Princeton Language Institute, ed. *21st Century Dictionary of Quotations*. New York: Laurel, 1993.

Rathje, William L. "Rubbish! An archeologist who excavates landfills believes that our thinking about garbage has been distorted by powerful myths." *The Atlantic*. December, 1989, 264, bi6, 99(10).

Robbins, Anthony. *Unlimited Power*. New York: Fawcett Columbine, 1986.

Sher, Barbara, with Annie Gottlieb. *Wishcraft: How to Get What You Really Want*. New York: Ballantine, 1979.

Stoddard, Alexandra. *Living a Beautiful Life: 500 Ways to Add Elegance, Order, Beauty and Joy to Every Day of Your Life*. New York: Avon Books, 1986.

Toffler, Alvin. *The Third Wave*. New York: Bantam Books, 1981.

Wilson, Mimi, and Mary Beth Lagerborg. *Once-a-Month Cooking: A Time-Saving, Budget-Stretching Plan to Prepare Delicious Meals*. Colorado Springs: Focus on the Family, 1992.

Young, Pam, and Peggy Jones. *Sidetracked Home Executives: From Pigpen to Paradise*. New York: Warner Books, 2001.

Index